Instant
Netscape
Dynamic HTML
NC4 Edition

Alex Homer
Chris Ullman

Wrox Press Ltd.®

Instant Netscape Dynamic HTML *NC4 Edition*

Published by Wrox Press Ltd. 30 Lincoln Road, Olton,
Birmingham, B27 6PA.

Printed in USA

ISBN 1-861001-19-3

Trademark Acknowledgements

Wrox has endeavored to provide trademark information about all the companies and products mentioned in this book by the appropriate use of capitals. However, Wrox cannot guarantee the accuracy of this information.

Credits

Authors
Alex Homer
Chris Ullman

Additional Material
Dan Kohn - *Javascript Reference*
David C Matthews - *Code Samples*

Editors
Anthea Elston
Jeremy Beacock

Technical Reviewers
Muffy Barkocy
Ron Phillips
Rick Stones

Design/Layout/Cover
Andrew Guillaume
Graham Butler

Index
Simon Gilks

Cover image by David Maclean. Digital processing by Andy Guillaume.

About the Authors

Alex Homer

Alex Homer is a software consultant and developer, who lives and works in the idyllic rural surroundings of Derbyshire UK. His company, Stonebroom Software, specializes in office integration and Internet-related development, and produces a range of vertical application software. He has worked with Wrox Press on several projects.

Chris Ullman

Chris Ullman is a computer science graduate who's not let this handicap prevent him becoming a fluent Visual Basic, Java and SQL programmer. Currently interested in all things web-based, he's trying to figure out how to design a web-bot which drags off every mention of his favourite soccer team, Birmingham City, from the web and displays it within a desktop component without him lifting a finger.

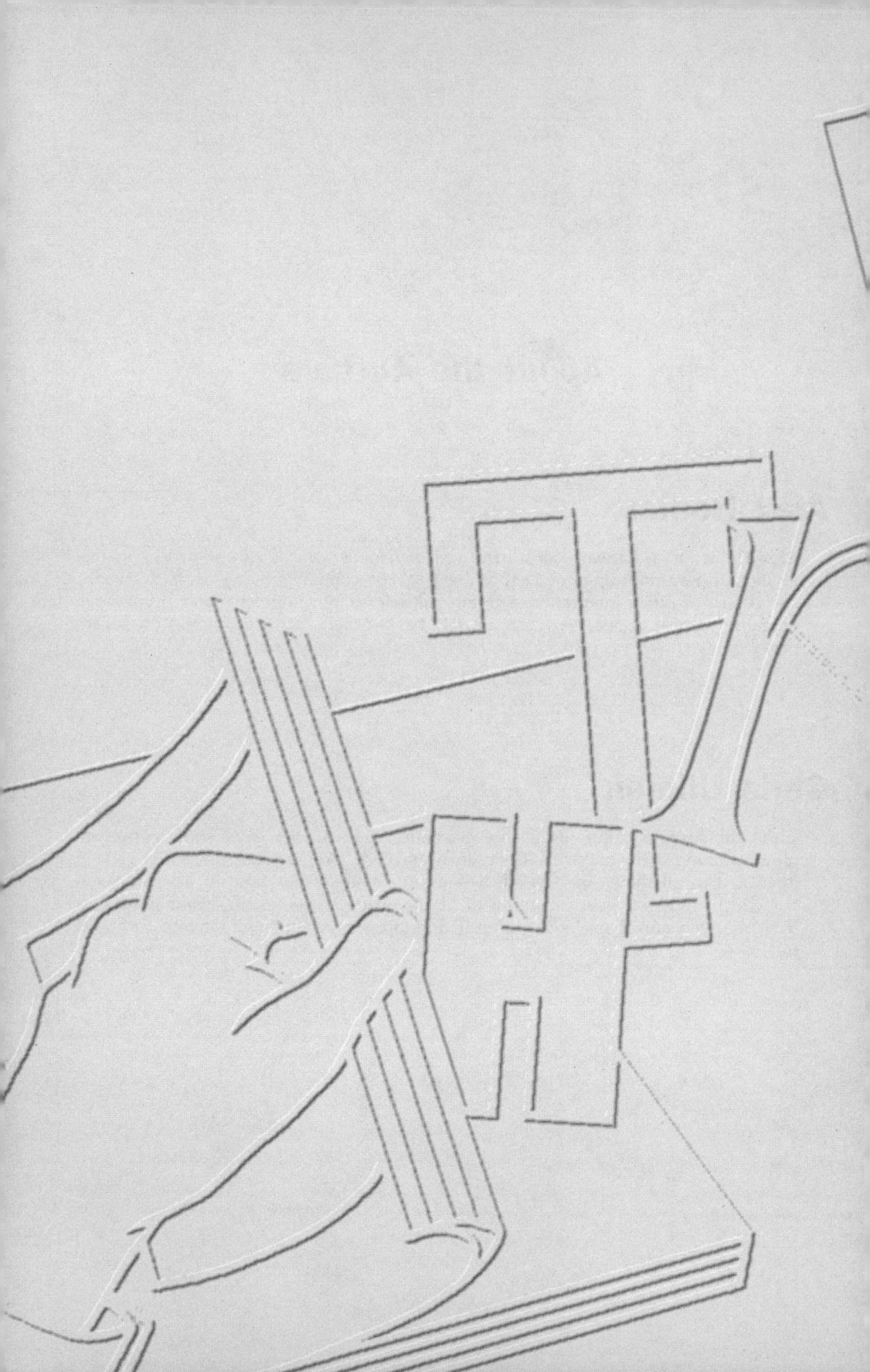

Table Of Contents

Chapter 4: The Dynamic HTML
Browser Object Model 67

Chapter 6: Scripts and Event Handling 131

Reference Section 225

Section A: Lists of Properties, Methods and Events 229

Section B: List of Dynamic HTML Tags 259

Section C: Style Sheet Properties 317

Section D: Common HTML Tags by Category 333

Section E: The Browser Object Model 339

Section F: HTML Color Names and Values 389

Section G: Special Characters in HTML 397

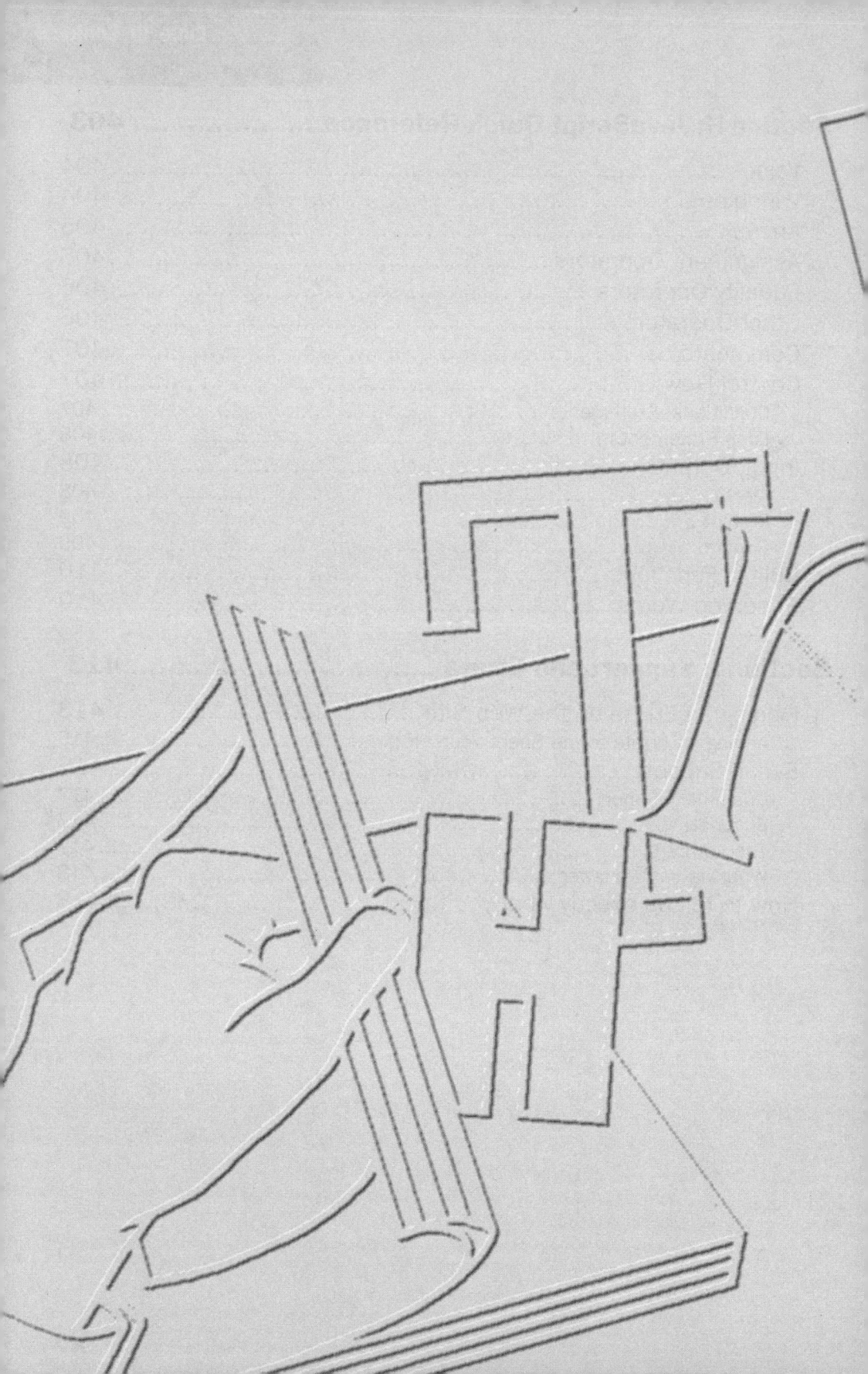

Introduction

Dynamic HTML is the latest and most exciting proposal for a language that can provide information in a Web browser. It releases the Web site creator from the strait-jacket that has previously limited so many of the things that could be done, and the effects that could be achieved. In fact, it provides a whole new way to make pages more interesting, more attractive, more like traditional documents, and—of course—more dynamic.

What is this Book About?

Since mid 1996, the World Wide Web Consortium (W3C) has been working on proposals for the next version of HTML, version 4.0, code named *Project Cougar*. One of the main innovations in HTML 4.0 is the ability to let the user update and manipulate text and graphics on a screen dynamically, without the need for a page refresh. This innovation is the reason behind why the new update to the language is known as Dynamic HTML.

Dynamic HTML differs from HTML in that it no longer relies on tags alone to achieve these effects, but makes use of JavaScript as well. This book aims to bring you up to date with the proposed standard outlines for Dynamic HTML, and to explain what it offers you and how closely the new proposals are followed in Netscape's new browser, Communicator 4. HTML 4.0 hadn't been finalized when Netscape released Communicator 4 on June 11th and since then several elements and attributes proposed by Netscape have been rejected by W3C. These elements are still supported in the final release of Communicator 4. While we aim to discourage the use of non-standard elements, we don't wish to completely ignore them either, so we have provided documentation of these features, where appropriate.

Dynamic HTML allows the Web author to work with the contents of the page in a fundamentally different way. This book isn't a dry list of specifications and discussion documents. You'll find that it's been split into two distinct sections. The first is a lightning tour and demonstration of all the new features that Dynamic HTML offers. We make references to the HTML standard, detailing what is and what isn't supported, throughout the book. The second section is a comprehensive reference guide to everything an HTML programmer could possibly need. This includes a cross reference of all the new and old properties, events and methods, a listing of all the Dynamic HTML tags that Communicator 4 supports, a browser object model reference and much much more.

Why Netscape Communicator 4 Edition?

When Netscape released Communicator 4, they beat all competitors by releasing the first browser capable of dynamically updating a page. Communicator 4 supports Dynamic HTML, in a way closely compliant with many of the proposals for HTML 4.0. Dynamic HTML is also supported within Microsoft Internet Explorer 4, but the definitions that the two companies have for the same language do vary – depending upon what their browser supports. We aim to cover the elements outlined in the standard and those unique to the Netscape browser, so that you can get the best out of it.

Browser Compatibility

However, this places HTML authors in a difficult position. We are used to minor differences in the tags and attributes that different browsers support, and the different ways that they sometimes interpret them, but the current situation means that there is very little common ground between the new features in the two main browsers. Producing pages and scripts that will work correctly on both browsers is a very difficult task during this transition period.

In Chapter 8 of this book, you'll see a more detailed discussion of browser, document and script compatibility, plus our opinions on what the future may hold.

What Do I Need to Use This Book?

All you'll need to create Dynamic HTML documents yourself is a text editor capable of saving files in ASCII format, and a browser which supports Dynamic HTML. This book uses Netscape Communicator version 4. This can be downloaded from:

```
http://home.netscape.com/
```

Apart from that, everything you need is here in this book. The examples and screenshots in this book were all taken from a PC running Windows 95, and using Windows Notepad as the text editor. However, HTML is a platform-independent language, so you can just as easily use a Macintosh or other operating system with the same results—again, as long as you have a suitable browser.

Who Should Read This Book?

You should read this book if you want to be able to create exciting and attractive web pages, using the latest techniques. Dynamic HTML is a combination (perhaps even a culmination) of two originally very different Web page coding techniques. The appearance of the page is created using **HTML**, but much of the control of the way it looks and works is down to embedded **scripting code**. On top of that, extensions to the way in which **style sheets** work add extra ways of controlling and specifying the final product's layout.

Therefore you should have at least a basic knowledge of a scripting language, preferably JavaScript as this is the one that Communicator 4 supports, and you should be reasonably familiar with HTML and style sheets. We won't be providing a full tutorial on these subjects. However, we have included some tips on how they work in our examples, and a full reference section at the back of the book.

If you've created a few web pages before, and have done a little scripting, you'll have no problems keeping up with what's going on.

Where you'll find the Samples and Tools

If you want to try out the examples in this book, you can run them straight from our web site or you can download them as compressed files from the same site. The index page can be found at: **http://www.rapid.wrox.com/books/1193/**

If you're located in Europe or the United Kingdom, or you find that the site in the United States is down for maintenance, then you may want to try our mirror site which can be found at: **http://rapid.wrox.co.uk/books/1193/**

What is the World Wide Web?

The concept of the World Wide Web, or simply the Web, was born in 1983 at the CERN laboratory in Geneva, when Tim Berners-Lee was looking for a way of disseminating information in a friendly, but platform-independent, manner. The scheme he devised was placed in the public domain in 1992, and the World Wide Web was born.

Most of the activity in developing the many standards and technologies that go into making the World Wide Web function have now been transferred from CERN to the World Wide Web Consortium (W3C). Their web site at **http://www.w3.org** is always a good starting place for discovering more about the Web. Here is the home page of the World Wide Web Consortium:

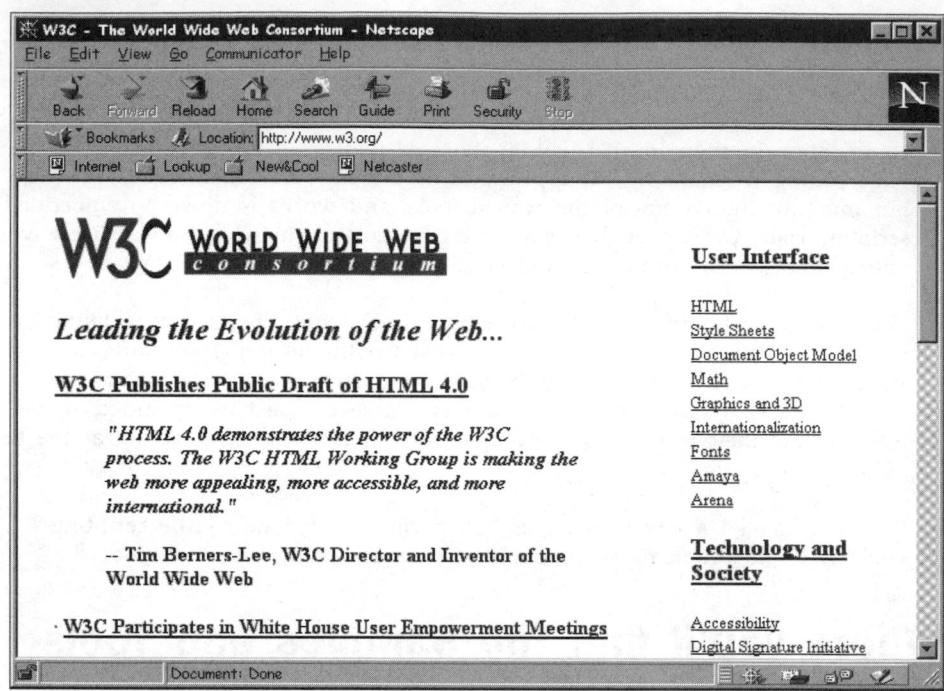

In this book, we aren't going to be examining how the World Wide Web works, but it is important to understand the basics that make it possible. There are three parts to this technology:

- The server that holds the information
- The client that is viewing the information
- The protocol that connects the two

Documents, including text, images, sounds, and other types of information are held on a server computer, viewed on a client computer, and transferred between the two using the HTTP (Hyper Text Transfer Protocol).

When a client (the computer or workstation being used by the person who wishes to view the document) makes a request to the server, it uses the HTTP protocol across a network to request the information—in the form of a URL—from the server. The server processes the request and, again, uses HTTP to transfer the information back to the client. As well as transferring the actual document, the server must tell the client the type of document being returned. This is usually defined as a MIME type. The client must then process the information before it presents it to the human viewer.

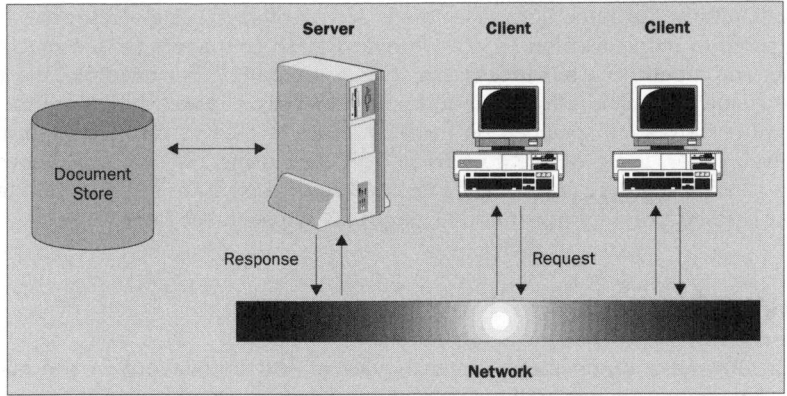

In this simplified diagram, we have shown the documents as fixed; however, in some cases, they can be dynamic documents, created 'on the fly' by the server as the client requests them. Perhaps the simplest example of a dynamic document is the ubiquitous 'hit counter' that appears on many pages.

Some Terminology

Before we go any further, it might be a good idea to define some terminology.

DTD (Document Type Definition)—a set of rules on how to apply SGML (see definition below) to a particular markup language. Again, you'll see more in Chapter 1.

HTML (Hyper Text Markup Language)—the basic subject of this book.

HTTP (Hyper Text Transfer Protocol)—this is the protocol used to transfer information between the client and server computer. Although vital for the operation of the Web, it is not generally necessary to know any details of HTPP to provide information across the Web.

MIME (Multimedia Internet Mail Extension)—this was originally intended as a way of embedding complex binary documents in mail messages, but is now used much more widely. When a server serves web information to a client browser, it first tells the client the type of information it is going to send using a MIME type and a subtype. The browser can then decide how it wishes to handle that document type. It may choose to process it internally, or invoke an external program to handle the information. MIME types consist of a main type and subtype. For example, plain text is 'text/plain', but 'image/mpeg' specifies an image stored in mpeg format.

RFC (Request For Comments)—this is something of a misnomer, as almost all of the protocols and conventions that make the Internet function are defined in documents called RFCs. For example, RFC1725 defines POP3, the protocol often used for retrieving Internet mail, and HTML 2.0 can be found in RFC1866. All RFC documents can be found on the Internet.

SGML (Standard Generalized Markup Language)—a standard for defining markup languages.

5

URL (Uniform Resource Locator)—this is a way of specifying a resource. It consists of a protocol name, a colon (**:**), two forward slash characters (**//**), a machine name, and a path to a resource (using **/** as a separator). For example, the Wrox Press home page can be found at **http://www.wrox.com/**. URLs are the way that all resources are specified on the web. Note that URLs can specify more than just web pages. For example, to retrieve RFC1866 using FTP, we could specify **ftp://ds.internic.net/rfc/rfc1866.txt**. URLs are often embedded inside web pages, to provide links to other pages, as we shall see later.

Conventions

We have used a number of different styles of text and layout in the book to help differentiate between the different kinds of information. Here are examples of the styles we use and an explanation of what they mean:

Advice, hints, or background information comes in this type of font.

> **Important pieces of information come in boxes like this**

- **Important Words** are in a bold type font
- Words that appear on the screen in menus like the File or Window are in a similar font to the one that you see on screen
- Keys that you press on the keyboard, like *Ctrl* and *Enter*, are in italics
- Code has several fonts. If it's a word that we're talking about in the text, for example, when discussing the **For...Next** loop, it's in a bold font. If it's a block of code that you can type in as a program and run, then it's also in a gray box:

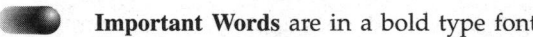

```
<STYLE TYPE="text/javascript">
... Some Javascript ...
</STYLE>
```

- Sometimes you'll see code in a mixture of styles, like this:

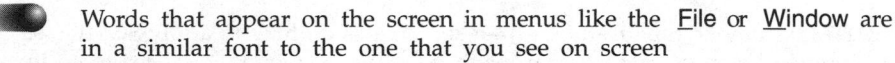
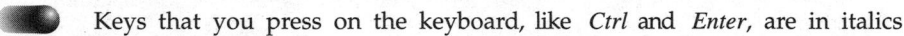

```
<HTML>
<HEAD>
<TITLE>Javascript Style Sheet Example</TITLE>
<STYLE  TYPE="text/javascript">
tags.BODY.color="black"
classes.base.DIV.color="red"
</STYLE>
</HEAD>
```

- The code with a white background is code we've already looked at and that we don't wish to examine further.

These formats are designed to make sure that you know what it is you're looking at. I hope they make life easier.

Tell Us What You Think

We've worked hard on this book to make it useful. We've tried to understand what you're willing to exchange your hard-earned money for, and we've tried to make the book live up to your expectations.

Please let us know what you think about this book. Tell us what we did wrong, and what we did right. This isn't just marketing flannel: we really do huddle around the email to find out what you think. If you don't believe it, then send us a note. We'll answer, and we'll take whatever you say on board for future editions. The easiest way is to use email:

feedback@wrox.com

You can also find more details about Wrox Press on our web site. There, you'll find the code from our latest books, sneak previews of forthcoming titles, and information about the authors and editors. You can order Wrox titles directly from the site, or find out where your nearest local bookstore with Wrox titles is located. The address of our site is:

http://www.wrox.com

Customer Support

If you find a mistake, please have a look at the errata page for this book on our web site first. Section I outlines how can you can submit an errata in much greater detail, if you are unsure. The full URL for the errata page is:

http://www.wrox.com/Scripts/Errata.idc?Code=1193

If you can't find an answer there, tell us about the problem and we'll do everything we can to answer promptly!

Just send us an email to **support@wrox.com**.

or fill in the form on our web site: **http://www.wrox.com/Contact.stm**

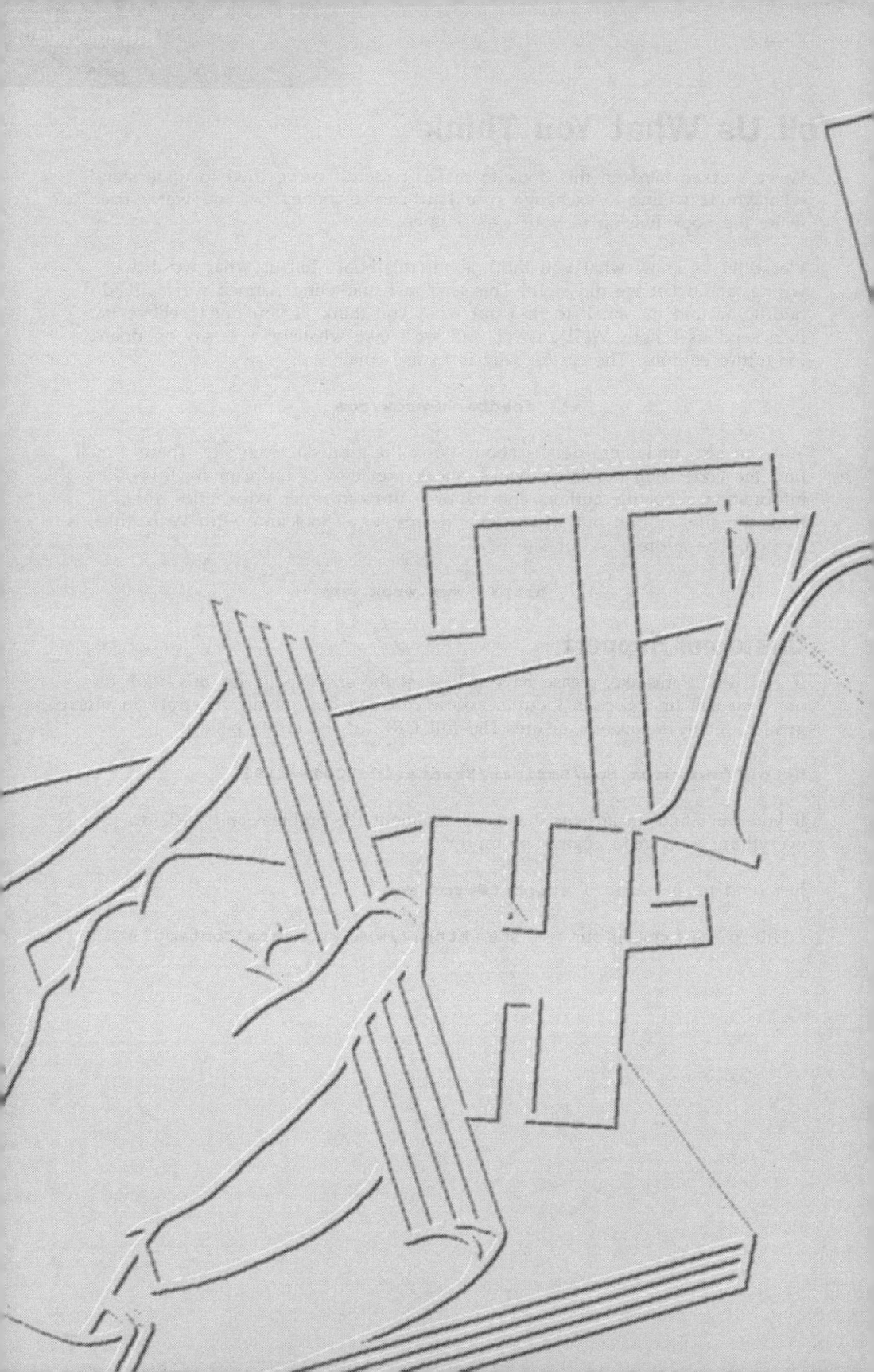

Introducing Dynamic HTML

It's always the same. You'd finally come to grips with all the new tags and attributes in HTML 3.2, and everything seemed to be settling down with the forthcoming ratification of this version of the language, when suddenly it's 'all-change time' once again. This has been precipitated by the release of Netscape's new browser, Communicator 4 (NC4) and Microsoft's browser Internet Explorer 4. Both these browsers support many of the proposals made in the draft of the new version of HTML standard, HTML 4.0.

This is a departure from the way things have tended to happen in the past. Usually, each new browser release carried with it some new HTML tags and a few new attributes. However, with HTML 4.0, both Netscape and Microsoft have been very active in proposing new additions to the language as part of the forthcoming standard. Previously, Netscape and Microsoft have tended to support each others new tags in their next release (with some exceptions), but—as any hardened HTML author knows—trying to build pages that will work correctly on different browsers is not as easy as it should be. So this time they've both contributed to the standards set by the World Wide Web Consortium to produce a new version of HTML although, sadly, still not one with which they both totally comply. The full draft of HTML 4.0 can be found at **http://www.w3.org**.

HTML 4.0 isn't really that different from the previous versions of HTML. The key changes can be summed up by the word **dynamic**. HTML 4.0 will now allow the user to manipulate and access the text and image elements directly. The web page has become dynamically updateable and the properties are easily accessible from code. This might seem like no big deal, as most operating systems have boasted this for years, but in web pages it's quite a major advance. However the adjustments required to the language aren't just in the form of a few new tags and attributes. While most of the tags in 3.2 remain present in 4.0, it's this new ability to manipulate and access elements with a scripting language that forms the unique innovation for HTML. As a result, both Netscape and Microsoft have christened the language Dynamic HTML.

So, why do we need these new features—and will they actually help to reduce compatibility problems in the future? We'll answer these two questions for you, but to do this we first need to show you what Dynamic HTML actually is, what it can do and how you use it. We'll show you how it fits into the overall scheme of things, and how it broadens existing concepts and techniques to let you achieve new kinds of effects in your web pages.

In this chapter, we'll aim to cover:

- The foundations of Dynamic HTML
- How it is the same as, and different from existing HTML
- What we can do with it, and what we need to learn

The Foundations of Dynamic HTML

Dynamic HTML is a development of the 'traditional' HTML we already use to create web pages of all kinds. HTML stands for **HyperText Markup Language**, and is designed to be a standard way of representing information so that many different types of client browser can display it. Before we go too deeply into Dynamic HTML itself, we'll take a brief look at the background to HTML and the other **document definition languages** from which it originated.

Document Definition Languages

The original documents that were used in the World Wide Web were in the format we call HTML—Hyper Text Markup Language. Perhaps the two most important features of this were that a basic HTML document was simple to create, and that HTML was almost totally platform and viewer independent.

HTML is a markup language that tells the client, in general terms, how the information should be presented. For example, to define a heading in an HTML document, you might write:

```
<H2>This is a heading</H2>
```

This tells the client that the text 'This is a heading' should be displayed as a level 2 heading, but leaves it up to the client to decide the most appropriate way of displaying it. As HTML has developed, this original concept is being diluted.

> *An important side-effect of this way of defining documents is that it allows people with visual disabilities to use special browsers that render the documents in a form which is easier for them to comprehend.*

The first version of HTML was a fairly loosely defined standard. Version 2 of HTML was more rigorously defined in terms of another standard, known as SGML.

SGML

SGML is the abbreviation for **Standard Generalized Markup Language**. This language, or meta-language as it should be called, was defined by International Standards in 1986 as ISO 8879:1986.

The purpose of SGML is very simple. At the time it was developed, there were several 'markup languages', none of which were particularly portable between platforms or even software packages. The purpose of SGML is to allow a formal definition of markup languages that can then be used to give complete flexibility and portability of information display between applications and platforms.

It is tempting for the newcomer to SGML to view it as a markup language in its own right—defining a set of tags, etc. and providing meanings for those tags. This is not the case. What SGML *does* do is describe the relation of components within a document. As such, SGML is not a competitor with the likes of TeX or Postscript, which define such things as layout, but a way of describing what the document 'is' rather than how it should be 'rendered'.

A markup language consists of a set of conventions that can be used together to provide a way to encode text. A markup language must also specify what markup is allowed, what markup is required and how the markup is distinguished from the text of the document. SGML does all this—what it doesn't do is specify what the markups are, or what they mean.

DTD

DTD stands for **Document Type Definition**. Its purpose is to define the legal productions of a particular markup language. A simple DTD would do nothing more than, say, define a set of tags that can be used by a particular markup language.

The HTML 3.2 standard is a formally defined SGML DTD. In other words, the definition of HTML 3.2 is itself specified using the SGML meta-language. This allows HTML specifications to be rigorously defined.

To fully define HTML 3.2, two different specifications are required. The first is the relatively small SGML definition that defines general features, such as the character set and size limits. The main information is contained in the DTD, which defines the detail, such as the tags and attributes, which we will learn more about later.

The HTML 3.2 DTD can be found at the following address:

```
http://www.w3.org/pub/WWW/TR/WD-html32
```

Hypertext Markup Language

HTML 3.2 is the latest standard awaiting final ratification by the World Wide Web Consortium. This has led to some confusion over what is now standard and what isn't. HTML 3.0 was never an official standard, it was always only a working draft. The Web developed so rapidly, with vendors implementing proprietary tags all the time, that the draft HTML 3.0 specification was left looking dated before it could even be issued. The consortium decided, probably wisely, that rather than continue work on HTML 3.0, they would move immediately to HTML 3.2. The HTML 3.2 standard incorporates all of HTML 2.0 (with some very minor changes) plus many of the proposals that were in the HTML 3.0 draft, and additional features such as tables and applets.

Since the 3.2 standard was proposed, more additions continue to be made to new browsers—over and above the requirements to meet the standard. In fact, the standard itself is now in danger of being completely overtaken before it ever reaches the stage of final ratification. Even though HTML 4.0 is not *that* different from HTML 3.2, there are several subtle changes that require a new standard to be defined. These standards are likely to be accepted by W3C, but considering 3.2 is still to be ratified, it could take a little while. Hopefully as there is less need for new tags and new attributes, HTML 4.0 should see the standard settling down at long last. Only once there is a stable standard that the major companies adhere to, do we have any chance of achieving a fully standardized and platform-independent way of viewing information from across the planet.

What's New in Dynamic HTML?

Having considered the background to the development of Dynamic HTML, it's time to see what's different. What can it do that we can't already do with HTML, JavaScript and Java applets? This is the subject of the next section, and you'll be pleased to know that—from some viewpoints—not much seems to have actually changed.

Netscape Communicator 4 looks quite similar to its predecessors. I will, of course display existing pages that employ almost any of the techniques currently used to make web pages more exciting. It hosts Java applets (which execute much quicker than in Navigator 3), runs code written in JavaScript, and supports all the other features that are becoming accepted requirements—such as tables and frames.

What Hasn't Changed

So, Dynamic HTML isn't a radical departure from the version of HTML that's currently awaiting ratification by the World Wide Web Consortium. If it were, we would be looking at all kinds of problems when different browsers accessed pages that exploited its features. Two main points to consider are:

- There is very little in the way of new tags to worry about and very few new attributes to go with them. However Communicator now supports the new HTML **<SPAN>** and **<LINK>** tags and introduces the **<LAYER>** tag. There is still no support for several tags such as **<OBJECT>**, although there are plans to support it in future releases. Also there is still no support for the Microsoft implemented scripting language VBScript, although there is a proprietary plugin.

- The same object model is available to JavaScript and components, but with extensions proprietary to Dynamic HTML. This means that existing scripts will still execute successfully.

What's Actually New

Much of the outward appearance of the Netscape Communicator browser remains very familiar. However, a lot of the structure of both the page and the browser has been exposed to the HTML author for the first time. This allows some very exciting new effects to be achieved. The illustration below shows a jigsaw puzzle that you can solve on our web site! With Dynamic HTML you can actually move pieces of the jigsaw about on the screen, as the instructions show:

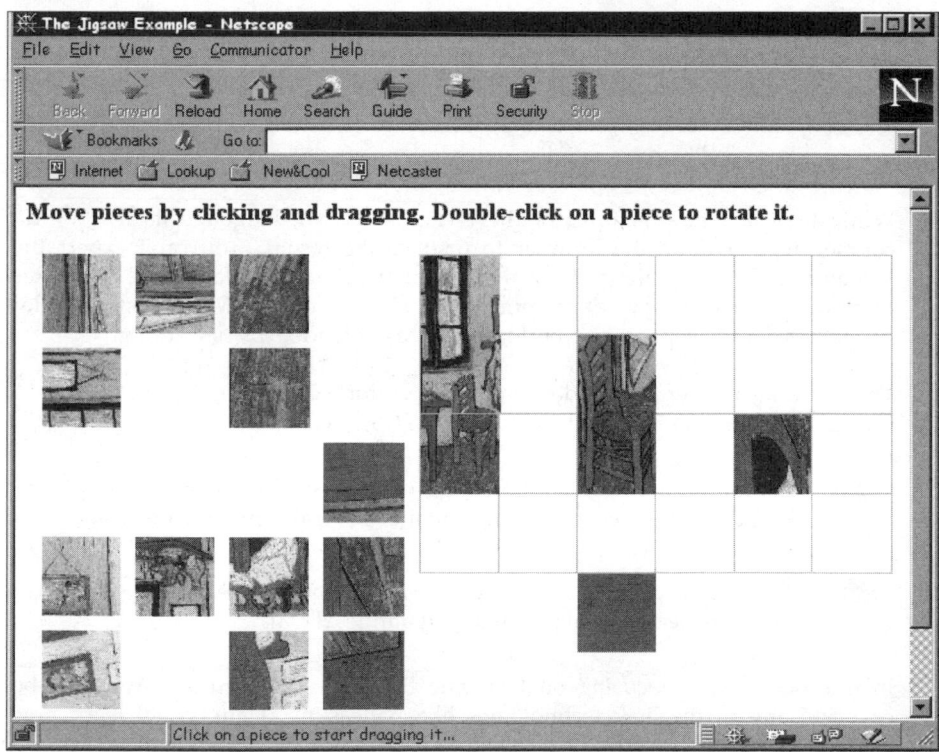

You can download, or just browse, all the samples for this book from our Web site at **http://rapid.wrox.co.uk/books/1193**

13

Dynamic HTML in Communicator 4 provides these new features:

- **Cascading Style Sheets**: these give the developer a lot more control over the positioning and format of elements on a page. They also provide hooks to the page elements from scripting code.

- **Absolute positioning of elements and layering**: allows developers to manipulate the x, y and z co-ordinates of objects on a page, allows a desktop publishing style of authoring via either style sheets, the `<LAYER>` tag or JavaScript.

- **The Document Object Model**: provides more programmability for elements on a page, by allowing their formatting and positioning properties to be altered by JavaScript.

- **Dynamic re-drawing of any or all parts of the page**: allows changes to a loaded page to be made visible. Pages no longer need to be reloaded to show the updated version.

- **New event-handling techniques are supported**: event capturing allows events to be passed along from one object to another. It also allows the capturing of events not supported by one object, from another, such as `onmousemove`.

- **Dynamic Fonts**: allow the developer to create new fonts for others to download, as they would do with image files. This can be used to enhance and vary the presentation of any web page.

- **Canvas Mode**: this lets the developer view the window or HTML page in a "full screen" mode, which takes up the entire screen.

While these are new features of the Dynamic HTML language itself, they do, of course, depend upon the browser to display the results. You can't expect the Dynamic HTML-specific parts of a page to do much in Navigator 3 or Internet Explorer 3. Like all new developments in HTML, the browser must provide support before the page can perform as was intended by its author.

There are also several new developments within Netscape's Communicator 4.01 browser, which interface with Dynamic HTML pages:

- Communicator 4.01 supports the new version (1.2) of the scripting language, **JavaScript**, which contains several new functions and methods.

- The e-mail package Messenger which comes as part of Communicator can also be manipulated with Dynamic HTML

In this book, we're focusing on Dynamic HTML as a language. We won't be covering any of the new technologies like Netcasting. Here, you'll learn how to create pages that conform to the Netscape proposals for Dynamic HTML. This doesn't mean we'll only be looking at the parts of HTML 4.0 that Netscape supports, as there are quite a few things in Communicator 4.0 that don't appear in the final standard.

In this chapter, we'll start by looking at the new features we listed earlier, and see how they provide opportunities to do things we can't do in existing HTML pages. In later chapters we'll get down to examining exactly how we can implement these new features in our pages—and you'll see how the examples we're using in this chapter work.

Accessing the Elements in the Page

In traditional HTML, it's impossible to 'get at' most of the contents of a web page once it's been rendered (i.e. displayed) by the browser. You can write scripts that read or change the values in HTML controls, such as text boxes and checkboxes. You can also include objects in the pages, such as Java applets, and access them through script code. And, of course, you can change the background color of the page, or the color of the links on the page, through script.

What you can't do is read or change anything else. You can't change the text on the page, either in headings, lists, tables, or body text. You can't change the font or style of the text, add or remove images, or change their position. In fact, you can't do much at all.

Of course, the Web—and therefore the browser that displays the pages—was originally designed as an information delivery system. The whole idea was that you got a page full of text and graphics to read. In those days, no-one expected you to want to *play* with it...

With Dynamic HTML, all this changes. Every part of the page that the browser displays can be accessed using a scripting language. You can change almost anything in the page, while it's being displayed. As an example, this page (named **ListChange.htm**) displays items in a list in a different color, size, and font style when the mouse pointer moves over them. Notice that they're not even hyperlinks, just a normal unordered list created with the **<UL>** tag. It's done using script code that detects the movements of the mouse, and changes the style of the text.

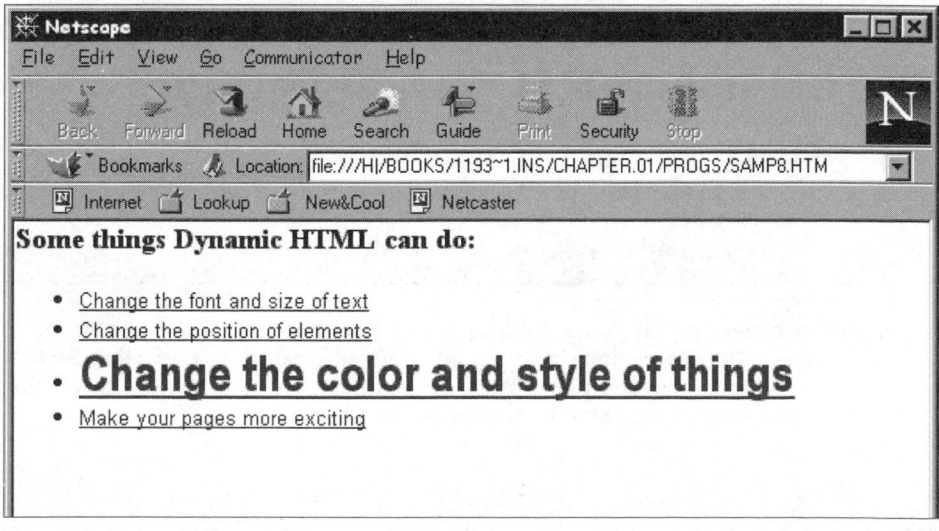

Properties, Styles and Style Sheets

In the Jigsaw example, we saw that JavaScript can change some relatively minor aspects of a loaded page by responding to the mouse moving over part of it. In the last couple of versions of the mainstream browsers it's been possible to control the size and font face of the text in a page, although it could only be set in a page as it was being designed, and not on-the-fly while it was being displayed.

This was done by using two HTML tags, **<FONT>** and **<STYLE>**. The simplest way was to enclose text in **<FONT> </FONT>** tags, and specify the font family, size, color and other effects:

```
<FONT  FACE="Arial Black" SIZE=4 COLOR=green>
    This is some text in big green letters
</FONT>
```

Instead of doing this every time, you could use the **<STYLE>** tag to define a set of named styles, then allocate them to different parts of the text. And using the standard formatting tag names avoided the need to specify which style applied to which part of the text. If you wanted all your **<H2>** text to be large and green you just defined this in a **<STYLE>** section at the start of the page:

```
<STYLE>
    .biggreen {font-family: Arial Black; fontSize: 18; color: green}
</STYLE>
<BODY>
    <P CLASS=biggreen>This is some text in big green letters</P>
    ...
```

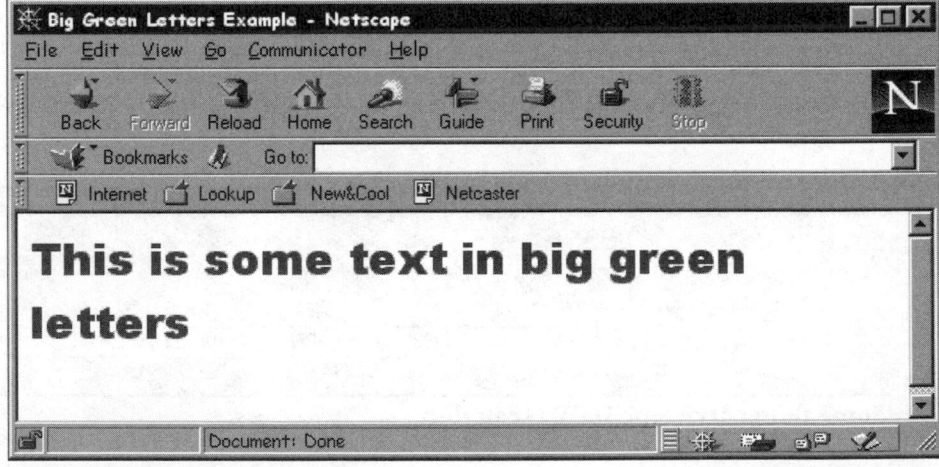

An even better way, if you wanted a lot of pages to have the same style, was to put the **<STYLE>** definition into a separate file, called a **Cascading Style Sheet** (CSS), and link it to each page. Then, you could change the styles in all the pages just by changing the entry in the style sheet file.

*Don't worry if you're not up to speed on using styles like this. We'll be
looking at how it's done in more depth in the next chapter, and we've included
full details in the reference section at the back of the book.*

But, why are we talking about existing methods? The point here is that
Dynamic HTML uses the characteristics you specify for the items in the page to
provide **properties** for each one. In other words, we now have to think of every
part of the page as an individual **element** or **object**, and not just as a tag. The
text between the **<H2>** and **</H2>** tags is now part of that heading element,
and it has a whole range of properties that are accessible from script code. The
fontSize is no longer just a number in a **<STYLE>** or **<FONT>** tag, but the
fontSize property of an **H2** element object.

For the moment, you just need to appreciate that style sheets provide a link
between the definition of all the parts of the page in HTML, and that they can
react to the script code within the page in a new way—as properties of that
element object.

The Extended Browser Object Model

So, all the pages we load into our shiny new browser are going to consist of
hundreds of different objects, rather than a static page full of text and graphics
with a few HTML controls or Java objects. It sounds like trying to program all
this in JavaScript will be a terrifying experience. As in most other programming
environments, the browser provides an object model which organizes all the
different objects and elements in a way that makes them manageable. If you've
programmed using JavaScript before, you'll have used this.

To cope with the flood of all kinds of new objects, Netscape Communicator 4
introduces several additions to the browser object model. Bear in mind that this
object model is designed around Dynamic HTML the language, so it must be
available in all browsers that will host Dynamic HTML. Providing it becomes
widely adopted, and there's little reason to suspect it won't, we'll find it
available in all the other browsers. This means that as long as we write our
pages and scripts to this model, they will work in all the other browsers that
support it.

*Web authors themselves can also help this process by sticking closely to the
standard. The standard helps web authors as well as browser developers,
because now webmasters have a definitive standard to work from, they should
no longer have to test their pages on different browsers to ensure cross
platform compatibility. They should therefore encourage conformity to the
standard by conforming themselves.*

We'll look in detail at the object model in later chapters, and it's fully
documented in the reference section at the back of this book. You'll see how it
becomes part of everything we do when we work with scripts in Dynamic
HTML.

Absolute Positioning and the Z-order

One of the biggest criticisms of existing HTML has been the difficulty of accurately controlling the appearance of a page. As we saw earlier, until the implementation of styles, everything was displayed in a default font (usually something like Times Roman), in default colors and almost at random within the browser window.

The most you could do was specify where a paragraph should start or end, and whether graphics or other elements should align to the left, center or right of the page. In the early versions of HTML this was an advantage, because the important thing was the page content, rather than the style, and having browsers on many different platforms was easier if the requirements on the browser developer where kept simple. The big problem was that, as the user resized the browser window, everything moved about again. To some extent, using tables helped to solve this, and when frames became more universally supported they allowed even more control.

One of the biggest advances in Dynamic HTML is the support for a method of placing elements on pages in fixed positions. As you'll see when we come to look at positioning in the next chapter, this very useful feature has evolved from these earlier techniques. This means that elements can be sized and positioned in the browser window exactly as the author requires. They can even be overlaid, something that could previously only be done by employing tricks with style sheets. The new concept of laying out pages is therefore very similar to desktop publishing techniques (unfortunately, however, the tools available to help still have some way to go). To see the difference it makes, here's one of the sample pages from this book as it appears in Netscape Communicator 4, followed by the same page loaded into Netscape Navigator 2:

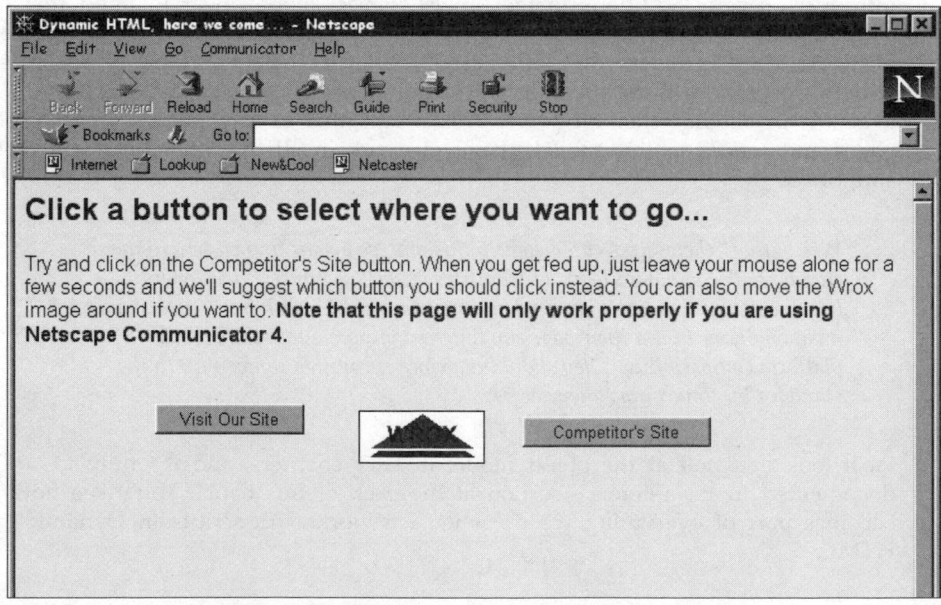

The Dancing Buttons page in Netscape Communicator 4

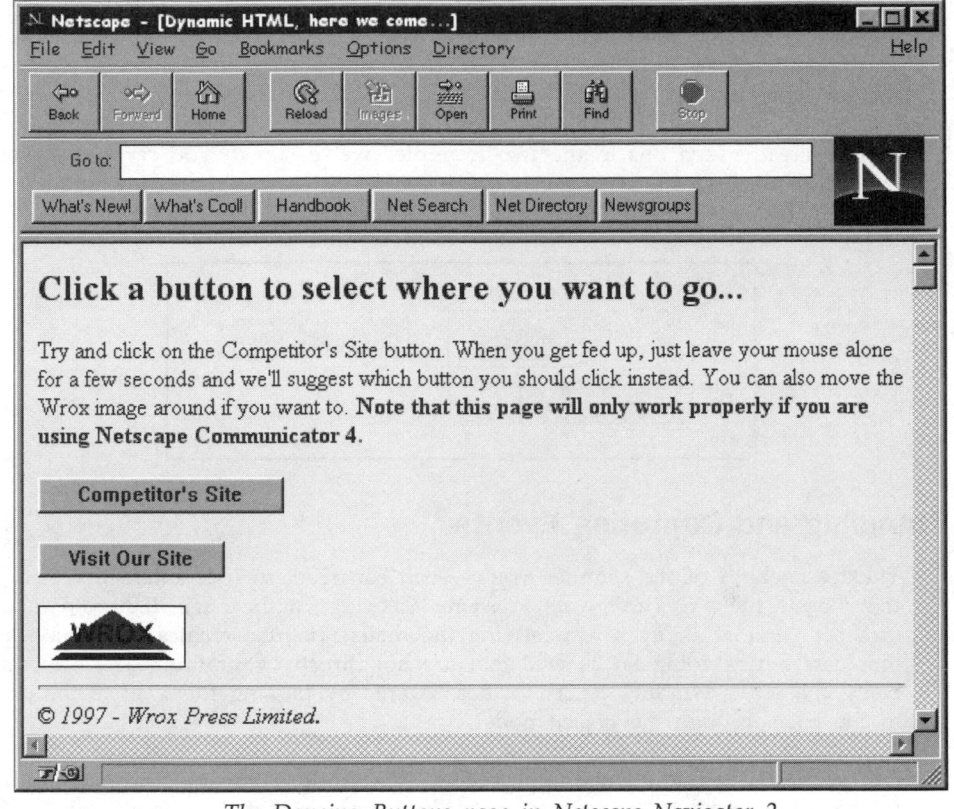

The Dancing Buttons page in Netscape Navigator 2

*You can download, or just browse, all the samples for this book from our Web
site at* **http://rapid.wrox.co.uk/books/1193**

Movement and Dynamic Page Re-drawing

The fact that we can accurately position elements on the page immediately
prompts the next question. If we can put them exactly where we want them,
can we move them around as well? This is probably the most visible advantage
that Dynamic HTML provides. It's linked to the fact that the browser will now
redraw all or part of the page using a stored representation of the contents,
rather than the original HTML source code stream.

This rather unusual effect can be seen if you load a Dynamic HTML page, then
carry out a task which changes the page—such as moving an element around.
The usual View Page Source option in the browser opens the original HTML
code, but it doesn't reflect the currently displayed page. It's just the original
source that created the page in the first place. And, as you'd expect, clicking the
Reload button in the browser just reloads this original version of the page
again.

19

Of course, the browser always had the ability to redraw parts of the page. The big difference now is that the entire stored page representation, which can itself be manipulated by the code, will show these updates on the screen as soon as the properties in the code are updated.

You've already seen this in the two examples we've shown you earlier. In the page with the two buttons, one of them jumps out of the way of your mouse, while the other creeps under it when you stop moving the pointer around.

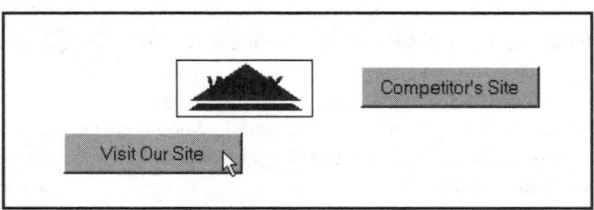

Handling and Capturing Events

The reason both of the samples you've seen can react to user interaction is that the code in the pages can react to **events**. Clicking on the page displayed in the browser window, or even just moving the mouse pointer, creates an event—and there are others going on as well that are not directly your fault. The browser, being the active window, reacts to these events by passing them on to the code in the page through the object model.

OK, so this happens in most applications. You could even get Navigator 3 and Internet Explorer 3 to react to events. What's new is that it is happening without reference to the originating site, so there is no transaction across the network, no CGI script and no network delays. There are also now a whole heap of options when it comes to reacting to the events in our scripting code. These not only give us more choice about how we create pages, but can also make the job of writing the code easier. We can provide one routine to handle an event in several objects, or several different events for one object.

Probably one of the most useful additions to Dynamic HTML is the ability to **capture** and **route** events. We can allow (or prevent) an event being 'captured' and passed through the browsers' object hierarchy, where it can be handled at different levels. We can identify which element on the page actually caused the event (or to be more exact, which one was the 'topmost' element that received it). Finally, we can identify which element is being 'routed' to, and which is being moved from, when we detect mouse movement events.

To see how useful event capturing can be, try the buttons sample page again. You'll find that you can push the Competitor's Site button over the central Wrox logo. It still responds to mouse movements even though the pointer is actually over the logo graphic. The button is still picking up events caused by the mouse, even though the image itself is responding to an event.

We've skipped through the list of new and exciting features in Dynamic HTML very briskly here. This is intentional, both to let you see what's new (and hence, what you're going to learn about in this book), and to give you an understanding of the terminology and how it all fits together. In the remainder of this chapter, we'll start the process of working through all these new features in detail.

Getting Started with Dynamic HTML

By now, you should appreciate that Dynamic HTML is not exactly a revolution, more an evolution of existing techniques and technologies. You don't need to sit down and learn a whole new language, just develop and extend your existing knowledge of HTML and browser scripting. What it does do is open up some new and exciting possibilities for creating much more interesting and varied web pages.

The Background Knowledge You'll Need

In this book, we're assuming that you already have some background in both of these areas—in other words that you know how to create a traditional Web page using HTML tags, and that you have at least a rudimentary grasp of how JavaScript is used in Web pages. We've included a Javascript reference section at the back of this book to help you. If you want to learn more about scripting or HTML up to version 3.2, look out for Instant JavaScript, ISBN 1-861001-274 and Instant HTML Programmer's Reference, ISBN 1-861000-766—both from Wrox Press.

The Tools You'll Need

When creating pages in HTML, many people use an authoring tool such as HotDog, HotMeTaL Pro, FrontPage, or even Microsoft Word 97. This is fine for a static page, which just uses the normal HTML tags to create the appearance the user sees.

However, these tools hide the actual structure of the page—the tags that do all the work—from the author. They are also unable to create much in the way of script and therefore the bad news is that none of these are going to be much help when we come to use Dynamic HTML.

In some ways, this is a good thing. To build a successful interactive page using JavaScript, you need to know how all the elements that make it up fit together. You also get a lot more freedom when using any programming language (and that's very much what Dynamic HTML is about) if you actually understand what's going on under the hood.

So, in this book, we're back to using the single most used web page development tool of all time, the NotePad text editor that comes with Windows. If you prefer, there's no reason why you can't use any other text editor. One that can provide line numbers is particularly useful, as you'll see when we come to look at finding and fixing script errors later on. You can even use Microsoft Word for this, as long as you remember to save your files with a `.txt` extension in Word 97. Otherwise, it will automatically convert them into HTML files, and, next time you open one, you'll see the results, rather than the actual source HTML tags and script which create the page.

Finally, of course, you'll need Netscape Communicator 4!

So, now that we've assembled our tool kit, both mental and physical, let's get on and look at how Dynamic HTML works in more detail. The first step is to understand more fully how style sheets and style tags are used in web pages, then see how this affects what we do in Dynamic HTML. This is the subject of the next chapter.

Summary

In this chapter we've examined the features that make Dynamic HTML different from earlier versions of HTML, and explored some of the ways we can use them to create more dynamic web pages. In the broadest terms, the major new features are:

- All the elements in the page (tags, images, text, etc.) are now accessible to script written in the page

- An extension to the implementation of styles and style sheets provides more hooks to the page elements from JavaScript

- Extensions to the browser object model are included, thus providing more programmability for JavaScript

- Absolute positioning of elements, including control of the z-order, allows a desk-top publishing style of authoring, and '2.5D' appearance

- Dynamic re-drawing of any or all parts of the page allows changes to a loaded page to be made visible. Pages no longer need to be reloaded to show the updated version

- New event-handling techniques are supported, including capturing events and routing them up through the object hierarchy

In the rest of the book, we'll explore each of these concepts in depth, and see how we can use them in the pages we create.

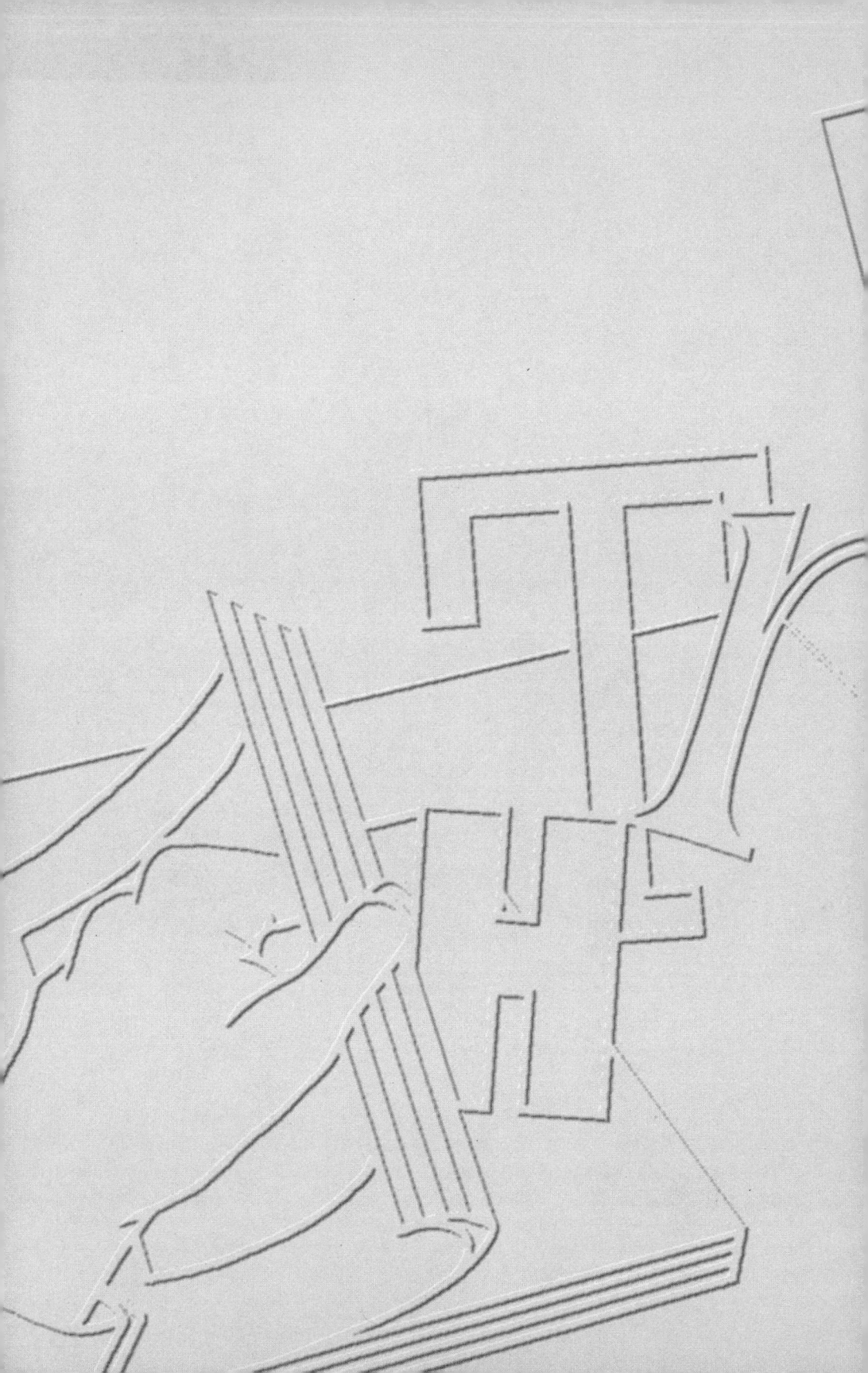

Style Sheets and Dynamic Fonts

In the previous chapter, we looked briefly at the new features in Dynamic HTML, saw some examples of dynamic pages, and discovered what we have to learn to start working with it. We're now ready to delve a little deeper. We'll begin with style sheets, which are used to connect the elements in the page to the scripts. Previously, in standard HTML, styles were either specified in the attributes of tags or in style sheets and couldn't be changed without refreshing the whole page. One of the main innovations in Dynamic HTML is that the user can now alter properties dynamically, which in turn allows elements on the page (such as text or graphics) to be changed or moved, without having to refresh the page every time. Dynamic HTML also allows much greater control over positioning of sheets on a page—to the nearest pixel in fact—and allows you to place and move elements on top of each other or to move one in front of another.

Style sheets form the basis for all of this. This chapter gives a quick overview of how they work and how they can be used to enhance the layout of your pages. We'll also look at Dynamic Fonts which are a rather nifty feature, introduced to allow us to create web pages with a more individual look, because we no longer have to rely on one of several standard fonts.

So we'll be covering:

- How styles and style sheets work in general
- The different features of Cascading Style Sheets
- The tags used to apply style sheets
- The different features of JavaScript style sheets
- How Dynamic Fonts can be added into a page

This will provide a comprehensive guide on the most important features of how styles are used, but we've also supplied a full style reference at the back of this book.

Using Styles and Style Sheets

As we discussed in Chapter 1, style sheets are the major method of linking the elements in our Dynamic Web pages with the code that manipulates them. In the next chapter, we'll consider how this link works in more detail, but for the moment we'll concentrate on how style sheets are used in the traditional way. You need to be familiar with this concept before you can start to take advantage of the extensions to the technique that Dynamic HTML offers.

There are currently two main ways to implement style sheets, both of which have ugly acronyms. The first is **Document Style Semantics and Specification Language**, or **DSSSL** for short. This is a remarkably large and complex standard, supported by the ISO, which also has a 'lite' version for use on the web called DSSSL-Online. The second way to implement style sheets is through **Cascading Style Sheets Level One**, or **CSS1** (in case you were wondering: no, there isn't a Level Two yet). CSS1 is designed to be easy to use and implement, so it has something of a lead over the more comprehensive (and difficult) DSSSL-Online.

CSS1 is currently a recommendation and will almost certainly become the de facto standard for Web style sheets, since the major browsers support them and W3C announced support for it in HTML version 3.2. Dynamic HTML, and the W3C proposals for the HTML 4 standard, extends style sheets by adding some new attributes. It also continues to omit some style properties implemented by Netscape in Communicator 4.

Communicator itself offers another form of style sheet, which allows styles to be defined using simple JavaScript statements within **<STYLE>** tags. Using JavaScript style sheets you can define styles for all HTML elements of one type, just as you can with Cascading Style Sheets (CSS). We'll look at JavaScript style sheets separately, later in the chapter.

What are Style Sheets?

A style sheet is essentially a declaration of display rules, specifying the display attributes of particular HTML constructs. These rules are easy to write, consisting of combination of tags, property names and values.

There are three main advantages of using style sheets. The first is their universality of application. This means that we can develop a style sheet and then apply it to any document or group of documents, by simply setting them so that they refer to the style sheet we have just created. This universality has an added benefit: we can change the appearance of all our pages by simply changing the style sheet. This enables us to create a 'house style' for documents that need the same look and feel.

The next advantage is that style sheets can convey greater typographic control than is normally possible. Both CSS and JavaScript provide a number of properties that can be used to create effects like drop-caps, overlapping text, shadowed text, and so on.

The third benefit that style sheets offer is smaller file sizes. In the following example, the HTML file doesn't contain any images. This is an example of the

sort of thing that we can do with style sheets, without resorting to special
workarounds or tricks. Anyone viewing this page would only have to download
a little over 1K, which is significantly smaller than the equivalent page
constructed from images. This reduces bandwidth use and the time spent
waiting for a page to download.

Cascading Style Sheets

We'll now take a look at an example of CSS in use. The following picture is
actually all text, with no bitmaps (the giant 'we' appears in red type in the
original).

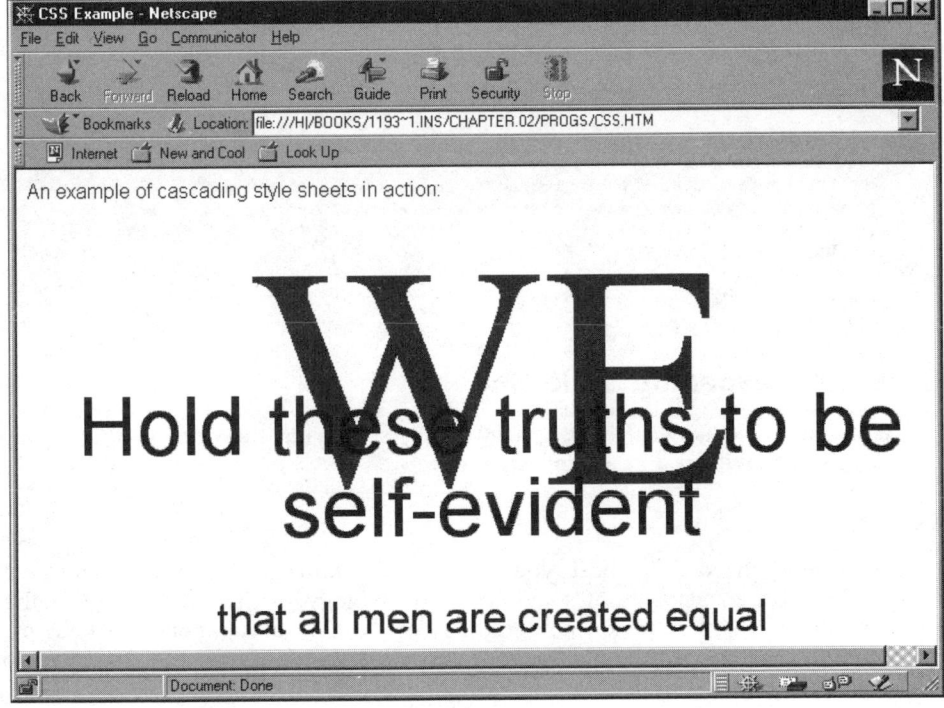

*You can run this page, called Simple Cascading Style Sheets, from our Web
site at:* **http://rapid.wrox.co.uk/books/1193**

The actual HTML file that generates this page is:

```
<HTML>
<HEAD>
<TITLE>CSS Example</TITLE>
<STYLE   TYPE="text/css">
<!--
BODY {        color: black;
    font-size: 16px;
    font-family: Arial }
.base {        color: red;
    weight: medium;
    margin-top: 10px;
    font-size: 250px;
    line-height: 250px;
```

```
        font-family: Times }
.layer1 { color: black;
    margin-top: -130px;
    weight: medium;
    font-size: 65px;
    line-height: 65px;
    font-family: Arial }
.layer2 { color: black;
    margin-top: 30px;
    weight: medium;
    font-size: 35px;
    line-height: 45px;
    font-family: Arial }
-->
</STYLE>
</HEAD>
<BODY>
An example of cascading style sheets in action:
<CENTER>
<TABLE WIDTH=730 CELLPADDING=0 CELLSPACING=0 BORDER=0>
<TR>
<TD ALIGN=CENTER VALIGN=TOP>
<DIV CLASS=base>WE</DIV>
<DIV CLASS=layer1>Hold these truths to be self-evident</DIV>
<DIV CLASS=layer2>that all men are created equal</DIV>
</TD></TR>
</TABLE>
</CENTER>
</BODY>
</HTML>
```

Creating Cascading Style Sheets

We'll start by looking at how you go about specifying the rules in this example that go to make up a cascading style sheet.

Syntax

When designing a style sheet, you only need to know a little HTML and understand the meanings of some basic terminology. We'll introduce all of the terminology you'll need to know, right now. All CSS declarations are known as **rules**. An example rule to change all text contained between **<H1>** tags to white would be as follows:

```
H1 { color: white }
```

Rules are broken up into two parts:

   the **selector** (the element to which the rule applies)

    the **declaration** (the part which defines what style the text should be)

The declaration itself is further split into two parts, the **property** of the text which is being affected, and the **value** to which it is being set. So looking back at our example, **H1** is our selector, the declaration is **{color: white}**, the property being affected is the **color** of the text and the value of the property is set to **white**.

All rules follow the same format:

```
TAG { property: value }
```

For example, to set all level 1 headings to white, we could use either of the following rules:

```
H1 { color: white }
H1 { color: #FFFFFF }
```

As you can see, both of these lines declare that everything enclosed by an **<H1>** tag will have the color white (or hex **#FFFFFF**) applied to it.

There's a list of the color names and values in Section F at the back of this book.

We can apply a single property to multiple tags simply by grouping those tags in the selector statement. In this example, we've just set all three headings to display in black:

```
H1, H2, H3 { color: #000000 }
```

As well as grouping tags, we can also group properties. We simply enclose our multiple property declarations inside the curly braces and separate them with semicolons:

```
H2 {
    color: #000000;
    font-size: 14pt;
    font-family: monaco;
    }
```

This example will display all level 2 headings in 14 point Monaco, in black. Note the use of a semicolon after each declaration to divide one property from another. In our example, we've spread the selector across multiple lines to make your code easier to read. It has the same effect as placing it all on one line. In both cases, though, don't forget the closing brace.

Inheritance

One of the best features of CSS is the ability to have one tag inherit the properties of an enclosing tag. This means that we don't need to specify every possible tag; if we neglect to set a property for **<EM>** it will simply acquire the characteristics of whatever tag encloses it. Consider the following:

```
<H3>Section Four: <EM>Colossal</EM> Widgets</H3>
```

If our style sheet specified that all **<H3>** items were to be in green, but didn't say anything about **<EM>**, then Colossal would be green, just like the rest of the line. If, on the other hand, we carefully specified that **<EM>** was blue, it would appear as such. This system of inheritance follows through all of the possible properties, allowing us to set default values. We then only need to worry about the exceptions to our rules (the best way to do this is to set all default properties for **<BODY>**, and then change things for all the usual tags where necessary).

Even better, we can specify that one property will have a value that is relative to its parent property:

```
P { font-size: 14pt }
P { line-height: 120% }
```

In this instance, line height is defined as a percentage of font size, which will ensure that the paragraph is easy to read. This is useful when we come to revise the styles later, since it automatically ensures that our line heights will instantly change whenever we change the font size. If we explicitly declared the line height, we would need to change it manually—easily forgotten in the heat of designing a site.

Contextual Selectors

Another useful feature of inheritance is that it can be used to apply styles contextually. For example, we can not only set **<H3>** to green and **<EM>** to blue, but we can also set all instances of **<EM>** that occur in **<H3>** as yellow, without affecting either of the other declarations. This is remarkably easy to achieve:

```
H3 EM { color: yellow }
```

Here the style sheet is specifying that any instance of **<EM>** that occurs inside **<H3>** will be shown as yellow. This does not affect any other instance of **<EM>**. You must be careful to omit the comma between the tags when using this method, or the selector will be interpreted as meaning that both **<H3>** *and* **<EM>** styles should be yellow.

This technique can be applied in great detail: it's possible to specify that all emphasized words are in red, in small print, but only when they appear in a listing that is itself enclosed by **<I>**. These types of declaration are termed **contextual selectors,** since they select values based on their context. It is also possible to specify values for several contextual selectors in a single statement by dividing them with commas. For example:

```
H3 EM, H2 I { color: yellow }
```

is the same thing as:

```
H3 EM { color: yellow }
H2 I { color: yellow }
```

One of the first things budding CSS designers do is to go crazy with the control they've just acquired. Sure, you can make your links all appear in pink 24pt Times, but do you really want to? Changing properties, simply because you can, is a recipe for reader dissatisfaction. If visitors can't figure out 'what is a link' versus 'what is just an emphasis', or 'why all of the lines are in 6pt type', they probably won't bother visiting your site again. A full list of style sheet properties can be found in Section C.

How do Style Sheets Cascade Anyway?

One of the niftiest, and most confusing, capabilities of CSS is the ability to have style sheets **cascade**—hence the name **Cascading Style Sheets**. This means that compliant browsers allow multiple style sheets to have control over the same document at the same time. It is possible, for example, to have three separate style sheets trying to format a document at once. This is actually more useful than it sounds.

The idea is this: when authors set up documents and refer to style sheets, they are expressing their preferred mode of display. Each browser may also have a 'default style' of its own that it will prefer to use to display pages. As the browser interprets documents on the Web, it will display them in its default style. If, however, it runs across a document that uses CSS, it will give way to the preferences stated in that style sheet. The basic idea appears to be that 'normal' HTML documents have nothing to lose by being formatted according to browser preferences, but that documents using CSS ought to be displayed according to the way the author intended (or else they wouldn't have been formatted that way in the first place).

Which style sheet 'wins' is determined on a selector-by-selector basis, so that the browser can win sometimes, and the author at others. This can be influenced by using the **important** mark—if the browser has been set to display all type in 24 point (in the case of user disability, for example), the user will probably not appreciate your documents overriding that preference and forcing a display in 10 point type. The user can, accordingly, enforce their preference by writing a default style sheet, so that the critical selectors are marked as such:

```
H1, H2, H3 { color: black }
EM { font-size: 24pt ! important }
```

In this case, the settings for **<H1>** and the others are of normal weight (they will be overridden by normal author settings), but **<EM>** is flagged important, and will override normal author settings. And yes, author settings marked **important** will override any user setting. (By the way, please don't use the **important** flag unless it is really very important. Using it just because you want to make sure you're forcing the user to see things the way you want them is asinine, to say the least.)

The sequence employed by browsers to determine which instructions will be used is as follows:

- Determine if the settings for any element actually conflict. If not, any inherited values (from 'parent' tags) are used instead. If there aren't any, the default values are used

- If there is a conflict, the values are sorted by weight (i.e. 'important' ones rank higher)

- Sort again by origin (author values are higher than reader values)

- Sort by specificity: if two values conflict, and one applies only to the situation at hand, but the other applies in all cases, then the restricted value will win

- Apply selectors according to their ranking

31

Notice that this system allows for the possibility of having effects from multiple style sheets all appearing at once on the page. This is actually a benefit, since it allows you to create multiple focused style sheets, and then apply them in different combinations.

Implementing Cascading Style Sheets

The next question is how do we actually incorporate the style sheet functionality into our HTML document? There are three ways to do this and they each have slightly different effects. It is important to decide which method suits your purpose, since they're not functionally identical.

Using <LINK>

The first method is a special use of the **<LINK>** tag. This can be used to reference alternative style sheets within the HTML code. To use the **<LINK>** method, we place the following in the **<HEAD>** of our document:

```
<LINK REL=STYLESHEET TYPE="text/css" HREF="http://foo.bar.com/style.css"
TITLE="Style">
```

Obviously, you would need to change the **HREF** to point to your own style sheet. Note that this means you can apply style sheets that reside on completely different servers. This can be particularly useful in an Intranet situation, where one department can set up several 'approved' styles for all documents to use. As a point of Internet etiquette, it would be a good idea to ask the original style sheet author for permission before 'borrowing' their style sheet in this manner.

Using <STYLE>

The next way to use style sheets is to use the **<STYLE>** element. The idea here is to enclose the style sheet data in the **<STYLE>** tag, so that it can be parsed and applied as the document is loaded. To this end, we use the following code, placed in the **<HEAD>** of our document:

```
<STYLE TYPE="text/css">
...style info goes here...
</STYLE>
```

This seems quick and easy (and indeed we used it in the earlier example that illustrated simple style sheets) but there are a few things you should be aware of. The first problem is that older browsers will ignore the **<STYLE>** tag, and will try to handle the style data as if it were normal text. This can be avoided by enclosing the whole line in HTML comment tags as we've done in our previous example, since style-aware browsers will still find the style information and handle it appropriately.

More problems arise from using the **<STYLE>** element, as we are required to include a complete style sheet in every document. This not only increases the time needed to create a document, but also increases the file sizes and makes it more difficult to change a complete site's appearance as well. In effect, this method erases two of the three advantages conferred by style sheets, and should be avoided if possible.

Using @import

Fortunately, there is a way to automatically apply style sheets and still keep the file sizes down: you can use a special notation in CSS1 that was designed for this very purpose:

```
@import url (http://foobar.com/style);
```

This notation tells the browser to get the style sheet 'style' from the server at **foobar.com**. If we place this line in the **<HEAD>** of our document, the style will automatically be retrieved and applied before our document is displayed. Even better, we can override the imported style by simply declaring any changes in the document itself, using the CSS1 description format we'll be covering shortly (this lets us set up a 'baseline' style sheet, from which individual documents can diverge).

In addition, all of the above methods apply their style sheets to the entire document, so we can't style just one paragraph unless we employ yet one more method of using style sheets.

Applying Cascading Style Sheets

Once you've linked the style sheets into the document, you still need a way of identifying the text to which you wish to apply the style.

Using STYLE with Individual Tags

One way of doing this is to specify the CSS1 information as part of the tag we want it to affect.

```
<P STYLE="color: green">This paragraph will be green</P>
```

This is extremely flexible and easy to use, but it does have the major drawback that we need to specify each tag individually (removing a major advantage of style sheets). In HTML 4.0, all text and graphics tags now support the **STYLE** attribute and the new properties, however we will refrain from discussing this further until the next chapter. The alternative, which provides more control over how things are formatted in CSS, is via the concept of a 'class'.

Classes

Lets start by looking at an example. If we specify that **<H3>** is blue, we can create a subset of **<H3>** that is white. This subset will retain any other properties we've given the parent, and must be referenced by name (in order to separate it from the parent.) For example this creates a new class named **second** to apply to **<H3>** tags:

```
H3 { font-size:14pt, font-family: monaco, color: #0000FF }
H3.second { color: #FFFFFF }
```

To implement our newly-created class, we must call it explicitly like this:

```
<H3 CLASS=second> This is in white fourteen-point monaco </H3>
<H3> This is in the default color and fourteen-point monaco </H3>
```

To round things off, you can specify properties on a class-wide basis, with any properties of that class applying to all instances of that class—even when used with different tags. Declaring the properties of a class is easy:

```
.second { color: #FFFFFF }
```

Notice the period that appears before **second**—this is needed to indicate that you are defining the properties of a class. You can now apply the properties of **second** wherever you call it, without having to set up every conceivable combination of tag and class:

```
<H1 CLASS=second> Level One </H1>
<EM CLASS=second> Emphasis </EM>
```

In this example, both items of text will be in white, and each will have whatever characteristics were previously defined, without having to explicitly define the properties of **H1.second** and **EM.second**.

JavaScript Style Sheets

As mentioned previously, Netscape Communicator 4 offers another form of style sheet, which allows styles to be defined using simple JavaScript statements within **<STYLE>** tags. To create a JavaScript style sheet, the **TYPE** attribute must be set to **"text/javascript"**. If you don't set the attribute, then Communicator will use the default style sheet type, Cascading. What we're going to do now is take a quick look at JavaScript style sheets, beginning by adapting our CSS example to a JavaScript style sheet.

```
<HTML>
<HEAD>
<TITLE>JavaScript Style Sheet Example</TITLE>
<STYLE  TYPE="text/javascript">

tags.BODY.color="black"
tags.BODY.fontSize=16
tags.BODY.fontFamily="Arial"
classes.base.DIV.color="red"
classes.base.DIV.weight="medium"
classes.base.DIV.marginTop=10
classes.base.DIV.fontSize=250
classes.base.DIV.fontFamily="Times"
classes.layer1.DIV.color="black"
classes.layer1.DIV.marginTop=-130
classes.layer1.DIV.weight="medium"
classes.layer1.DIV.fontSize=65
classes.layer1.DIV.fontFamily="Arial"
classes.layer2.DIV.color="black"
classes.layer2.DIV.marginTop=30
classes.layer2.DIV.weight="medium"
classes.layer2.DIV.fontSize=35
classes.layer2.DIV.fontFamily="Arial"

</STYLE>
</HEAD>
<BODY>
An example of JavaScript style sheets in action:
<CENTER>
<TABLE WIDTH=730 CELLPADDING=0 CELLSPACING=0 BORDER=0>
<TR>
<TD ALIGN=CENTER VALIGN=TOP>
```

```
<DIV CLASS="base">WE</DIV>
<DIV CLASS="layer1">Hold these truths to be self-evident</DIV>
<DIV CLASS="layer2">that all men are created equal</DIV>
</TD></TR>
</TABLE>
</CENTER>
</BODY>
</HTML>
```

As you can see from the screenshot, the JavaScript and CSS implementations are virtually indistinguishable apart from the titles (the spacing is slightly different):

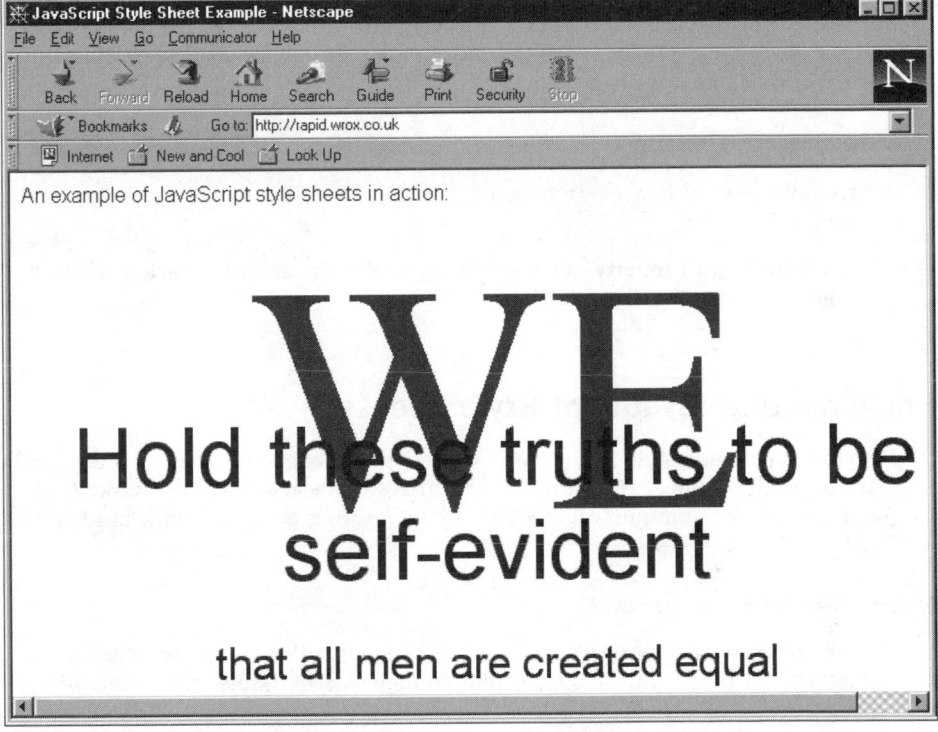

You can run this page, called Simple JavaScript Style Sheet, from our Web site at **http://rapid.wrox.co.uk/books/1193**

Creating a JavaScript Style Sheet

The biggest difference between Cascading and JavaScript style sheets is the syntax used to define the styles.

Syntax

You can change and set styles with simple JavaScript statements. The different styles that are used within the style sheets are in fact properties of the **document object**. We're not going to look at the document object until Chapter 5, but it's enough to know that JavaScript style sheets utilize arrays of properties of the document object to set styles. The **tags** array is particularly useful. It is a list of all of HTML tags that form the document object. You can set the various properties of tags using the **tags** array as follows:

```
tags.P.color = "blue"
```

This line sets the color property of the **<P>** tag to blue. This means that each time you use a **<P>** tag to enclose text on your page, its color will be changed to blue. The same can be done for all text-related tags. You can change the values of the properties of these tags, just as though you were changing them in HTML. For instance, the line:

```
tags.H3.fontSize = 18
```

changes the **fontSize** of all **<H3>** tags to 18. As the **<BODY>** tag forms the superset of all tags, if you want one setting to apply across the whole page, you can just set a property of the **<BODY>** tag to ensure that everything on the page has that style applied.

```
tags.BODY.fontFamily=Arial
```

This would ensure that everything on the page was in Arial.

> As the **tags** property always applies to the document object, you don't have to specifically call it each time.

Implementing JavaScript Style Sheets

You can link these style sheets into your pages using only one of three methods used by CSS, as the **TYPE** attribute of **<LINK>** doesn't recognize **text/javascript** in Communicator 4 and the **@import** notation only applies to CSS1.

Using the <STYLE> element

This is done in an identical way to CSS; the only differences are the setting of the **TYPE** attribute and, of course, the contents of the style definition itself.

```
<STYLE TYPE="text/javascript">
... Some JavaScript...
</STYLE>
```

The same shortcomings of increased file size and reduced customizability apply, as they did to CSS, but as you have little choice in the matter, there's not much that can be done about it.

Applying JavaScript Style Sheets

To identify the text you wish to style, as with CSS, you can use a class definition. It's possible to set up classes which define multiple features of a style and can then be applied to different tags. This is done by defining a named style in a tag such as **<DIV>** using the **CLASS** attribute. Then, within the **STYLE** definitions, you can set the **CLASS** properties as follows:

```
<STYLE TYPE="text/javascript">
classes.class1.DIV.fontSize=12
```

```
classes.class1.DIV.fontFamily=Arial
classes.class1.DIV.color=yellow
classes.class2.DIV.fontSize=18
classes.class2.DIV.color=green
</STYLE>
<BODY>
<DIV=class1>This is class1's styles</DIV>
<DIV=class2>This is class2's styles</DIV>
</BODY>
```

This gives you greater flexibility than you might otherwise have using just the **tags** array.

Which is better: Cascading or JavaScript?

The first, and perhaps most important, point is that CSS have been accepted by W3C and are already regarded as recommendations. This means that they will be implemented across platforms and across browsers. At the time of writing, JavaScript style sheets don't form part of the standards ratified by the W3C organization. However, HTML 4.0 does allow you to set the **STYLE TYPE** to any valid MIME type and this would presumably include JavaScript. Currently no other browser supports JavaScript style sheets although, if Microsoft support all of the HTML 4.0 draft, they would probably include JavaScript style sheets with Internet Explorer 4. So, for the time being, while it isn't invalid HTML 4.0 to use JavaScript style sheets, neither is it certain whether they will form part of the standard.

Secondly, as of Communicator release 4.01, JavaScript style sheets don't implement all of the properties present in CSS. For example, the **background** property of the **BODY** tag seems to function perfectly normally in a cascading style sheet:

```
<HEAD>
<STYLE TYPE="text/css">
BODY { background: green}
</STYLE>
</HEAD>
<BODY>
Some Text on a green background
</BODY>
```

but the equivalent code won't work in the JavaScript style sheet and the text will remain in its default color.

```
<HEAD>
<STYLE TYPE="text/javascript">
tags.BODY.background = "green"
</STYLE>
</HEAD>
<BODY>
Some Text on a green background
</BODY>
```

For more information on which properties are supported in CSS and which are supported in JavaScript style sheets, please refer to Section C in the second part of this book.

Also some properties implemented in both types of style sheet, such as the **lineHeight** property, exhibit different behaviors depending on the type of style sheet being used.

So, until JavaScript style sheets do officially become part of the W3C standard and properties under JavaScript style sheets work in an identical manner to Cascading Style Sheets, we suggest strongly that you stick to using Cascading Style Sheets wherever possible.

Using Tags to Apply Style Sheets

We've already seen that you can use a **STYLE** attribute with all text and image tags to deploy elements of the CSS1 styling. However, if you applied a style to the **H2** tag, you'd still get the effects of the **H2** styling as well.

```
<H2 STYLE="color: green">This heading will be green</H2>
```

The good news is that there are three tags that are ideal for identifying text because they don't add any styling of their own. We're only going to look at two of the tags now, as they are the two defined in the HTML 4.0 standard, and the third already has some new features of Dynamic HTML built into it that we don't wish to consider yet.

The <DIV> Tag

This tag was introduced in the HTML 3.2 standard. It is used to define an area of the page, or **document division**. Anything between the opening and closing tag is referred to as a single item. The **<DIV>** tag doesn't allocate any particular style or structure to the text, it just allocates an area. When used together with the **CLASS** attribute, you can apply sets of styles (such as colors, font sizes) to this 'area' or to individual items of text.

This tag was used in our style sheets example to enclose each of the separate lines of text and to allow them to be layered on top of one another.

```
<DIV CLASS=base>WE</DIV>
<DIV CLASS=layer1>Hold these truths to be self-evident</DIV>
<DIV CLASS=layer2>that all men are created equal</DIV>
```

The current standard bars **<DIV>** from controlling the display in any way (all information should be set in the style sheet), apart from using the **ALIGN** attribute.

The <SPAN> tag

This tag was originally introduced by Microsoft, but it is now present in the HTML 4.0 standard. It's been adopted in Communicator 4 as another way of applying style sheets to an area of text. The way this is done is very similar to the **<DIV>** tag. The **<SPAN>** tag defines localized style information, and anything between the open and closing tags is referred to as a single item. As this is pretty much what the **<DIV>** tag does, you'd be forgiven for wondering exactly what the difference is between the two? The HTML 4.0 standard is quite explicit, the **<DIV>** tag groups blocks together, **<SPAN>** only groups words inside a block together. The best way to illustrate this is to go back to our Style Sheets example and change each of the **<DIV>** tag definitions to **<SPAN>**

```
<SPAN CLASS=base>WE</SPAN>
<SPAN CLASS=layer1>Hold these truths to be self-evident</SPAN>
<SPAN CLASS=layer2>that all men are created equal</SPAN>
```

and see what happens:

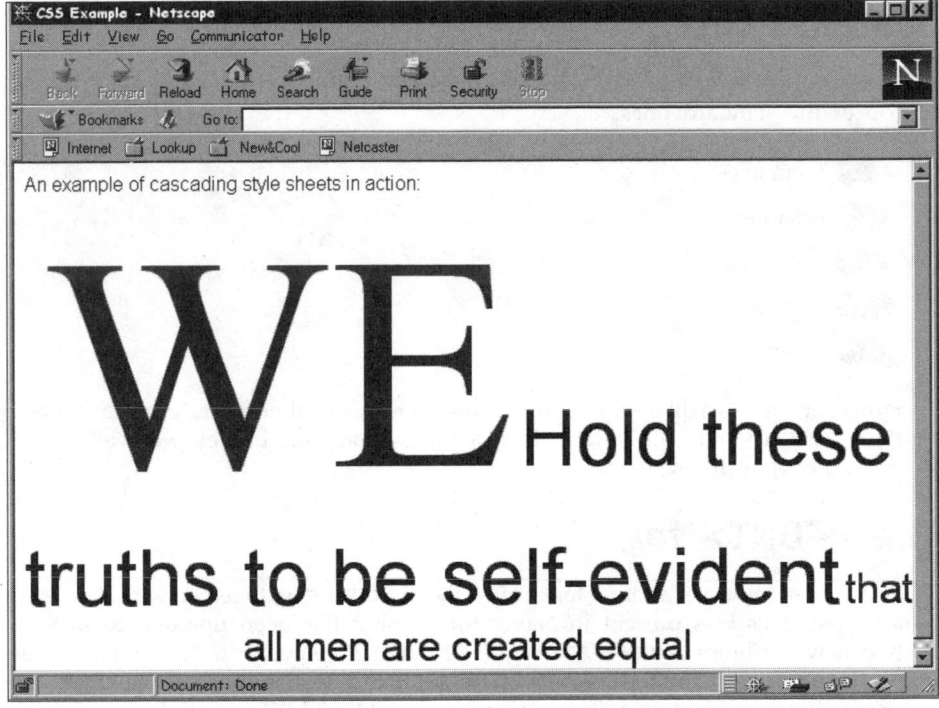

The effects are immediately noticeable. As the **<SPAN>** tag just covers the text involved and not the area around it, the text, instead of being overlaid, follows on from the text in the previous tag, causing an unsightly wraparound.

You should use the **<SPAN>** and **<DIV>** tags to apply style sheets, as they don't impose any extra structure on your page, and both are present in the HTML 4.0 standard. There is a non-standard third element **<LAYER>**, which we will look at in the next chapter and discuss fully within chapter 7, but it isn't recommended as a way of implementing style sheets. This concludes our look at style sheets. Next, we'll now turn our attention to something that falls very loosely under the style sheet banner—Dynamic Fonts.

Dynamic Fonts

Although not strictly related to style sheets, dynamic fonts are a great way of enhancing the layout and look of your document. They provide a way of linking fonts into your document, or appending them to a document in the same way you would an image. You can use them in one of two ways. You can either incorporate them with a style sheet or add them with the **<FONT FACE= >** definition.

The advantages of using Dynamic Fonts (apart from the greater variety offered), are that they allow web authors to format text without having to use graphics and they reduce the download time. The downside is that, to view Dynamic Fonts you'll need a True-Doc enabled browser. Communicator 4 is the only one currently available.

System Fonts

Netscape Communicator already provides the following five additional fonts, on top of the standard ones:

- cursive
- fantasy
- monospace
- sans-serif
- serif

However, this is still fairly limiting considering the thousands of web pages out there, which would all start to look a bit monotonous if they were all compiled from the same fonts.

The <FONT> tag

You can specify a standard font using the **<FONT>** tag together with the **FACE** attribute. This was present in Navigator 3.0, but has been updated to include two new attributes **POINT-SIZE** and **WEIGHT**. Previously in Navigator 3 there was a **SIZE** tag which allowed you to set the font size, but the new tag allows you to specify point sizes by adding to or subtracting from the original size, i.e. +1 or –1. **WEIGHT** is an attribute that allows you to set how bold a tag is meant to be, in values between 100 and 900 (100 being the lightest, 900 being the heaviest). It can be used as follows:

```
<FONT FACE = "sans-serif" POINT-SIZE = 24 WEIGHT = 750> Sans-serif 24 point
</FONT>
```

However it's very important to note that the **<FONT>** tag has been deprecated in HTML 4.0 and it causes erratic and erroneous behavior on some browsers, including Communicator. We recommend very strongly that you use style sheets to define your font type instead, and use the **<LINK>** tag to include dynamic fonts in your documents.

Including Dynamic Fonts in Style Sheets

Currently W3C are still considering how best to implement Dynamic Fonts within style sheets so it's best to define your font type in a style sheet, using the **font-family** property, as follows:

```
<STYLE TYPE="text/css">
.title1 {font-family: Clarendon BT; font-size: 20pt}
</STYLE>
```

Then you can include a font definition file within the **<HEAD>** of the document.

Font Definition Files

To link a dynamic font to a document, you need to attach it to a **font definition file**. First, the browser looks for a font in your browser's cache. If it fails to find the specified font there, it can then download it from the site specified in a URL placed in the tag. This is the same way your browser would download an image. The URL of the font definition file is placed with the **SRC** attribute of the **LINK** tag.

The **LINK** tag also has a **REL** attribute, which is used to define the document's relationship with other documents. The **REL** attribute has a new setting in Communicator 4, **fontdef**, which is used to indicate that a font definition is being made. An example definition would look like:

```
<LINK REL=fontdef SRC="http://netscape.com/examplefont.pfr">
```

The font definitions are stored in files known as **PFRs (Portable Font Resources)** and these files can include more than one font definition at a time. Once the font definitions have been linked together in a file, they can then be used with the non-standard **FACE** attribute.

How To Use Dynamic Fonts

Having said this all of this, you might now be wondering where you can find some dynamic fonts to link into your pages. The catch is that dynamic fonts aren't freely available. Currently you can't go to a site and download a PFR and use it in your own web pages. The problem is that as dynamic fonts are the intellectual property right of the font author, the fonts are associated with a domain name or directory. This physically prevents their use in any pages other than the original author's. You can view other people's page with their dynamic fonts, but you can't save the PFRs. You can't even link into them using their URL from your own page, since their format physically prevents you from doing this. This differs quite considerably from images, where you can go to any page, save an image to your hard drive and then use it in your own pages (providing you're not infringing the copyright!).

What you can do is create your own font files using a suitable tool. To create a font file is beyond the scope of this book. However one such tool for doing this can be found at the site **http://www.hexmac.com**.

Or if you're just interested in seeing an example of some dynamic fonts in action, you can go to the Netscape site and view the Stockwatch demo, which shows them off to good effect. The URL is:

**http://home.netscape.com/comprod/products/communicator/fonts/
stockwatch_demo/index.html**

41

Shortcomings of Dynamic Fonts

One problem with Dynamic Fonts is that when you first view the page, you get to see all of the default fonts and, despite reducing download times, you still have to wait for the text to be updated with the new fonts – it isn't instantaneous. It means pages containing many dynamic fonts are likely to be slow, but this is the usual trade-off in web pages, improved presentation against increased download times.

Summary

Many HTML authors have shunned style sheets in the past, but now is the time to understand them better, because they offer several significant advantages that will reward those authors that take the trouble to understand and use them. Previously, the benefits they offered were mainly aesthetic, but now that they've been linked with JavaScript, it's essential to understand them if you're going to make full use of Dynamic HTML.

In this chapter we gave a quick overview of both cascading style sheets and JavaScript style sheets. We looked at the syntax used to define styles first, then we looked at the different methods you can use to link a style sheet into a document. We also covered how you apply style sheets to specific text, rather than the page as a whole. We considered which of the style sheet proposals is the best for the Communicator 4 user and concluded that Cascading Style Sheets currently offer more features. We concluded the chapter with a look at how Dynamic Fonts are used to improve the presentation of a page, often in combination with style sheets.

In the next chapter we'll be looking at the new properties that Dynamic HTML offers for positioning and how you can use JavaScript to manipulate these properties and dynamically position elements on a page.

Chapter

3

Positioning HTML Elements using Style Sheets or Layers

We looked at style sheets in the last chapter and found that, while they present the user with more precise control over positioning of elements and application of styles, they still don't free the user from the 'strait-jacket' of static pages. Style sheets don't provide X and Y type coordinates in HTML for specifying where an element is to be positioned on a page. Also, there is no way of updating that information without a full page refresh. This all changes with HTML 4.0 which introduces a series of new properties and attributes that not only specify positions on the page in absolute terms, but are also dynamically updateable via script, allowing effects such as animation to become easily achievable.

We'll start by looking at what style sheets can't do and what new properties HTML 4.0 offers to get around this. We'll then look at how you would go about incorporating a script into your page and how you'd update the new properties with scripts. This chapter covers:

- Shortcomings of style sheets
- The new properties that HTML 4.0 offers
- The `<LAYER>` element and its attributes
- How we can use style sheets to achieve absolute positioning
- How we can control the z-order of elements
- How to use style sheets to connect scripts to page elements

Shortcomings of Style Sheets

Style sheets have two main shortcomings. The first one can be illustrated by referring back to the Style Sheets example in the previous chapter. In this example, the text in the sheet labeled `layer1` appears over the top of the text in the sheet labeled `base`. However, rather than being able to specify which sheet should appear on top of another in the code, the order of the `<DIV>` tags is all that the browser has to go by.

```
<DIV CLASS=base>WE</DIV>
<DIV CLASS=layer1>Hold these truths to be self-evident</DIV>
<DIV CLASS=layer2>that all men are created equal</DIV>
```

If we changed around the <DIV> tags attached to the **base** and **layer1** sheets, then the text layering would also be reversed. This is all very well, but what if you wanted to alter this ordering mid program, without going back to reload the page? Dynamic HTML deals with this by using something called **2.5-D layering**, which we'll look at later in this chapter.

Secondly, as mentioned previously, it isn't possible to specify exactly where a style sheet should appear on a page. It's possible to define the height, width and margin size of a sheet and even where they can be positioned in relation to each other, but not much more. So, while style sheets offer greater flexibility in these terms over standard HTML, they're still not the answer to everything. That's why you'll need something extra.

New Communicator 4 Style Properties

Netscape Communicator 4 provides support for six completely new properties, which appear in the working draft for HTML 4.0, and extends the existing properties available for formatting the background and setting margins (or borders) around elements.

The six all-new properties that we'll be looking at in particular are:

```
left            top                 z-index
position        visibility          overflow
```

You can find a list of all the properties available in Section A.

The extensions to existing border properties are:

```
border-color           border-style
border-right-width     border-left-width
border-top-width       border-bottom-width
```

The extensions to the background formatting properties are:

```
background-attachment  background-color
background-image       background-position
background-repeat
```

We won't be spending time on these last two sets of properties. They really only duplicate existing properties, although making them easier to use. You'll find a complete listing of all the style properties available in the reference section at the end of the book. So, instead, let's look at what is really new.

Displaying and Positioning Elements

The six all-new style properties allow us to create pages in a way more akin to desktop publishing than existing Web page authoring techniques. The reason is simple, and can be seen in the names of just three of the new properties: **left**, **top** and **z-index**. Instead of depending on the browser to place our elements in consecutive order as they are progressively rendered in the page, or using a style sheet with positive or negative margin settings, we can simply specify the x, y, and z coordinates in pixels of each element on the page.

This is just like the way we design the forms or dialogs for a normal Windows application, using a 'heavy weight' programming language. The new **top** and **left** properties of the **STYLE** attribute can be used to define—to pixel point accuracy—where on a page a tag should go.

- The **left** property (the X coordinate) is used to specify, in pixels, how far away from the left of the window (or a container) an element should be placed. Values are stored as strings, in the form of **100px** which would denote 100 pixels

- The **top** property (the Y coordinate) specifies, in pixels, how far from the top of a window (or container) an element should be placed

- The **z-index** property adds a new dimension, or more accurately, a series of layers to the page. The higher the value set for the **z-index** property of an element, the 'closer' it appears on the page. By this we mean elements with higher **z-index** properties will appear on top of elements with lower **z-index** properties.

The W3C draft of the standard proposed that these properties should be supported through the means of Cascading Style Sheets. Now let's look at an example which utilizes these properties to create a 3D effect.

Easy 3D Text Effects

By using document divisions and the absolute positioning abilities of HTML 4.0, we can achieve better results, much faster. Here's an example page, named **3dtitles.htm**:

You can run this page from our Web site at:
http://rapid.wrox.co.uk/books/1193

Here's the HTML that creates this page. It consists of a **<STYLE>** section that defines the three text styles, and three document divisions denoted by the **<DIV>** and **</DIV>** tags. The style section defines a standard paragraph format using a large red font, then two subclasses with the same font but in different colors:

```
<!DOCTYPE HTML PUBLIC "-//IETF//DTD HTML//EN">
<HTML>
<HEAD><TITLE> Cheating with 3D Titles </TITLE></HEAD>

<STYLE TYPE="text/css">
  P { color:red; fontfamily:"Impact", "sans-serif"; fontsize:96 }
  P.highlight { color:silver }
  P.shadow { color:darkred }
</STYLE>

<BODY BGCOLOR=408080>

<DIV STYLE="position:absolute; top:5; left:5; width:600; height:100; margin:10">
<P CLASS=shadow>Wrox Press</P>
</DIV>

<DIV STYLE="position:absolute; top:0; left:0; width:600; height:100; margin:10">
<P CLASS=highlight>Wrox Press</P>
</DIV>

<DIV STYLE="position:absolute; top:2; left:2; width:600; height:100; margin:10">
<P>Wrox Press</P>
</DIV>

</BODY>
</HTML>
```

The three divisions are identical except for their **top** and **left** properties, and—since they are all defined with a **position** property of **absolute**—they will appear at these slightly different positions, but display different colored text. The order that they are defined in the page controls the **z-index**, so we end up with the silver highlight overlaid by the dark red shadow and then by the top-level bright red text.

Changing the appearance, shadow depth or colors is simply a matter of changing the **top**, **left**, **z-index** and **color** properties, and this can create some very different appearances. You should always, where possible, use the **<DIV>** and **<SPAN>** elements to implement style sheets. However, there is a third element, **<LAYER>**, and it's sometimes necessary to use this to take advantage of some of the new Dynamic HTML features.

The <LAYER> Element

Netscape introduced the **<LAYER>** element in early Communicator 4 betas. It worked both as a simpler means of implementing absolute positioning and also as a way of exposing properties to the programmer, which could be altered by JavaScript. Unfortunately it was rejected by the W3C standards committee and its future now seems bleak, considering Netscape have issued a statement saying that the only reason that it was included in the final release of Communicator 4 was for reasons of backwards compatibility. However that's not quite the whole story and, until future releases of Communicator allow you to manipulate the new style properties by script directly, this element is the only way to take advantage of some of Dynamic HTML's new features.

Like the **<DIV>** element, everything between the opening and closing **<LAYER>** element is treated as one item (a layer in this case). Layers allow you to think of your web page almost like a book, with various pages stacked on top of each other. Everything on the top layer obscures the other layers. But, if there are gaps, you can see the pages underneath. Each layer can be peeled away to reveal another layer. This allows quite complex manipulation of screen content, especially as you can make layers visible or invisible. Layers can also be made transparent or opaque and, with the opaque layers, you can set the colors as well. At the moment, we're only interested in how they're used in positioning. Layers can be positioned by the use of attributes or properties manipulated by JavaScript.

LEFT, TOP, WIDTH, HEIGHT and Z-INDEX attributes

Instead of having to set the properties such as **LEFT** and **HEIGHT** through the **STYLE** attribute of the **<STYLE>** tag, or via a Cascading Style Sheet definition, these properties are actually attributes of the **<LAYER>** tag. This can be used to directly alter the positioning of a graphic or some text on the page. It's more direct than having to declare a separate style and then setting it up inside a style sheet.

```
<LAYER ID=Layer1 LEFT=100 TOP=150 WIDTH=40 TOP=10 ZINDEX=2>
This is a Layer
</LAYER>
```

We've already used the new properties to produce a fake 3-D style page layout using just the **<DIV>** element. However there's no way you can actually manipulate the style properties with JavaScript, unless you use the **<LAYER>** element. Before we go as far as that, we'll create another 3-D layout, but this time demonstrating the use of both the **<DIV>** element and the **<LAYER>** element.

While the following example does provide a 'kind' of 3D appearance, we can actually only specify the three standard x, y, and z co-ordinates—we can't achieve real 3-D. For this reason, it's often referred to as **two-and-a-half-D** layout.

Going 2.5-D in a Web Page

For each division and layer we want to create on a page, we can specify the top, left, width and height. With divisions we set the **left**, **top** and **z-index** properties of the elements, with layers we use the **LEFT**, **TOP** and **Z-INDEX** attributes. We can then create a display, using either or both of these features, that will look like it was created using frames. This sample page, called **2point5d.htm**, uses both layers and divisions.

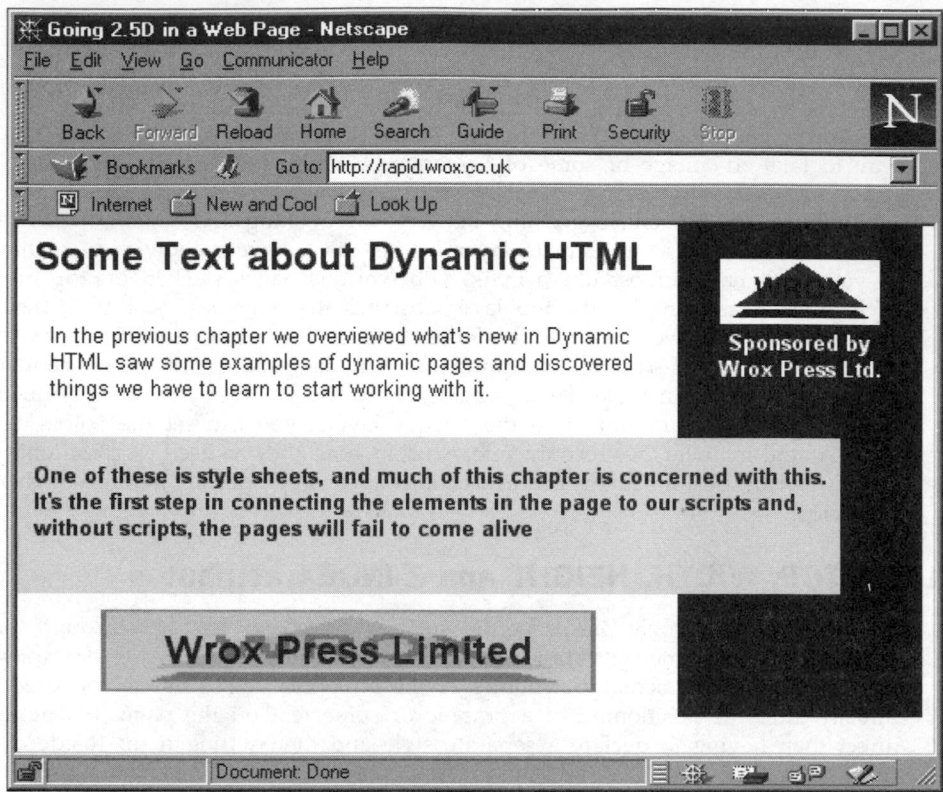

You can run this page from our Web site at:
http://rapid.wrox.co.uk/books/1193

Notice how the central band of text overlaps the right-hand dark-colored column. This kind of layout would be just about impossible to achieve with tables. However, it's easy using Dynamic HTML. In fact, this page demonstrates several ways of using the new properties to build more free-form, desktop-publishing-like web pages. Here is the complete HTML source for this page:

```
<HTML>
<HEAD><TITLE> Going 2.5D in a Web Page </TITLE></HEAD>

<STYLE>
   P                    { fontfamily:Arial;
                          fontsize:14 }
   .bluetext            { fontweight:Bold;
                          color:darkblue;
                          position: absolute;
                          top:10;
                          left:10;
                          width:480;
                          height:60}
   .reverse             { fontweight:Bold;
                          color:white }
   H2                   { fontfamily:Arial;
                          fontsize:24;
                          fontweight:Bold;
```

```
                        color:darkblue
                        z-index: 1}
        .class1         {position:absolute;
                        top:0;
                        left:0;
                        width:400;
                        height:100;
                        margin:10}
        .class2         {position:relative;
                        top:20;
                        left:25}
        .class3         {position:absolute;
                        top:235;
                        width:400;
                        left:90;
                        z-index:3}
        .class4         {position:absolute;
                        top:225;
                        left:50;
                        z-index:2}
</STYLE>

<BODY>

<DIV CLASS=class1>
  <H2> Some Text about Dynamic HTML </H2>
  <P > In the previous chapter we overviewed what's new in Dynamic HTML
saw some examples of dynamic pages and discovered things we have to learn
to start working with it.</P>
</DIV>

<LAYER top=0 left=400 width=150 height=300 bgcolor=darkblue>
<DIV CLASS=class2>
  <IMG SRC="wrox0.gif">
</DIV>
<CENTER>
    <P CLASS=reverse>Sponsored by<BR>Wrox Press Ltd.</P>
  </CENTER>
</LAYER>

<LAYER top=130 left=0 width=500 height=80 bgcolor=yellow >
  <P CLASS=bluetext> One of these is style sheets, and much of this chapter is
concerned with this. It's the first step in connecting the
elements in the page to our scripts and, without scripts, the
pages will fail to come alive  </P>
</LAYER>

<DIV CLASS=class3>
    <H2 STYLE="color=darkred; line-height:200%"> Wrox Press Limited</H2>
</DIV>

<DIV CLASS=class4>
<IMG SRC="wrox1.gif">
</DIV>

</BODY>
```

As you can see, there are five main sections to the code. The first is the **STYLE**
element that sets the font styles, sizes, colors, etc. for each kind of text style we
are going to use in the page. You'll notice that it creates a style for the standard
<P> paragraph element, then two sub-class styles based on this. These have a
bold font weight, and different colors. The fourth style is just used to create the
headline **<H2>** style.

51

Of course, these style definitions could be included in a separate style sheet to permit easier updating of several pages in one go if required. However, what we're really interested in are the other five sections of the page—the 'working parts'. These are the `<LAYER>` and `<DIV>` elements.

Working with Divisions

One of the easiest ways to think of the `<DIV>` element is that it creates a section within the page where we can place other elements and these sections can overlap each other. Each section becomes a **container**, and its contents can be placed accurately within this section using the Communicator 4 `left` and `top` style attributes. This is how we've divided our page up into separate sections that overlap.

Document divisions also act in a different way to the normal page. While text will flow across layer boundaries, if it won't all fit within the layer in which it has been declared, other elements such as images are cropped. When the browser window is resized, text in a division does not repaginate like text displayed directly on the page. With careful design, both of these properties can be used to advantage in our pages. In particular, it means that our designs are now independent of the size of the browser window, and the user must adjust the size, or scroll the page to see it all. However you must be careful as this can force people to maximize their browser window to see your whole design, which can prove irritating.

To present the page as separate divisions, we need to use another of the new style properties, **position**. This is used to specify where the browser will place the division, and applies equally to any other elements that can be positioned using the `left` and `top` properties.

The Position Property

This new property allows us to position elements at fixed positions within the browser window, in conjunction with the `top` and `left` property. It can be set to one of three possible values: **relative**, **absolute**, or **static**.

 relative means that the element will be placed in a position relative to its position within the HTML source for the page. In other words, if an image follows three lines of text in the HTML source, has its **position** property set to **relative**, and the `left` and `top` set to zero, it will appear in the same position with respect to the text as if there were no positioning attributes included. If we specify **relative**, and set the `left` and `top` properties to non-zero figures (positive or negative), it will be placed at this horizontal and vertical offset from the normal position. Other elements in the HTML source that follow it will still be placed after this element in the usual way, and hence initially offset by the same amount.

- **absolute** means that the element will be placed at an absolute position with respect to the top left hand corner of its container. This effectively removes it from the HTML source as far as its influence on following elements is concerned. For example, specifying **left** and **top** values will position the element at those *x* and *y* coordinates with respect to the division that contains it. If it is not within a division, it is placed in that position with respect to the top left corner of the page. Its actual position will not affect any elements that follow it in the HTML source.

- **static** means that the element will be placed in the usual position with respect to the HTML source for the page, and is the default value if **position** is not specified in the **<STYLE>** tag.

The **position** property applies to the **<DIV>** element, as well as to other elements, so we can use it to place our document divisions accurately in the page. In the example above, we used these four divisions to build up the basic structure of the page:

```
.class1      {position:absolute;
             top:0;
             left:0;
             width:400;
             height:100}
...
<DIV CLASS=class1>
...
</DIV>


.class2      {position:relative;
             top:20;
             left:25}
...
<DIV CLASS=class2>
...
</DIV>


.class3      {position:absolute;
             top:235;
             width:400;
             left:90;
             z-index:3}
...
<DIV CLASS=class3>
...
</DIV>


.class4      {position:absolute;
             top:225;
             left:50;
             z-index:2}
...
<DIV CLASS=class4>
...
</DIV>
```

Notice that there is no **height** property set for the last three definitions. If we omit any properties like this, the division will assume default values. For example, if we omit the **width** property, it will span the width of the browser window by default.

Working With Layers

Layers are very similar to document divisions and indeed Netscape probably intended them as an alternative to document divisions. However, as they won't be replacing divisions, we haven't used them except when there are no other alternatives. If you do use layers you must remember that they aren't compatible with any proprietary browsers other than Communicator 4 and, in all likelihood, will be removed from future Communicator releases. But like it or not, sometimes they're the only way you can do things...

For example one thing that the document division doesn't do in this example, that makes it necessary for us to use layers, is to set a background color block. The following code should, in theory, create two identically sized colored blocks (and indeed in Internet Explorer 4, the **<DIV>** element would be the same size as the **<LAYER>** one here):

```
<DIV STYLE="position:absolute; top:100; left: 100; width: 100; height:100;
background:red; color: white">
This is a division
</DIV>

<LAYER TOP= 100 LEFT=300 WIDTH=100 HEIGHT=100 BGCOLOR=RED >
This is a layer
</LAYER>
```

However, in Communicator, if you specify a background color with a document division it simply surrounds the text as follows:

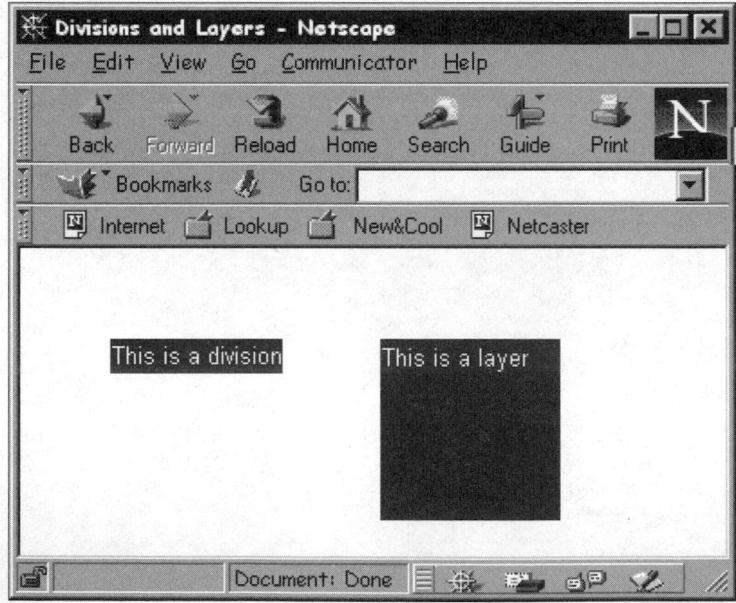

One point to note is that document divisions respond to adjustments in the size of the browser window, layers don't. So, if you resize the browser window to make both the division and the layer go off the screen and then resize it again to make them appear, the text in the division will have been displaced but the text in the layer will stay the same. This can be a good or bad thing depending on how the web page author intends the screen to be viewed.

Positioning and Layers

Using the **LEFT** and **TOP** attributes of the **<LAYER>** element avoids the need to specify the type of positioning. By default, it's always going to be absolute, as the coordinates you specify are always going to correspond directly to a position on the page. If you need to specify a **<LAYER>** relative to another **<LAYER>** then you have to use the **<ILAYER>** element (inflow layer). We'll look at this in more detail in chapter 7, as we don't need to use it now.

Using Divisions and Layers in Specifying Dynamic HTML Layout

Having placed our document division and layer containers on the page, we can now fill them with our page elements. Anything enclosed in a **<DIV>** and **</DIV>** tag pair will appear within the area of the screen designated to that layer. The first division is simple enough—it just displays the heading and some introductory text:

```
.class1      {position:absolute;
             top:0;
             left:0;
             width:400;
             height:100}
...
<DIV CLASS=class1>
  <H2> Some Text about Dynamic HTML </H2>
  <P > In the previous chapter we overviewed what's new in Dynamic HTML
saw some examples of dynamic pages and discovered things we have to learn
to start working with it.</P>
</DIV>
```

The next section that is rendered is the dark colored layer to the right of the page, containing a logo and some text. Notice that we've specified the image element with a **position** property of **relative**. This just offsets it while 'reserving' its place in the HTML source, so that the text that follows will appear below it:

```
.class2      {position:relative;
             top:20;
             left:25}
...
<LAYER top=0 left=400 width=150 height=300 bgcolor=darkblue>
<DIV CLASS=class2>
  <IMG SRC="wrox0.gif">
</DIV>
<CENTER>
    <P CLASS=reverse>Sponsored by<BR>Wrox Press Ltd.</P>
  </CENTER>
</LAYER>
```

If we had declared the **position** property as **absolute** for the image, instead of **relative**, it would appear in the same place, but the text would be displayed at the top of the division, overlaid by the image.

The image could have 'disappeared' from the HTML source as far as its effect on the following text is concerned:

You'll also see that the usual formatting tags work normally within a division. We've used the **<CENTER>** tag to center the text in the division, and applied the **P.reverse** style we defined earlier, just as we would in a traditional web page.

The second layer is very similar to the first. It uses the **<LAYER>** attributes, so that it fits nicely into the One of these Style sheets... division:

```
<LAYER top=130 left=0 width=500 height=80 bgcolor=yellow >
  <P CLASS=bluetext> One of these is style sheets, and much of this chapter is
concerned with this. It's the first step in connecting the
elements in the page to our scripts and, without scripts, the
pages will fail to come alive </P>
</LAYER>
```

Layer Control with the Z-index Property

The final division demonstrates one more technique. Here, we have an **<IMG>** tag overlaid by text. In traditional web pages, this is not possible. In traditional HTML, the text is wrapped around any images on the page, unless you arrange for the image to be used in the **<BODY>** tag as the page background.

There is a new property, called **z-index**, in both Communicator 4 and Internet Explorer 4, which allows the web page author to specify at what level (or layer) an element is displayed. This can be in relation to the body text or headings in the page, or any other elements. The body text and titles are displayed in level zero, or layer **0**, and so have a **z-index** of zero.

Specifying the Z-index

By specifying positive numbers, we can arrange for our elements to appear above the text, and by specifying negative numbers, they will appear below it. And, of course, we can layer individual non-text elements in relation to each other by using higher or lower **z-index** values.

In the third and fourth divisions of our example page, we have some text, and a logo inside an **<IMG>** tag. The text is defined first in the HTML, and uses the **line-height** style property to place it in the correct vertical position inside the division. Then the logo is specified, using absolute positioning to get it centered with respect to the text. Then, to make it appear with the text rendered on top, we set its **z-index** property to a value lower than that of the text:

```
.class3     {position:absolute;
            top:235;
            width:400;
            left:90;
         z-index:3}
```

```
.class4        {position:absolute;
               top:225;
               left:50;
          z-index:2}
...
<DIV CLASS=class3>
   <H2 STYLE="color=darkred; line-height:200%"> Wrox Press Limited</H2>
</DIV>

<DIV CLASS=class4>
<IMG SRC="wrox1.gif">
</DIV>
```

The result isn't terribly pretty, but it serves to demonstrate the point.

Overlaying Document Divisions or Layers

As mentioned previously, the browser sets the **z-index** of elements automatically as it renders the page. When two elements with an equivalent 'default level', such as two image tags, are defined in the HTML source for the page, the one that comes last will have the highest **z-index**. Therefore, if these two elements are made to overlap, using any of the positioning techniques, the second one will appear on top of the first one.

So, by setting the **z-index** in a style tag, or as an attribute of the **<LAYER>** tag—or, as you'll see later on, dynamically with script code—we can control this layering process to provide exactly the effect we want. If you look back at the previous example, you'll see that the third (yellow) document division overlays the second (dark blue) one, because it was declared later in the HTML.

Controlling Overflow and Visibility

In this chapter, we've seen how four of the six new Dynamic HTML style properties can be used to create pages in a fundamentally new way by accurately positioning elements and controlling the layering. The properties we use are the **left**, **top** and **z-index** properties/attributes, which effectively define the x, y, and z coordinates. When using Cascading Style Sheets we also use the **position** property, to define how the coordinates are used and what effect the positioning has on other elements that follow in the HTML source. The other two new properties are used to control the **overflow** and **visibility** of elements.

Using the Overflow Property

The **overflow** property is used to determine what should happen when an element's contents exceed the height or width of a window. It can be set to one of three values:

 A value of **none** indicates that no clipping is to be performed. For example, preformatted text that extends past the right edge of an element's boundaries would be rendered anyway

57

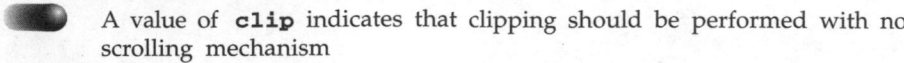

A value of **clip** indicates that clipping should be performed with no scrolling mechanism

A **scroll** value causes a scrolling mechanism to be invoked

Using the Visibility Property

The last new style property in Dynamic HTML is **visibility**. As the name suggests, this controls whether the element will be visible on the page. When we create static pages, using absolute positioning, it isn't terribly useful. After all, if we don't want to show an element, there's not a great deal of point in including it in the HTML source.

Where the **visibility** property is useful is when we come to add scripting code to our page. It can change the properties of the elements in the page, thereby making them visible or invisible as required, while the page is displayed.

However, there is one case where the **visibility** property can be useful in a static page. Looking back at our 'two-and-a-half-D' example, we found that the text below the *Wrox* image in the right-hand division depended on the image tag having a **position** property value of **relative**, to prevent it appearing at the top of the division. If we remove the image tag, the text will not be in the same position, because there is no relative image to move it down the page.

If, for some reason, we wanted to hide the image and not move the text, we can set its
visibility property to **hidden** (the default is **visible**). The result is that everything else stays the same, but the image itself is not rendered on the page:

Using the VISIBILITY Attribute

The **<LAYER>** element also supports a **VISIBILITY** attribute, which has three settings as follows:

- **SHOW**
- **HIDE**
- **INHERIT**

HIDE hides the layer, just as the **HIDDEN** setting does in style sheets, **SHOW** displays the layer but the default is **INHERIT** which means that a layer has the same visibility setting as its parent.

We've now considered the six new properties that Communicator 4 introduces, so it's time to look at how we can take advantage of them by adding some script to your pages, which allows you to change properties dynamically.

Adding Script to HTML Pages

So far, you might be forgiven for thinking that many of the effects we've demonstrated could have been achieved – albeit with a little more effort - with Cascading Style Sheets and without any of the new HTML 4.0 properties. While this is true to some extent, it's because we haven't yet covered the real power it offers—being able to dynamically manipulate properties with a **script** and update their positions/styles on screen.

At its most basic, a scripting language is just a way of making your pages reactive, enabling them to interact with the user so they are more than just code. They've been present in both Internet Explorer and Netscape Navigator/ Communicator since version 3. Internet Explorer 4 supports both JavaScript and VBScript, while Communicator 4 only supports JavaScript (without the aid of proprietary add-ins). As the focus of the book is Netscape Communicator 4, we'll be using examples in just JavaScript.

Rather than talk about how to make your page react to events, we've chosen to describe how to manipulate the new Dynamic HTML properties first and include only simple code. In Chapter 6, Scripts and Event Handling, we'll look in more detail at how JavaScript is used with the object model.

However, there are a couple of things you will need to know before you start. We'll briefly show you how script code appears in a page, and how we create code routines. This will be enough to carry you through to Chapter 6.

Where to Place Your Script

Scripting code is placed in the page within the HTML `<SCRIPT>` and `</SCRIPT>` tags. These tell the browser that the code between the tags is to be interpreted and the script is executed as the page is loaded.

```
...
<SCRIPT LANGUAGE=JAVASCRIPT>
   ... JavaScript code goes here
</SCRIPT>
...
```

The script section can be placed almost anywhere in the page. The favorite position is often at the end, so that the rest of the page is loaded and rendered by the browser before the interpreter loads and runs the code.

If this page is loaded into a browser that doesn't support JavaScript, the code itself will simply be displayed as text on the page. The traditional way to prevent this is to enclose the contents of the `<SCRIPT>` section in a comment tag. Non-script enabled browsers will then ignore it, while browsers that do support scripting will still be able to interpret and execute it.

```
...
<SCRIPT LANGUAGE=VBSCRIPT>
<!-- hide from older browsers
   ... script code goes here
-->
</SCRIPT>
...
```

Of course, we're aiming our pages at Dynamic HTML-enabled browsers, and support for a scripting language is a prerequisite for this anyway. However, it doesn't hurt to hide it in case the page is loaded by an older browser—even though it will probably still look odd because the browser won't support the other layout features of Dynamic HTML either.

Creating Script Routines in a Page

The other technique you need to be familiar with is how we create separate code routines in a page, which are *not* executed as the page is loading. Much of the dynamic nature of modern web pages is due to script code that reacts to **events** occurring within the browser. Changing the contents of a page by executing script as the page is loading does provide a dynamic page in some ways, but not in the sense we're looking for, where the page will also react to events occurring within the browser.

To prevent code being executed as the page loads, we place it inside a **function**.

```
<SCRIPT LANGUAGE=JAVASCRIPT>

function MyNewRoutine()
{
   .. JavaScript code goes here;
}

function window_onLoad()
{
   .. JavaScript code to run when the window object gets an 'onLoad' event;
}

function GetAnyNumber()
{
   .. JavaScript code goes here, including setting the return value;
   return 42
}

</SCRIPT>
```

Using a Script to Manipulate the Dynamic HTML Properties

We're going look at an example, which shows how we can dynamically update properties of an element on the page with a script to make it move across the screen. However, before we can do that we need to understand how we can update properties using code. This is all done via the **layers** object.

Using the Layers Object

The real power behind the **<LAYER>** element is the **layers** object. Currently in Communicator 4 it just isn't possible to use script to dynamically alter the style properties and attributes as you can in Internet Explorer 4. The properties aren't exposed to the programmer, so to get around this, you need to use the **layers** object.

It's important to realize that there are different ways of setting the properties for the **<LAYER>** element in the HTML source, and correspondingly two different ways to access these properties in our code.

If we define a **<LAYER>** element like this:

```
<LAYER ID=MyLayer SRC="Mypic.gif" WIDTH=100 HEIGHT=100>
```

we are controlling the width and height using traditional HTML attributes. The width and height properties are then direct properties of the object, and we can refer to them in our code using the **layers** object:

```
document.layers["MyLayer"].width
document.layers["MyLayer"].height
```

Don't be put off by the rather ponderous method that is needed to access each property or method. The reason the **document.layers** bit is needed is really quite simple. You need to consider that for each layer in a page, there is a corresponding JavaScript layer object. The layer object can be accessed in the following ways:

layerName.methodName
layerName.propertyName

However each layer has a document property and that property has a layers array, which contains all the layer names. So when you reference a specific layer, by name, you need to preface it with **document.layers** as we're referencing the name using the layers array.

document.layers["*LayerName*"**].***property/methodName*

For the purposes of this example, that's all you need to know—we look at the **layers** object in greater detail in later chapters.

> *There's a full listing of the properties and methods of the layers object in the reference section at the end of this book.*

Moving Elements around a Page

Here's the bit you've been waiting for! If we define an **<LAYER>** tag like this:

```
<LAYER LEFT=200 TOP=100>
<IMG SRC="MyPic.gif">
</LAYER>
```

not only can we retrieve the image's `left` and `top` properties, we can also change them—effectively moving it around the screen while the page is displayed.

Moving Elements Around a Page Example

Right, it's time to take a look at an example. We're going to 'move' an element across the screen, making it move behind one element and then in front of another, by simply updating one property. The element will start its journey on the far left hand side of the screen and will move gradually rightwards. Here the message is already halfway across the screen:

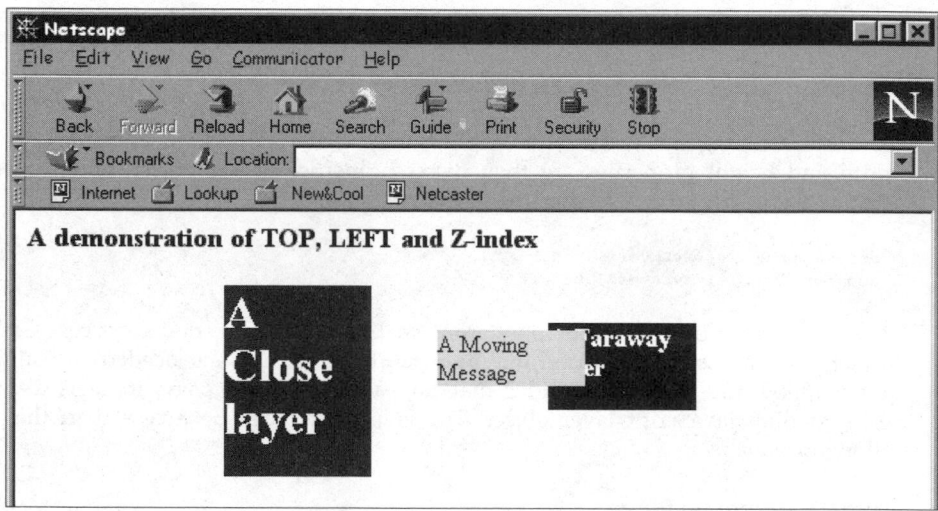

You can run this page from our Web site at:
`http://rapid.wrox.co.uk/books/1193`

The initial 'X 'and 'Y' co-ordinates of the tags are set out in the `LEFT` and `HEIGHT` attributes of the `<LAYER>` tags and the Moving Message `<LAYER>` tag is assigned a unique name, with an ID attribute so it can be identified within the script.

```
<!DOCTYPE HTML PUBLIC "-//IETF//DTD HTML//EN">
<HTML>
<HEAD>

</STYLE>
<TITLE></TITLE>
</HEAD>

<BODY>
<H3>A demonstration of TOP, LEFT and Z-index</H3>

<LAYER top=50  left=140  height=130 width=100  bgcolor= red  z-index= 4>
A Close layer
</LAYER>

<LAYER top= 75 left=360 height= 70 width=100  bgcolor= blue z-index= 2>
A Faraway layer
```

```
</LAYER>

<LAYER ID=MovingMessage  top= 80 left=0 height= 30 width=100  bgcolor=yellow z-
index= 3 >
A Moving Message
</LAYER>

<SCRIPT>
function moveLeft()
{
    document.layers["MovingMessage"].left++
    if(document.layers["MovingMessage"].left !=500)
    {
    setTimeout("moveLeft()",10)
    }
}
window.onload=moveLeft;
</SCRIPT>
</BODY>
</HTML>
```

The script is very simple. It just obtains the **left** property of the
MovingMessage element and then increments it by one. This moves the
element rightwards by one pixel. The procedure is then executed again.

```
document.layers["MovingMessage"].left++
  if(document.layers["MovingMessage"].left !=500)
```

So, after this procedure had been executed 10 times the message would be in this position:

Left Property = 10 pixels

The script checks to see if it's reached 500 pixels across the screen, stops if it
has and runs the procedure again if it hasn't.

```
    if(document.layers["MovingMessage"].left !=500)
    {
    setTimeout("moveLeft()",10)
    }
```

There is one minor thing that complicates the script. If you just went ahead and
moved the block across the screen and simply called the procedure again, the
screen wouldn't have time to display the block as it moved across the screen.
So we need to slow its journey across the screen by calling a **setTimeout**
function, which gives Dynamic HTML time to update the position of the
element on the screen. This function arranges for the **moveLeft()** function to
be called after a delay of 10 milliseconds. So, instead of not being able to
update the screen in time, the 10 milliseconds allow the browser to redraw the
element, one pixel to the right.

63

There's one final line, which we're going to gloss over now, as we don't want to talk about it until Chapter 6, where we discuss events. This basically starts the function as soon as the page is opened, otherwise the function would never be called:

```
window.onload=moveLeft;
```

Admittedly, this is a very simple example, but it demonstrates something that just wasn't possible in HTML or style sheets previously and shows that Dynamic HTML opens up a lot of possibilities. What happens if you get the movement to be triggered by the click of a mouse, for instance? However before we get carried away, we need to look at the HTML object model and how scripting makes use of it. That is the subject of the next chapter.

Summary

In this chapter, we've seen how the formatting of pages in Dynamic HTML is far more dependent on using **styles** than earlier versions of HTML. In particular, the six new properties provide ways to control the positioning, layout, and z-order (or z-index) of the various elements in the page.

Dynamic HTML provides six new style properties that control the layout and appearance of pages:

- **left** and **top** define the x and y coordinates of the element within its container. This can be a document division, or the page itself

- **z-index** defines the z coordinate, or layer, in which the element will appear. It's set initially by the ordering of the elements in the HTML, if not specified directly

- **position** defines how the **left** and **top** values are interpreted in relation to the element's position within the HTML source, and how it affects the elements that follow

- **overflow** defines whether an element is clipped to window boundaries or if it is to be displayed off-screen with or without a scrolling mechanism

- **visibility** defines whether the element will be visible in the page when it is rendered. An element can be **hidden**, but still keep its place in the HTML source

And of course, we can still use the existing style properties from HTML 3.2 to control the other aspects of our design—as we did throughout this chapter. We also looked at how to manipulate some of these new properties with the aid of a script. We used the **style** property to access all of the new properties and dynamically update the screen as it did so. However, to understand how we can get the best out of scripting, we need to understand the **object model** on which the browser is built—and this is the subject of the next two chapters.

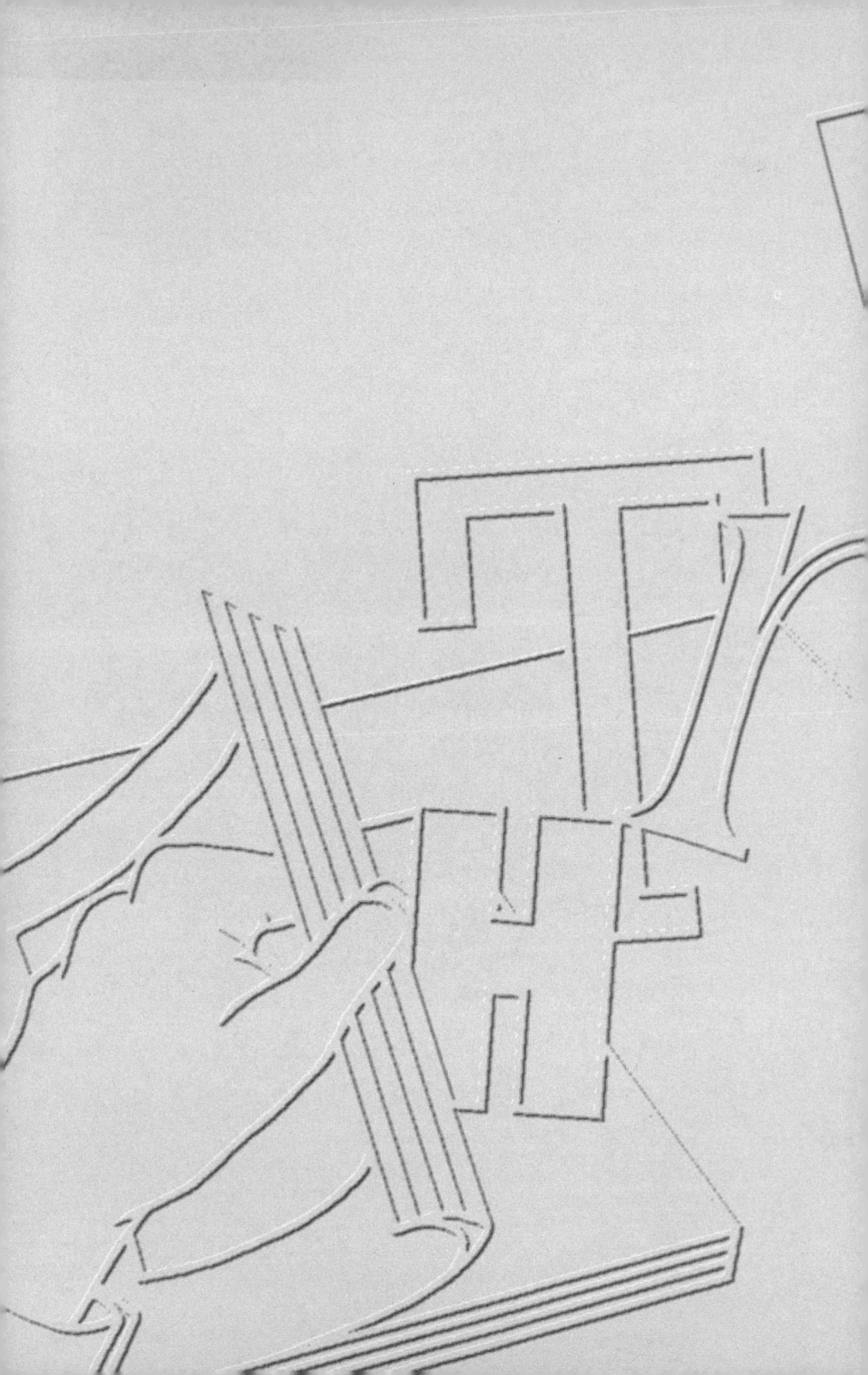

The Dynamic HTML Browser Object Model

Now that we've explored the new properties that are available in the Dynamic HTML implementation of style sheets, we can move on to look at the other major difference between traditional and Dynamic HTML. Since the advent of Netscape 2, the browser has provided a documented **object model**, which can be used by the scripting code in a page to access both the browser environment and the contents of the page itself. This access was severely limited when it came to the non-control elements in the page—while you could access such things as HTML text boxes and list boxes, and Java applets, you couldn't get at the real contents of the document. The text, images, headings and other page contents remained temptingly out of reach.

Much of this has changed in Dynamic HTML. Many of the things that are visible in the page, and some that aren't, can be accessed through the new extensions to the object model. This is the subject of this chapter. We'll take an overview of the whole structure, then investigate the new and the most useful objects. In the next chapter, we'll continue this process, to look at the other objects that are most useful for integrating our script into a web page.

In this chapter, we'll cover:

- The browser object model in outline, with a comparison to older browsers
- A brief tour of the basic window objects, generally unchanged from earlier versions
- A look at some of the more useful new objects and arrays

We can't hope to give an in-depth explanation of the entire structure in this book, and there is no real need to do this anyway. Much of the structure is simple, and some is only used in very special cases. You will, however, find definitions and listings of the items which make up the structure in the reference section at the back of this book.

Introducing the Browser Object Model

If you haven't used scripting code in a web page before, you may not have realized that the browser is built around a structured set of **objects**. It's these objects that provide an interface between the scripting languages and the internal workings of the browser itself. To make the whole thing easier to visualize and work with, the various objects are organized into a structure called the **object model**.

Why Do We Need An Object Model?

When we just define a normal static web page with HTML, we don't need to know about the object model or the structure of the browser itself. Even when we display several documents in different frames, we just give each frame a name, and **TARGET** new pages to the appropriate one. For example, if we have defined a frameset which contains a frame named **mainwindow**, like this:

```
<FRAMESET>
  <FRAME NAME="mainwindow" SRC="http://www.wrox.com">
  ...
</FRAMESET>
```

we can load a different page into it using the **TARGET** attribute of the **<A>** tag:

```
<A HREF="http://rapid.wrox.co.uk" TARGET="mainwindow">The Wrox Rapid site</A>
```

The Object Model and Scripting

If you've used a scripting language like JavaScript before, you'll know that this is an extremely simplified view. In reality, the browser stores the frames in the browser window as an **array** (a specially defined structure, which we'll be looking at later), and they become child objects of the main window. To refer to the main window in a scripting language, we have to reference it using the keywords **parent** or **top**. The keyword **parent** refers to the window immediately above the current window in the hierarchy, which may be the top window, while **top** always refers to the topmost window :

```
parent.frames["mainwindow"].location.href = "http://rapid.wrox.co.uk"
```

> You'll no doubt have met the 'page targeting' keywords _**top**_ and _**self**_
> before. In the **TARGET** attribute of an **<A>** tag, _**top**_ is used to load a page
> into the main browser window, instead of into a frame within the window—
> effectively replacing the frameset. _**self**_ can be used to load a page into the
> current window, though this is rarely used. The **top** and **self** keywords in
> scripting languages have the same meaning as these.

So the concept of things being stored as arrays, and having parents and children, implies that there is an underlying object model structure—even if you haven't actually seen it before. Don't worry about the code we've used here for the time being. In this chapter, we'll start to explore the object model, and see how to use it in Dynamic HTML.

The Object Model in Overview

The browser object model can be thought of as physically part of the software that is the browser. HTML 4.0 will be (in theory at least) a universal browser-independent document definition language. This means that all browsers which host HTML 4.0 must provide the same object model. Otherwise, it would be impossible to create pages that performed properly on different browsers.

> *In actual fact, at the present time, the two newest browsers—Netscape Communicator and Microsoft Internet Explorer—don't implement all of the proposals made in the draft of HTML 4.0 and what they both refer to as Dynamic HTML is in fact subtly different as well. The object models in these two browsers are therefore also different. You'll see more about this in Chapter 8.*

However, the object model is in fact just an **interface** between the scripting language, and the browser software routines that create the window and fill it with the elements defined in the page. How it does this filling of the window, or **rendering** of the page, is unimportant. Dynamic HTML simply defines what the results should be, not how the processes should be implemented.

So, we can think of the browser's object model simply as a way of connecting our pages to the browser. It exposes a range of **objects**, **methods**, **properties** and **events** that are present within the browser's software to the HTML and scripting code in the page. We can use these to communicate our wishes back to the browser, and therefore to the viewer. The browser will carry out our commands and update the page(s) it displays.

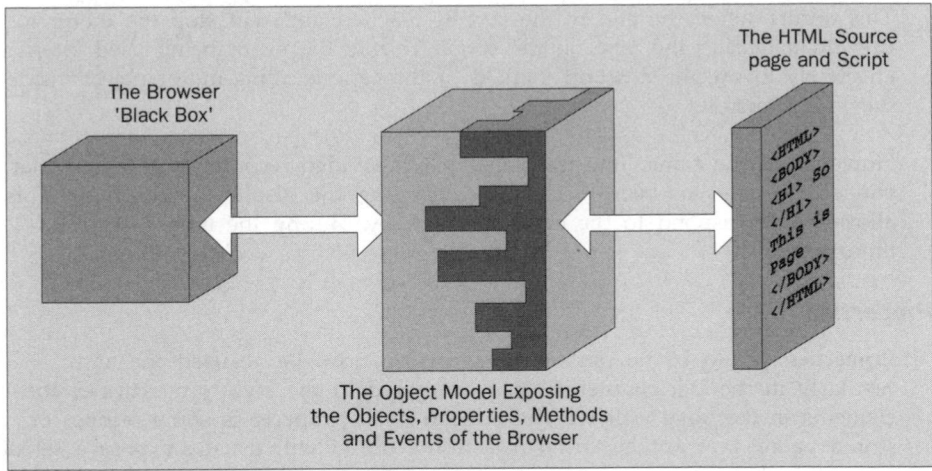

Objects, Methods, Properties and Events

So far we've talked about objects, methods, properties and events—and assumed that you are familiar with these terms. No doubt you've heard them used many times, but we'll recap briefly here before going on to look at the browser object model itself.

69

Objects

Modern software design is very much concerned with **objects**. You can think of these as being self-contained parts of a program such as the browser, which carry out specific functions. The key is that they will usually store their own data, in their own format, and contain the code routines called **methods** (see definition below) required to manipulate that data.

You can think of an object as being rather like a video recorder, in that we put the tapes in and set the timer, but all the work of recording and playing back goes on inside the black box. We just tell it to record or play back, and we don't need to know what's actually going on inside. The video recorder stores its data (our TV program) itself, in its own format, without us having to worry about how it's doing it.

Methods

Methods are an object's way of letting us do something with it. Our video recorder has methods built in that allow us to record or play back TV programs. The big advantage of having an object provide methods is that it takes away the worry of knowing what's going on inside the object. Rather than telling the video recorder the exact patterns of magnetism to lay down on the tape or how to interpret the sound signal, we just execute its **Record** and **Play** method by pressing a couple of buttons.

Events

If methods are our way of telling an object what to do, **events** can be thought of as the object's way of telling us that something happened. It's likely that our trusty video recorder will have something we could term an **EndOfTape** event. This occurs when the end of the tape is reached and will stop the motor to prevent it tearing the tape off the spool. This is the event being used internally, effectively to execute a **Stop** method of the tape-winding-motor object inside the video recorder.

However, at the same time it's likely that the video recorder will tell us that the end of the tape has been reached, by changing the display on the front. This allows us to respond to the event, perhaps by putting the tape back in its library case.

Properties

Properties should be no problem to grasp by now. We've used the term regularly in the last chapter when we referred to the style properties of the elements in the page. All we really mean by a property is some setting, or stored value, that applies to an object. The object will usually expose a set of properties that affect the appearance or behavior of the object, and some that just provide information about it. These properties are either read-only or properties that can be written to, which are termed read/write.

In our video recorder example there are properties we can just observe (read) or use to change (write) the behavior or appearance. Read-only properties could be the age, the price and the working condition. Read/write properties might include the record speed setting, and the time setting on the clock. As you can see, there are often read-only properties that we would like to be able to change, but can't—and Dynamic HTML is no exception.

The Object Model Diagram

Being able to describe the object model of the browser is, as you've seen, a necessity if we are to understand how all the parts of the hierarchy fit together. The usual way to do this is to show a tree-style diagram, with the main objects at the top and the subsidiary ones below.

This is what we've done here. The top-level object in the browser hierarchy is the **window**. This is the parent object for every other object in the structure.

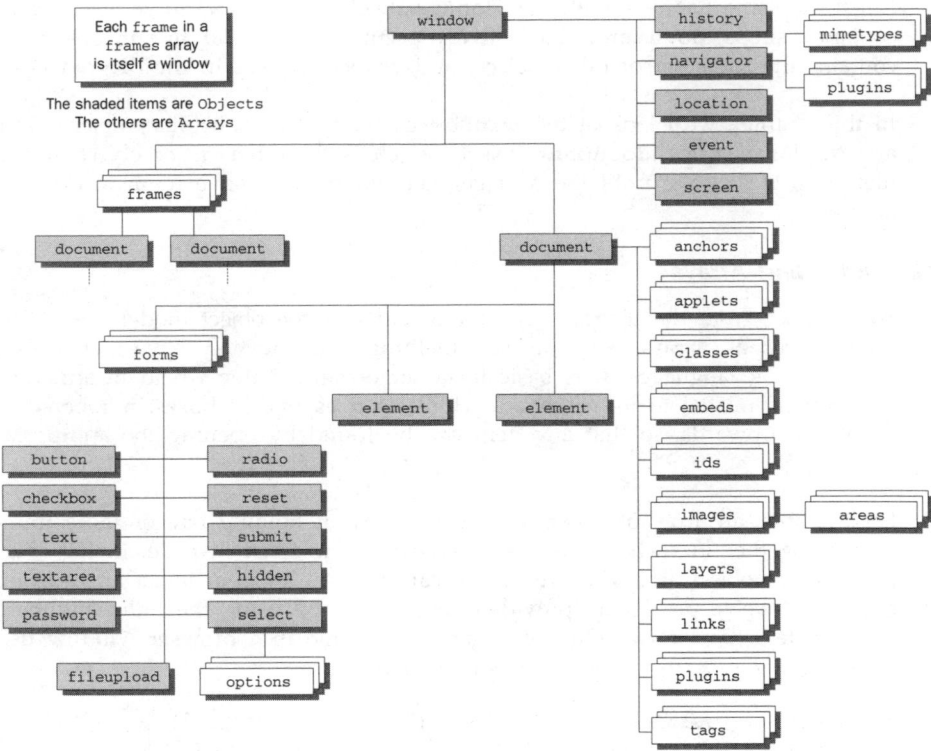

*You'll notice that some of the 'things' in the object hierarchy are **objects**, and some are **arrays**. Arrays have a plural name, i.e. **anchors** rather than anchor.*

The diagram shows how each of the objects is related—and there are quite a few of them altogether. If you've used JavaScript in any depth before, you'll recognize many of them. To maintain backwards compatibility with pages designed for older browsers, the object model for Dynamic HTML is a superset of that found in Netscape Navigator 3 (and Internet Explorer 3).

Looking at the Structure

Looking at the diagram, you can see that although the **window** object is at the top of the tree, it's the **document** object that is really at the heart of things. This isn't surprising, because the bulk of our page and its contents are part of the **document** itself. The **window** is just the container that holds it.

If you are worried about remembering this structure, don't panic. A lot of it is of only minor importance when creating pages, and much of it is repeated. For example, a window can hold a selection of **frames**, but each frame is actually a **window** in its own right. Therefore, once you understand how to use the **window** object, it works the same in the separate windows created by a frameset document.

Much the same happens with the **document** object. Each **window** object can contain a single **document** object. Every occurrence of a **document** object contains the same set of other objects and arrays you see in the diagram.

In this chapter, we'll look at the **window** object and its subsidiary objects and arrays. However, the **document** object, which is the other major object in the hierarchy, we'll leave until the next chapter where we'll have room to do it justice.

Understanding Arrays

You can see from the diagram that many parts of the object model are implemented as **arrays**. An array is something that you may have met in other programming languages. It is basically a set of similar items held in structure, and each is related to its neighbors. Think of it as pile of boxes, numbered from zero upwards, so that any item can be found by opening the appropriate box.

For example, an array of **frames** is just a way of holding one or more frame objects together in such a way that they can be accessed in code. In the case of the browser object arrays, however, we can refer to an item in an array using a name that we've previously provided—as well as by using the index number for that item. So we can retrieve details of a frame in a browser window using either its name or its numerical position in the array:

```
window.frames["mainframe"]    // both of these refer to frames in a window
window.frames[0]              // this is the first frame, with index zero
```

The browser assumes that the *active* **window** object (which may, of course, be a frame inside another window) is the default object for script in the page. Therefore, in most cases we don't need to specify it. The following lines have the same meaning as those above:

```
frames["mainframe"]
frames[0]
```

In the browser object model's arrays, the first item is indexed zero. The actual ordering of the frames in an array depends on their order in the HTML source. Frame zero will be the first frame defined in the **<FRAMESET>** tag. The same applies to other arrays, such as the **forms** or **images** in a document.

Understanding Parents and Children

The expression
window.frames[0] that we
used above refers to the first
frame in a window. However,
this is the *current* window,
which may not be the window
at the top of the object tree.
Imagine a case where there are
three frames in a window. As
far as we are concerned, they
are indexed **0**, **1** and **2** in the
frames array.

window.frames[0]	
window.frames[1]	window.frames[2]

However, this is the **frames** array of the main (top) window. If we are using
scripting code in the page in the lower-left frame, **window** refers to our own
window and not the *top* main window. Our window is a **child** of the main
(top) window, and script running in it has to refer to other frames in relation
to the current frame. Remember, each frame is in effect a **window** in its own
right.

To refer to an object one step up the hierarchy, such as the **window** that holds
the **frames** array that created our frame, we use the **parent** keyword. To go
up the hierarchy two steps, we can refer to the **parent** of the **parent**, etc.:

```
parent.window.frames[0]        // this is the first frame in the parent window
parent.parent.window.frames[0] // and in the parent of this window if there is one
```

We can always refer to the *topmost* window in the object model (the browser
window itself, in effect) by using the keyword **top**, instead of having to specify
the correct number of parent keywords. This is useful in a complex page with
several layers of frames. However, remember that **top** may not refer to the
topmost frame in your layout. If the viewer loads your page into a frame
created by somebody else—for example by clicking a link to it on their site—it
could refer to that page. Therefore, if you load a new page into the top
window, you'll remove *their* frameset as well.

The Window Object

The **window** object is the 'top-of-the-tree' as far as the browser object model is
concerned, and everything else in the Dynamic HTML object model revolves
around it. Once we understand the **window** object, we'll have a pretty good
grasp of how we relate to the object model in our pages.

The **window** object refers to the current window. This may be the top-level
window, but it might equally be a window that is within a frame created by a
<FRAMESET> in another document. If the window is divided into frames (i.e. its
document does contain a frameset) it will have a frames array—as we saw
earlier:

Array	Description
frames	Array of all the frames defined within a **<FRAMESET>** tag.

The **window** object also has a range of properties, methods and events. We'll look at these next, concentrating on the most useful ones.

The Properties of the Window Object

The following two tables show all the properties of a **window** object. You'll see the **parent**, **self**, and **top** properties we mentioned earlier, which allow us to refer to objects elsewhere in the hierarchy, and the **name** property which reflects the name we give to a window in a **<FRAMESET>** tag. On top of these, there are quite a few new properties available, when compared to earlier versions of the browser. We'll look at the existing ones first:

Properties	Description
closed	Indicates if a window is closed.
defaultStatus	The default message displayed in the status bar at the bottom of the window.
name	Specifies the name to use to refer to the window.
opener	Returns a reference to the window that created the current window.
parent	Returns a reference to the parent window.
self	A reference to the current window.
status	The text displayed in the current window's status bar.
top	Returns a reference to the topmost window object.

The **opener** and **closed** properties are usually used when we create new browser windows, as you'll see later in this chapter. Finally, the **status** and **defaultStatus** properties refer to the text displayed in the status bar at the bottom of the browser window. **status** is useful when we want to display progress messages to the user, or for debugging script. We can display anything we like in the status bar while the script is running:

```
window.status = "The value of the variable 'MeaningOfLife' is usually 42";
```

The new properties for the **window** object provide us with more control over the way the browser window appears, and provide information about its size and the position of the page within it:

New Properties	Description
innerHeight	Height of the window excluding the window borders.
innerWidth	Width of the window excluding the window borders.
outerHeight	Height of the window including the window borders.

New Properties	Description
`outerWidth`	Width of the window including the window borders.
`pageXOffset`	Horizontal offset of the top left of the visible part of the page within the window in pixels.
`pageYOffset`	Vertical offset of the top left of the visible part of the page within the window in pixels.
`locationbar`	Defines whether the address bar will be displayed in the browser window.
`menubar`	Defines whether the menu bar will be displayed in the browser window.
`personalbar`	Defines whether the user's personal button bar will be displayed in the browser window.
`scrollbars`	Defines whether the window will provide scrollbars if all the content cannot be displayed.
`statusbar`	Defines whether the status bar will be displayed in the browser window.
`toolbar`	Defines whether the toolbar will be displayed in the browser window.

Only the first four of these properties are read/write (i.e. can be changed directly), and then only as long as they don't make the window smaller than 100 pixels square. To change the size of the browser window using script we can write code like this:

```
window.innerHeight = 300;     // set the available page width
window.outerWidth = 600;      // set the overall browser height
```

The other properties are read-only unless we are using signed scripts. To access the **toolbar** property, we query its own **visible** property—the following line produces an **alert** dialog showing true if the browser toolbar is visible:

```
alert(window.toolbar.visible);
```

> *Signed scripts* are a new feature of Communicator, which we'll be coming to later in this chapter and also in Chapter 7. They allow us set all the properties for new windows, including resizing them to less than 100 pixels square.

The Methods of the Window Object

The **window** object's methods provide many ways of manipulating a window, and carrying out tasks within it.

New Browser Windows

If we want to work with new browser windows from a web page, we can use the **open** and **close** methods. We'll come back to closing a window in a while. In the mean time, the following code creates a new browser window containing the page **newpage.htm**:

75

```
window.open("newpage.htm");
```

We can also add other arguments to the method to get more control over how the new window is presented. The full syntax is:

window.open (*URL, windowname, features*)

where *features* can be a string of instructions concerning the position, size and type of window, and whether it should contain scrollbars, a toolbar, etc.

```
strFeatures = "toolbar=yes,menubar=no,screenX=10,screenY=10";
window.open("untitled.htm", "newwin", strFeatures);
```

The *windowname* argument we provide to the **open** method is simply the name we use to **TARGET** new pages to this window, such as from an **<A>** tag:

```
<A HREF="http://www.wrox.com" TARGET="newwin">Load a page into the new window.</A>
```

If we want to refer to the window later in script code, we have to store a reference to it. This reference is returned by the **open** method, and allows us to manipulate the new window later on. This example displays the inner height of the new window in an **alert** dialog:

```
strFeatures = "toolbar=yes,menubar=no,screenX=10,screenY=10";
mywindow = window.open("untitled.htm", "newwin", strFeatures);
alert("Inner height of new window is: " + mywindow.innerHeight);
```

While we've got a reference to the new window, we can query its properties. The **opener** and **closed** properties we mentioned earlier are available for all windows, including our new one:

```
alert(mywindow.closed);                  // displays false while the window is open
alert(mywindow.opener.document.URL);     // displays the URL of the original page
```

The second example uses the **window** object's **opener** property, which returns a reference to the window that opened the current window, or **null** if the window was opened by the user directly. Here, we're querying the **URL** property of the window's **document** object. We'll be covering the document object in depth in the next chapter.

Dependent Browser Windows

We can use the **open** method of a **window** object to create a new browser window that is dependent on the main window (i.e. closes when the main window is closed). Under *Windows* 95 or NT4.x, these windows do not appear in the taskbar:

```
strFeatures = "dependent=yes,...";
```

There are several other properties that we can specify in the features string we use when creating a new browser window, but these require us to use a **signed script**. This means that we have packaged the script up so that it can't be tampered with, and signed it digitally so that the end user can identify where it came from. In Chapter 7, we'll be looking at signed scripts in more detail.

Disabling Signed Scripts

While we are developing our pages, we can disable the signed scripts security feature by closing Communicator and editing the 'preferences' file. In Windows, this is named **prefs.js** and is in the **Users/Default** or **Users/**_username_ sub-folder of the **Netscape** folder. All we need to do is add the line:

```
user_pref("signed.applets.codebase_principal_support", true);
```

Then restart Communicator, and we can avoid the security restrictions and allow our code to access the features that normally require signed scripts. We still need to request permission first, however, by placing the following line within the script itself:

```
netscape.security.PrivilegeManager.enablePrivilege("UniversalBrowserWrite")
```

This gives the script full access to the browser and its contents for that page.

> **Remember to remove the line you added to your preferences file before you browse the Web again, to protect yourself from malicious scripts. Of course, in a controlled environment like an Intranet, you may wish to leave it disabled to avoid having to keep resigning scripts.**

Features Available in Signed Scripts

When we use signed scripts, or disable them as shown above, Dynamic HTML adds support for new features in browser windows. They can be displayed 'always on top' (i.e. overlaid by) or 'always underneath' (i.e. covered by) the existing windows. This is done by adding the **alwaysRaised=yes** or **alwaysLowered=yes** arguments to the features string that creates the new window. We can also create windows that have no title bar, and which do not respond to the usual 'hotkeys' (such as _Ctrl-O_ and _Ctrl-S_ to open and save a page):

```
strFeatures = "alwaysRaised=yes,hotkeys=no,titlebar=no";
strFeatures += "toolbar=yes,menubar=no,screenX=10,screenY=10,alwaysLowered=yes";
```

> _Note that we have to specify **titlebar=no** as well, before the **hotkeys=no** option will have any effect. This does not disable the security and quit hot keys, however. If you get stuck with a window that has no title or menu bar open, just press Ctrl-W to close it._

As an example, the following code opens a new window to display a splash screen when the page has loaded. It requests the security privilege **UniversalBrowserWrite**, so that it can set the restricted properties of the new window:

```
netscape.security.PrivilegeManager.enablePrivilege("UniversalBrowserWrite");
strFeatures = "alwaysRaised=yes,dependent=yes,hotkeys=no,titlebar=no,";
strFeatures += "screenX=100,screenY=100,innerWidth=300,innerHeight=185";
mywindow = window.open("Splash.htm", "newwin", strFeatures);
```

When the browser executes the **enablePrivilege** request, the user gets a confirmation dialog to indicate that the script is not safe. They can avoid this appearing every time by ticking the 'Remember this decision' checkbox:

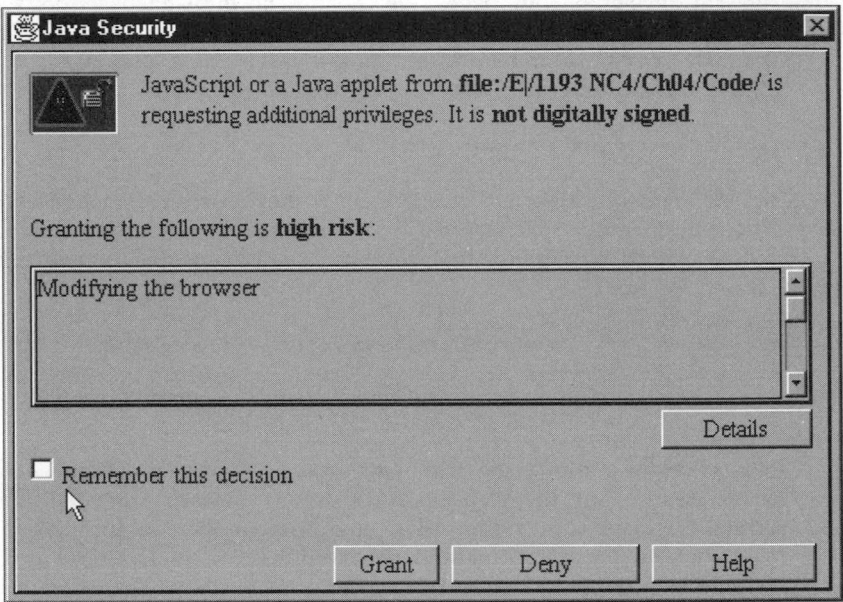

Here's the result of our code, showing the contents of the page **splash.htm**. This window has no title bar, border or other furniture, and stays on top of all the other windows:

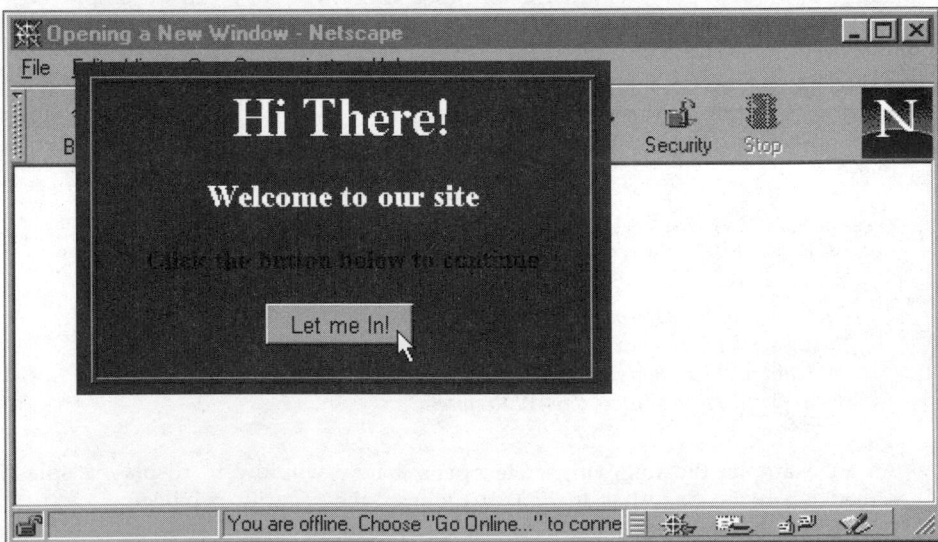

You can run this example, called NewWin.htm, from our Web site at http://rapid.wrox.co.uk/books/1193.

Closing Windows from a Script

The splash window itself contains script, which runs when the Let Me In! button is clicked. All it does is call the **close** method of the **window** object to close the new window:

```
<INPUT TYPE="BUTTON" NAME="cmdEnter" VALUE="Let me In!" ONCLICK="LetmeIn()">
...
<SCRIPT LANGUAGE=JAVASCRIPT>
function LetmeIn() { window.close() };    // close the window
```

Because the code is running in the same window, the one that will be closed, we don't need to get the **UniversalBrowserWrite** privilege. However, if it is the main window, the browser will prompt the user before closing it:

We can't then close another window using script, without obtaining the **UniversalBrowserWrite** privilege. This has to be done by altering the **prefs** file. Only then will the following code work:

```
mywindow = window.open("splash.htm", "newwin", strFeatures);
...
// do something with the window
...
mywindow = close();   // requires UniversalBrowserWrite privilege
```

Summary of Features for window.open

To help you see the whole picture, the following table shows all the properties that can be used with the **window.open** method:

Feature	Requires Signed Scripts?	Description
alwaysLowered	Yes	Defines if the window is always below (overlaid by) all other windows.
alwaysRaised	Yes	Defines if the window is always on top (overlaying) all other windows.
dependent	No	Defines if the window closes when the main browser window does, and doesn't appear on the taskbar.
directories	No	Defines if the window will have the directory buttons available.

Feature	Requires Signed Scripts?	Description
hotkeys	Yes	Defines if the window will respond to hot keys like Ctrl-O and Ctrl-S.
innerHeight (replaces height)	If less than 100 pixels	Sets the height excluding window furniture (menus, title bar, borders, etc.) of the new window.
innerWidth (replaces width)	If less than 100 pixels	Sets the width excluding window furniture (menus, title bar, borders, etc.) of the new window.
location	No	Defines if the window shows the address text box.
menubar	No	Defines if the window will have a menu bar.
outerHeight	If less than 100 pixels	Sets the height including window furniture (menus, title bar, borders, etc.) of the new window.
outerWidth	If less than 100 pixels	Sets the width including window furniture (menus, title bar, borders, etc.) of the new window.
resizable	No	Defines if the window will be resizable or fixed size.
screenX	If window will be off-screen	Sets the horizontal position of the window on screen.
screenY	If window will be off-screen	Sets the vertical position of the window on screen.
scrollbars	No	Defines if the window will display scroll bars.
status	No	Defines if the window will have a status bar.
titlebar	Yes	Defines if the window will have a title bar and frame.
toolbar	No	Defines if the window will display the normal toolbar.
z-lock	Yes	Defines if the window will remain below other windows even when activated.

The previous **width** and **height** properties have been replaced with **innerWidth** and **innerHeight**, although they are still supported for backwards compatibility. The settings for the **innerWidth**, **innerHeight**, **outerWidth**, **outerHeight**, **screenX** and **screenY** properties are all in pixels. The rest are set using either **yes** or **no**, or **1** or **0**. There must be no spaces in the complete string and the settings must be separated by a comma.

Built-in Dialogs

Built-in dialogs are available as methods of the **window** object, which we can display using **alert**, **prompt**, and **confirm**:

```
window.alert("You'll have to choose where to go next.");
strLocation = window.prompt("Enter your preferred location", "Birmingham");
blnResult = window.confirm("Are you ready to load this page ?");
```

Here's an example that uses these dialogs to load a new page. The page **Dialogs_js.htm** consists of a single script section, containing this code:

```
<SCRIPT LANGUAGE=JAVASCRIPT>
window.alert("You'll have to choose where to go next.");
strLocation = window.prompt("Enter your preferred location", "Birmingham");
if (strLocation != null)
{
  if (strLocation == "Birmingham")
    strAddress = "http://www.wrox.co.uk"
  else
    strAddress = "http://www.wrox.com";
  window.status = "New location will be " + strAddress;
  if (window.confirm("Are you ready to load this page ?"))
    window.location.href = strAddress;
}
</SCRIPT>
```

You can run this example, **Dialogs_js.htm**, *from our Web site at*
http://rapid.wrox.co.uk/books/1193/

The code in this page runs when it is loaded, and the first line displays an **alert** dialog with a simple message.

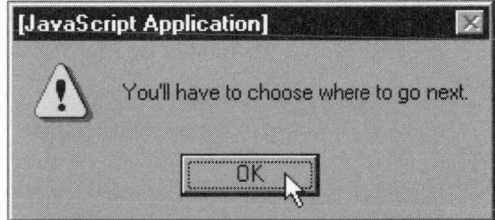

The second line uses the **window** object's **prompt** method to display a dialog where the user can enter some information. The first argument is the prompt itself, and the second is the default value for the text box within the dialog.

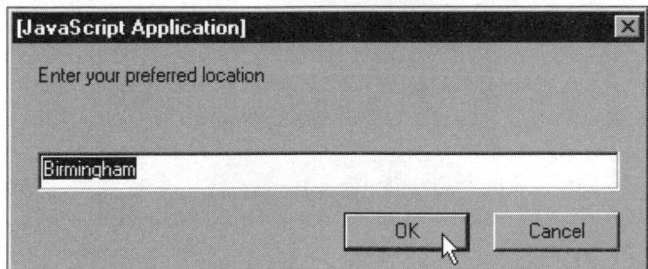

The value in the text box is returned to our code when the user clicks the OK button, and we assign it to a variable named **strLocation**. Now we can see what the user actually entered—if anything. If they clicked the Cancel button in the dialog, we'll get the special value **null** (no value) back from the **prompt** method. We test for this first by comparing **strLocation** to **null**, and only execute the following code if there actually is a value. The exclamation mark in JavaScript means **NOT**, so **!=** means 'not equal to':

81

```
if (strLocation != null)
{ ...
```

If the value is still Birmingham, the default, we set the value of another
variable, **strAddress**, to the address of our UK Web site. If not, we'll use the
main US site address:

```
...
if (strLocation == "Birmingham")
  strAddress = "http://www.wrox.co.uk"
else
  strAddress = "http://www.wrox.com";
...
```

By now, we know we've got an address to go to, so we can display a message
in the browser's status bar, by setting the **window** object's **status** property. We
use some text and add the address string from the variable **strAddress** to the
end of it like this:

```
window.status = "New location will be " + strAddress;
```

Now we can perform a final check to see if they really want to do it. We use
the **window** object's **confirm** method to display the OK or Cancel dialog. The
string argument is the message displayed, and it returns **true** or **false**
depending on which button the user clicks. Once they've clicked a button, we
can check the result and load the new page if it is **true**. Notice in the
screenshot that the status bar is displaying our message as well.

```
if (window.confirm("Are you ready to load this page ?"))
  window.location.href = strAddress;
```

The line that actually loads the new page does so by setting a property of
another object in the browser's object model hierarchy. We're changing the **href**
property of the **window.location** object to the value of the string variable
strAddress we set earlier, and this loads the new page:

```
if (window.confirm("Are you ready to load this page ?"))
   window.location.href = strAddress;
```

You'll meet the **location** object and its properties later on in this chapter.

Focus, Scrolling and Timers

If there is more than one browser window open, we can switch the focus between them using the **blur** and **focus** methods. These effectively change which is the 'active' window. **blur** moves the focus from the window where the code is to the next window (like pressing *Tab*), while **focus** moves it to the window where the code is.

There are some useful new methods which allow us to move and resize the browser window while it's open, and move (or scroll) the document that is being displayed within the window. These are the **moveBy**, **moveTo**, **resizeBy**, **resizeTo**, **scrollBy** and **scrollTo** methods. For example, to scroll the page so that the point 250 pixels across and 150 pixels down is at the top left of the browser window, we could use:

```
window.scrollTo(250, 150);
```

Remember that you have to use a signed script with these methods if you wish to move a window off-screen, or resize it to less than 100 pixels square.

Timeout Methods

We can set **timers** in a window that will cause part of our code to be executed after a certain number of milliseconds. The previous **setTimeout** method survives from earlier versions of the browser, and Dynamic HTML adds a new version of this—**setInterval**. This makes using repeated timeouts easier, because you don't have to keep resetting it each time it fires. It just goes on firing every specified number of milliseconds until disabled with a call to the **clearInterval** method.

This example creates a timer that will run for five seconds, and tells it to execute a function named **MyTimer()** after the five seconds are up:

```
timeoutID = window.setTimeout("MyTimer()", 5000);
```

We can react to the timer event by writing a subroutine that catches the **MyTimer** event:

```
function MyTimer()
  { alert("Time's up!") };
```

Once the timer has fired, we need to reset it again if we want to repeat the process. Alternatively, we can cancel it before it fires using the **clearTimeout** method, and supplying the **timeoutID** we saved earlier when we set the timer:

```
window.clearTimeout(timeoutID);
```

The Interval Timer

The original way to get a timer to repeat over and over was to call the **setTimeout** method within the function that ran each time the **timeout** event occurred. In Communicator 4, we can use the new **setInterval** method instead:

```
timeoutID = window.setInterval("MyInterval()", 5000);
...
function MyInterval()
  { alert("Interval's up!") };
```

When we're ready to stop the timer running, we use the **clearInterval** method:

```
window.clearInterval(timeoutID);
```

Capturing Events

Dynamic HTML can give us extra control over our pages because of the new ways that events work in the browser. Six of the **window** object's new methods, **captureEvents**, **releaseEvents**, **routeEvent**, **handleEvent**, **enableExternalCapture** and **disableExternalCapture** are concerned with this technique of event capturing. However, we aren't ready to get involved in this in detail yet. Instead, we're devoting a whole chapter (Chapter 6) to it later in the book.

The Built-in 'Button' and find Methods

The **window** object also provides a set of methods that are the equivalent of some of the toolbar buttons. We can move to the previous or next page stored in the user's history list by using the **back** and **forward** methods. We can open the user's Home page using the **home** method, stop the download of a page using the **stop** method, or print the contents of a window using the **print** method. This solves the perennial problem of deciding which frame to print if there is more than one displayed. For example, we can print just the contents of the third frame using:

```
window.frames[2].print;
```

Finding Text in a Page

Finally, we can use the **find** method to find text within a window's document. This is useful if you have large quantities of text in a page, because you can allow a user to search for particular topics themselves. In its simplest form, the single code line:

```
window.find()
```

produces a Find dialog. The user can enter the text to be found, select which direction to search in, and opt to match the case of the text. In this example, we've provided a button that simply executes the code you saw above:

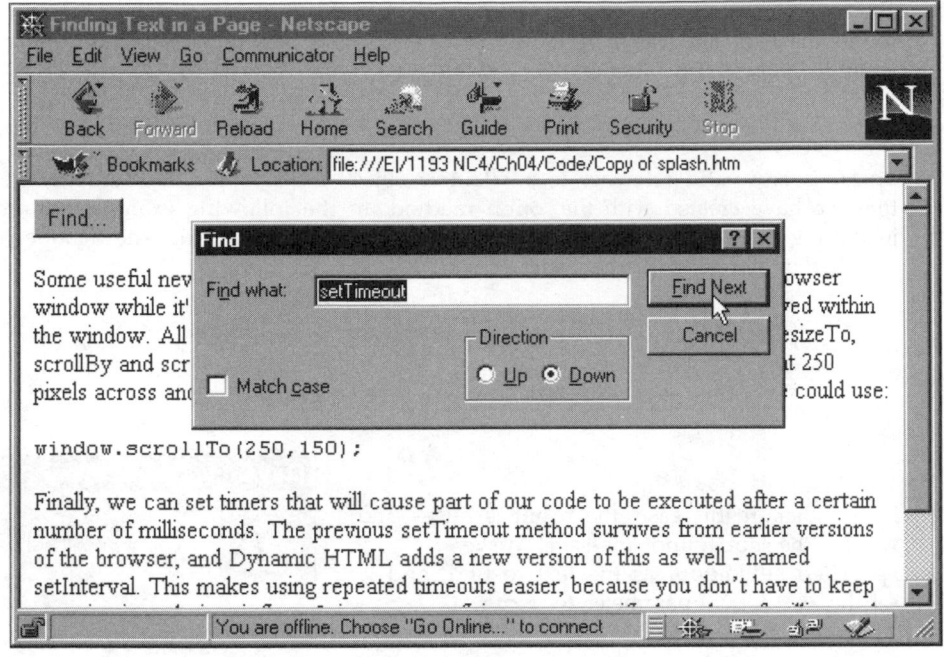

*You can run this example, named **FindText.htm**, directly from our Web site at **http://rapid.wrox.co.uk/books/1193**.*

If the text does occur in the currently loaded document, the browser scrolls the page so that it is visible and selects it:

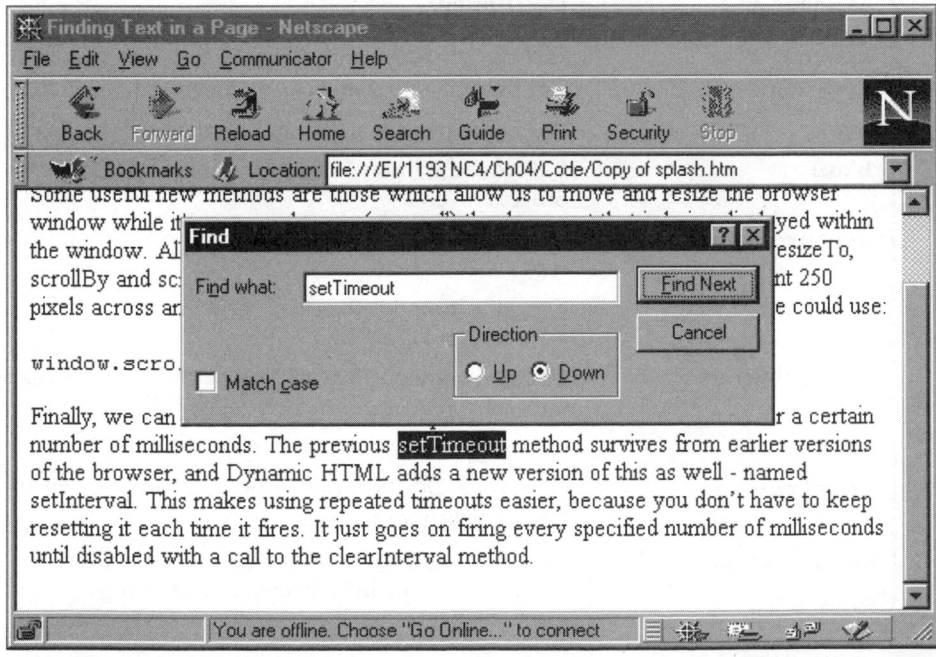

The **find** method also returns **true** or **false**, depending on whether or not it found the text, and can accept two parameters that indicate which direction we want to search, and whether we want to match the case of the text:

```
result = window.find("text_to_find", match_case, search_backwards)
```

window is any valid reference to a **window** object; for example, it could be one that we have created with the **open** method. In the following example we are just using the current window. The code displays a message depending upon whether or not it finds the text:

```
if (window.find("settimeout", true, false))
   alert("Found it!")
else
   alert("Sorry, it's not there.");
```

Notice that in this case, the result is false—and we get the 'not found' message. We've specified settimeout as the text to find, and set the *match_case* parameter to **true**.

Window Methods Summary

Here's a full list of the methods of the **window** object:

MethodName	Description
alert	Displays an Alert dialog box with a message and an OK button.
back	Loads the previous URL in the browser's history list.
blur	Causes the window to lose the focus, and fire its **onBlur** event.
captureEvents	Instructs the window to capture events of a particular type.
clearInterval	Cancels a timeout that was set with the **setInterval** method.
clearTimeout	Cancels a timeout that was set with the **setTimeout** method.
close	Closes the current browser window.
confirm	Displays a Confirm dialog box with a message and OK and Cancel buttons.
disableExternalCapture	Prevents a window that includes frames from capturing events in documents loaded from different locations.

MethodName	Description
enableExternalCapture	Allows a window that includes frames to capture events in documents loaded from different locations.
find	Returns true if a specified string is found in the text in the current window.
focus	Causes the window to receive the focus, and fire its onFocus event.
forward	Loads the next URL in the browser's history list.
handleEvent	Invokes the appropriate event handling code of the object for this event.
home	Loads the user's Home page into the window.
moveBy	Moves the window horizontally and vertically.
moveTo	Moves the window so that the top left is at a position x, y (in pixels).
open	Opens a new browser window.
print	Prints the contents of the window, equivalent to pressing the Print button.
prompt	Displays a Prompt dialog box with a message and an input field.
releaseEvents	Instructs the window to stop capturing events of a particular type.
resizeBy	Resizes the window horizontally and vertically.
resizeTo	Resizes the window to a size x, y specified in pixels.
routeEvent	Passes an event that has been captured up through the normal event hierarchy.
scrollBy	Scrolls the document horizontally and vertically within the window by a number of pixels.
scrollTo	Scrolls the document within the window so that the point x, y is at the top left corner.
setInterval	Denotes a code routine to execute every specified number of milliseconds.
setTimeout	Denotes a code routine to execute once only, a specified number of milliseconds after loading the page.
stop	Stops the current download, equivalent to pressing the Stop button.

Window Object Events

The **window** object has nine events. We can react to these events in our code to make our pages interact with the user. We'll be looking at events in general in Chapter 6. In the mean time, we'll show you some simple examples that demonstrate the different ways that we can react to the actions of the user.

Blur and Focus Events

Two of these occur when the user switches between the windows. This initiates the **onBlur** and **onFocus** events. The easiest way to connect code to a window or frame's events is to define the handlers in the **<BODY>** tag of the page:

```
<BODY ONBLUR="BlurFunction()" ONFOCUS="FocusFunction()">
```

We can use any names for the functions in the **<BODY>** tag, and then write functions with these names in a **<SCRIPT>** section within the page:

```
function BlurFunction() { window.status = "I've now got the focus." };
function FocusFunction() { window.status = "Oh no, I've lost it again." };
```

> *Notice that these can also be fired when the **window** object's **blur** and **focus** methods are called by our code.*

Load, Unload and Error Events

These are events that occur when the window loads a page, and when it unloads one—either before opening a new page or when the browser is closing down. If the loading of a page fails, either through a network error or the user clicking the Stop button, the **onError** event occurs. Again, we can connect to these events by placing our function names in the **<BODY>** tag of the page:

```
<BODY ONLOAD="LoadFunction()" ONUNLOAD="UnloadFunction()"
ONERROR="ErrorFunction()">
...
function LoadFunction() { alert("Finished loading the page.") };
function ErrorFunction() { alert("About to unload the page.") };
function UnloadFunction() { alert("About to unload the page.") };
```

Move, Resize and Mouse Events

When the user moves the browser window or resizes it, we can react to events that these actions produce in a similar way:

```
<BODY ONMOVE="MoveFunction()" ONRESIZE="ResizeFunction()"
ONERROR="ErrorFunction()">
...
function MoveFunction() { window.status = "You moved the window." };
function ResizeFunction() { window.status = "You re-sized the window.") };
```

When the user moves the mouse over the page, this causes **MouseMove** events. To react to these, however, we first have to turn on event capturing. This is a subject we'll be saving for Chapter 6.

Managing Drag and Drop

The final event is **onDragDrop**. This provides information about files that the user drags onto the browser window using the mouse. Normally, the browser will unload the current page and load the item dropped onto it as though it were a document. If you drag an HTML file or an image onto the browser window, it opens in the same way as if you had typed the URL for it into the browser's Address box.

Instead, you can cancel loading of the document by creating a function that runs when the events occurs, and setting the return value of the function to **false**. You can also use the **Event** object to look at the files that were dropped onto the window—providing that you are using a signed script. You'll see more later.

EventName	Description
onBlur	Occurs when the window loses the focus.
onDragDrop	Occurs when the user drops a file or object onto the Navigator window.
onError	Occurs when an error arises while loading a document.
onFocus	Occurs when the window receives the focus.
onLoad	Occurs when a document has completed loading.
onMouseMove	Occurs only when event capturing is on and the user moves the mouse pointer.
onMove	Occurs when the window is moved.
onResize	Occurs when the window is resized.
onUnload	Occurs immediately prior to the current document being unloaded.

The Window's Subsidiary Objects

The **window** object has several subsidiary objects, which are referenced through it. Three of these, the **history**, **navigator** and **location** objects, are all basically unchanged from earlier versions of the object model—with just a couple of additional properties and methods. **event** and **screen** are two completely new objects, that are added in Dynamic HTML.

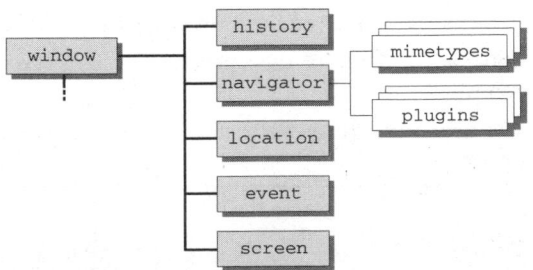

The History Object

The **history** object contains information about the URLs that the browser has visited in this session, as stored in the History list. It allows us to move through the list using script code, loading the pages it contains. The properties return references to various pages in the history list, and the **length** of the list:

Properties	Description
current	The current item in the browser's history list.
length	Returns the number of items in the browser's history list.
next	Refers to the next item in the browser's history list.
previous	Refers to the previous item in the browser's history list.

Methods	Description
back	Loads the previous URL in the browser's history list.
forward	Loads the next URL in the browser's history list.
go	Loads a specified URL from the browser's history list.

To move through the list, we can use these properties and methods. Here, we'll go to entry number one in the list, then jump to the fourth one (the current item is, of course, numbered zero in the list). Notice that we have omitted the default **window** object from the code:

```
history.go(1);
history.forward(3);
```

The Navigator Object

The **navigator** object represents the browser application itself, providing information about its manufacturer, version and capabilities. It has just six properties:

Properties	Description
appCodeName	The code name of the browser.
appName	The product name of the browser.
appVersion	The version of the browser.
language	Returns the language the browser was compiled for.
platform	Returns the name of the operating system the browser was compiled for.
userAgent	The user-agent (browser name) header sent as part of the HTTP protocol.

Because the browser can support different types of documents (MIME types) and plugins that add extra functions to the browser, there are two arrays that hold references to these objects:

Array	Description
`mimeTypes`	Array of all the MIME types supported by the browser.
`plugins`	Array of all the plugins that are installed.

For example, this code displays information about each type of document that the browser can support, including the properties that hold the file extensions (**suffixes**) and the **description**. Just to warn you, there are lots of them and you'll be clicking OK for quite a while:

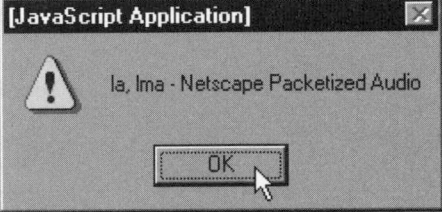

```
for (x = 0; x <= navigator.mimeTypes.length; x++)
alert(navigator.mimeTypes[x].suffixes + " - " +
navigator.mimeTypes[x].description);
```

The same kind of code can be used to identify the installed plugins. Here, we're displaying the **filename** and **description** properties of each one:

```
for (x = 0; x <= navigator.plugins.length; x++)
alert(navigator.plugins[x].filename + " - " + navigator.plugins[x].description);
```

Finally, the single method provides us with a way to test whether the browser can support Java code and applets:

Methods	Description
`javaEnabled`	Indicates if execution of Java code is enabled by the browser.

The Location Object

The **location** object contains information about the URL of the current page. It also provides methods that will reload the current or a new page. The properties consist of one that holds the complete URL string, **href**, and several which hold various parts of the URL string:

Properties	Attribute	Description
hash		The string following the # symbol, the anchor name, from the **HREF** value.
host		The **hostname** part of the location or URL.
hostname		The **hostname:port** part of the location or URL.
href	HREF	The destination URL or anchor point.
pathname		The file or object path name following the third slash in a URL.
port		The **port** number in a URL.
protocol		The initial sub-string indicating the URL's access method.
search		Any query string or form data following the **?** in the complete URL.

Methods	Description
reload	Reloads the current page.
replace	Loads a page replacing the current page's session history entry with its URL.

We can use the properties to change the page that is being displayed. The usual way is to reset the **href** property to a new value, as you saw earlier in this chapter:

```
window.location.href = "http://rapid.wrox.co.uk";
```

The two methods provided by the **location** object can be used to reload the current page or replace it in the browser's history list.

The Event Object

The first new object is the **event** object. This allows the scripting language to get more information about any event that occurs in the browser—in effect it is global to all the objects. The **event** object provides a range of properties:

Properties	Description
layerX	Horizontal position of the mouse pointer in pixels with respect to the containing layer.
layerY	Vertical position of the mouse pointer in pixels with respect to the containing layer.
pageX	Horizontal position of the mouse pointer in pixels with respect to the document.

Properties	Description
`pageY`	Vertical position of the mouse pointer in pixels with respect to the document.
`screenX`	Horizontal position in pixels of the mouse pointer on the screen for an event.
`screenY`	Vertical position in pixels of the mouse pointer on the screen for an event.
`type`	The type of event, as a string.
`which`	ASCII value of a key that was pressed, or indicates which mouse button was clicked.
`modifiers`	String containing the names of the keys held down for a key-press event.
`target`	The name of the object where the event was originally sent.
`data`	The URLs of the objects dropped onto the Navigator window, as an array of strings. This only applies to the `ondragdrop` event.

The first six properties return values that indicate where the mouse pointer was when the event occurred. They give the position in relation to the screen, the current document (the page) and the layer within the page.

The next three properties, **type**, **which** and **modifiers**, tell us what was going on when the event occurred. We can query the **type** property to find out the name of the event. If it was a mouse event, the **which** property will tell us which of the mouse buttons was pressed. If it was a key-press event, this property returns the ASCII code of the key that was pressed—and the **modifiers** property indicates if the *Alt*, *Ctrl* and/or *Shift* keys were being held down at the time.

Next comes the **target** property, which returns the name of the element where the event first occurred. Finally, the **data** property provides an array of string values that represent the URLs of files that were dropped onto the browser window in an **onDragDrop** event. We'll cover the way that the **event** object is used in Chapter 6.

The Screen Object

The **screen** object is also new in Dynamic HTML, and provides information about the viewer's screen resolution and rendering abilities. There are just six properties. The first four are useful when we want to create new browser windows, or change the size of the existing one, in code. For example, we can use them to decide where to put a new window:

```
if (screen.width >= 800)
    window.open("newpage.htm", "newwin", "screenX=200,screenY=200,outerWidth=400")
else
    window.open("newpage.htm", "newwin", "screenX=170,screenY=100,outerWidth=300");
```

Properties	Description
height	Overall height of the user's screen in pixels.
width	Overall width of the user's screen in pixels.
availHeight	Height of the available screen space in pixels (excluding screen furniture).
availWidth	Width of the available screen space in pixels (excluding screen furniture).
colorDepth	Maximum number of colors that are supported by the user's display system.
pixelDepth	Returns the number of bits used per pixel by the system display hardware.

The last two properties, **colorDepth** and **pixelDepth**, are useful for deciding which images to display, to get the best out of the user's screen capabilities. Without going into a discussion of how colors are represented, just accept that the browser can display images in a variety of color depths—2 colors for a monochrome display, 16 colors, or upwards in steps to 16 million colors ('True Color'). These two read-only properties describe the color depth in terms of the number of colors, and the number of bits per pixel (where **8** means 256 colors and **32** is 'True Color', for example).

If we display an image containing 256 colors, but the color depth of the user's system is only set to 16 colors, they will see a degraded version of the image. If we query the **colorDepth** property first, we can use the result to decide which of a series of images we display:

```
if (screen.pixelDepth < 8)
    // display monochrome image
else
    //display 256 color image;
```

This can help to minimize download times as well. There's no point downloading a 'true-color' image if the user is working in 256 colors—we might as well send them a 256 color version instead.

A Window Object Example Page

To finish up this chapter, here's another page **BrowsInf.htm** that we've provided on our Web site at **http://rapid.wrox.co.uk/books/1193/** for you to try out. It simply retrieves the values of properties from several of the objects we've looked at in this chapter, and displays them in a table:

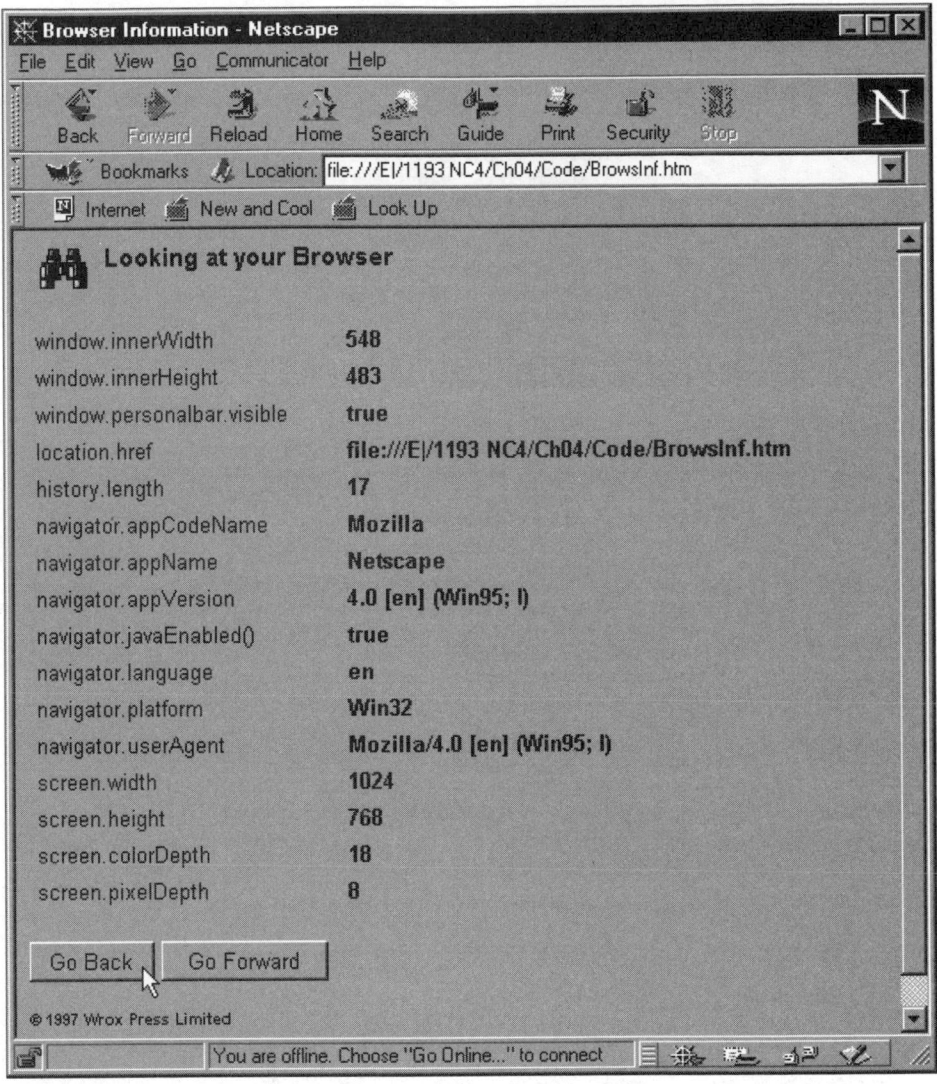

How It Works

The code that creates the page looks like this:

```
<HTML>
<HEAD><TITLE> Browser Information </TITLE>
<STYLE>
<!--
   H1 {fontFamily:"Arial"; fontSize:16; color:blue}
   H2 {fontFamily:"Arial"; fontSize:10}
   TD {fontFamily:"Arial"; fontSize:14}
   BODY {fontFamily:"Arial"; fontSize:14}
-->
</STYLE>
</HEAD>
<BODY BGCOLOR=#FFC0A0>
<H1> <IMG SRC="binocs.gif" HSPACE=5 ALIGN=MIDDLE> Looking at your Browser </H1>
```

```
<SCRIPT LANGUAGE="JAVASCRIPT">
<!-- hide from non-JavaScript Browsers

var strInfo = "<CENTER><TABLE WIDTH=100%>" +
              "<TR><TD>window.innerWidth</TD>\n" +
              "<TD><B>" + window.innerWidth + "</TD></TR>\n" +
              "<TR><TD>window.innerHeight</TD>\n" +
              "<TD><B>" + window.innerHeight + "</TD></TR>\n" +
              "<TR><TD>window.personalbar.visible</TD>\n" +
              "<TD><B>" + window.personalbar.visible + "</TD></TR>\n" +
              "<TR><TD>location.href</TD>\n" +
              "<TD><B>" + location.href + "</TD></TR>\n" +
              "<TR><TD>history.length</TD>\n" +
              "<TD><B>" + history.length + "</TD></TR>\n" +
              "<TR><TD>navigator.appCodeName</TD>\n" +
              "<TD><B>" + navigator.appCodeName + "</TD></TR>\n" +
              "<TR><TD>navigator.appName</TD>\n" +
              "<TD><B>" + navigator.appName + "</TD></TR>\n" +
              "<TR><TD>navigator.appVersion</TD>\n" +
              "<TD><B>" + navigator.appVersion + "</TD></TR>\n" +
              "<TR><TD>navigator.javaEnabled()</TD>\n" +
              "<TD><B>" + navigator.javaEnabled() + "</TD></TR>\n" +
              "<TR><TD>navigator.language</TD>\n" +
              "<TD><B>" + navigator.language + "</TD></TR>\n" +
              "<TR><TD>navigator.platform</TD>\n" +
              "<TD><B>" + navigator.platform + "</TD></TR>\n" +
              "<TR><TD>navigator.userAgent</TD>\n" +
              "<TD><B>" + navigator.userAgent + "</TD></TR>\n" +
              "<TR><TD>screen.width</TD>\n" +
              "<TD><B>" + screen.width + "</TD></TR>\n" +
              "<TR><TD>screen.height</TD>\n" +
              "<TD><B>" + screen.height + "</TD></TR>\n" +
              "<TR><TD>screen.colorDepth</TD>\n" +
              "<TD><B>" + screen.colorDepth + "</TD></TR>\n" +
              "<TR><TD>screen.pixelDepth</TD>\n" +
              "<TD><B>" + screen.pixelDepth + "</TD></TR>\n" +
              "</TABLE></CENTER><P>\n";
document.write(strInfo);

function HistoryButtons(dir, dirs)
{
  intPlaces = Math.floor((Math.random() * 3) + 1);
  alert("Trying to go " + dirs + " " + intPlaces + " places.");
  window.history.go(dir * intPlaces);
}

// stop hiding -->
</SCRIPT>

<FORM>
  <INPUT TYPE=button VALUE="Go Back" NAME="cmdBack"
         onClick="HistoryButtons(-1, 'back')">
  <INPUT TYPE=button VALUE="Go Forward" NAME="cmdForward"
         onClick="HistoryButtons(1, 'forward')">
</FORM>

<H2>&copy; 1997 Wrox Press Limited</H2>
</BODY>
</HTML>
```

The first section, up to the opening **<SCRIPT>** tag, provides the title and heading for the page, and defines the styles for the text. Inside the script section, we've defined a string variable named **strInfo**, and then filled it with a set of **<TABLE>**, **<TR>** and **<TD>** tags to create a two-column table.

```
var strInfo = "<CENTER><TABLE WIDTH=100%>" +
              "<TR><TD>window.innerWidth</TD>\n" +
              "<TD><B>" + window.innerWidth + "</TD></TR>\n" +
              ...
```

In the first column is the text of the object and property we are querying, and in the second column is the actual value. These two lines are repeated for each object property we want to query. Notice that the **javaEnabled** entry is actually using a *method*, rather than a property—you can tell it's a method because it is followed by brackets:

```
              ...
              "<TR><TD>navigator.javaEnabled()</TD>\n" +
              "<TD><B>" + navigator.javaEnabled() + "</TD></TR>\n" +
              ...
```

Once we've got the table into our string variable, we can print it into the page. The browser doesn't know that the information is coming from our code, it just accepts it as though it were part of the HTML source stream coming from the server in the usual way. To put it into the page, we use the **write** method of the **document** object. You'll see more about this in the next chapter:

```
document.write(strInfo);
```

Jumping to Another Page in the History List

At the end of the page are two push buttons, created with the usual **<INPUT>** tag. These are named **cmdBack** and **cmdForward**:

```
<INPUT TYPE=button VALUE="Go Back" NAME="cmdBack"
       onClick="HistoryButtons(-1, 'back')">
  <INPUT TYPE=button VALUE="Go Forward" NAME="cmdForward"
       onClick="HistoryButtons(1, 'forward')">
```

When one is clicked, the browser looks for a function named **HistoryButtons()**, and passes it two values—a number indicating the direction to move and a string describing the direction. The function simply creates a random number and uses the **back** and **forward** methods of the **navigator** object to load the relevant page. Here's the function again:

```
function HistoryButtons(dir, dirs)
{
   intPlaces = Math.floor((Math.random() * 3) + 1);  // create a random number
   alert("Trying to go " + dirs + " " + intPlaces + " places.");
   window.history.go(dir * intPlaces);
}
```

This code uses the **random** and **floor** methods of the JavaScript **Math** object to produce a pseudo-random number between 1 and 3, then stores it in a variable named **intPlaces**. Finally it displays a message, and executes the **go** method of the **history** object to jump that number of places multiplied by the direction provided in the **dir** parameter. If you are new to JavaScript, and this code seems a little complex at the moment, don't worry. You'll learn more about creating JavaScript functions in Chapter 6

97

Summary

In this chapter, we've begun our tour of the Dynamic HTML **object model**. If you have used scripting languages before, you'll be familiar with much of this—and so we've tried to concentrate on the new objects, properties, methods and events. However, we've included some examples of the existing ones to help you if you've previously only ever used HTML, and not tried scripting. Section H contains a JavaScript quick reference to help you out.

We started with the main browser object, the **window**, and looked at its properties, methods and events. Then we covered its subsidiary objects and arrays, consisting of:

- The **frames** array, which holds details of all the windows in a frameset within the current window
- The **history** object, which represents the browser's History list
- The **navigator** object, which represents the browser application itself
- The **location** object, which represents the URL of the page being displayed in the browser
- The **screen** object, which represents the hardware's size and color rendering abilities
- The **event** object, which represents the events that occur in the browser

However, the main object we use in much of our code is actually the **document** object, and its subsidiary objects and arrays. These are the subjects of the next chapter.

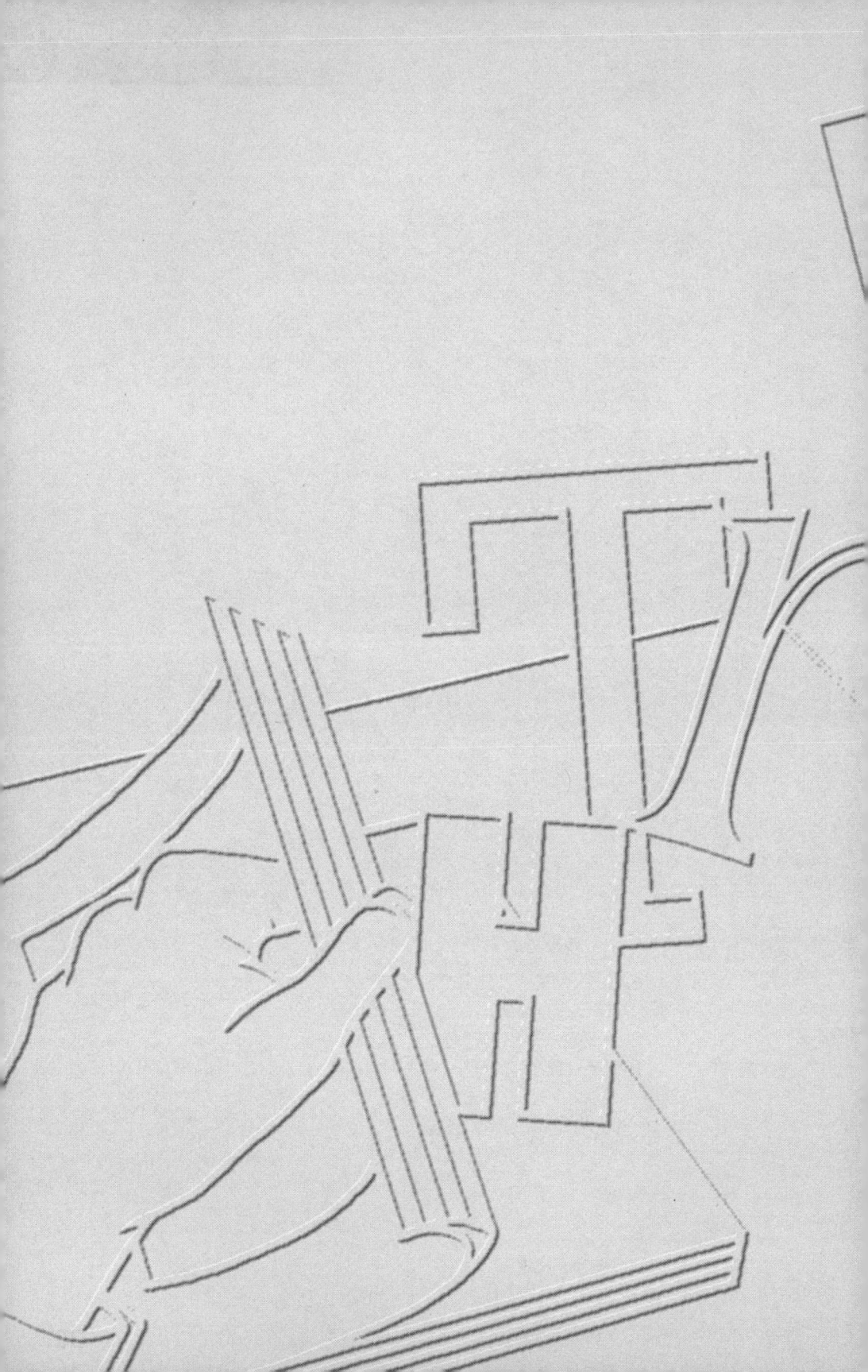

The Dynamic HTML Document Object

In the previous chapter, we discovered why we need an **object model** to use Dynamic HTML, and saw what it looks like. We also examined the top-level **window** object and its subsidiary objects. By now, you should be familiar with some of the techniques for using scripting code like JavaScript in your web pages.

Of course, there is still a lot to learn. Most of what we do in Dynamic HTML revolves around using scripting to modify a loaded document. We've supplied a JavaScript quick reference at the back of the book in case you aren't familiar with the traditional ways in which scripting can be used.

In this chapter, we'll continue our exploration of the browser object model by moving on to the central object in the hierarchy, the **document** object. In this chapter, you'll see:

- The properties, methods and events supported by the **document** object
- The arrays it provides to organize all the other items that are part of the page
- More about the new **layers** feature that is part of Netscape Communicator

There are other objects available to our code in Dynamic HTML, but these are not strictly part of the object model. We'll look at these in this and subsequent chapters, when we come to explore event handling and dynamic scripting in more depth. Here, we'll start with the **document** object itself.

The Document Object

The whole reason for using Dynamic HTML, or any other version of HTML, is to produce pages that we can display in a browser that the user can interact with directly. The page itself is technically referred to as the **document**, and the object model provides a document object, plus subsidiary objects and arrays, to organize the document itself and all the contents.

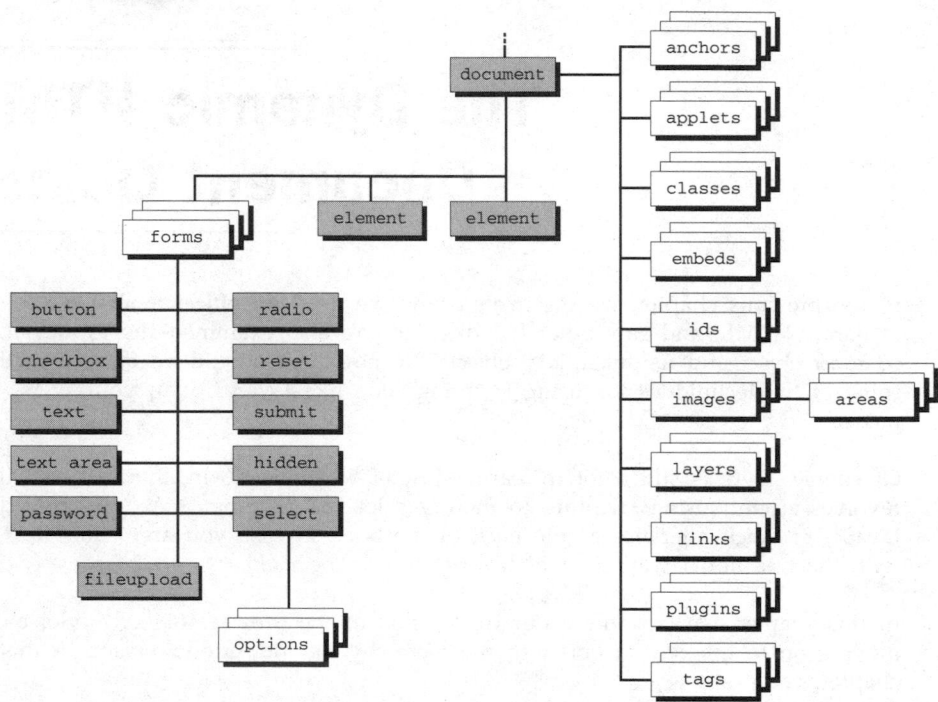

We'll start with a look at the properties, methods and events of the **document** object, then move on to look at the arrays and subsidiary objects it supports. The reference section at the back of the book lists them all in alphabetical order and provides a full list of their properties, methods and events.

The Properties of the Document Object

The document object's properties can be grouped in the following way:

- **General** properties which hold information about the document and the disk file that it is stored as

- **Color** properties that define the color of various parts of the document

The General Document Properties

The general properties are mainly concerned with the document and its disk file, and provide information that can help the HTML author decide how to handle it. Most of them are self-explanatory, and you'll find an example that demonstrates several of these properties later in this chapter:

General Properties	Description
cookie	String value of a cookie stored by the browser.
domain	Security domain of the document.
lastModified	Date the document was last modified.
referrer	URL of the page containing the link that loaded this page, if available.
title	The title of the document as defined in the <TITLE> tag
URL	Uniform Resource Locator of the page.

The Document Color Properties

These properties provide access to the colors of various parts of the page. In particular, they allow the code to read and change the color of the page background, and the color of the unvisited hyperlinks, visited hyperlinks and active hyperlinks (i.e. while the mouse button is held down over the link).

> • Note that some browsers (including Internet Explorer) do not support the 'active' link colors, but do allow dynamic changes to the foreground color of the page. Changing link colors is not advisable as it creates a serious risk of confusing the user, who has probably set the color to their own preference, and doesn't want it overridden by an over-zealous web page constructor.

Color Properties	Description
alinkColor	Color of the active links on the page, i.e. those where the mouse button is held down.
bgColor	Background color of the page.
fgColor	Color of the document foreground text.
linkColor	The color of the unvisited links in the page.
vlinkColor	Color of the visited links in the page.

These properties are really leftovers from earlier versions of the object model. We would normally use style properties to change the colors, as you saw in Chapter 3.

The Methods of the Document Object

The **document** object's methods also fall neatly into two groups, general **methods** and **event handling methods**. We'll look at the general methods first, because these are the ones you'll probably be most familiar with already.

Writing Text and HTML to the Document

As you've seen in the previous chapter, we can write text and HTML into a page using the **write** method of the **document** object. This is often used to create pages where the content is only decided by the browser's environment, such as the current date and time, or the properties of the browser itself.

There is a second related method, **writeln**, which acts in the same way, but appends a carriage return to the string it writes into the page. Of course, this has no effect most of the time, unless the string is being placed inside HTML tags such as **<PRE>**, which preserve line formatting.

Connected with the **write** and **writeln** methods are two others, **open** and **close**. These allow the code to open an existing document, after the browser has finished rendering it, and insert text and HTML into it. This replaces any existing content—in other words it clears the document first. Once we have completed writing the new content, the **close** method is used to update the browser display.

The **open** method also accepts two optional parameters. The first is a MIME type, indicating the type of contents that will be displayed. If the MIME type isn't specified, then the default is **text/html**. The second is either **true** or **false**, and indicates if we want the new document to replace the existing one's entry in the history list.

```
// open the document to insert new HTML content, replacing this history entry.
document.open("text/html", true)
document.write "Some text and HTML"        // write some text into the document
document.close                             // close it and update the display
```

The **open** method also has a return value that indicates success or failure. This is handy for handling errors for MIME types that aren't supported by the browser.

> *In older versions of HTML, we could remove the complete HTML source of the page using the **clear** method. This is still supported for backward compatibility, but isn't required as the content is automatically cleared when the document is opened. To clear a document without writing new content, we just have to open and close it.*

You'll see more ways of using these methods later in the chapter, where we've included a simple example that uses them to create a listing of the some of the contents of the document in a new browser window.

General Methods	Description
open	Opens a new browser window.
write	Writes text and HTML to a document in the specified window.
writeln	Writes text and HTML followed by a carriage return.

General Methods	Description
close	Closes an output stream to a document and updates the display.
getSelection	Returns a string containing the text currently selected in the document.

Reading the User's Selection

One brand new method of the document object is **getSelection**. This allows us to retrieve the contents of the user's selection in the page. For some time, it's been possible to drag the mouse over a loaded web page and copy the contents to the clipboard to paste into another document. Now, it is possible to automate the process, or provide new ways to interact with the user.

For example, we could provide some text and allow the user to make a choice by selecting the items of interest, then send this selection back to the server for further processing—perhaps to return more information on a topic, or to use it as input to another page.

The only problem with using **getSelection** is that we have to react to a mouse event, rather than putting a button or link into the page. Otherwise, the selection would disappear when the user clicked on the button or link. In the example below, we're reacting to the **onMouseUp** event. Drag over some text using the left mouse button as usual. When you release the button, an **alert** dialog displays the text you selected.

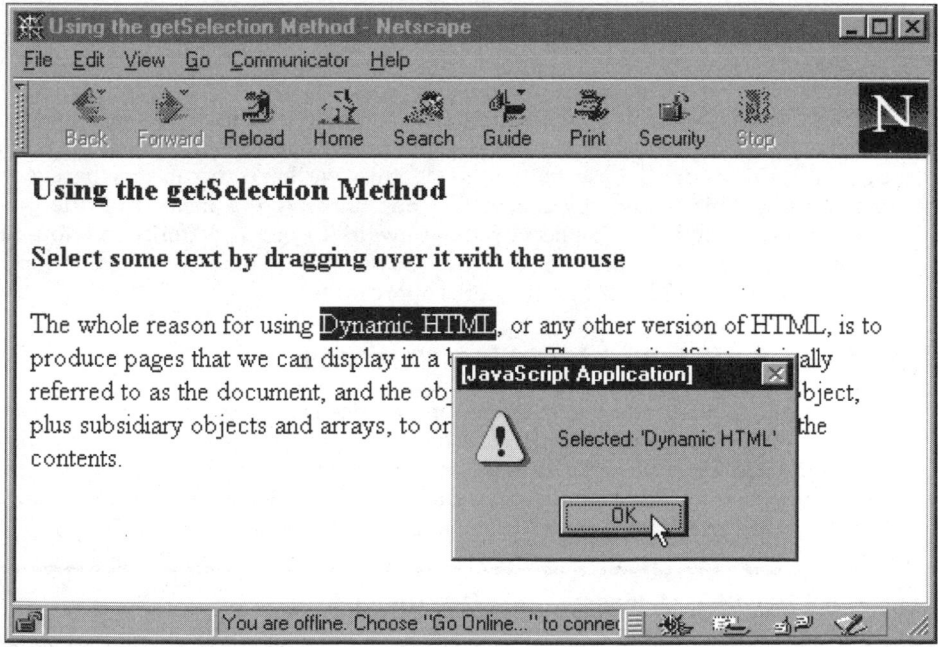

How It Works

This page demonstrates the **document** object's **getSelection** method at work. It also introduces us to **event capturing**. This is the main topic of the next chapter, and so we'll be skipping over it briefly here. However, it will give you some idea of just how powerful Dynamic HTML is when we come to work with the **document** and **window** objects.

The page is made up of the usual heading tags, and **<BODY>** followed by some sample text. The **<SCRIPT>** section contains a simple function that retrieves the user's current selection into a variable named **strSelection**. Then, providing it is not of zero length, the browser displays it using an **alert** dialog:

```
<BODY BGCOLOR=FFFFFF>
<H3>Using the getSelection Method</H3>
<H4>Select some text by dragging over it with the mouse</H4>
The whole reason for using Dynamic HTML, or any other version of HTML, ...
...

<SCRIPT LANGUAGE=JAVASCRIPT>

function ShowSelection(e)
{
  strSelected = document.getSelection();
  if (strSelected.length > 0)
    alert("Selected: '" + strSelected + "'");
}

// Turn on event capturing for onMouseUp in the window
// Note that the event name has to be all upper-case!
window.document.captureEvents(Event.MOUSEUP);

// Now we can connect the event with our function
window.onMouseUp = ShowSelection;

</SCRIPT>
```

To execute this function at the appropriate moment, we need to react to one of the mouse events, and the ideal one is the **onMouseUp** event, which occurs after the user releases the mouse button. To do this, we have to capture the event in the window. This is done by calling the **captureEvents** method of the **window** object and then connecting these events to our new function. You can see both of these statements in the code above. We'll come back to this topic in the next chapter, and see how it works more fully.

The Document Event Handling Methods

In the previous example, we saw one of the **document** object's event capturing methods, **captureEvents**, at work. There are four of these methods in all, and between them they allow us to react to events occurring almost anywhere in the browser object hierarchy, and channel them to other objects as required. You'll see this demonstrated in detail in the next chapter.

Event Handling Methods	Description
captureEvents	Instructs the document to capture events of a particular type.

Event Handling Methods	Description
`handleEvent`	Invokes the appropriate event handling code of the object for this event.
`releaseEvents`	Instructs the document to stop capturing events of a particular type.
`routeEvent`	Passes an event that has been captured back up through the normal event hierarchy.

The Events of the Document Object

The **document** object provides us with a wide range of events, and we can use these to react to almost any action taken by the user. We've divided them up into two groups here—**mouse** events and **key-press** events. Remember that, unlike many other languages, Dynamic HTML can capture events and pass them up or down through the object hierarchy—so these events can occur for the **document** even when the user targets their actions to an element on the page. Don't worry if this seems a strange concept, because we'll be covering event capturing and event handling in the next chapter.

Mouse Events in the Document

As you would expect, these events occur when the user performs some action using the mouse. Four new events, **onDblClick**, **onMouseDown**, **onMouseMove** and **onMouseUp** provide us with a whole raft of new opportunities for making our pages more interactive. Notice, however, that the **onMouseMove** event only occurs when we have enabled event capturing for the document.

Mouse Events	Description
`onClick`	Occurs when the mouse button is clicked on the document.
`onDblClick`	Occurs when the user double-clicks on the document.
`onMouseDown`	Occurs when the user presses a mouse button.
`onMouseMove`	Occurs when the user moves the mouse pointer, and event capturing is enabled.
`onMouseUp`	Occurs when the user releases a mouse button.

The mouse events also provide information regarding the position of the mouse pointer, the button pressed, and the state of the *Shift*, *Ctrl* and *Alt* keys. We'll be looking at how we handle all the document mouse and key-press events in detail in the next and subsequent chapters.

Key-press Events in the Document

As well as providing information on the events created by the mouse, the document object also provides a set of key-press events that run in order.

Key-press Events	Description
onKeyDown	Occurs when the user presses a key.
onKeyPress	Occurs when the user presses a key and that keyboard input is translated. i.e. multiple events occur if the key is held down, unlike **onKeyDown**.
onKeyUp	Occurs when the user releases a key.

Like the mouse events, the key-press events provide information on the state of the *Shift*, *Ctrl* and *Alt* keys. The **onKeyPress** event occurs when a key is pressed and then released, and provides an ASCII code modified to take account of the state of the *Shift*, *Ctrl* and *Alt* keys.

The Document Arrays

Having covered the properties, methods and events of the document, it's time now to look at the range of **arrays** that the **document** object provides. A web page contains a vast amount of information, and to allow us to access it using Dynamic HTML, it has to be organized in a sensible and usable way. This organization is done through eleven arrays:

Arrays	Description
anchors	Array of all the anchors defined in the document.
applets	Array of all the objects in the document, including intrinsic controls, images, applets, embeds and other objects.
classes	Array of all the style classes defined in the document.
embeds	Array of all the **<EMBED>** tags/plugins in the document.
forms	Array of all the forms defined in the document.
ids	Array of all the individual element styles defined in the document.
images	Array of all the images defined in the document.
layers	Array of all the layers defined in the document.
links	Array of all the links and **<AREA>** blocks defined in the document.
plugins	An alias for the array of all the plugins defined in the document.
tags	Array of all the elements defined in the document.

We'll look at how we can work with these arrays next, although some are intrinsically more useful that others. We'll be concentrating on those you are likely to come across most often.

Working with Document Arrays

We looked briefly at arrays in the previous chapter, where we saw how we can access other frames in a window using the **window** object's **frames** array. We considered these two ways of accessing the members of the **frames** array:

```
window.frames[1]              // the index of a frame in the array
window.frames["mainframe"]    // the name of a frame in the array
```

The **document** object supports a range of arrays, and we can use the same techniques to access them. For example, to access the second image on a page, we can use:

```
document.images[1]            // the index of an image in the array
```

If we have named the image, using the **NAME** attribute in the HTML **<IMG>** tag, we can even access it like this:

```
document.images["MyImage"]    // the name of an image in the array
```

As an example, here's part of a page that includes a single image:

```
<IMG SRC=element.gif NAME="MyImage">

<SCRIPT LANGUAGE=JAVASCRIPT>
   function ImageInfo() { alert(document.images["MyImage"].src) };
   document.onClick = ImageInfo;
</SCRIPT>
```

Clicking on the page executes the **ImageInfo()** function. This function uses the **images** array to get a reference to the image named **MyImage**. It then displays the value of the image's **src** property (the URL of the image), which is the Dynamic HTML equivalent of the value of the **SRC** attribute in the **<IMG>** tag. The function has an **onclick** event which is called in the line:

```
document.onClick = ImageInfo;
```

which means that whenever the **onclick** event of the document is detected, the **ImageInfo** function is executed.

109

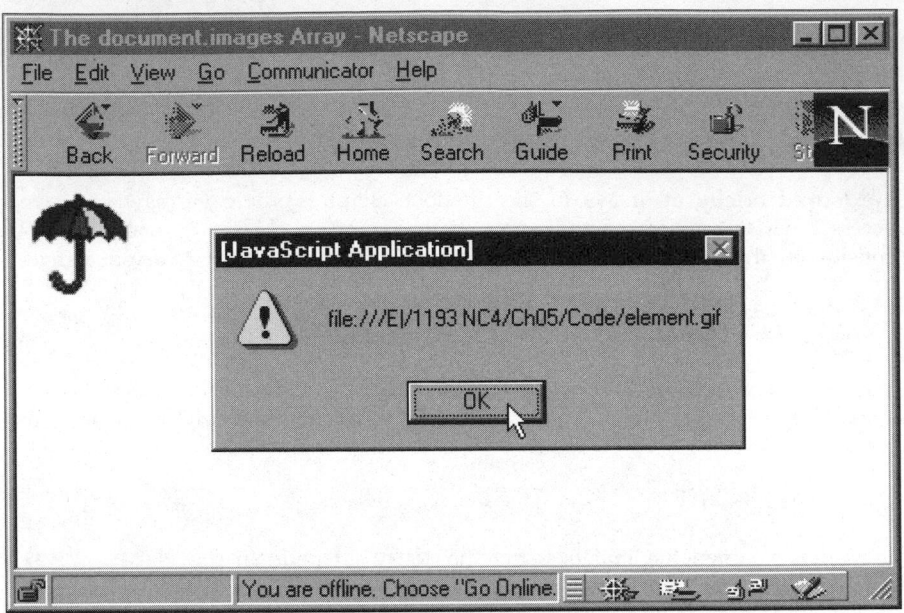

Using the Layers Array

One of the most exciting of the new features in Netscape's implementation of Dynamic HTML is the concept of **layers**. As you saw in Chapter 3, we can use the **<LAYER>** and **<ILAYER>** tags to create either absolute-positioned or in-line layers within a page. Each acts like a separate window, and holds a document and arrays of that document's contents. They are like frames in that respect, but do not need to be created using a separate **<FRAMESET>** page.

To keep track of the layers in a document, the object model provides a **layers** array. It holds a reference to each **Layer** object in that page. A layer holds a document that can itself contain other layers, in other words each layer's **document** object can contain an array of its 'child' layers. In the following code, we create a single layer in the document, with the **ID** of **MainLayer**, and then, within its document, two layers **InnerLayer1** and **InnerLayer2**:

```
<BODY BGCOLOR=FFFFFF>
   The actual HTML document
   <LAYER ID="MainLayer">
     A single layer contained within the document.
     <LAYER ID="InnerLayer1">
       A layer contained within the main layer.
     </LAYER>
     <LAYER ID="InnerLayer2">
       Another layer contained within the main layer.
     </LAYER>
   </LAYER>
</BODY>
```

We can think of this as forming a hierarchy of layers, as illustrated by the next diagram:

110

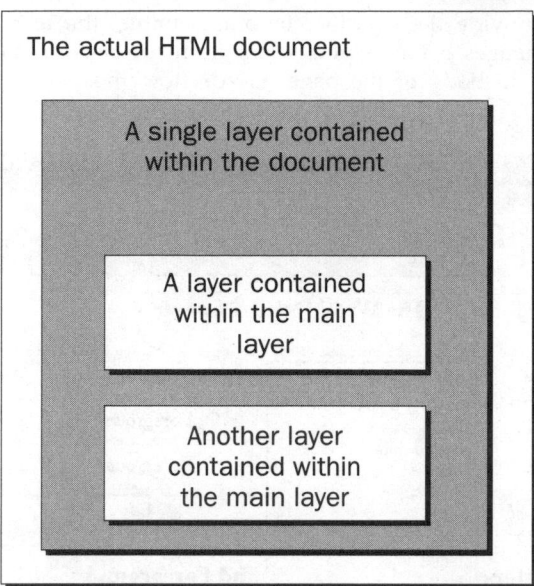

Accessing Layers and Their Contents

To access a layer, we use the **layers** array of the **document** object and—in the
case of contained layers—the **layers** array of each layer's **document** object.
The layers are indexed by their position within the document, and within each
layer. They can also be accessed using either their **ID** or their **NAME**, which are
interchangeable:

```
// the top property of the main layer in the document
document.layers[0].top;
document.layers["MainLayer"].top;

// the top property of the second layer within the main layer
document.layers[0].document.layers[1].top;
document.layers["MainLayer"].document.layers["InnerLayer2"].top;
```

Notice how, in the last two examples, we have to refer to the **document** object
within the layer to get at *its* **layers** array.

A Dynamic Layers Example Page

On our samples site at **http://rapid.wrox.co.uk/books/1193** we have
supplied a page that can be used to preview what different colors look like in
the browser. It changes the foreground and background colors of a sample of
text dynamically—while the page is being displayed.

While changing the background color is easy—we just need to assign the new
color to the **bgColor** property of the document object—it's not so easy with the
foreground color. Some browsers, like Internet Explorer, reflect changes in the
page. Unfortunately, Netscape's browser doesn't in Communicator 4. Instead, we
have to find a different method.

Of course, layers provide the solution. In our example, the text at the bottom of the page, which changes color as you select from the lists, is contained within a **<LAYER>** in the main body of the page. Here's how the page looks when you are using it:

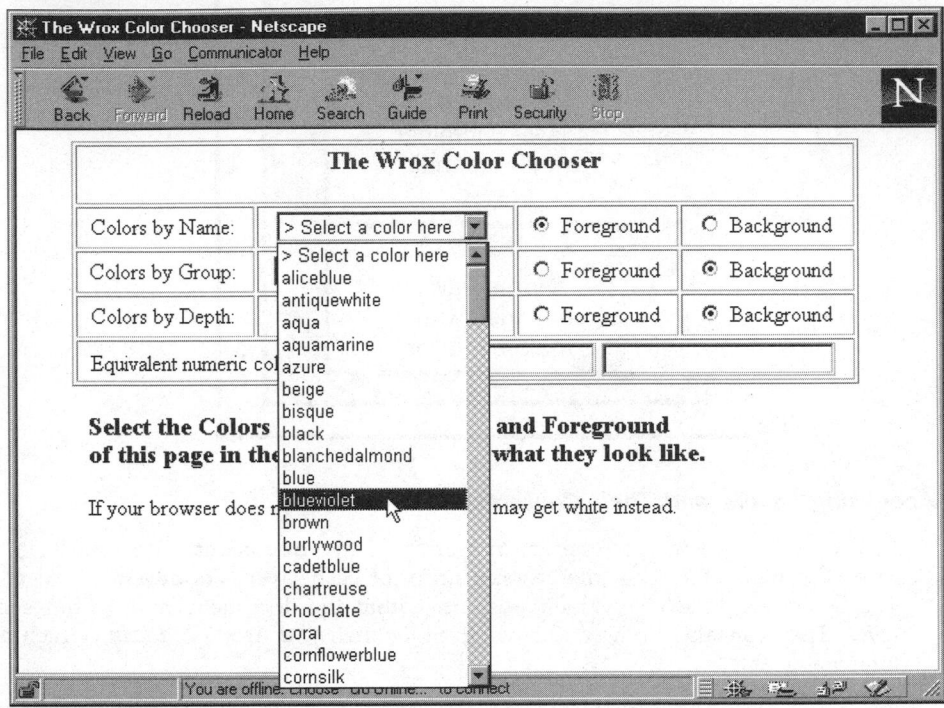

The HTML Part of the Color Chooser Page

The HTML that creates the page is pretty huge, because it contains the 100+ color names for each list box. However, the important part as far as we're concerned here is the section that creates two layers—one absolute-positioned and one in-line. In the first layer, we place the text you see on the page. The second layer simply has the background color set to the default white. It's also invisible, because we've set the **VISIBILITY** attribute to **HIDDEN** in the **<LAYER>** tag:

```
...
<!-- The layer that holds the text that will change color -->
<!-- Note: you can't write to an ILAYER, you must use a LAYER -->
<LAYER ID="textlayer" LEFT=50>
  <H3>Select the Colors for the Background and Foreground<BR>
  of this page in the Lists above, to see what they look like.</H3>
  If your browser does not support the color, you may get white instead.
</LAYER>

<!-- Hidden layer that is used to convert the color name to a value -->
<!-- There is no content, because we're just changing its bgColor -->
<ILAYER NAME="convertlayer" VISIBILITY="HIDDEN">
  <BODY BGCOLOR=FFFFFF>
  </BODY>
</ILAYER>
...
```

You can see how close layers are to frames and windows here. We can use a
<BODY> tag to set their appearance just as we would with a document
displayed in a window object.

The reason for that hidden frame is shown when you select a color for the foreground. The two text boxes in the table show the numerical equivalent of the colors as RGB triplets (**#RRGGBB**):

The Wrox Color Chooser		
Colors by Name:	blueviolet ▼	⦿ Foreground 〇 Background
Colors by Group:	> Select a color here ▼	〇 Foreground ⦿ Background
Colors by Depth:	> Select a color here ▼	〇 Foreground ⦿ Background
Equivalent numeric color values:	Foreground: #8A2BE2	Background: #FFFFFF

To convert the color name selected in the list into a numerical value is easily done by assigning it to the color property of an object like the background of the page (**bgColor**), then reading it back. It's returned as the RGB triplet value we want. However, we can't do this in Communicator with the foreground color, because it's read-only once the page has been rendered. Instead, we assign the color to the background of our hidden in-line layer, then read it back from there.

The Script in the Color Chooser Page

Here's the code of the first of two functions in the page that perform all this magic. It creates a whole new page for the visible fixed layer, with the correct foreground color. Because layers are transparent, if we don't apply a background color we will see the background color of the main page through it:

```
function ChangeTextLayer(fgcol)
{
    // create a string containing the new layer content
    newcontent = '<BODY TEXT="' + fgcol + '"><H3>Select the Colors for the ';
    newcontent += 'Background and Foreground<BR> of this page in the Lists ';
    newcontent += 'above, to see what they look like.</H3> If your browser ';
    newcontent += 'does not support the color, you may get white instead.</BODY>';

    // then write it to the layer's document, and close it to update the display
    document.layers["textlayer"].document.write(newcontent);
    document.layers["textlayer"].document.close();

    // now change the background of the hidden layer to the new foreground color
    // so that we can read back the converted RRGGBB value from it for the textbox
    document.layers["convertlayer"].document.bgColor = fgcol;
}
```

Once we've created the string, we write it to the layer using the **write** method of that **Layer** object and then **close** it—just as we would with a **document** object. Notice how we refer to the methods of the document in the layer, using:

```
document.layers["textlayer"].document.write(newcontent);
document.layers["textlayer"].document.close();
```

The final line then changes the background color of the other (hidden) layer. Again, we refer to the layer by name, though we could just as easily have used **document.layers[1]** because it is the second layer in the document:

```
document.layers["convertlayer"].document.bgColor = fgcol;
```

The other function does the work of extracting the values from the list boxes and radio buttons when a selection is made. You'll see these techniques described later in the chapter, and you may wish to come back to this example once you've read about them. In particular, we refer to the Foreground radio button using its index, which is one more than the associated list box element:

```
thisform.elements[listnumber + 1].checked
```

The rest of the function is concerned with retrieving the RGB color triplet values from the **bgColor** property of the main page, and the background of the hidden layer:

```
function ChangeColor(listnumber)
{
  // get a reference to the form, and then to the color selector list
  thisform = document.forms[0];
  thislist = thisform.elements[listnumber];

  // find out which entry is selected, and get the text for it
  thisindex = thislist.selectedIndex;
  thiscolor = thislist.options[thisindex].text;

  // change appropriate setting and update two text boxes with new values
  // but only if a color is selected, not an entry starting with '>'
  if (thiscolor.indexOf('>') == -1)
    { if (thisform.elements[listnumber + 1].checked) ChangeTextLayer(thiscolor)
        else document.bgColor = thiscolor;

      // to get foreground color query background color of hidden layer
      thisform.elements['txtFG'].value = 'Foreground: ' +
        document.layers["convertlayer"].document.bgColor.toUpperCase();
      thisform.elements['txtBG'].value = 'Background: ' +
        document.bgColor.toUpperCase();
    }
}
```

Layer Properties, Methods and Events

As you will appreciate by now, layers give an enormous boost to the capabilities of the browser for client-side scripting with JavaScript or other languages. Unsurprisingly, they have many properties, methods and events to make this possible. We've provided a full list in the reference section of this book, and reprinted the common ones here. We'll be using layers, and seeing how we work with them in more detail, throughout the rest of this book.

The Properties of the Layer Object

Layers have many properties, some of which reflect the values we set in the attributes in the **<LAYER>** tag. Here, we've grouped them into three sections—

114

position properties, **clipping** properties and **content** properties. A full alphabetical list is provided in Section E at the end of this book.

The position properties allow us to access information about the physical position of the layer in relation to the page (**pageX** and **pageY**), or a layer and document that contains it (**top** and **left**). We can also get information about the z-order of the layer, using the **above**, **below** and **zIndex** properties. Finally, we have properties that provide references to other layers that are parents or children of the current layer:

Position Properties	Description
left	Position in pixels of the left-hand side of the layer in relation to its containing layer or the document.
top	Position of the top of the layer in relation to its containing layer or the document.
pageX	Horizontal position of the layer in relation to the document window.
pageY	Vertical position of the layer in relation to the document window.
above	Indicates that the layer should be above another element in the z-order of the page, or returns the element above it.
below	Indicates that the layer should be below another element in the z-order of the page, or returns the element below it.
zIndex	Position in the z-order or stacking order of the page, i.e. the z co-ordinate.
parentLayer	Reference to the layer that contains the current layer.
siblingAbove	Reference to the layer above the current layer if they share the same parent layer.
siblingBelow	Reference to the layer below the current layer if they share the same parent layer.

Each layer has a clipping rectangle, beyond which the contents are not visible. It's possible to control the size of this rectangle by setting the clipping properties:

Clipping Properties	Description
clip.bottom	Y co-ordinate of the bottom of the clipping rectangle for the layer.
clip.top	Y co-ordinate of the top of the clipping rectangle for the layer.
clip.left	X co-ordinate of the left of the clipping rectangle for the layer.

Table continued on following page

Clipping Properties	Description
clip.right	X co-ordinate of the right of the clipping rectangle for the layer.
clip.height	Height of the clipping rectangle for the layer.
clip.width	Width of the clipping for the layer.

Finally, the remaining properties provide us with a way of accessing the background image and color of the layer (if these are set to **null**—the default—the layer is transparent). We can also access the **NAME** or **ID**, as provided in the **<LAYER>** tag, the URL of a separate page that provides the contents for the layer if available, and the visibility of the layer:

Content Properties	Description
background	URL of an image to display behind the elements in the layer.
bgColor	Specifies the background color to be used for the layer.
name	Specifies the name to use to refer to the layer.
src	An external file that contains the source data for the layer.
visibility	Defines whether the layer should be displayed on the page.

You've seen many of these properties used in our earlier example, and we'll be working with layers in the remainder of this book. You'll see a lot of different ways that they can be used.

The Methods of the Layer Object

We've divided the methods of the **Layer** object into three groups. The first group is concerned with moving and resizing the layer. We can move a layer in script by relative amounts, or to an absolute position in relation to the containing layer or the main document itself (if the layer is contained within another document, for example).

We can also move a layer in the z-plane, so that it lies below or on top of other layers. This can provide the 2.5-D effect in pages, by overlapping different layers.

Move and Size Methods	Description
moveAbove	Changes the z-order so that the layer is rendered above (overlaps) another element.
moveBelow	Changes the z-order so that the layer is rendered below (overlapped by) another element.

116

Move and Size Methods	Description
`moveBy`	Moves the layer horizontally and vertically by a specified number of pixels.
`moveTo`	Moves the layer so that the top-left is at a position x, y (in pixels) within its container.
`moveToAbsolute`	Moves the layer to a position specified in x and y in relation to the page and not the container.
`resizeBy`	Resizes the layer horizontally and vertically by a specified number of pixels.
`resizeTo`	Resizes the layer to a size specified by x and y (in pixels).

A layer contains a document, and this document is the HTML that creates the content of the layer. To make our pages dynamic, we can change this content while the layer is displayed. We can write to it by using the **write** and **writeln** of the **document** object within the layer, or load a whole new document using the **Layer** object's **load** method:

Load Method	Description
`load`	Loads a file into the layer, and can change the width of the layer.

The third group of methods are those that we use when working with events that occur in the layer. We'll be coming back to these in the next chapter, when we examine the whole concept of event handling in more detail.

Event Handling Methods	Description
`captureEvents`	Instructs the layer to capture events of a particular type.
`handleEvent`	Invokes the appropriate event-handling code of the object for this event.
`releaseEvents`	Instructs the layer to stop capturing events of a particular type.
`routeEvent`	Passes an event that has been captured back up through the normal event hierarchy.

The Events of the Layer Object

Layers, like windows and frames, have several events available for scripting. We'll be looking at how we work with script and events in a lot more detail in the next chapter. However, as you can see from the table below, the list of events is similar to those of the **window** object we met in the previous chapter:

117

Events	Description
onBlur	Occurs when the layer loses the focus.
onFocus	Occurs when the layer receives the focus.
onLoad	Occurs immediately after the layer's contents have been loaded.
onMouseOut	Occurs when the mouse pointer leaves the layer.
onMouseOver	Occurs when the mouse pointer first enters the layer.

Of course, layers cannot be resized or moved by the user using script alone. Therefore they don't have the **onMove** and **onResize** events. Notice, though, that there is an **onLoad** event that we can use to trigger a script once the layer has completed loading. Because we can change the contents of a layer to a different URL, or write new content into it directly, the **onLoad** event allows us to manage the process and detect when it is properly complete before we manipulate these new contents.

Using an Array's Length Property

We've talked about arrays, and how we can access them, in several places in this and previous chapters. As we work with arrays, we'll often want to retrieve a list of the objects that are available in that array. For example, we might consider using a **for** loop to read the **src** property of each image on the page. We use the array's **length** property to return the number of items in the array:

```
for (item = 0; item < document.images.length; item++)
   alert(document.images[item].src);
```

*Notice that, as arrays are indexed from zero and the **length** property returns the number of items in the array, we use*
*__item < document.images.length__. as the condition for stopping the loop. This is because the last item in the array will have an index one less than the value of the **length** property.*

We'll be using this technique in the example at the end of this chapter. Most of the document arrays work in the same way as this, providing easy access to any element on the page. However, there are some that are different—the **forms** array and the three arrays used to set the styles of the page elements. We'll look at the **forms** array first.

Using the Forms Array

Web page authors can create pages that contain one or more sections defined as **forms**, by enclosing then in the **<FORM>** and **</FORM>** tags. Forms have special abilities, in that they can contain the **SUBMIT** and **RESET** types of **<INPUT>** tag, which either send the contents of the controls in that form to the server for processing, or reset them to their default values.

This means that the forms in a document can themselves act as containers to hold other elements and objects. To manage this, each member of the **forms** array (i.e. each **Form** object) has its own sub-array of **elements**:

elements   An array of all the controls and other elements in a form.

This array can be accessed in the same way as the **document** arrays, this time with the **elements** array added to the end of the statement:

```
// access the third element in the first form on the page
document.forms[0].elements[2]

// access the element named MyTextBox in the second form on the page
document.forms[1].elements["MyTextBox"]

// access the element named MyTextBox in a form named MyForm
document.forms["MyForm"].elements["MyTextBox"]
```

Accessing Properties and Methods

Of course, like all arrays, the items in the array are themselves objects. Therefore, we need to specify to which property or method of the object we are referring—as we did earlier to retrieve the source file from an image element. Here are some property retrievals:

```
strFileName = document.images["MyImage"].src        // image source
strTheValue = document.forms[0].elements[2].value    // control value
blnChecked  = document.forms[3].elements[0].checked  // control setting
strAddress  = document.links["MyLink"].href          // URL of a hyperlink
strPlugin   = document.plugins[0].name               // name of a plugin
```

And here's how we can call a method of an object in an array. In this example we're calling the **focus** method of the third element in the first form:

```
document.forms[0].elements[2].focus      // set the focus to this control
```

The Options Array

Finally we also need to consider a list box control, as created by a **<SELECT>** tag. This has an array of entries, or **options**, that are shown in the list. These entries are stored as an array as well—the **options** array of the **Select** object.

We access these using the same syntax as with other arrays. For example, if we have created a page that contains a form and a **<SELECT>** element using this code:

```
<FORM NAME="MyForm">
  <INPUT TYPE=RADIO VALUE=1 NAME="MyRadio">
  <INPUT TYPE=RADIO VALUE=2 NAME="MyRadio">
  <SELECT NAME="MyList" SIZE=4>
    <OPTION VALUE="1"> Text of item 1
    <OPTION VALUE="2"> Text of item 2
    <OPTION VALUE="3"> Text of item 3
    <OPTION VALUE="4"> Text of item 4
  </SELECT>
</FORM>
```

119

we can access the values in the list using:

```
// text of fourth option in list control which is third element on first form
document.forms[0].elements[2].options[3].text        // returns 'Text of Item 4'

// value of fourth option in the list named MyList on the form named MyForm
document.forms["MyForm"].elements["MyList"].options[3].value // returns '4'
```

In the first case, we're using the **text** property of the **Option** object that is the fourth item in the list. In the second case, we're using the **value** property, i.e. that which is set with the **VALUE** attribute. In the next screenshot, we're using the form that we created above, and displaying the value of the **document.forms[0].elements[2].options[3].text** property in an **alert** dialog:

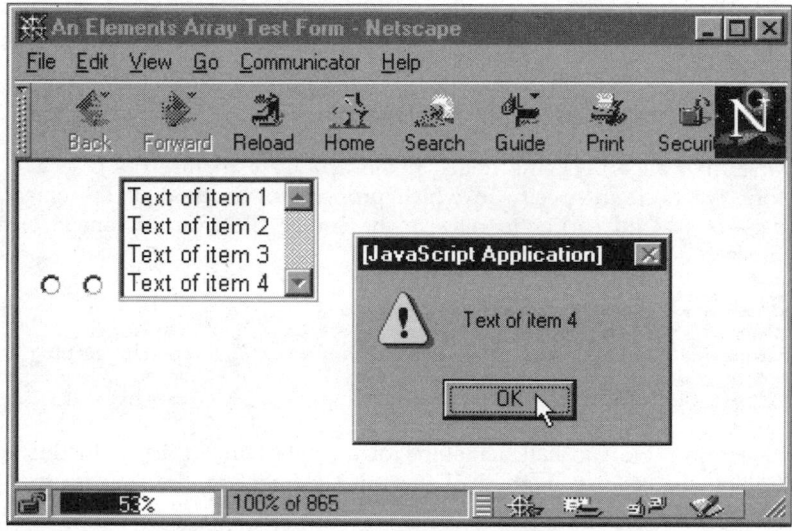

You can see that by using names for the controls, and in the script that accesses them, we can avoid problems of the index of the element changing when we add or remove other controls on the form.

Radio Button Groups

The form we used above also has two option buttons, or **radio** buttons as they are more commonly known. Radio buttons are grouped by giving them the same name. This won't prove a problem if we are accessing them using their index within the **elements** array. Using our sample form again:

```
<FORM NAME="MyForm">
  <INPUT TYPE=RADIO VALUE=1 NAME="MyRadio">
  <INPUT TYPE=RADIO VALUE=2 NAME="MyRadio">
  <SELECT NAME="MyList" SIZE=4>
    <OPTION VALUE="1"> Text of item 1
    <OPTION VALUE="2"> Text of item 2
    <OPTION VALUE="3"> Text of item 3
    <OPTION VALUE="4"> Text of item 4
  </SELECT>
</FORM>
```

120

The first radio button (in our case) is **elements[0]**, and the second is **elements[1]**. We can get at their value using:

```
// value of first element on the form named MyForm
document.forms[0].elements[0].value        // returns '1'

// value of second element on the form named MyForm
document.forms[0].elements[1].value        // returns '2'
```

However, when we come to access them using their name, things are a bit more difficult—they both have the same name. In this case, we take advantage of the fact that JavaScript creates a sub-array of all the elements that have the same name:

```
// value of the first element named MyRadio on the form named MyForm
document.forms[0].elements["MyRadio"][0].value      // returns '1'

// value of the second element named MyRadio on the form named MyForm
document.forms[0].elements["MyRadio"][1].value      // returns '2'
```

Managing Specific Element Types

While each element on a form is part of the **elements** array, they are not all the same *type* of object. This is unlike the other arrays, such as **images**, where each member is of the same type—an **Image** object. In the **elements** array, the members can be any type of form control element, such as a **Radio** object, a **Select** object, a **Textbox** object, a **Submit** object, etc.

The different types of elements have different properties, methods and events. This means that we can't always iterate through the array (using, for example, a **for** loop), and read the properties. If we try to read the **checked** property, we'll only get a result for checkboxes and option buttons, and not for text boxes and lists.

> *Section E lists the various control types, showing their respective properties, methods and events. It also contains a useful cross-reference which shows the different properties, methods and events categorized by type, and the controls to which they are applicable.*

Using the Document's Style Arrays

Three of the document arrays are not true arrays. The **tags**, **classes** and **ids** arrays are used in JavaScript style sheets to apply a style to specific elements, or groups of elements, as we saw back in Chapter 2.

We can't iterate through these arrays in the same way as we can with the other document arrays. To access them, we have to know the actual member we want to query. There are four basic ways that we can set the style of an element using JavaScript Style Sheets:

 We can assign a value to that tag type using the **tags** method:

```
<STYLE TYPE="text/javascript">
  tags.H1.color = "red";
```

121

```
</STYLE>
...
<H1> This is some red text </H1>
```

 We can assign a value to a **class** which covers all types of tag, then apply that **class** to any element using an inline **STYLE** attribute in the element tag:

```
<STYLE TYPE="text/javascript">
  classes.MyClass.all.color = "red";
</STYLE>
...
<H1 CLASS="MyClass"> This is some red text </H1>
```

 We can also mix the two previous techniques by assigning a value to a **class** for a single tag type, then applying that **class** to an element of the appropriate type:

```
<STYLE TYPE="text/javascript">
  classes.MyClass.H1.color = "red";
</STYLE>
...
<H1 CLASS="MyClass"> This is some red text </H1>
```

 Finally, we can assign a value to an individual element by applying it to that element's **ID**, as set in the attribute of the element, using the **ids** method:

```
<STYLE TYPE="text/javascript">
  ids.MyHeading.color = "red";
</STYLE>
...
<H1 ID="MyHeading"> This is some red text </H1>
```

Reading Style Information from the Style Arrays

Once we've set the style for an element, we can read it back directly using the relevant array. In the case of our examples above, we can use:

```
document.tags.H1.color                  // returns 'red'
document.classes.MyClass.all.color       // returns 'red'
document.classes.MyClass.H1.color        // returns 'red'
document.ids.MyHeading.color             // returns 'red'
```

You'll see this technique used in the final example of this chapter. It's also possible to change the values of the style properties, but only before that element has been rendered. For example, we could use code to decide on the customer's access level privileges (perhaps by pre-processing the page on the server or with a cookie) to set the value of a **customer_access_level** variable. This can then be tested to decide on the color of the text:

```
<STYLE TYPE="text/javascript">
  tags.H1.color = "red";
</STYLE>
```

```
<BODY BGCOLOR=FFFFFF>
<SCRIPT LANGUAGE=JAVASCRIPT>
  // code here to decide on access level for this customer
  ...
  if (customer_access_level == 1) document.tags.H1.color="green";
</SCRIPT>
<H1> Prepare to enter our site. </H1>
```

A Document and Arrays Example

To show you how we can use some of the **document** object's arrays, and demonstrate several of the properties of the **document** object at the same time, we've provided a simple example page called The Document Object and Arrays (**DocObject.htm**) on our Web site at **http://rapid.wrox.co.uk/books/ 1193/**:

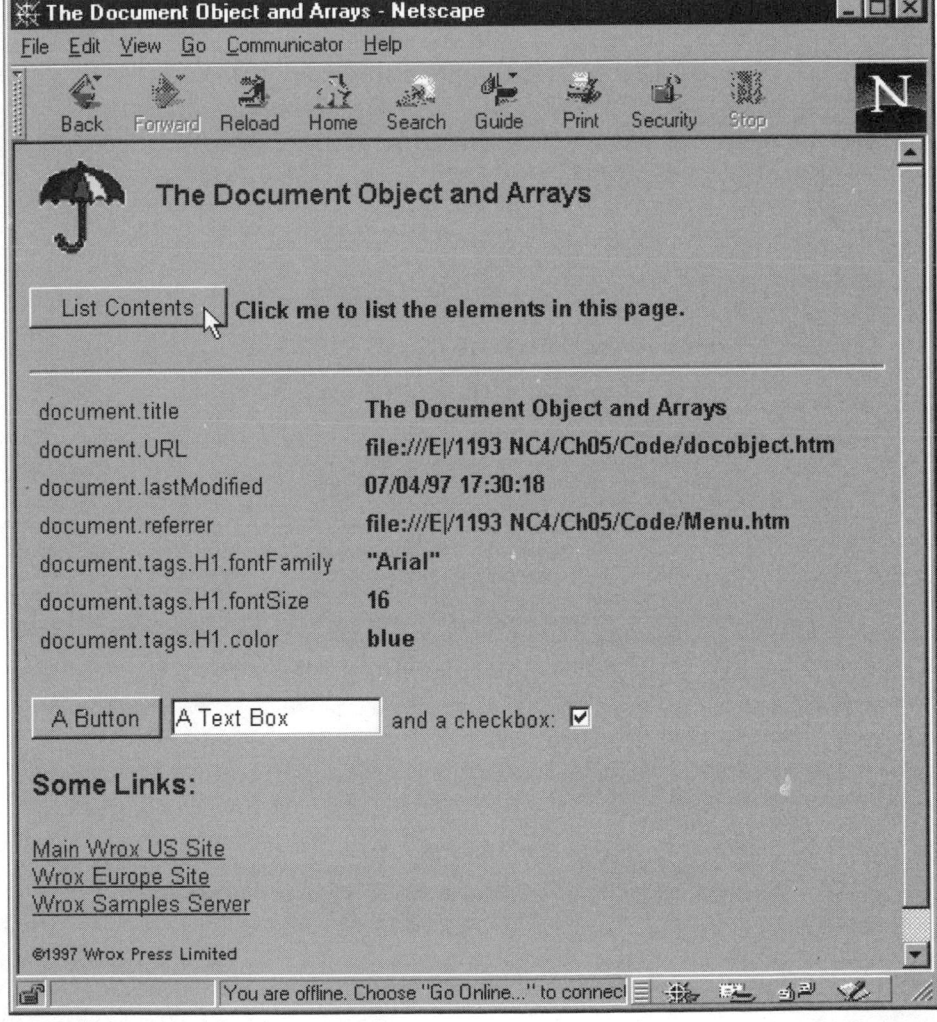

This page uses the same techniques as the similar example in the previous chapter to display the values of several properties from the **document** object, and from several of the document arrays. The text box, checkbox and buttons at the bottom of the page, and the various anchors and links, are included simply so that you can see how their tags and attributes appear within the **forms** and **elements** arrays. Here's the HTML and script code for the page—we're omitting the code for the List Contents button for the time being:

```
<HTML>
<HEAD><TITLE> The Document Object and Arrays </TITLE></HEAD>
<STYLE>
<!--
   H1 {fontFamily:"Arial"; fontSize:16; color:blue}
   H2 {fontFamily:"Arial"; fontSize:10}
   TD,A {fontFamily:"Arial"; fontSize:14}
-->
</STYLE>

<BODY BGCOLOR=#FFC0A0>
<A NAME="MyAnchor1">
<H1><IMG SRC="element.gif" HSPACE=5 ALIGN=MIDDLE NAME="ImageElement">
The Document Object and Arrays</H1>
<FORM NAME="FirstForm">
  <INPUT TYPE=button VALUE="List Contents" NAME="cmdContents"
         ONCLICK="ListContents()">
  <B> Click me to list the elements in this page.</B>
</FORM>
<HR ID=HRule1>

<SCRIPT LANGUAGE="JAVASCRIPT">
<!--

  strInfo = "<CENTER><TABLE WIDTH=100%>" +
            "<TR><TD>document.title</TD>" +
            "<TD><B>" + document.title + "</TD></TR>" +
            "<TR><TD>document.URL</TD>" +
            "<TD><B>" + document.URL + "</TD></TR>" +
            "<TR><TD>document.lastModified</TD>" +
            "<TD><B>" + document.lastModified + "</TD></TR>" +
            "<TR><TD>document.referrer</TD>" +
            "<TD><B>" + document.referrer + "</TD></TR>" +
            "<TR><TD>document.tags.H1.fontFamily</TD>" +
            "<TD><B>" + document.tags.H1.fontFamily + "</TD></TR>" +
            "<TR><TD>document.tags.H1.fontSiz</TD>" +
            "<TD><B>" + document.tags.H1.fontSize + "</TD></TR>" +
            "<TR><TD>document.tags.H1.color</TD>" +
            "<TD><B>" + document.tags.H1.color + "</TD></TR>" +
            "</TABLE></CENTER><P>";
  document.write(strInfo);
  // stop hiding -->
</SCRIPT>

<A NAME="NextToForm">
<FORM NAME="BottomForm">
  <INPUT TYPE=button VALUE="A Button" NAME="cmdButton">
  <INPUT TYPE=text VALUE="A Text Box" SIZE=10 NAME="txtTextBox">
  and a checkbox: <INPUT TYPE=checkbox NAME="chkCheckBox" CHECKED>
</FORM>
```

```
<H1>Some Links:</H1>
<A HREF="http://www.wrox.com">Main Wrox US Site</A><BR>
<A HREF="http://www.wrox.co.uk">Wrox Europe Site</A><BR>
<A HREF="http://rapid.wrox.co.uk">Wrox Samples Server</A>
<H2>&copy;1997 Wrox Press Limited</H2>

</BODY>
</HTML>
```

How It Works

The page is relatively simple, using the same techniques as we saw in the
Browser Information page from the previous chapter. A string is created with
the name of each property in the first cell of a table row, and the value of that
property in the second cell. Once the complete string has been built, it's written
to the page using the **write** method of the **document** object.

You can see that we are querying three properties of the **<H1>** heading tag's
style, using the contents of the **tags** array. This works because we have
previously assigned values to these properties in a **<STYLE>** section at the top
of the page. It's interesting to see that they are still applied to the **tags** array,
even though we assigned these styles using:

```
H1 {fontFamily:"Arial"; fontSize:16; color:blue}
H2 {fontFamily:"Arial"; fontSize:10}
TD,A {fontFamily:"Arial"; fontSize:14}
```

instead of the more formal syntax:

```
tags.H1.fontFamily = "Arial";
tags.H1.fontSize = 16;
tags.H1.color = blue;
... etc.
```

Using the Document Arrays

So, if you click the List Contents button at the top of the page, this will open a
new browser window, which lists the contents of several of the **document**
object's arrays for the original document:

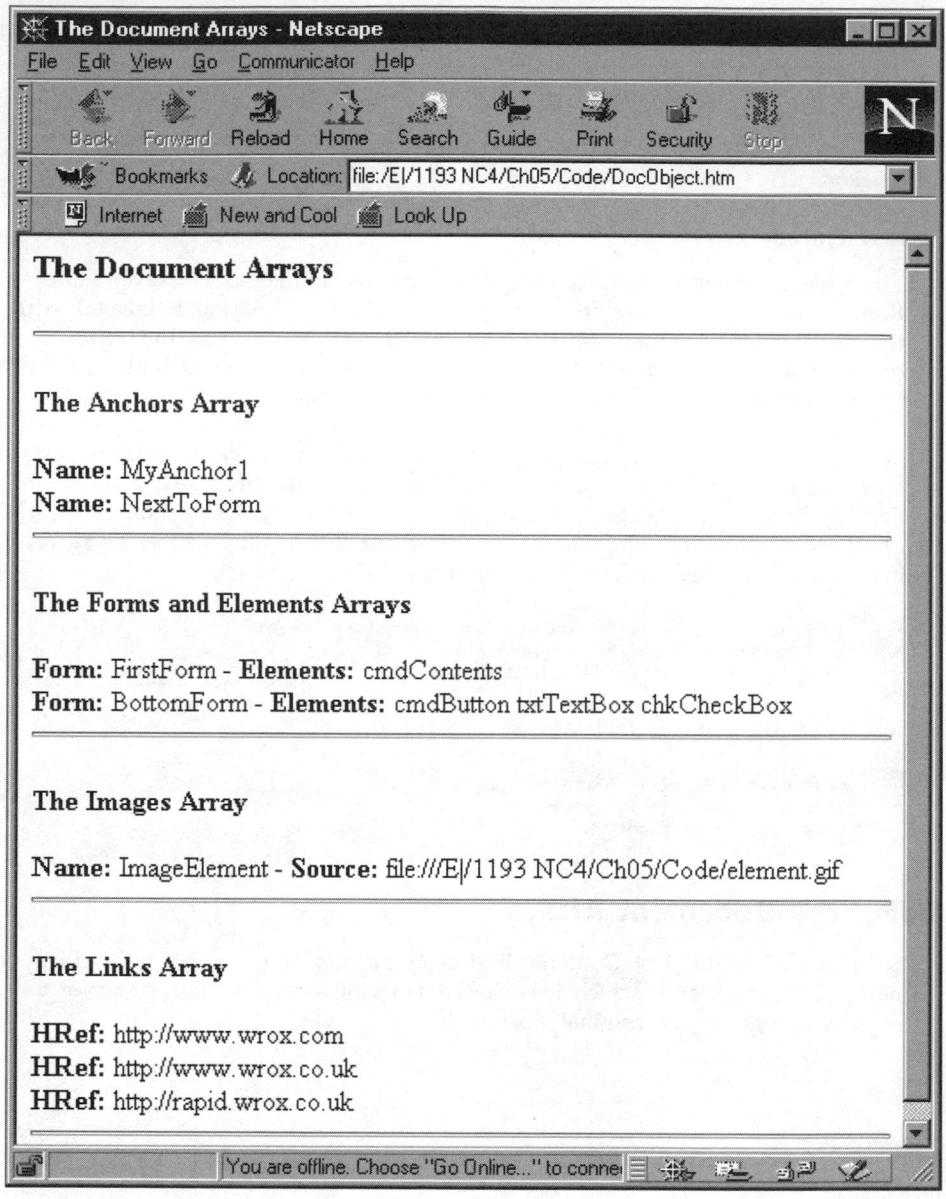

How It Works

Here's the complete code of the **ListContents()** function, which runs when the List Contents button is clicked:

```
function ListContents()
{
  NewWin = window.open("");
  NewWin.document.write("<HTML><HEAD><TITLE>The Document Arrays" +
                        "</TITLE></HEAD><BODY>");
  NewWin.document.write("<H3>The Document Arrays</H3>");
```

```
    NewWin.document.write("<HR><H4>The Anchors Array</H4>");
    for (objItem = 0; objItem < document.anchors.length; objItem++)
      NewWin.document.write("<B>Name:</B> " + document.anchors[objItem].name +
                            "<BR>");

    NewWin.document.write("<HR><H4>The Forms and Elements Arrays</H4>");
    for (objItem = 0; objItem < document.forms.length; objItem++)
    {
      strFormName = document.forms[objItem].name;
      NewWin.document.write("<B>Form:</B> " + strFormName + "<B> - Elements:</B> ");
      for (objElement = 0; objElement < document.forms[strFormName].elements.length;
         objElement++)
        NewWin.document.write(document.forms[strFormName].elements[objElement].name
                              + " ");
      NewWin.document.write("<BR>");
    }

    NewWin.document.write("<HR><H4>The Images Array</H4>");
    for (objItem = 0; objItem < document.images.length; objItem++)
      NewWin.document.write("<B>Name:</B> " + document.images[objItem].name +
                            "<B> - Source:</B> " + document.images[objItem].src +
                            "<BR>");

    NewWin.document.write("<HR><H4>The Links Array</H4>");
    for (objItem = 0; objItem < document.links.length; objItem++)
      NewWin.document.write("<B>HRef:</B> " + document.links[objItem].href +
                            "<BR>");

    NewWin.document.write("<HR></BODY></HTML>");
    NewWin.document.close();

};
```

The code in the page iterates (or loops) through several of the document arrays, placing the value of some of their properties into the page. We're using:

- The **anchors** array, and displaying the name of each member—as set in the **NAME** attribute of each **<A NAME="...">** tag.

- The **forms** array, and displaying the name of each member—as set in the **NAME** attribute of each **<FORM>** tag. Then, within that form we're iterating through the **elements** array and displaying the **NAME** of each element we find in that form.

- The **images** array, and displaying the source file of each image—as set in the **SRC** attribute of each **<IMG>** tag.

- The **links** array, and displaying the target URL of each link—as set in the **HREF** attribute of each **<A HREF="...">** tag.

The first stage is to open a new browser window using the **window** object's **open** method. We don't need to specify a source file, because we're going to create the contents of the window dynamically using the **write** method of the new, blank **document** object. At the same time, we assign the new window object to a variable **NewWin** so that we can then access it in our code later on.

Once we've got our new window, we can start to write to it. We're going to create the content using code running in the original page, and write it to the new page. Of course, the new page is in the new browser window, not our existing (current) one, so we need to call the write method of the **NewWin.document** object.

127

Listing the Contents of the Array

The next step is to list the members of the array, and add some property values where appropriate. The **for** loop will step through the complete array, from zero to **array.length - 1**, and for each iteration it sets the variable **objItem** to the index of that member of the array.

```
for (objItem = 0; objItem < document.anchors.length; objItem++)
   - code to write the property values to the new window goes here - ;
```

All we have to do in the loop is **write** the property we want to the new page. In the case of the **anchors** array, this is the **name** property:

```
NewWin.document.write("<B>Name:</B> " + document.anchors[objItem].name + "<BR>");
```

The only complexity is the **forms** array, where we need to iterate through each form's **elements** array as well. The code to do this first saves the name of each **Form** object in the **forms** array as a string, **strFormName**, then uses it in an inner loop to retrieve all the elements. This is an example of an alternative way to access the members of the **forms** array, instead of using the numerical index as we did with the **anchors** array:

```
for (objItem = 0; objItem < document.forms.length; objItem++)
   {
   strFormName = document.forms[objItem].name;  // get the form name
   ...
   for (objElement = 0; objElement < document.forms[strFormName].elements.length;
        objElement++)     // and loop through the elements array
      NewWin.document.write(document.forms[strFormName].elements[objElement].name);
   }
```

When complete, we close the document using the **close** method. You can see that the code creates a properly formatted page, including the opening and closing **<HTML>** and **<BODY>** tags. Of course, we could easily add code to create a more attractive result, but that would only have clouded the issue here.

Summary

In this chapter, we've completed our tour of the Dynamic HTML **object model** by looking at the central character it provides—the **document** object. We've also looked at the other subsidiary objects and arrays that it supports, and seen some ways we can use them in our pages. We looked at:

- How the entire content of the page being displayed by the browser is accessible through the **document** object and various other objects and arrays

- How we can use the **document** object's properties, methods and events to manipulate the document, or just get information about it

- How we can access the various elements on the page, using the **document** object's arrays

- How we can get access to the style of elements on the page, using the **document** object's **tags**, **classes** and **ids** arrays

You've probably also seen some new ways of using scripting in this chapter. We're actually going to be concentrating on scripting in the next chapter, and in the remainder of the book. Now you know what's inside the browser, it's just waiting for you to play with it through scripting code. OK, so there are a few more things to learn—so turn the page, and let's get started.

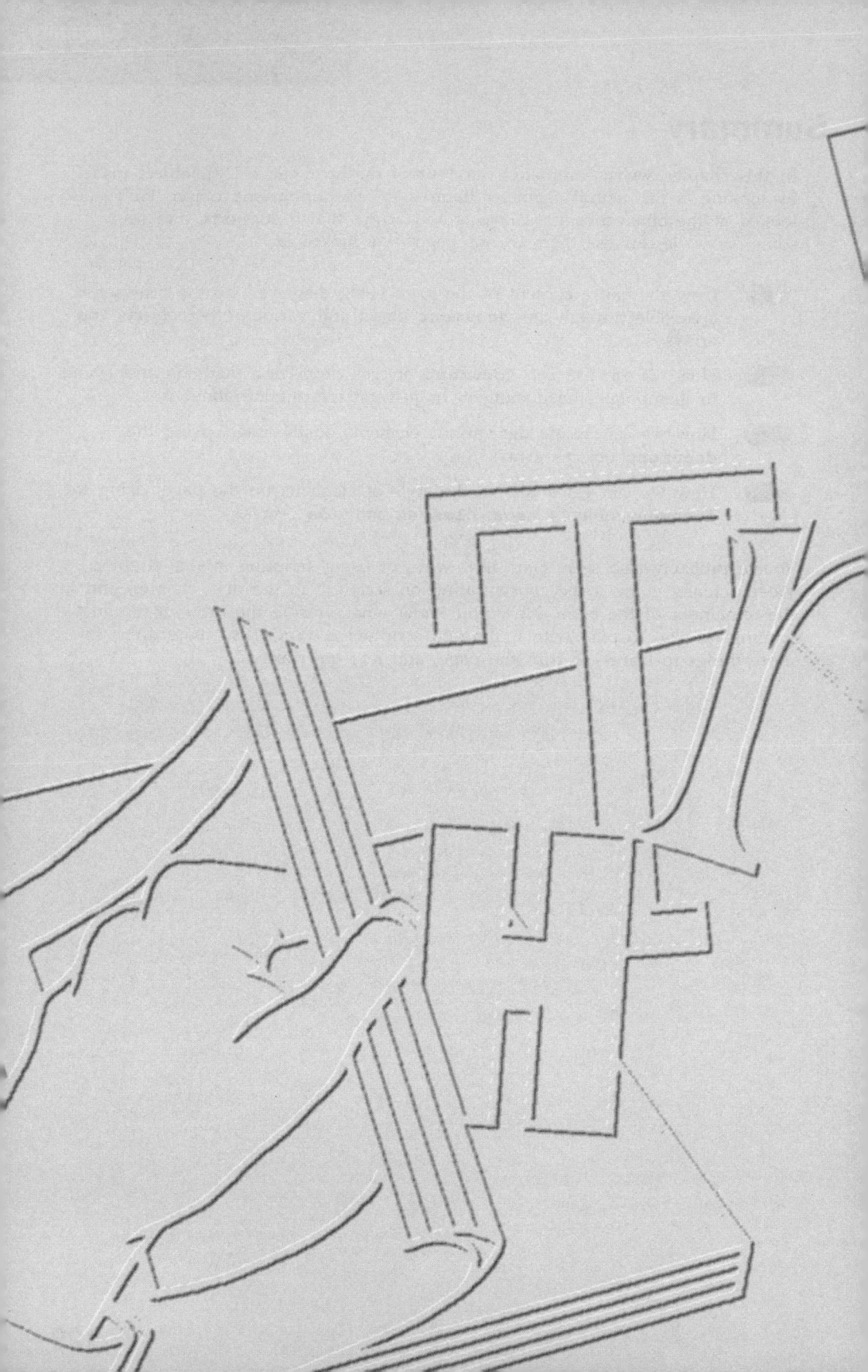

Scripts and Event Handling

So far, we've covered a lot of the basics of Dynamic HTML. We've studied style sheets and style tags, looked at the new design opportunities they offer for static pages, and discovered the object model that lurks inside the browser and how we get at it. We've also seen some ways of taking advantage of all these techniques. What we still haven't done is create any really wild dynamic pages.

Well, the time has now come to start doing so. We know enough about the way Dynamic HTML interfaces with the browser and the pages it displays to start getting into script code in a big way. Most of what happens in script is in response to **events**. These can be initiated by the viewer of our page, by the browser they are using, by a component within the page or even by Windows itself.

When an event occurs, the browser passes it to our script code through the object model we've been exploring, and we can then choose to react to it if we want to. To do this, we need to know more about how we hook our scripts up to events, and how we use the exposed methods and properties that the object model provides to actually manipulate the page contents.

In this chapter, you'll see:

- What events are, and where they come from
- How we connect our script to an event
- How we can decide which events to react to
- The kinds of things we can do when reacting to an event

Understanding the nature of events, and how we create the link between an event and our code, are the crucial steps. It's these that we'll look at first.

What are Events?

Most people have heard the term **event driven programming**, and connect this with the way operating systems such as Windows work. But what does this actually mean? Why should a program be driven by events, rather than by any other method? And what other alternatives are there anyway?

These are questions that don't normally concern the web page author, but you need to know a little about how Windows works to use Dynamic HTML to anything like its full potential. We'll take a brief overview of the subject, then see how we can use events in our pages.

What is Event Driven Programming?

In pre-Windows times, and pre-graphical user interface days, users generally worked with one application at a time—rather than having several open as we tend to these days. In that single application, the user carried out tasks by navigating from one 'menu' screen to another, and had only a finite set of choices available at any one time.

In a graphical user interface like Windows, users can run several applications at the same time, change the size of the screen windows as they go along and switch from one to another. More importantly, the applications have no fixed 'route' through them. The user can click different buttons, or select from any of the menus, to decide for themselves which course they want to take in the program.

As an example, consider a program which carries out technical calculations. In the years BW (before Windows), on starting the application we would have been presented with a main menu from which there were a fixed number of choices. Selecting an option would display more screens collecting information, then display the result. We would have followed this same course every time we wanted to carry out the query.

In the equivalent Windows program, or one in other graphical user environments, we can generally choose which windows to open and open several at once. We can fill in text boxes, make selections from lists, set other controls and click a range of buttons—in almost any order we like. To keep control of all this, the operating system has to work in a fundamentally different way.

Where Do Events Come From?

When we carry out some action in Windows, say clicking on a window with the mouse, the operating system raises an **event**. This is simply a signal that something has happened. Windows examines the event to decide what caused it and what to do about it.

This isn't always as simple as it may seem, for example we may have clicked on a window that was not currently active (i.e. not part of the application we were working with). In this case, Windows has to work out where the mouse pointer is on the screen, and which application is under the pointer, then bring this application's window to the front and tell the other application that it is no longer the active one. And this is only a simplified view. In reality there will be a lot more happening 'under the hood'—a stream of messages is being sent to all the applications by the operating system. Each application can choose to do something about the message, or just ignore it.

However, some events may not be aimed at any application in particular. For example pressing a key when Microsoft Word is active will normally cause that character to appear in the page. But if there is another application running at the same time, and the key-press is *Alt-Tab*, Windows brings up its own task-switching window instead of passing the event onto Word.

Events in Dynamic HTML

In the case of the browser and Dynamic HTML, this constant barrage of messages provides a way for us to react to things that are going on in the browser. We can link code in our pages to the events that are occurring, and use them to interact with the viewer.

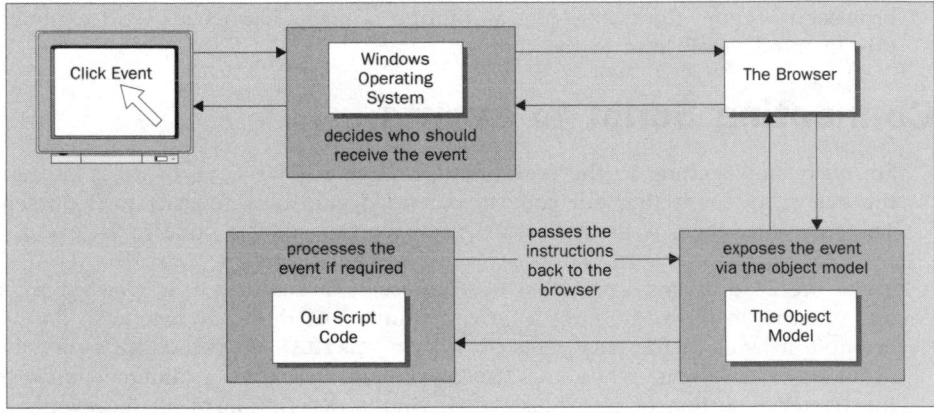

For example, just clicking the mouse button creates several events—descriptively named **onmousedown**, **onmouseup** and **onclick**. Each message is collected by the Windows operating system, which then decides what to do with it. If the user pressed the mouse button while the pointer was on the screen over the browser window, Windows sends a message to the browser. It includes information on which button was pressed, what other keys were held down and where the pointer was on the screen.

The browser then decides if it is going to handle the event. If the user clicked on one of the browser toolbar buttons, it just gets on and does whatever is required—perhaps printing the page, refreshing it or loading the user's Home page. If, however, the click was over the page itself, the browser then **exposes** it, by passing it on to our script code via the browser's object model. At this point, we can react to the event ourselves if we want to.

The reverse path is taken if we actually do decide to respond. The instructions in our code are passed back to the browser via the object model. It decides what effect this will have on the page and tells Windows—which then updates the screen to show the new page. The great thing is that, as Dynamic HTML programmers, all we have to do is decide which events to respond to and what instructions to give the browser. Everything else is looked after automatically.

Reacting to Browser Events

To be able to react to an event, we have to be able to detect it happening. If we don't react to it, the browser will just carry on regardless—perhaps carrying out some action of its own. And even if we do decide to react, we can still let the browser carry out the original task as well. If this sounds confusing, think about the following example.

When we have a Submit button on a page, and the user clicks it, the browser sends the information from all the HTML control elements on the form to the server. However, it also provides an event that we can react to—called **onsubmit**. If we want to, we can have a look at what the user entered, and decide if we want to submit the form or not. If we don't, we can instruct the browser to ignore the event—just as though it never happened. We'll explore this in more detail later in the chapter.

Connecting Script to Events

So, we're now getting to the crux of the matter. All we have to do is capture the event, by connecting our code to it, and decide how to react to it ourselves. The first step, then, is to understand how we can connect code to an event.

There are 24 different events that the browser exposes to our script—but for any one element in the page, only a limited number of these are available. For example a layer in the page, created with a **<LAYER>** or **<ILAYER>** tag, only provides eight events; while an **<INPUT>** tag can provide 10 different ones. In the reference section of this book, you'll find a description of all the events, and a list of those available for each HTML element tag.

We used one event handling routine in the last example of Chapter 3, but deferred explanation of it, and we used several in Chapters 4 and 5 to demonstrate the object model in action. Here, we'll summarize the way event handlers are written, and show you the other ways you can link your code to events.

Event Handling in JavaScript

In JavaScript, we can use several techniques to connect up our events and code. The connection between a function and an element can be made by defining the name of the function in the element tag itself, as the value of an event name attribute. For example, you've seen how we can connect a function named **MyClickCode()** to the **onClick** event of a button:

```
<FORM>
<INPUT TYPE=BUTTON VALUE="Click Me" ONCLICK="MyClickCode()">
</FORM>
...
<SCRIPT LANGAGE=JAVASCRIPT>
  function MyClickCode()
  {
    alert("You clicked me!");
  }
</SCRIPT>
```

Notice that we need **MyClickCode()**, not just **MyClickCode**, to satisfy the JavaScript syntax requirements. We can also use **inline** code within the element tag:

```
<INPUT TYPE=BUTTON VALUE="Click Me" LANGUAGE=JAVASCRIPT ONCLICK="alert('You
clicked me!');">
```

And because JavaScript is the default language in the browser, we can omit the **LANGUAGE** attribute if we want to, making our code more compact:

```
<INPUT TYPE=BUTTON VALUE="Click Me" ONCLICK="alert('You clicked me!');">
```

Notice that Communicator does not support the FOR and EVENT attributes introduced in Internet Explorer as an alternative way of connecting event handlers to elements. The following code will display the alert dialog as soon as the page loads, and not when the button is clicked.

```
<SCRIPT LANGUAGE=JAVASCRIPT FOR=MyButton EVENT=onClick>
  alert("You clicked me!");
</SCRIPT>
```

Finally, we can create **javascript:** pseudo functions which can be placed in a link, such as an **<A>** (anchor) tag. The code is executed when the link is clicked. These are often referred to as **JavaScript URLs**:

```
<A HREF="javascript:alert('You clicked me!');"> Click Me </A>
```

JavaScript Versions

Netscape Navigator 2 used version 1.0 of JavaScript, and this is the default for our script sections if we just use **LANGUAGE=JAVASCRIPT** (or omit the **LANGUAGE** attribute altogether). Navigator 3 introduced an updated version of JavaScript called version 1.1. Communicator brings with it another new version, 1.2. Each version is backward compatible with earlier ones, and in our examples so far we've used the default version 1.0.

If we want to use the features added in the newer versions, however, we can specify the minimum version that the browser must support. This is very useful if we decide to use the new features of the language. To tell the browser it must support the latest version, we just use **LANGUAGE=JAVASCRIPT1.2** in the **<SCRIPT>** tag. Likewise, we can use **LANGUAGE=JAVASCRIPT1.1** to specify the Navigator 3 version of the language.

When we use a specific version tag, the way that some features JavaScript work changes. In other words, the version specified in the **LANGUAGE** attribute actually makes the language interpreter behave differently. In Communicator, for example, the interpreter will pretend to be version 1.0 if we don't specify a version, or 1.1 if we specify this. Only if we use **LANGUAGE=JAVASCRIPT1.2** will the new features be available to our script code.

You'll see the **LANGUAGE=JAVASCRIPT1.2** attribute used in several of the examples in Chapter 8—where it also provides opportunities to redirect a browser to a specific page based on its capabilities.

Changes to JavaScript in Version 1.2

While this isn't a book about JavaScript itself, we'll briefly cover the changes to the language that appear in version 1.2. These are:

- The statement **new Array**(*value*) creates a new array with the first element (indexed zero) set to the specified value. You can create a new array with several elements by listing them in the brackets separated by commas, using **new Array**(*value0, value1, value2, ...*).

- The **Number** object now returns **NaN** (not a number) if a string being converted is not a legal number, rather than an error.

- The equality operators **==** and **!=** no longer try and convert the values to the same type before comparison. They are just compared 'as is'.

- The new **break** and **continue** statements can be used to jump out of a loop or other construct, and continue execution at a specific line:

```
while (count < 4)
{
  if (anothervalue == 2 ) break skipitall;
  somevalue = somevalue + anothervalue;
}
skipitall :
//execution continues here outside the loop
```

```
while (count < 4)
{
  if (anothervalue == 2 ) continue skipit;
  somevalue = somevalue + anothervalue;
  skipit :
  //execution continues here within the loop
}
```

- JavaScript now contains the **do..while** construct and the **switch** construct:

```
do
  somevalue = somevalue + anothervalue;
while (anothervalue != 2 );
```

```
switch (language)
{
  case "Java" :
    alert("One program for all.");
    break;
```

```
   case "C" :
     alert("Speed is king.");
     break;
   case "VB" :
     alert("Anyone can do it.");
}
```

The **String** object has three new methods, **charCodeAt**, **fromCharCode**, and **substr**. **charCodeAt** returns the ASCII code of the character at the specified position, **fromCharCode** constructs a string from a comma-separated list of ASCII code values, and **substr** returns a specified number of characters from a string:

```
MyString = "ABCDE";
alert(MyString.charCodeAt(2))   // produces 66 (decimal).
```

```
MyString.fromCharCode(65, 66, 67)   // returns "ABC"
```

```
MyString = "ABCDE";
MyString.substr(2, 5)   // returns "BCD"
```

Other changes are:

- the **substring** method no longer swaps over the indexes when the first is greater than the second
- the **sort** method now works on all platforms and converts undefined elements to null and sorts them to the top of the array
- the **split** method now removes more than one white-space character when splitting a string
- the **toString** method now converts the object or array into a string literal

Using External Script Files

The **<SCRIPT>** tag in Communicator can accept an **SRC** argument which loads the script code from a plain text file on the server. For example, the following code uses a script file called **MyScript.js**, which is stored in a separate directory on the server.

```
<SCRIPT SRC="./JScripts/MyScript.js" LANGUAGE=JAVASCRIPT1.2> </SCRIPT>
```

It's a good idea to specify the language version, and use **1.1** or **1.2**, because older browsers will not understand the **SRC** attribute in a **<SCRIPT>** tag. You may also have to set up your server to supply the files in the correct MIME-type format. This technique is also used with signed scripts, which we'll be looking at in more depth in the next chapter.

Canceling an Event Action

Some events, such as **onSubmit**, **onClick**, **onKeyPress** and **onMouseUp**, allow us to provide a return value which controls how the browser behaves. In JavaScript, we return a value from a function using the **return** statement.

This example defines a form section with a single text box named **txtEmailAddress**, and a Submit button:

```
<FORM NAME="MyForm" ACTION="http://somesite.com/scripts/doit.pl"
ONSUBMIT="SubmitEvent()">
  <INPUT TYPE=TEXT NAME="txtEmailAddress">
  <INPUT TYPE=SUBMIT>
</FORM>

<SCRIPT LANGUAGE=JAVASCRIPT>

function SubmitEvent()
{
  strEmailAddress = document.forms["MyForm"].txtEmailAddress.value;
  // see if the text box contains the @ symbol somewhere
  if (strEmailAddress.indexOf("@") != -1)
    retval = true
  else
  {
    retval = false;
    alert("You must supply a valid email address.");
  }
  return retval;
}
</SCRIPT>
```

This code uses the **indexOf()** method to find the position of the first @ character in the string the user enters into a textbox named **txtEmailAddress** on the form. If there isn't a @ character in the string, we can assume it's not a valid email address, display a message, and cancel the submission of the form by returning **false**. Otherwise, we return **true**.

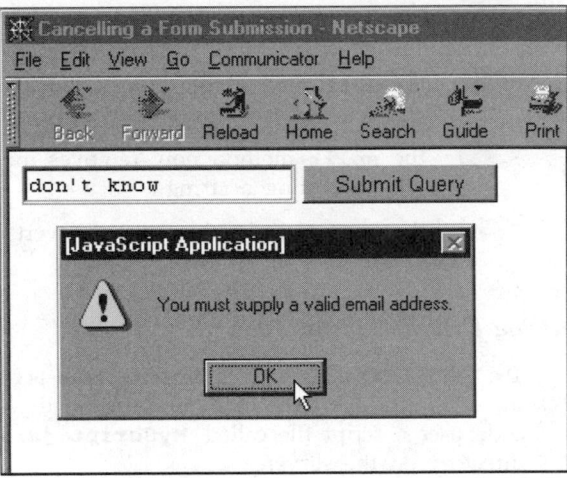

Notice how we have to use the browser's object model to get at the text in the text box. The string we want is the **value** property of the **txtEmailAddress** control, on the form named **MyForm**, which is stored in the **forms** array of the **document** object. (We could have started with **window.document**, but—as you'll recall—the **window** object is the default anyway).

Using the Event Object

The ways you've seen so far of connecting our code to an event were equally valid in earlier releases of browsers that supported scripting, though only a very limited subset of controls exposed their events previously. Dynamic HTML now adds another way of getting information about an event.

In Chapter 4, we briefly mentioned the **Event** object, which is part of the new object model and a subsidiary object to the top-level **window** object. The **Event** object is constantly being updated to include information about each event that occurs in our page—it is global to all events in this sense. So, when an event occurs we can query the **Event** object's properties to learn more about the event.

Using the Event Object Properties

Some events, such as the **onMouseDown** event, produce values that we would like to be able to use in our code, such as detecting which mouse button was pressed, and where the pointer was on the screen when the event occurred. These values are available as properties of the new **Event** object, which can be queried in code inside the event handlers we create.

As an example, this code uses properties of the **Event** object to gather information about an **onMouseUp** event. Notice how we create a reference to the **Event** object, **e**, by declaring it as a parameter of the function. Within the function, we can then use **e.***propertyname* to retrieve the various properties of the global **Event** object:

```
<SCRIPT LANGUAGE="JavaScript1.2">

function MouseEvent(e)
{
  strMesg = "You clicked the "
  if (e.which == 1) strMesg += "left ";
  if (e.which == 3) strMesg += "right ";
  strMesg += "mouse button, at position x = " + e.pageX;
  strMesg += ", y = " + e.pageY + String.fromCharCode(10);
  strMesg += "The keyboard modifiers value is " + e.modifiers;
  alert(strMesg);
}

document.onmouseup = MouseEvent;
</SCRIPT>
```

For a mouse event, the **Event** object's properties include **which**, which holds **1** if the left button was pressed, and **3** if the right button was pressed. There is also the position in relation to the document (**pageX** and **pageY**), as well as the position on the screen (**screenX** and **screenY**). In our example, we're using the **pageX** and **pageY** properties. Finally, our code reads the **modifiers** property, which indicates which keys (such as *Ctrl*, *Shift* or *Alt*) were being held down at the time the button was clicked.

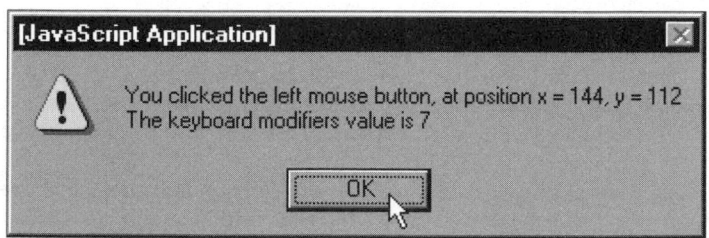

139

*If your mouse has a middle button, you might like to experiment to see if this produces **2** for the* **which** *property, although we could not confirm this.*

Using the modifiers Property

The value of the **modifiers** property is not terribly useful as it is. What does **7** mean anyway? In the case of the message shown above, we were holding down the *Ctrl, Shift* and *Alt* keys at the time. In fact, the value is a combination of special constant values, each one defining a particular key. These constants are:

Constant	Key	Value
ALT_MASK	*Alt* key	1
CONTROL_MASK	*Ctrl* key	2
SHIFT_MASK	*Shift* key	4
META_MASK	*Meta* or *Command* key	8

So it's pretty easy to figure out that we were holding down *Ctrl, Shift* and *Alt* by adding together the key values. However, there is a far better way, and it is in fact the reason the constants names take the form *key*_**MASK**. We can use them as masks with **bit-wise arithmetic** to pick out the combination of keys very easily.

And, Or, and Bit-wise Arithmetic

Computers store numbers as patterns of 'on' and 'off' states, usually represented by a series of **1**'s and **0**'s in a **byte**. This is what we term **binary notation**.

Each byte consists of 8 bits, numbered **0** to **7** from right to left. Each bit represents double the value of the bit to its right. In the diagram, bits **0, 2, 3** and **5** are 'set' (i.e. are one, rather than zero), so the number being stored is **1 + 4 + 8 + 32 = 45**. The largest number that can be stored in one byte is 255.

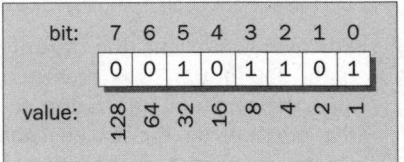

The whole point of bit-wise arithmetic, however, is to ignore the total value of the byte—and consider each *bit* within it separately. For example, if our **modifiers** property has the value **5**, we can soon figure out that the *Shift* and *Alt* keys were pressed. However, rather than testing for each of the 64 possible values of the **modifiers** property (count them if you don't believe there are 64 different combinations), we can test for each key individually instead.

It's no coincidence that the 'key' values are **1, 2, 4** and **8**—these are the first four binary bit values. All we do is use the **and (&)** and **or (|)** operators to see if these individual bits are set within the parameter value. The **&** operator returns a value where each individual bit is set only if *both* the values have that bit set (one **and** the other). The | operator sets the bits if *either* of the values has that bit set (one **or** the other). In our case, **and** (**&**) is the useful one:

```
 parameter value: 5 = 00000101
SHIFT_MASK value: 4 = 00000100
 result of 'and':   = 00000100 = 4 (= True)

 parameter value: 5 = 00000101
 CTRL_MASK value: 2 = 00000010
 result of 'and':   = 00000000 = 0 (= False)
```

You can see that the **&** operator only returns a non-zero value if the appropriate bit is set. In scripting code, all non-zero values are considered to be **true**, while zero is **false**. So, now we have a way to handle our **modifiers** parameter:

```
function MouseEvent(e)
{
   strMesg = "You clicked the "
   if (e.which == 1) strMesg += "left ";
   if (e.which == 3) strMesg += "right ";
   strMesg += "mouse button, at position x = " + e.pageX;
   strMesg += ", y = " + e.pageY + String.fromCharCode(10);
   if (e.modifiers > 0)
   {
     strMesg += "while holding down the ";
     if (e.modifiers & Event.SHIFT_MASK) strMesg = strMesg + "Shift key ";
     if (e.modifiers & Event.CONTROL_MASK) strMesg = strMesg + "Ctrl key ";
     if (e.modifiers & Event.ALT_MASK) strMesg = strMesg + "Alt key ";
     if (e.modifiers & Event.META_MASK) strMesg = strMesg + "Meta key ";
   }
   alert(strMesg);
}
```

Here's the result, using our modified code for the **modifiers** property (if you see what we mean):

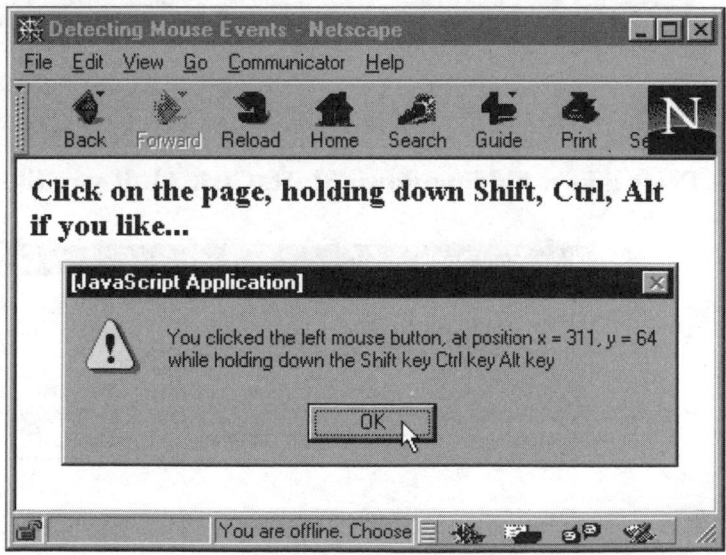

Key-press Information and the Event Object

The **Event** object has more uses than just providing information about mouse events. For example, if we query it for a **key-press** event, we can still find out where the mouse pointer is, and use the **modifiers** property. However, more than that, we can use the **which** property this time to find out which key was pressed. It returns the ASCII code of the key, altered to take account of the other keys (such as *Shift*) that are being held down at the same time:

```
<SCRIPT LANGUAGE="JavaScript1.2">

function KeyEvent(e)
{
  strMesg = "You pressed the " + String.fromCharCode(e.which)
          + " key, which has an ASCII value of "
          + String(e.which) + "." + String.fromCharCode(10);
  if (e.modifiers > 0)
  {
    strMesg += "while holding down the ";
    if (e.modifiers & Event.SHIFT_MASK) strMesg = strMesg + "Shift key ";
    if (e.modifiers & Event.CONTROL_MASK) strMesg = strMesg + "Ctrl key ";
    if (e.modifiers & Event.ALT_MASK) strMesg = strMesg + "Alt key ";
    strMesg += ". " + String.fromCharCode(10);
  }
  strMesg += "The mouse pointer is at position x = " + e.pageX + ", y = " +
e.pageY;
  alert(strMesg);
}

document.onkeyup = KeyEvent;
</SCRIPT>
```

Notice how the technique of detecting the *Ctrl*, *Shift* and *Alt* keys in the **modifiers** property is repeated here. The next screenshot shows the result. Look where the mouse pointer is, and at the values of the mouse position retrieved from the **Event** object. It still works if the pointer isn't over the page:

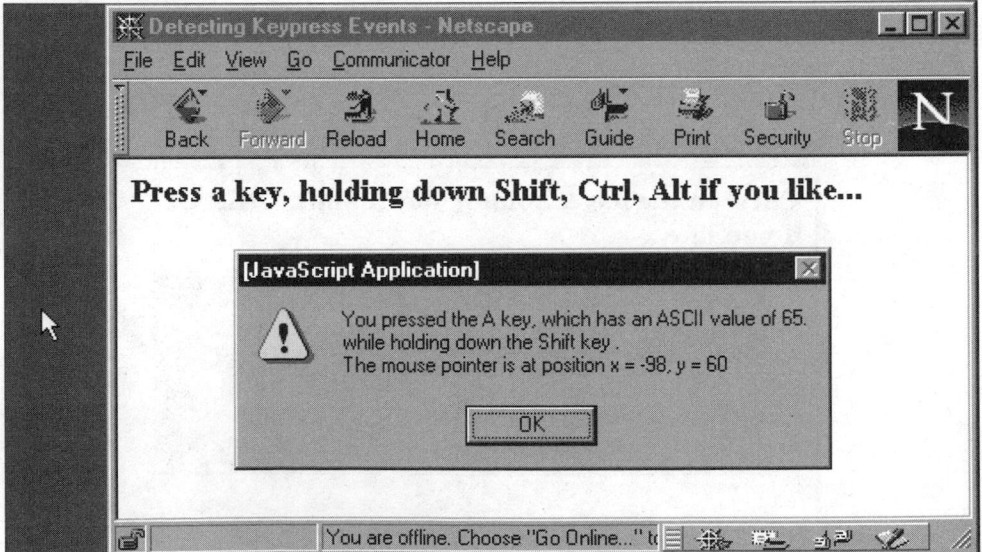

Both of the pages demonstrating the **Event** *object,* **Mdown.htm** *and*
Kpress.htm, *can be run directly from our Web site at:*
http://rapid.wrox.co.uk/books/1193

Responding to Events

Now that we've found ways of connecting our code to an event, and getting
the information we need about that event, we can write the code to generate
the instruction that will tell the browser what we want to do. In general, this
involves three tasks—finding out about the element the event occurred for,
deciding what to do about it (if anything), and carrying out the task. This is
where the links between our code and the elements in the page (as exposed by
the object model) come into play.

Accessing an Element's Properties

Often the first step in reacting to an event is to find out more about the *event*
itself, and the element it came from. We've seen how we can find out more
about the event from the **Event** object. The next question is, how do we find
out more about the *element* that raised the event?

Every element in a page has a set of **properties**, and you'll find a complete list
of these in the reference section at the back of the book. For example, an
<IMG> has a **src** property, which indicates which file is used as the source for
that image. When we apply styles to our pages, the styles are made available as
properties as well. In the previous chapter, we saw the **document.tags** array
used to retrieve these:

```
document.tags.H1.fontFamily    // returns the font family for the element
document.tags.H1.fontSize      // returns the font size for the element
document.tags.H1.color         // returns the font color for the element
```

Of course, of more interest in dynamic pages are properties like the position
and size of elements. A layer object has top and left properties, which we can
retrieve using:

```
document.layers["layername"].top     // returns position of the top of the layer
document.layers["layername"].left    // returns position of the left of the layer
```

This is one useful way in which Dynamic HTML exposes the properties of the
elements within the page, and allows them to be changed in our code. There
are a whole range of different properties available for different element tags,
depending on which HTML attributes are valid for that tag.

An **<IMG>** tag has (among many others) the **width**, **height** and **src**
properties—while the **<BODY>** tag can have **aLink** and **bgColor** properties.
Updating the properties causes the change to appear dynamically on the page
where appropriate.

One point you need to watch out for is that many properties return null if a
value has not been set explicitly in the HTML or in script code—irrespective
of the default property values assumed by the browser.

Generating Our Own Pseudo-Events

As well as setting the values of properties, and calling the methods of various objects within the browser's object model, our code can also generate its own pseudo-events. Because all the event routines we write are available to our code, we can call them directly. They will run just that same way as if that event had occurred, though of course the browser and Windows itself won't behave as if they had received the event.

As an example, imagine we have a page with a button which updates some part of the page. We can call this code directly from elsewhere in the page like this:

```
<INPUT VALUE="Update Page" ONCLICK="UpdateButtonCode()">

<SCRIPT LANGUAGE=JAVASCRIPT>

function UpdateButtonCode()
{
   // ... some code to update the page
};

function DoSomethingElse()
{
   // ... do something else to change the page
   // now run the 'Update Page' button event handler code
   UpdateButtonCode()
};

</SCRIPT>
```

Capturing and Routing Events

One major topic that makes Dynamic HTML different from scripting in earlier versions, either with JavaScript or any other language, is the way that the browser manages the events that are occurring in the page. We've already seen this to some extent when we looked at the **Event** object earlier.

However, there is another innovation that plays a major role in the way we create script routines in Dynamic HTML. The **Event** object comes into play again here by providing two properties, **target** and **type**.

The Itinerary of an Event

In everything we've done in this chapter so far, and in most of the previous chapters, we've assumed one fundamental fact. When an event occurs in a page, the object that gets first look at it is the element that was current at the time. For example, this would be the object under the mouse pointer for a mouse event, a **<TEXTAREA>** control on a form for a key-press event or a layer within the page:

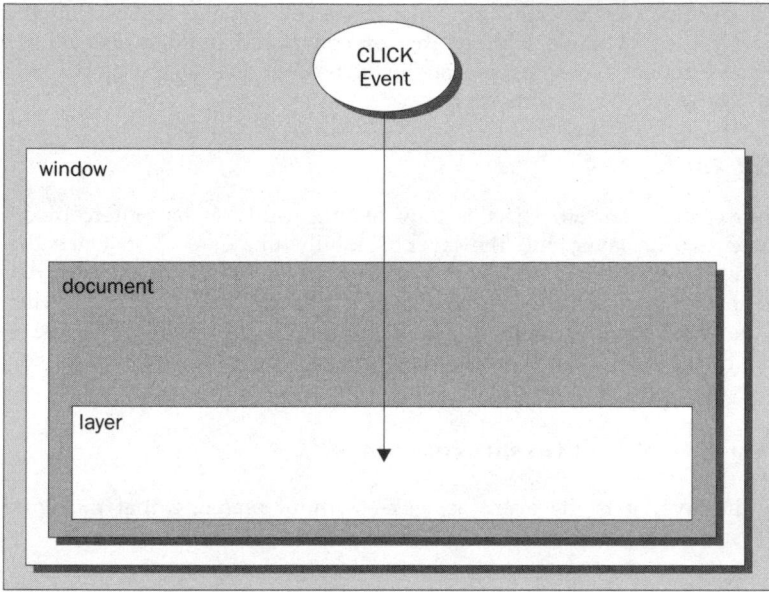

Capturing an Event

This is the case by default, if we don't do anything to change it. However, as the name suggests, the new **event capturing** feature of Dynamic HTML means that we can allow other objects to see the event before it gets to it's intended target. This is done using the **captureEvents** method. If we execute the code:

```
window.captureEvents(Event.CLICK)
```

the browser will divert all the **onClick** events occurring in the window to the **window** object first, rather than sending them to the intended objects—in our example the layer on the page. It's as if the window just sticks out its hand as the event goes past and grabs it. The layer doesn't get to see it at all:

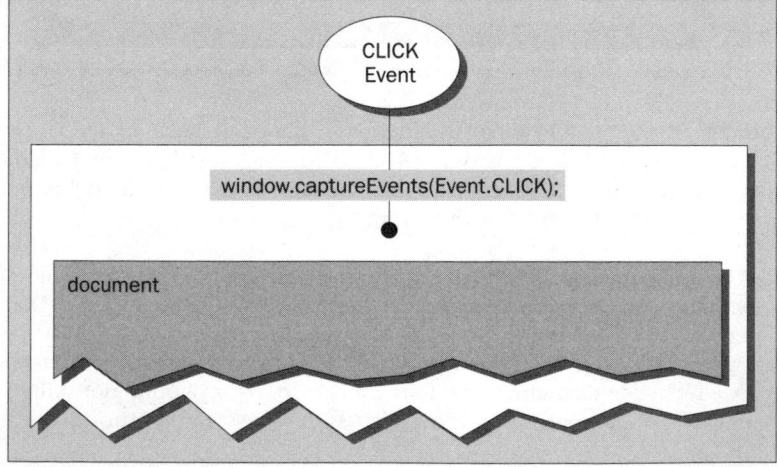

In this example, we're capturing only **onClick** events. Notice that the code requires the event name without the 'on' part, and it must also be in wholly upper-case letters. These events are in fact properties of the global **Event** object, hence the syntax of **Event**.*eventname*.

Routing an Event

Of course, the **window** object is now feeling guilty. It has intercepted the event destined for the layer, and the layer is totally unaware of it. Once the window has finished examining the event, and reacting to it if it wants to, it can pass it on to the original intended recipient as if nothing had happened. This is done with the **routeEvent** method. The argument is the reference to the event originally passed to the window's event handling function (you'll see some explicit examples in a while):

```
window.routeEvent(event_reference)
```

Now, the layer gets the event as well—without realizing that the window has had a sneak preview:

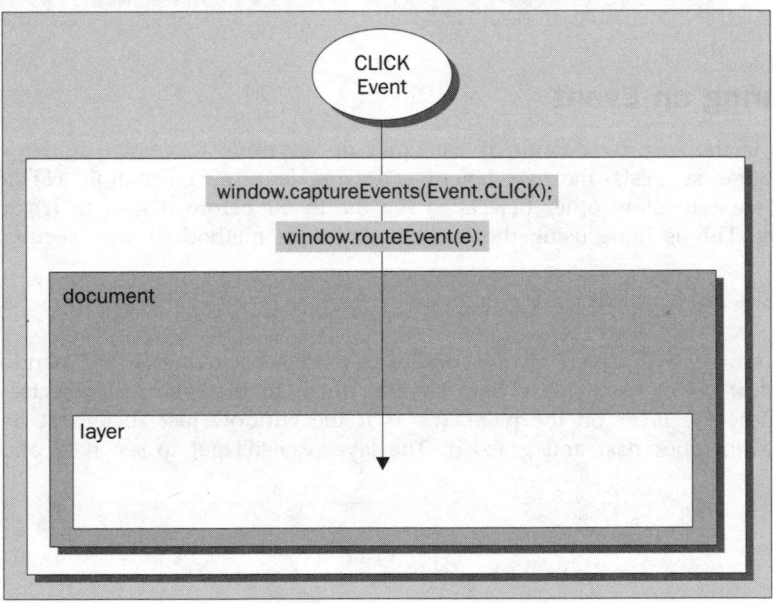

By routing an event, the window effectively hands it back to the browser. The event then continues on its way. It will go to the intended target element, as if nothing had happened. Notice that the window doesn't need to know which element this is when it routes the event.

Of course, the window isn't the only object that can capture an event like this. The document can do the same. In the next diagram, you can see that the document is grabbing the event after the window has routed it—the window always gets first look in. Once the window routes the event, the browser hands it on to whichever element is next in the chain. This would normally be the layer, but our document has interrupted the process by capturing the event itself:

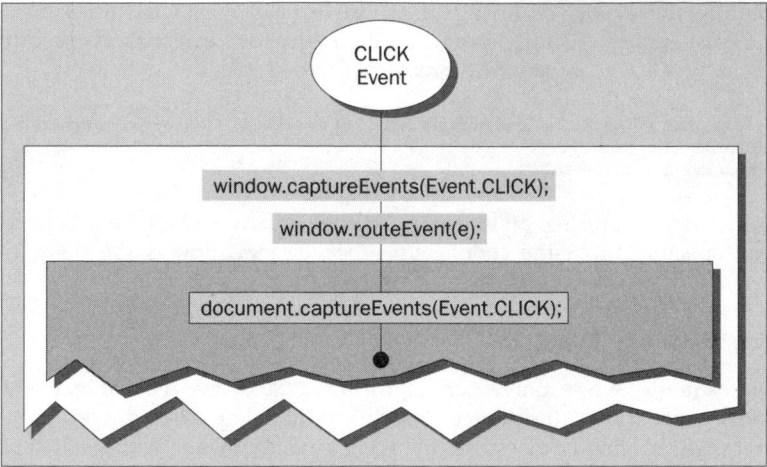

Of course, once the document has finished with the event, it too can route it. This time the next element in the chain is the layer, the original target:

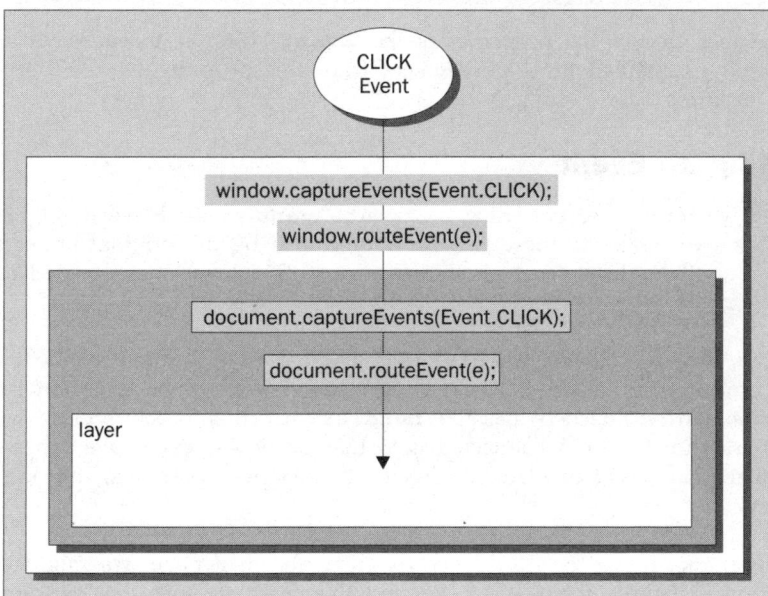

In fact layers can also capture events, so the process could have continued if the original target had been an element within the layer—but no doubt you've grasped the concept by now.

Capturing Events in Other Windows

So, the **window** object can capture events within its own window, followed by the document and then any layers. But event capturing can also be established in windows other than the one that is running our script. This requires a signed script to be used (see chapter 7), even if the other window is just a separate frame within the same frameset.

To capture the events occurring in all the frames in a window, for example, we would first request security privilege, then turn on **external event capturing**. Finally, we call the **captureEvents** method as usual:

```
netscape.security.PrivilegeManager.enablePrivilege("UniversalBrowserWrite");
enableExternalCapture();
captureEvents(Event.CLICK);
```

External event capturing only works for the **window** object, and this is why we haven't specified it in the code. Remember, the **window** is the default object anyway.

Capturing Different Events

In our example, we've only been capturing **CLICK** events. Other events are passed directly on to the target element, as usual. However, we can capture several different kinds of events by specifying them all in the call to the **captureEvents** method, separating each one with vertical bar (|) character, which acts as the logical OR between the event identifiers:

```
captureEvents(Event.KEYPRESS | Event.MOUSEDOWN | Event.MOUSEUP);
```

Remember, one of the properties of the **Event** object is **type**. When an event occurs, we can read the type of event from this property, as you'll see in the next example.

Directing an Event

When we route an event using the **routeEvent** method, we don't have any control over where it goes. The destination will be the original target element, unless another object (such as the document or a layer) has enabled event capturing as well.

Instead, we can call the **handleEvent** method of a different element instead. Every element or object that can support events (to which an event handler function can be attached) has the **handleEvent** method. Providing we have written a function and connected it to that particular event, we can send an event to that object or element directly. It no longer passes to the original target.

For example, if we have 20 checkbox elements on a page, we might create one function to handle them all. To connect this function with the **onMouseDown** events for all the checkboxes, we might decide to capture the event at document level:

```
document.captureEvents(Event.MOUSEDOWN);
document.onMouseDown = MyMouseCode;
...
```

Now, the function **MyMouseCode()** will run every time an **onMouseDown** event occurs in the entire document. By examining the **target** property of the **Event** object, we can tell which element the event was aimed at. If we decide to send it to a different element, we can simply use **handleEvent**:

```
function MyMouseCode(e)
{
  strTarget = " " + e.target    // convert target property into a string
  if (strTarget.indexOf("MyCheck1") != -1)
    document.forms["MyForm"].elements["MyCheckMaster"].handleEvent(e);
  ...
}
```

This code checks to see if the original target for the event was the checkbox named **Check1**, by examining the target property of the **Event** object. This property contains the complete element tag, and we are implicitly converting it to a string by linking it with a space character. If it contains the name **Check1**, we send the event to the element named **MyCheckMaster** instead.

Event Return Values

You'll recall that events can return either **true** or **false** to attempt to change the outcome of that event. Our earlier example returned **false** to cancel submission of a form if there wasn't enough information. Several events can be cancelled this way, including **onClick** for links, **onKeyDown**, **onKeyPress**, **onMouseDown**, **onMouseUp**, **onReset**, **onSubmit**, and **onDragDrop**.

When we have enabled event capturing, these effects still apply. If the user clicked on a link, the link will not be followed. However, many events are not cancelable. In this case, returning **false** from a routine that has captured that event will end event handling for that event.

Releasing Event Capture

We can turn on event capturing at any time in code, it doesn't have to be set when the page is first loaded. Event capturing becomes effective as soon as the **captureEvents** method has been called. If we then decide to stop capturing events, we just need to call the equivalent method, **releaseEvents**. Again, we specify which event or events we wish to release, and we don't have to release all the ones we're currently capturing:

```
// release just CLICK events, or release several events in one go
releaseEvents(Event.CLICK);
releaseEvents(Event.KEYPRESS | Event.MOUSEDOWN | Event.MOUSEUP);
```

If we have previously enabled external event capturing, we can turn this off using the **disableExternalCapture** method. Of course, we still need to switch off event capturing for the **window** object itself first:

```
releaseEvents(Event.CLICK);
disableExternalCapture();
```

An Event Capturing Example

To give you a chance to experiment with event capturing and routing, try this example called **RouteCap.htm**. It can be run or downloaded from our Web site at **http://rapid.wrox.co.uk/books/1193/**:

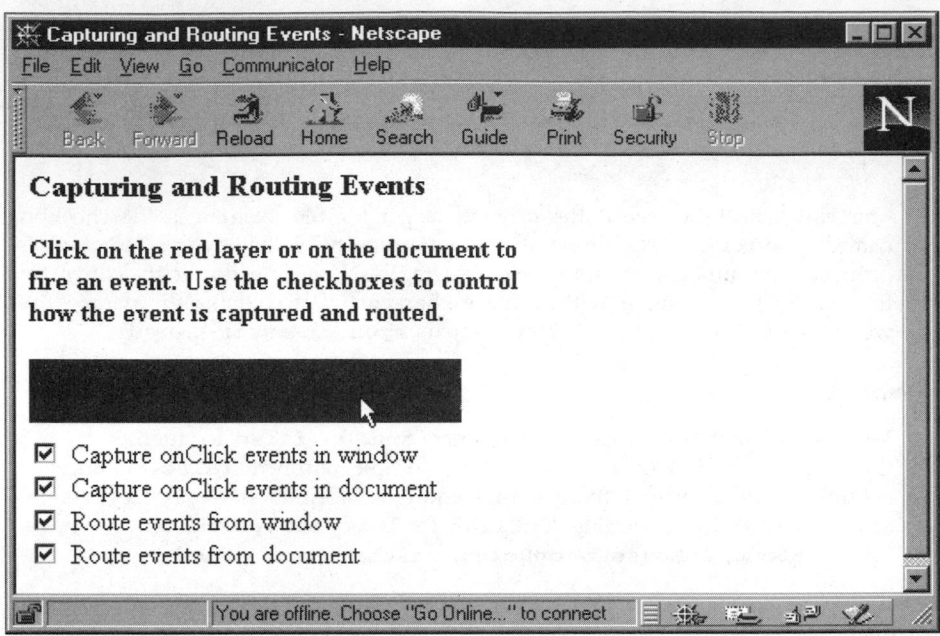

The page contains some introductory text, and a layer named **MyLayer**, which has a red background. We've included the two 1-pixel wide horizontal rules to force the layer to be a couple of 'lines' high:

```
...
<!-- the layer to target events to -->
 <LAYER NAME="MyLayer">
  <BODY BGCOLOR="red">
    <!-- make the layer two rules high -->
    <HR WIDTH=1><HR WIDTH=1>
  </BODY>
</LAYER>
...
```

At the bottom of the page is a form named **MyForm** containing four check boxes. This form is inside another layer, named **FormLayer**, which is positioned below the first one using the **TOP** attribute:

```
...
<!-- the layer to hold the checkboxes -->
<LAYER ID="FormLayer" TOP=170>
  <FORM NAME="MyForm">
    <INPUT TYPE="CHECKBOX" NAME="InWindow" CHECKED ONCLICK="setRouting();">
    Capture onClick events in window <BR>
    <INPUT TYPE="CHECKBOX" NAME="InDocument" CHECKED ONCLICK="setRouting();">
    Capture onClick events in document <BR>
    <INPUT TYPE="CHECKBOX" NAME="FromWindow" CHECKED>
    Route events from window <BR>
    <INPUT TYPE="CHECKBOX" NAME="FromDocument" CHECKED>
    Route events from document
  </FORM>
</LAYER>
...
```

The remainder of the page is script code that runs when an **onClick** event occurs. To see the full sequence, click on the red layer. The next screen shot shows the combined result, with the three **alert** dialogs that appear:

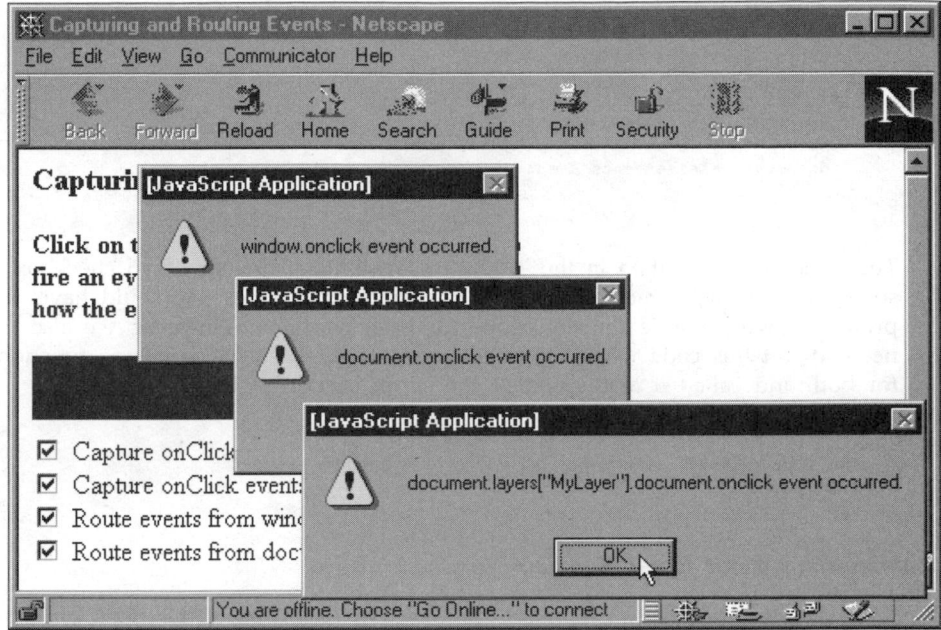

You can see that the window handled the event first, even though it was destined for the layer. Then, after the window routed the event, the document intercepted and handled it as well. Finally, it reached its intended target, the document inside the layer. Try turning on and off the various checkboxes and clicking in different parts of the page. By comparing the results to the diagrams of event handling we used earlier in this chapter, you'll be able to see how each combination affects the routing of the event.

How It Works

To see how this example works, we'll look at each part of the code in turn. It's made more complex by the need to dynamically enable and disable event capturing while the page is loaded. The script first creates a global reference to the form in the second layer, making it easier to handle the checkboxes later in the script.

```
// create a reference to the form containing the checkboxes
objForm = document.layers["FormLayer"].document.forms["MyForm"];
...
```

Turning Event Capturing On and Off

Next, there is a function named **setRouting**, which enables or disables event capturing for the window and document as appropriate. Using the **objForm** global reference, it retrieves the current setting of the two checkboxes, to see it event capturing is selected. If it is, it calls the **captureEvents** method of that particular object. Otherwise, the **releaseEvents** method is called:

```
...
function setRouting()
// sets or releases capturing when checkboxes are changed
{
  if (objForm.elements["InWindow"].checked)
    window.captureEvents(Event.CLICK)
  else
    window.releaseEvents(Event.CLICK);

  if (objForm.elements["InDocument"].checked)
    document.captureEvents(Event.CLICK)
  else
    document.releaseEvents(Event.CLICK);
}
...
```

This function is specified in the **ONCLICK** attribute of the first two checkboxes, so it will run each time the value of one of them changes. We could have produced two separate functions, one for each checkbox. However, we also need to run this code when the page is first loaded, so we used one function for both and called it at the end of the script section of the page:

```
...
// set the default capturing for window and document
setRouting()
...
```

Connecting up our Event Handlers

The page also contains event handling code for **onClick** events. Just because we've enabled event capturing doesn't mean that the events will be handled, however. We have to make the explicit connection between the event and the code that will handle it at each point. This is done in the usual way, by assigning them in code within the script section:

```
...
// connect event handler functions with appropriate events
window.onClick = windowEvent;
document.onClick = documentEvent;
document.layers["MyLayer"].document.onClick = layerEvent;
...
```

Handling the onClick Events

Now we can create the events handlers specified in the code above. The two functions for the **window** and the **document** are almost identical. Because we are capturing all **onClick** events, and these will also occur when the user changes a setting in one of the checkboxes, we look for this occurrence and don't display the **alert** dialog:

```
...
function windowEvent(e)
// runs when the window gets a click event
// displays a message indicating an event occurred
{
  // get the target and make it into a string
  strTarget = ' ' + e.target;
  // if it's one of the checkboxes don't show message
  if (strTarget.indexOf('input') == -1)
    alert('window.on' + e.type + ' event occurred.');
```

```
    // if routing checkbox is set, route event to next element
    if (objForm.elements["FromWindow"].checked) window.routeEvent(e);
}

function documentEvent(e)
// runs when the document gets a click event
// displays a message indicating an event occurred
{
    // get the target and make it into a string
    strTarget = ' ' + e.target;
    // if it's one of the checkboxes don't show message
    if (strTarget.indexOf('input') == -1)
      alert('document.on' + e.type + ' event occurred.');
    // if routing checkbox is set, route event to next element
    if (objForm.elements["FromDocument"].checked) document.routeEvent(e);
}
...
```

Notice that, in each case, we get the name of the event from the **Event** object's **type** property—adding the on part to turn click into onclick. The **target** property provides the HTML source of the 'clicked' element, and we only need to look for the word input in it to see if it's a checkbox. The **type** and **target** properties return wholly lower-case values.

> In fact, the **target** property contains an object in its own right. In our code, we are converting the entire object into its string equivalent. Later in this chapter, we'll see how we can get more specific information from the **target** property.

The third event handler for the **layer** is less complicated. If the user clicks the layer, they can't have clicked a checkbox—so we don't need to check for this. Neither do we have to worry about routing the event to another object:

```
...
function layerEvent(e)
// runs when the red layer gets a click event
// displays a message indicating an event occurred
{
    alert('document.layers["MyLayer"].document.on' + e.type + ' event occurred.');
}
...
```

Summary of Event Object Properties

To end this look at the way we capture and handle events in Dynamic HTML, here is a summary of the properties provided by the **Event** object:

Properties	Description
type	The type of event, as a string.
target	The name of the object where the event was originally sent.
screenX	Horizontal position in pixels of the mouse pointer on the screen for an event.
screenY	Vertical position in pixels of the mouse pointer on the screen for an event.

Properties	Description
pageX	Horizontal position in pixels of the mouse pointer or a layer in relation to the document's window.
pageY	Vertical position in pixels of the mouse pointer or a layer in relation to the document's window.
layerX	Horizontal position of the mouse pointer in pixels in relation to the containing layer.
layerY	Vertical position of the mouse pointer in pixels in relation to the containing layer.
which	ASCII value of a key that was pressed, or indicates which mouse button was clicked.
modifiers	String containing the names of the keys held down for a key-press event.
data	The URLs of the objects dropped onto the Navigator window, as an array of strings.

Dynamic Element Positioning

To finish off this chapter, we'll take a brief look at another sample that uses events and style properties to provide a dynamic page—which includes moving button elements around as well as moving an image. We saw what this page does in Chapter 1, and here we'll see how some of the effects are achieved with techniques we've learned in this chapter.

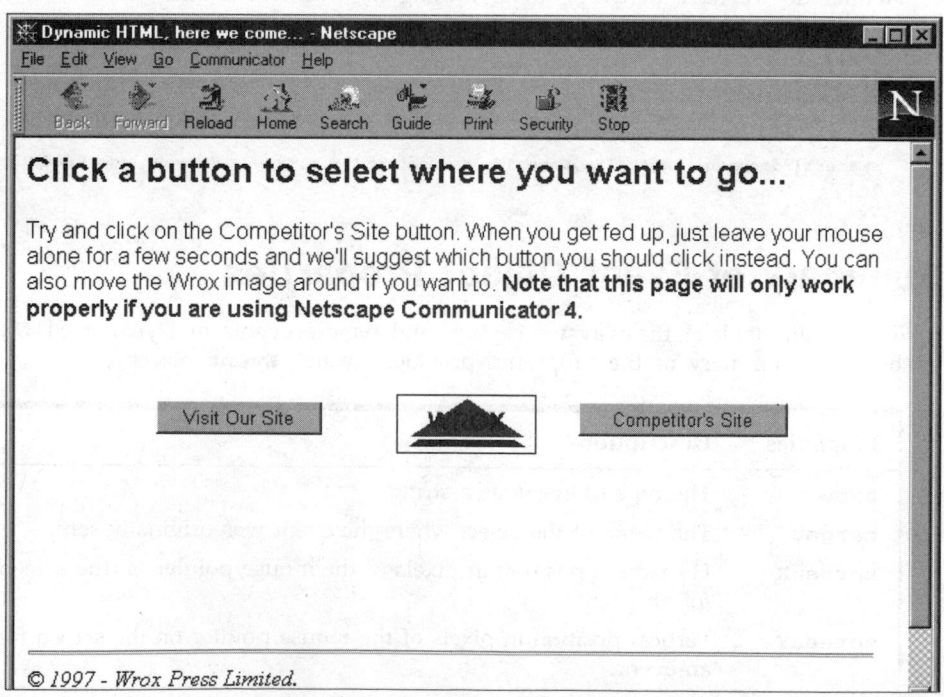

*You can run or download this example, called **Buttons.htm**, from our Web
site at* **http://rapid.wrox.co.uk/books/1193**

The Dancing Buttons Page

The Dancing Buttons page, **Buttons.htm**, consists of a layer that fills the
majority of the page. Within it are three more layers—two containing normal
HTML buttons created with **<INPUT>** tags, and one containing an image. They
are absolutely positioned within the main layer using the **TOP** and **LEFT**
attributes. Finally, we've used a separate layer to position the **<HR>** horizontal
rule and our **<CITE>** tag:

```
...
<LAYER ID="layDoc" TOP=0 LEFT=0 WIDTH=600 HEIGHT=350>
  <LAYER ID="layImg" TOP=180 LEFT=270>
    <IMG SRC="wrox0.gif" NAME="imgWrox">
  </LAYER>
  <LAYER ID="layTheirs" TOP=185 LEFT=400>
    <FORM>
      <INPUT TYPE=BUTTON VALUE="Competitor's Site" ONCLICK="cmdTheirsClick()">
    </FORM>
  </LAYER>
  <LAYER ID="layOurs" TOP=185 LEFT=100>
    <FORM>
      <INPUT TYPE=BUTTON VALUE="Visit Our Site" ONCLICK="cmdOursClick()">
    </FORM>
  </LAYER>
</LAYER>

<LAYER TOP=355 LEFT=10 WIDTH=600 HEIGHT=100>
  <HR><CITE>&copy; 1997 - Wrox Press Limited.</CITE>
</LAYER>
...
```

Inside the **<SCRIPT>** section of the page, a function named **MouseMove()** is
used to respond to the **onMouseMove** event. This event is only available if we
have event capturing turned on, so we set this up first. We're going to capture
the **MOUSEMOVE** event for our main layer **layDoc**:

```
<SCRIPT LANGUAGE=JAVASCRIPT>
...
// capture the mouse move events for the main layer
document.layers["layDoc"].captureEvents(Event.MOUSEMOVE);
document.layers["layDoc"].onMouseMove = MouseMove;
...
```

Here's the outline of the function **MouseMove()**. It sets up some variables to be
used within the code, then looks to see if the target element of the event is our
Wrox image. If so, we need to move the image around and not worry about
moving the buttons:

```
function MouseMove(e)
{
  objLay = document.layers["layDoc"];    // get a reference to the layer
  db = 15;                               // how close to the edge to get
  dw = 600;                              // main layer width
  dh = 350;                              // main layer height
  x = e.pageX;                           // get x and y position of
  y = e.pageY;                           // mouse pointer as of now
```

```
...
if (e.target.name == "imgWrox")
{
// move the Wrox image element around
...
}
else
{
// move the Competitor's Site button away from the mouse pointer
...
}
};
```

Storing References to Objects

Notice how, in the first few lines of the code, we use the browser object model to get at the **layer** object we're interested in, and through it the properties we are going to need for our page. We use the **layers** array of the **document** object, which contains all the layers in the page. Remember that the **window** is the default object, so we don't need **window.document.layers["layDoc"]** in this case.

Querying the Event Object

We want to allow the user to drag the *Wrox* logo around the page, but allow the mouse to 'chase' the Competitors Site button if the mouse pointer is not over the image. To do this, we need to know which element was the source of the **onMouseMove** event.

We've seen how to discover this earlier in this chapter, using the **Event** object's **target** property. However, here, we're being a little cleverer. As we suggested earlier, the **target** property of the **Event** object is itself an object—and it has its own properties. Amongst these is the **name** property, which returns the name we gave to an element in the HTML source. So, instead of converting the **target** object into a string representation, we can read the **name** property directly:

```
<IMG SRC="wrox0.gif" NAME="imgWrox">
...
if (e.target.name == "imgWrox")
```

In fact, we can do a lot more than this with the **target** property. Many of the attributes we use with a tag to create an element in the HTML source are available as properties of the **Event** object's **target** object. In this small example, we're reading the **BORDER** and **SRC** properties as well:

```
<IMG BORDER=5 SRC="wrox0.gif" NAME="imgWrox">

<SCRIPT LANGUAGE=JAVASCRIPT>
window.onKeyDown = doit;
window.captureEvents(Event.KEYDOWN);

function doit(e)
{
  strMesg = "The element is named '" + e.target.name + "'\n"
        + "The SRC property is '" + e.target.src + "'\n"
          + "The BORDER property value is '" + e.target.border + "'\n";
  alert(strMesg);
```

```
}
</SCRIPT>
```

Here's the result, showing the values of the properties:

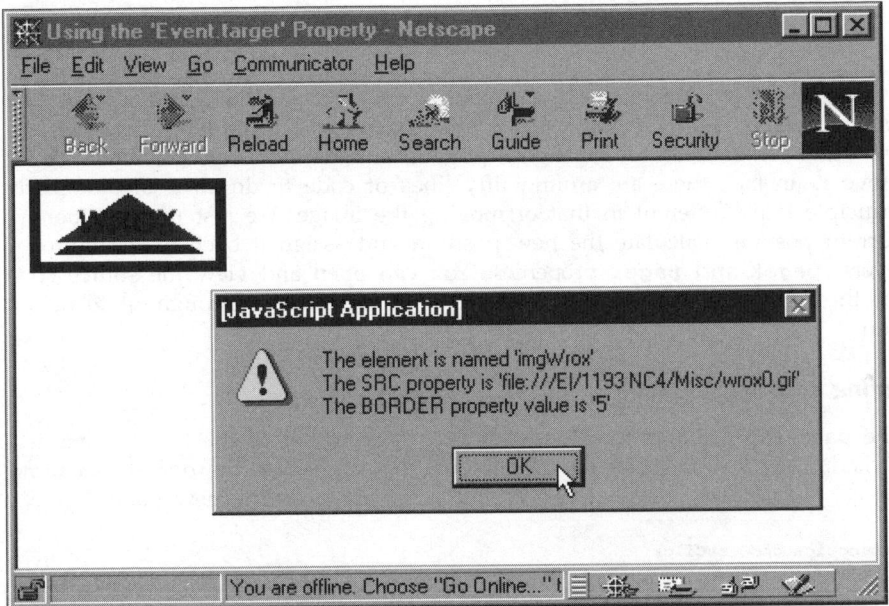

However, going back to our Dancing Buttons page, we also need to know the
position of the mouse pointer with respect to the entire page (not just the
current layer). The *x* and *y* coordinates are available from the **Event** objects
pageX and **pageY** properties.

Moving the Elements

Moving the *Wrox* logo is easy enough. Here's the code we use—it simply places
some text in the window's status bar, then calculates the new horizontal and
vertical positions for the image using the **width** and **height** properties and
the **x** and **y** mouse coordinates. We've set the values of three variables **dh**, **dw**,
and **db** previously, to refer to the height and width of the main document layer
layDoc, and the minimum distance we want to get to the edge of it. Once
we've calculated the new position, we just assign it back to the image layer's
pageX and **pageY** properties:

```
...
if (e.target.name == "imgWrox")
{
    // move the Wrox image element around
    window.status = "Drag me to a new position";
    window.clearInterval(timMoveID);          // reset the creep interval
    timMoveID = window.setInterval(timMove, 4000);
    objImage = document.layers["layDoc"].document.layers["layImg"];
    iw = objImage.document.images[0].width;  // width of the image
    ih = objImage.document.images[0].height; // height of the image
    nx = x - (iw / 2);                        // new horizontal position
    if (nx < db) nx = db;                     // stop at left and right edges
    if (nx > (dw - db - iw)) nx = (dw - db - iw);
```

157

```
    ny = y - (ih / 2);                        // new vertical position
    if (ny < db) ny = db;                     // stop at left and right edges
    if (ny > (dh - db - ih)) ny = (dh - db - ih);
    objImage.pageX = nx;
    objImage.pageY = ny
}
else
...
```

Moving the Competitors Site button follows the same process, but is complicated by the fact that we need to find out the position of the sides of the button in relation to the mouse pointer, and decide in which direction to move it. In fact, there are around fifty lines of code to do all this, though the principle is no different to that of moving the image. We just retrieve the current position, calculate the new position and assign it back to the button layers' `pageX` and `pageY` properties. You can open and view the source code for the page to see it in detail, and we've commented it throughout to help you.

Reacting to Button Clicks

The page also contains functions that run when either of the two buttons is clicked. The Visit Our Site one is obvious, it just changes the default **window** object's **location** object's **href** property, which loads the new page:

```
function cmdOursClick()
{
  location.href = "http://www.wrox.com"
};
```

The Competitors Site button shouldn't need any code, because the whole idea is that the user won't be able to get the mouse pointer over it. However, we're going to cover the occasion where they load the page into a non Dynamic HTML-savvy browser:

```
function cmdTheirsClick()
{
  strMsg = "You aren't using Netscape Communicator 4 then ?\n" +
           "If you were, you wouldn't have been able to click the button.\n" +
           "To see why you'll have to install it and come back again...";
  alert(strMsg);
  location.href = "http://www.wrox.com"
};
```

Here is what happens when the page is running in Internet Explorer 3, for example:

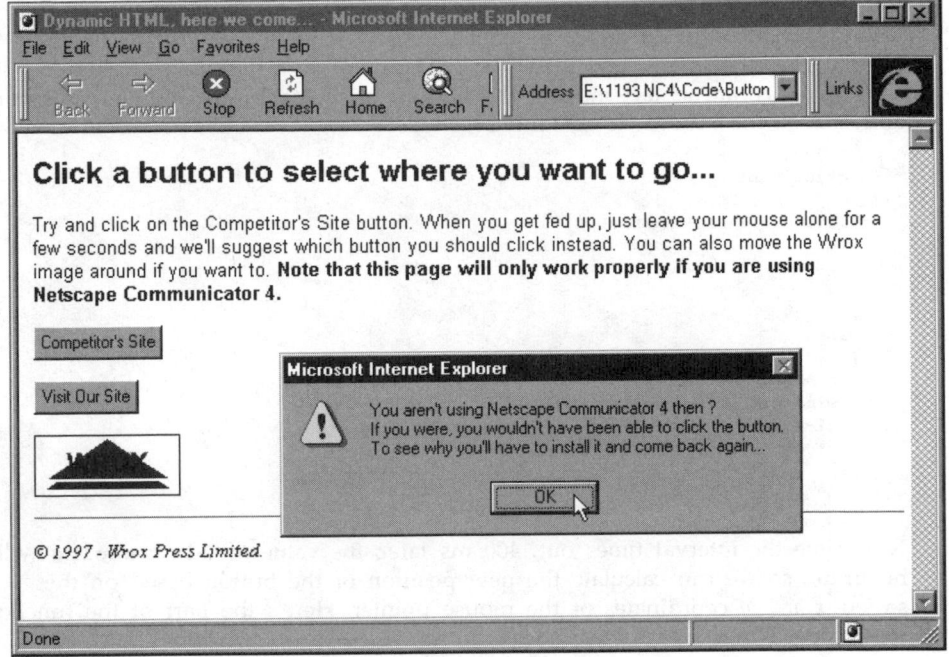

Moving the Visit Our Site Button

Of course, we haven't yet considered how the Visit Our Site button moves around in the page. It's obviously not responding to an event that we are causing, because it happens when we aren't doing anything.

In fact, this event is powered by an interval timer in the page—created with the new **setInterval** and **clearInterval** methods of the **window** object. At the beginning of the script section, we declare three variables. Two will store the last position of the mouse pointer as it passed out of our layer, or when it stopped moving if it's still over the layer. The third variable will hold the state of the 'creep' timer we're setting up.

Then, we start the creep timer going by calling the **setInterval** property of the window with a timeout value of 4 seconds. The function we want to run when it times out is **timMove()**, and the reference to the timer we save for use later is **timMoveID**:

```
...
var blnCreeping;    // our button is creeping
var lastX;          // last kown X position
var lastY;          // last know Y position
timMoveID = window.setInterval(timMove, 4000);
...
```

When the interval is up, the **timMove()** function runs. This first checks the value of **blnCreeping** to see if we are already moving the Visit Our Site button. The first time round it will be **false**, so we just set it to **true** to show that we are in fact moving the button, place a message in the status bar, and change the interval to 400 milliseconds.

```
function timMove()
{
  if (blnCreeping == true)
  {
    // move the 'Visit Our Site' button
    ...
  }
  else
  {
    blnCreeping = true;
    window.clearInterval(timMoveID);
    timMoveID = window.setInterval(timMove, 400);
    window.status= "Please click me ...";
  };
};
```

Next time the interval times out, 400 ms later, the value of **blnCreeping** will be **true**, so we can calculate the new position of the button based on the saved x and y coordinates of the mouse pointer. Here's the part of the function we removed in the previous code:

```
function timMove()
{
  if (blnCreeping == true)
  {
    // move the 'Visit Our Site' button
    db = 5;                                        // how close to go to the edge
    dt = 1;                                        // number of pixels to creep
    objLay = document.layers["layDoc"];
    dw = 600;                                      // main layer width
    dh = 350;                                      // main layer height
    objOurs = objLay.document.layers["layOurs"];
    hw = 130 / 2;                                  // half button width
    hh = 30 / 2;                                   // half button height
    nx = objOurs.pageX;                            // left of button
    ny = objOurs.pageY;                            // top of button
    cx = nx + hw;                                  // center of button x pos
    cy = ny + hh;                                  // center of button y pos
    if (lastX > cx)                                // move right
    {
      nx = nx + dt;                                // new x position
      if (nx + hw + hw + db > dw)                  // at edge of layer
        nx = dw - hw - hw - db;                    // so stay there
    }
    if (lastX < cx)                                // move left
    {
      nx = nx - dt;                                // new x position
      if (nx < db)                                 // at edge of layer
        nx = db;                                   // so stay there
    }
    if (lastY > cy)                                // move down
```

```
        {
          ny = ny + dt;                        // new y position
          if (ny +hh + hh + db > dh)           // at edge of layer
            ny = dh - hh - hh - db;            // so stay there
        }
        if (lastY < cy)                        // move up
        {
          ny = ny - dt;                        // new y position
          if (ny < db)                         // at edge of layer
            ny = db;                           // so stay there
        }
        objOurs.moveToAbsolute(nx, ny)
      }
      else
      {
        blnCreeping = true;
        window.clearInterval(timMoveID);
        timMoveID = window.setInterval(timMove, 400);
        window.status= "Please click me ...";
      };
    };
```

As you can see, it uses the **MoveToAbsolute** method of the layer object to
move it to a new position, rather than setting the **pageX** and **pageY** properties
directly. This has the same effect.

The only other things we need to do are to reset the interval back to 4 seconds
when we detect that the user has woken up, and has moved the mouse again.
We also need to save the new 'last position' coordinates ready for when they
fall asleep again. All this is done in the main **MouseMove()** function we
looked at earlier:

```
function MouseMove(e)
{
  ...
  blnCreeping = false;                   // reset the global creep flag
  x = e.pageX;                           // get x and y position of
  y = e.pageY;                           // mouse pointer as of now
  lastX = x;                             // store x and y position of
  lastY = y;                             // mouse for timer routine

  if (e.target.name == "imgWrox")
  {
  // move the Wrox image element around
  window.status = "Drag me to a new position";
  window.clearInterval(timMoveID);       // reset the creep interval
  timMoveID = window.setInterval(timMove, 4000);
  ...
```

Summary

In this chapter, we've spent a lot of time studying the basics we need to know to work with script code in Dynamic HTML. As you'll appreciate, scripting is at the heart of any Dynamic HTML page where we want to make it interactive and responsive to the user. Only pages that use just the absolute positioning abilities of Dynamic HTML, and are not truly *dynamic*, can manage without some code.

Thankfully, the changes to the object model and workings of Dynamic HTML from earlier versions of browsers that supported scripting, mean that we can often create these exciting pages using very little actual script code. In particular, the new **Event** object makes it easier than ever before to get information about the elements in the page, and manipulate them.

We've seen how:

- Events are Windows' way of telling applications that something has happened

- The browser exposes many events to our script code through its **object model**

- We can respond to these events if we want to, or just ignore them

- Each element maintains a set of **properties** whose values we can access, and often change to make the page dynamic

- We can **capture** and **route** events through the browser object hierarchy as required, allowing them to be handled at **window**, **document** or **layer** level.

- We can use the **Event** object to get information about an event, including the position of the mouse and the key that was pressed, where appropriate

With this chapter, we've completed our tour of the main parts of Dynamic HTML. It's now time to look at layers in more detail and see how we can achieve some quite complex effects, such as dragging images on the screen from one side to the other.

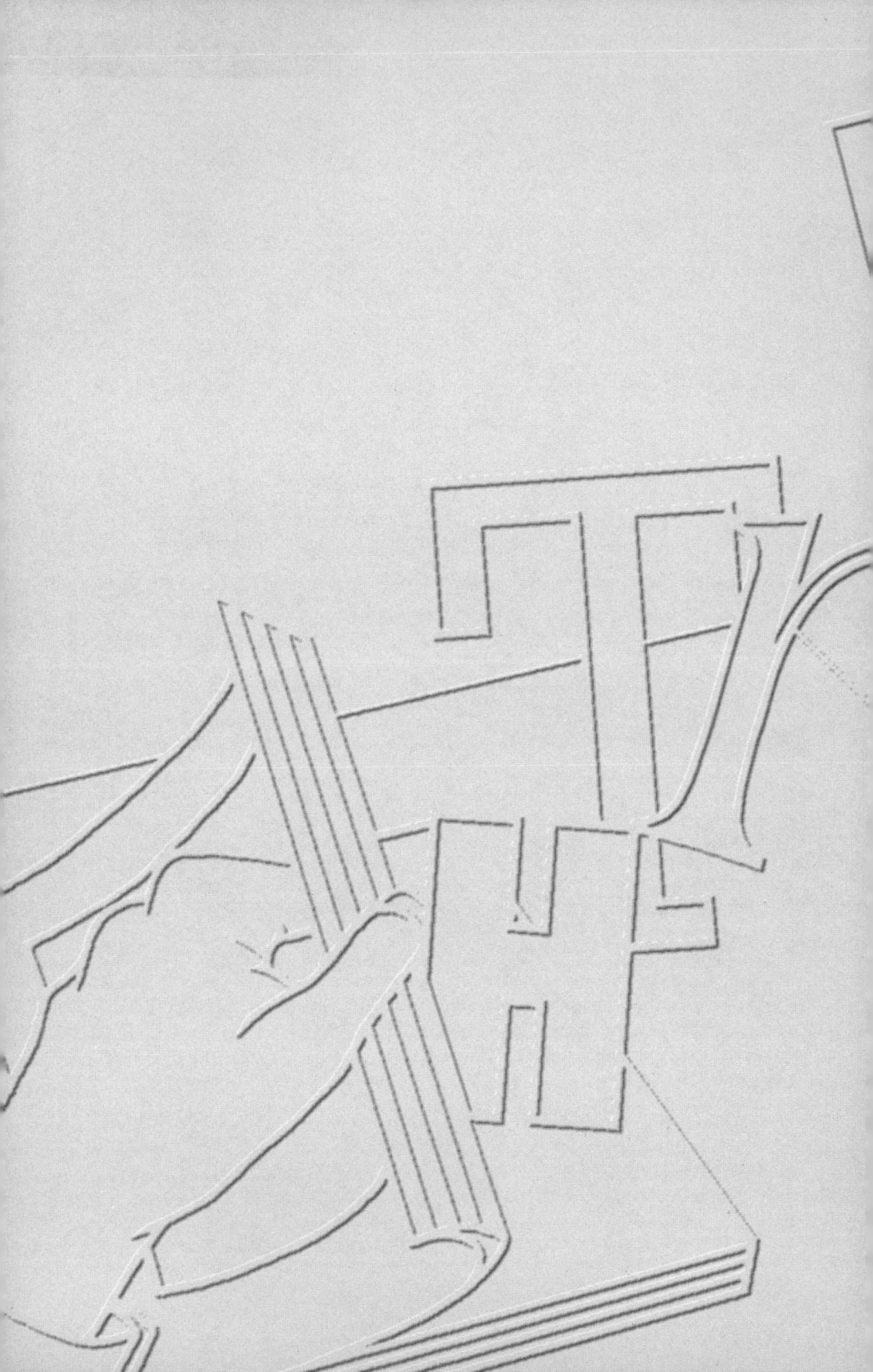

Working with Layers

In the previous chapters, we've covered just about all the basic techniques that provide Dynamic HTML with the ability to create more exciting and interactive web pages. We've seen how scripts are used with the events that the browser exposes, looked at how we can create better looking pages using styles and explored the abilities of the browser to redraw parts of the page as we move elements around and change their appearance.

Much of the magic is connected with the use of the major advance in Netscape Communicator 4, namely **layers**. These provide all kinds of new opportunities to produce dynamic pages—you've seen many examples already. In this chapter, we're going to look at two more complex pages, which use a combination of many of the techniques we've already seen in action.

The first is the Jigsaw page, introduced back in Chapter 1 as an indication of some of the things that are possible with Dynamic HTML. The second is the Book List page, which takes advantage of some of the more advanced properties of layers. We'll also be filling in some of the gaps in the theory as we go along. So you'll see:

- An overview of how **layers** can be used to provide more interactive pages
- How we used layers and scripting code to create the Jigsaw example page
- How the Book List page uses the more advanced features of layers
- How we can create signed scripts to get more out of the browser

First let's take a look at what layers have to offer us.

An Overview of Layers

In order to create a more interactive environment within web pages, Netscape have added several features to the new browser. These combine to create the language called Dynamic HTML, but by far the most useful of all the new features is the addition of **layers**. These allow us to place elements and scripts into separate containers within the page, and update them in real time—while the page is loaded. The changes are reflected on screen as they happen, providing our dynamic content.

As mentioned in Chapter 3, Netscape introduced the **<LAYER>** element in early Communicator 4 betas. Unfortunately it was rejected by the W3C standards committee and it seems likely to be discontinued in future releases, as Netscape have issued a statement saying that the only reason that it was included in the final release of Communicator 4 was for reasons of backwards compatibility. However there are several things you can do in layers that you can't do easily using standard methods, or in some cases, such as manipulating the new style properties by script—you can't do at all. So this leaves us with a dilemma. While we strongly discourage deviating from the HTML 4.0 standard, we don't want to ignore the power that layers offer. So bear this in mind as you read this chapter. If you don't want to use layers, for compatibility reasons, then that's fine, but if you know your audience is going to be using Communicator 4 then you will certainly be interested in what they have to offer.

The Capabilities of Layers

Layers provide two main features. Firstly, we can use the **<LAYER>** tag to precisely position elements within a page, as you can when using a desktop publishing package. Secondly, we can **animate** the layers, by changing their content or appearance in various ways, while that page is loaded.

Absolute Positioning of Layers

We've seen in earlier chapters how we can position layers, using the **TOP** and **LEFT** attributes of the **<LAYER>** tag. We can also specify the default size of the layer, although it will grow to accommodate the content if it won't all fit:

```
<LAYER NAME="MyLayer" TOP=100 LEFT=50 HEIGHT=200 WIDTH=300>
```

Layer Properties

Before we move on to look at the ways we can animate layers, we need to see how their properties provide us with access to the various attributes defined in the **<LAYER>** tag. Back in Chapter 5 we examined the various properties in some detail. As a refresher, the following table shows the attributes we can use, and the equivalent properties and descriptions:

Attribute	Property	Description
NAME	name	Specifies the name to use to refer to the layer.

Attribute	Property	Description
ID	name	Same as the **NAME** attribute.
LEFT	left	Position in pixels of the left-hand side of the layer in relation to the document.
TOP	top	Position of the top of the layer in relation to the document.
PAGEX	pageX	Position in pixels of the left-hand side of the layer in relation to the containing layer, or the document if no container.
PAGEY	pageY	Position in pixels of the top of the layer in relation to the containing layer, or the document if no container.
BACKGROUND	background	URL of an image to display behind the elements in the layer.
BGCOLOR	bgColor	Specifies the background color to be used for the layer.
SRC	src	An external file that contains the source data for the layer.
VISIBILITY	visibility	Defines whether the layer should be displayed on the page.
ABOVE	above	Indicates that the layer should above be another element in the z-order of the page, or returns the element above it.
BELOW	below	Indicates that the layer should be below another element in the z-order of the page, or returns the element below it.
Z-INDEX	zIndex	Position in the z-order or stacking order of the page, i.e. the z co-ordinate.
CLIP	clip.bottom	Y co-ordinate of the bottom of the clipping rectangle for the layer.
	clip.left	X co-ordinate of the left of the clipping rectangle for the layer.
	clip.right	X co-ordinate of the right of the clipping rectangle for the layer.
	clip.top	Y co-ordinate of the top of the clipping rectangle for the layer.
	clip.height	Height of the clipping rectangle for the layer.
	clip.width	Width of the clipping for the layer.

Notice how we can set the clipping rectangle for a layer, so elements that will not fit do not cause the layer to grow in size. They are simply chopped off at the clipping boundary.

167

Stacking Layers

You can think of a layer as being a separate page, which is displayed on top of the document. The layer may not cover the entire document, depending on its size and position. When there are several layers in a page, they may also overlap each other. This introduces the concept of a **stacking order**, or **z-order**, as we've seen in earlier chapters.

> *The background of each layer is initially transparent, unless we apply a background color or load a background image. This means that the contents of layers underneath, and the document itself, show through. We can also make a layer transparent again by setting the* **bgColor** *and* **background** *properties to* **null**.

We can control the stacking order by setting the **zIndex**, **above** or **below** properties (we can only specify one of these properties in any **<LAYER>** tag). To place the second layer below the first, we can use several methods in the HTML:

```
<LAYER NAME="TopLayer" Z-INDEX=2 TOP=100 LEFT=50></LAYER>
<LAYER NAME="BottomLayer" Z-INDEX=1 TOP=100 LEFT=50></LAYER>
```

```
<LAYER NAME="TopLayer" TOP=100 LEFT=50></LAYER>
<LAYER NAME="BottomLayer" ABOVE="TopLayer" TOP=100 LEFT=50></LAYER>
```

In fact, the default stacking order is the order of the layers in the HTML, so the final example doesn't actually need the **ABOVE** attribute to be set. Of course, when we come to animate our layers, this will provide a way to change the stacking order while that page is loaded and displayed.

Animating Layers

The previous section has hinted at one way that we can animate layers, by changing the stacking order while the page is displayed. We can bring different layers to the top, or move them below other layers, as required. But we can do a lot more than this with layers. As you saw from earlier examples, we can change almost all the properties of layers in code. This means that we can:

- Change the stacking order of the layers, as mentioned earlier
- Hide or show layers, by changing their **visibility** property
- Move and resize layers, by changing their **top**, **left**, **pageX**, **pageY**, and clipping properties
- Change the background color or picture in a layer, or make it transparent again
- Change the entire contents of a layer, either by loading a different page or writing new content to it from script with the **document.write** method

Using Layer Methods

Layers have a set of methods that allow us to manipulate them in many ways. We can move and resize them using these methods, rather than by setting the size and position properties directly. We can also load a new page into the layer—remember each layer contains its own, separate, document:

Method	Description
`moveBy`	Moves the layer horizontally and vertically by a specified number of pixels.
`moveTo`	Moves the layer so that the top left is at a position x, y (in pixels) within its container.
`moveToAbsolute`	Moves the layer to a position specified in x and y with respect to the page and not the container.
`resizeBy`	Resizes the layer horizontally and vertically by a specified number of pixels.
`resizeTo`	Resizes the layer to a size specified in x and y (in pixels).
`moveAbove`	Changes the z-order so that the layer is rendered above (overlaps) another element.
`moveBelow`	Changes the z-order so that the layer is rendered below (overlapped by) another element.
`load`	Loads a file into the layer, and can change the width of the layer.

Handling Events in Layers

Layers provide a limited range of events that we can react to, and they support event capturing—as we saw in the previous chapter. This means that we can easily react to the common user actions, such as moving the mouse over a layer.

Event	Description
`onBlur`	Occurs when the layer loses the focus.
`onFocus`	Occurs when the layer receives the focus.
`onLoad`	Occurs immediately after the layer's contents have been loaded.
`onMouseOut`	Occurs when the mouse pointer leaves the layer.
`onMouseOver`	Occurs when the mouse pointer first enters the layer.

Often, however, we'll react to events by capturing them at other levels in the hierarchy. We might decide to capture them in the document or the window for all elements, including all the layers. That way, we can react to the event in different ways depending on which layer received the event. This is something you'll see used to advantage in both the sample pages in this chapter.

But, as the layer contains its own document, we might decide to capture events in the layer for that document and all its contents. This is done with the four event capturing methods we've seen in action in the previous chapter:

Method	Description
captureEvents	Instructs the layer to capture events of a particular type.
handleEvent	Invokes the appropriate event handling code of the object for this event.
routeEvent	Passes an event that has been captured back up through the normal event hierarchy.
releaseEvents	Instructs the layer to stop capturing events of a particular type.

We'll look at a simple example of animating layers before we move on to the two main sample pages in this chapter. First, detecting the **onMouseOver** and **onMouseOut** events.

Detecting Mouse Events for a Layer

We can add event handlers to the **<LAYER>** tag, just as we can to any other element that supports events. In our case, we have a layer with a white background, and we want to react to the **onMouseOver** and **onMouseOut** events:

```
<LAYER NAME="MyLayer" BGCOLOR="white" TOP=50 LEFT=50
  ONMOUSEOVER="colorlayer('red')" ONMOUSEOUT="colorlayer('white')" >
<P>Wrox Press
</LAYER>
```

Notice that the two events call the same function, **colorlayer**, but with different colors as the argument. The idea is that the **onMouseOver** event will cause the **colorlayer** function to change the background color of the layer to red, and the **onMouseOut** event will cause it to return to white.

The code for the **colorlayer** function is simple enough. It just has to set the **bgColor** property of the layer. However, it's worth considering how we are going to reference this property. If the **colorlayer** function is in a **<SCRIPT>** section in the main document, it will have to access the layer using the **layers** array of the document, and know exactly where to find it. If our layer is within the document that is itself in another layer, the script has to go through two levels of the hierarchy to get to our layer:

```
document.layers["mainlayer"].document.layers["MyLayer"].bgColor = 'red';
```

If we later redesign the page, we may have to change all the references to our layers so that the code still works properly.

Writing Scripts in Layers

The easy answer to this problem is to write the code within the layer it applies to. It becomes local to the layer, and cannot be accessed from anywhere outside the layer. This is useful if we use global variables in the code, because they won't conflict with global variables in other layers.

In our case, the code is also a lot simpler now because the **bgColor** property applies to the layer the code is running in:

```
<LAYER NAME="MyLayer" BGCOLOR="white" TOP=50 LEFT=50
   ONMOUSEOVER="colorlayer('red')" ONMOUSEOUT="colorlayer('white')" >
   <P>Wrox Press
   <SCRIPT LANGUAGE=JavaScript1.2>
     function colorlayer(changeto)
       { bgColor=changeto }
   </SCRIPT>
</LAYER>
```

And here's the result. The layer background turns red when the mouse pointer moves over it and white when it moves out again. Because the layer contains text, the mouse pointer changes to an I-beam when over it:

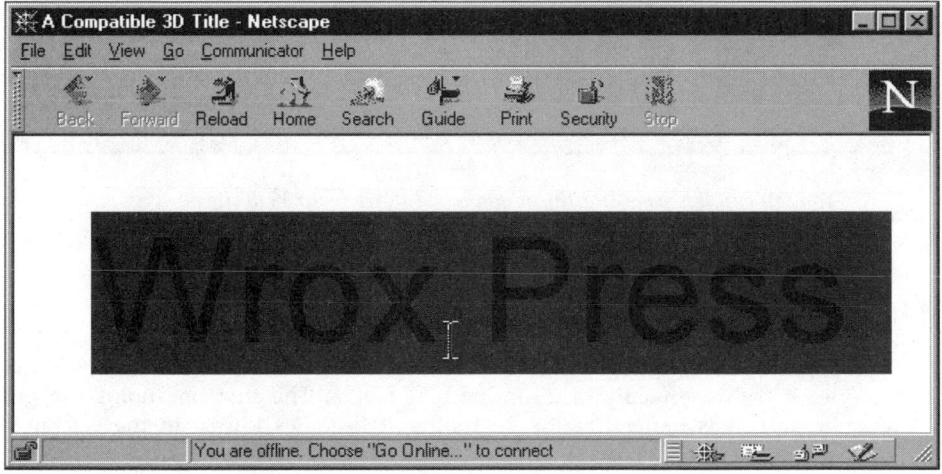

The Jigsaw Example Page

It's time to move on to look at the first of our sample pages for this chapter. The Jigsaw page contains a famous Van Gogh picture divided up into 24 square pieces. All you need to do is click on a piece, drag it to the grid (without holding the mouse button down) and click again to place it. It's automatically aligned to the grid for you. To rotate a piece, just double-click on it:

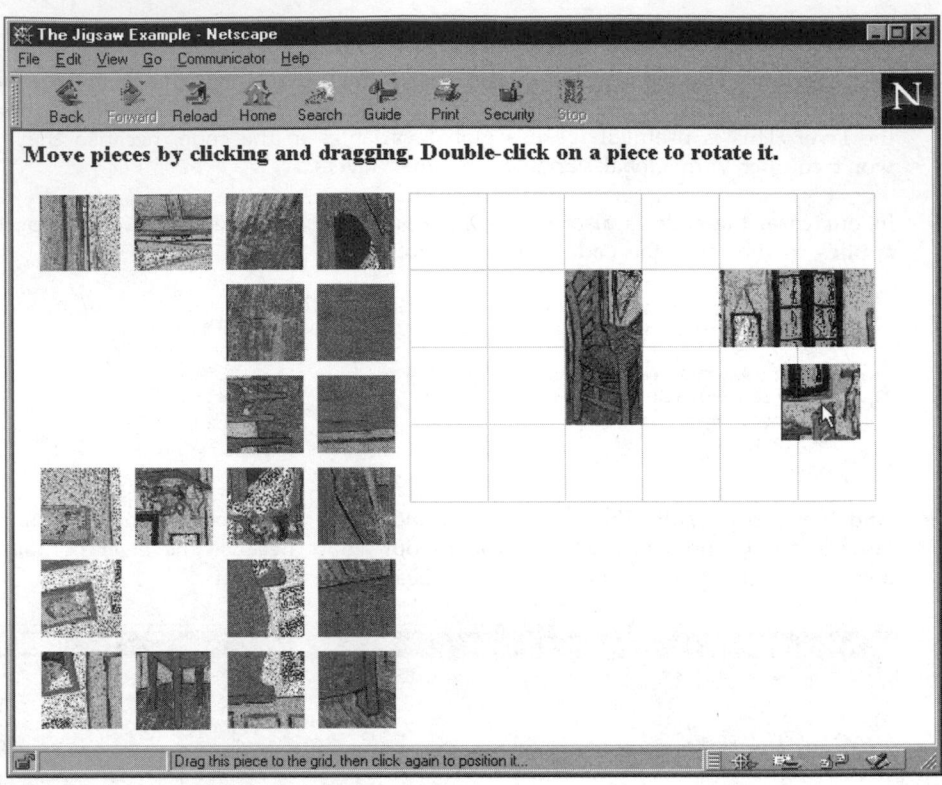

You can run this page directly, or download it, from our Web site at
http://rapid.wrox.co.uk/books/1193/

Creating the Jigsaw Page

Although it looks complicated, the HTML that creates the Jigsaw page is quite simple. It consists mainly of 25 individual layers. The first one holds the grid, and because it is defined at the beginning it becomes lowest in the stacking order. This is what we want, so that the individual pieces will lie on top of it. The other 24 layers hold these individual pieces. We've removed some of the duplication from the code to save space and make it easier to see what's going on:

```
<!DOCTYPE HTML PUBLIC "-//IETF//DTD HTML//EN">
<HTML>
<HEAD><TITLE>The Jigsaw Example</TITLE></HEAD>
<BODY>
<H3> Move pieces by clicking and dragging. Double-click on a piece to rotate it.</
H3>
<LAYER NAME="Grid" TOP=50 LEFT=300 WIDTH=380 HEIGHT=290><IMG NAME="Grid"
SRC="jig1.gif"></LAYER>
<LAYER NAME="P1" TOP=50 LEFT=20 WIDTH=60 HEIGHT=60><IMG NAME="P1"
SRC="gogh11.gif"></LAYER>
<LAYER NAME="P2" TOP=120 LEFT=20 WIDTH=60 HEIGHT=60><IMG NAME="P2"
SRC="gogh22.gif"></LAYER>
...
<!-- Layers P3 to P22 defined here -->
...
```

```
<LAYER NAME="P23" TOP=330 LEFT=230 WIDTH=60 HEIGHT=60><IMG NAME="P23"
SRC="gogh233.gif"></LAYER>
<LAYER NAME="P24" TOP=400 LEFT=230 WIDTH=60 HEIGHT=60><IMG NAME="P24"
SRC="gogh241.gif"></LAYER>
</BODY>
...
```

We've given each layer a name, with the grid being in the layer named **Grid**
and the jigsaw pieces in layers named **P1** to **P24**. Inside each layer, we've
placed an image tag and included the name of the layer in this tag as well.
This is because the layer name is often not returned if there is no actual
content, other than an image, defined in the **SRC** attribute. By using an **<IMG>**
element, we can access the name of the image, and hence retrieve the name of
the layer. You'll also see that the original pieces are placed in the grid in a
random order. We'll discuss the naming of the images for the pieces in a while.

The Script Section

The script section of the page implements three functions. At the beginning is a
definition of a global variable **strImgDragging**, which we'll use to indicate if
the user is dragging a piece of the jigsaw. At the end of the script section are
the statements that turn on event capturing for the document and define the
event handlers. Here's the complete script section so you can see how it fits
together. We'll discuss each part afterwards:

```
...
<SCRIPT LANGUAGE=JavaScript>

var strImgDragging;   // indicates if we are currently moving a piece

function MouseUpEvent(e)
{
  if (strImgDragging == null)    // not currently dragging, so start
  {
    // image name is same as layer name, and can be retrieved from target
    strImgDragging = e.target.name
    // however, we don't want to move the grid, so we ignore this image
    if (strImgDragging == "Grid") strImgDragging = null;
  }
  else
  {
    // stop dragging, and position the piece in line with grid.
    posLeft = Math.floor((document.layers[strImgDragging].left - 270) / 59) * 59;
    posTop = Math.floor((document.layers[strImgDragging].top - 20) / 59) * 59;
    document.layers[strImgDragging].left = posLeft + 301;
    document.layers[strImgDragging].top = posTop + 51;

    // reset the global 'dragging' variable
    strImgDragging = null;
  };

  // put a message in the status bar
  if (strImgDragging == null)
    window.status = "Click on a piece to start dragging it..."
  else
    window.status = "Drag this piece to grid and click again to position it...";
}

function MouseMoveEvent(e)
{
  if (strImgDragging != null)      // if we are dragging
  {
```

173

```
        // move the layer to the new position
        // assume the mouse pointer is in middle of image
        document.layers[strImgDragging].left = e.pageX - 30;
        document.layers[strImgDragging].top = e.pageY - 30;
    }
}

function DblClickEvent(e)
{
    // get the image file name
    strSrc="" + e.target.src

    // if it's not the grid image itself, then we'll rotate it
    if (strSrc.indexOf("jig1.gif") < 0)
    {
        // extract just the image number as a string
        intStart = strSrc.indexOf("/gogh");
        if (intStart != -1) strSrc = strSrc.substr(intStart + 5);
        intEnd = strSrc.indexOf(".");
        if (intEnd != -1) strSrc = strSrc.substr(0, intEnd);

        //split into image and attitude numbers
        strImgNum = strSrc.substr(0, strSrc.length - 1);
        strAttNum = strSrc.substr(strSrc.length - 1, strSrc.length - 1);

        // calculate the new image attitude number
        intAttNum = strAttNum.valueOf();
        intAttNum ++;
        if (intAttNum > 4) intAttNum = 1;
        strAttNum = intAttNum.toString();

        // create and assign the new image name
        e.target.src = "gogh" + strImgNum + strAttNum + ".gif";
        document.routeEvent(e);
    }
}

// turn on event capturing from the document
document.captureEvents(Event.DBLCLICK | Event.MOUSEMOVE | Event.MOUSEUP);

// then define the event handlers
document.onMouseUp=MouseUpEvent;
document.onDblClick=DblClickEvent;
document.onMouseMove=MouseMoveEvent;

</SCRIPT>
</HTML>
```

How It Works

The heart of the Jigsaw example page is the way we handle events for the 24 pieces of the jigsaw. We don't want to write any more code than necessary, and it would be nice to have one event handler that could manipulate all the pieces. This is where event capturing, which we met in the previous chapter, proves very useful. We capture all the appropriate mouse events at document level, then determine which piece was under the mouse pointer at the time—and move that piece.

Capturing the Mouse Events in the Document

To capture events at document level, we use the **captureEvents** method, and specify the events we're interested in:

```
// turn on event capturing from the document
document.captureEvents(Event.DBLCLICK | Event.MOUSEMOVE | Event.MOUSEUP);
```

Then we can connect the event handlers that will react to these events to the events themselves:

```
// then define the event handlers
document.onMouseUp=MouseUpEvent;
document.onDblClick=DblClickEvent;
document.onMouseMove=MouseMoveEvent;
```

Now all **onMouseUp**, **onMouseMove** and **onDblClick** events will be intercepted by the document, rather than being passed to the element that the mouse was over at the time.

Moving the Jigsaw Pieces

Once we capture the events, we can manipulate the pieces of the jigsaw. We want to allow the user to move a piece by simply moving the mouse. By reacting to the **onMouseMove** event, we only need to retrieve the current mouse pointer co-ordinates from the **Event** object, and apply them to the layer that contains our jigsaw piece.

We've previously declared a global variable, **strImgDragging**, at the start of the **<SCRIPT>** section. When the user clicks on a piece, this will hold the name of the layer that we need to move—you'll see how in a moment. If it's **null**, however, we know that they haven't yet selected a piece to move, so we can ignore the event:

```
function MouseMoveEvent(e)
{
  if (strImgDragging != null)       // if we are dragging
  {
    // move the layer to the new position
    // assume the mouse pointer is in middle of image
    document.layers[strImgDragging].left = e.pageX - 30;
    document.layers[strImgDragging].top = e.pageY - 30;
  }
}
```

The code simply uses the **strImgDragging** variable to reference the correct layer, and sets its **left** and **top** properties using the values in the **Event** object's **pageX** and **pageY** properties. Because each jigsaw piece is 59 pixels square, we subtract half of this so that the mouse pointer is in the center of the piece, rather than the top-left corner. This makes it look better when the piece is moving, although it does cause the piece to jump when first selected if the user doesn't click exactly in the center of it.

We could get round this by storing the offset of the mouse pointer position with respect to the top left corner when the user first clicks the piece to select it, then applying these offsets instead of assuming 30 pixels. You might like to adapt the code yourself along these lines.

Handling an onMouseUp Event

OK, so we can move a jigsaw piece once it's been selected, and the **strImgDragging** variable is not **null**. The trick now is to be able to select it, and drop it again when the user clicks a second time. The document doesn't expose an **onClick** event, so we do this in the code that runs for an **onMouseUp** event instead. In outline, the code looks like this:

```
function MouseUpEvent(e)
{
  if (strImgDragging == null)     // not currently dragging, so start
  {
    // set strImgDragging to the name of the piece's layer
    ...
  }
  else
  {
    // stop dragging, and position the piece in line with grid.
    // and reset the global 'dragging' variable strImgDragging to null
    ...
};
```

It examines the current value of **strImgDragging**, which will be **null** if the user has not yet clicked on a piece to select it. In this case, it just has to set **strImgDragging** to the name of the layer that needs to be moved. If it's not already **null**, however, we are already dragging a piece, so we need to drop it at this point and reset the variable back to **null** again.

The actual code is a little more complex, because it has a couple of other things to do. Firstly, we need to make sure we don't allow the user to drag the grid image, which is also in a layer. We do this by checking the name of the layer, and setting **strImgDragging** back to **null** if it's the grid:

```
...
if (strImgDragging == null)     // not currently dragging, so start
{
  // image name is same as layer name, and can be retrieved from target
  strImgDragging = e.target.name
  // however, we don't want to move the grid, so we ignore this image
  if (strImgDragging == "Grid") strImgDragging = null;
}
...
```

Dropping a Piece into the Grid

If, on the other hand, we are already dragging an image, we need to drop it. We're going to assume that the user will click when the piece is over the grid, and we'll help them by aligning it to the grid automatically. This is done using the original coordinates of the grid (**300**, **50**), and the fact that each piece is 59 pixels square.

We calculate where the mid-point of the piece is, in terms of rows and columns, by subtracting the grid layer's top and left co-ordinates (each minus half the width and height) from the current layer's co-ordinates, and then dividing the result by the width and height of the piece. Then, we can add back the co-ordinates of the grid, plus one pixel to place the piece inside it, and assign these values directly to the layer's **top** and **left** properties:

```
...
else
{
    // stop dragging, and position the piece in line with grid.
    posLeft = Math.floor((document.layers[strImgDragging].left - 270) / 59) * 59;
    posTop = Math.floor((document.layers[strImgDragging].top - 20) / 59) * 59;
    document.layers[strImgDragging].left = posLeft + 301;
    document.layers[strImgDragging].top = posTop + 51;

    // reset the global 'dragging' variable
    strImgDragging = null;
};
...
```

Notice that we also need to set the value of **strImgDragging** back to **null**, so that the next **onMouseMove** event will ignore it. But we haven't quite finished yet. To help the user along, we want to put a message in the status bar to indicate what they must do next. By re-examining the value of **strImgDragging**, we can correctly handle the situation where the grid layer was clicked on by keeping the value of **strImgDragging** as **null**:

```
...
// put a message in the status bar
if (strImgDragging == null)
    window.status = "Click on a piece to start dragging it...";
else
    window.status = "Drag this piece to grid and click again to position it...";
}
```

Rotating a Jigsaw Piece

The final event we have to handle is **onDblClick**, when the user wants to rotate a jigsaw piece. To achieve this, we've actually provided four images for each piece of the jigsaw, one for each orientation (or attitude). The pieces have names that reflect this—for example piece 17 in the jigsaw is actually one of the images **gogh171.gif**, **gogh172.gif**, **gogh173.gif** or **gogh174.gif**. They're all the same piece, but rotated through 90 degrees.

So, when a double-click occurs, all we have to do is retrieve the filename of the current image, and increment the last digit. If it exceeds **4**, we set it back to **1** again. Then we can load the new image into the layer's **<IMG>** tag by simply assigning it to the **src** property. The **target** property of the **Event** object contains a reference to the object that was the original target for the event, in this case the image the user double-clicked. We can get the file name from the **src** property of this image element:

```
function DblClickEvent(e)
{
    // get the image file name, forcing it into a string
    strSrc = "" + e.target.src

    // if it's not the grid image itself, then we'll rotate it
    if (strSrc.indexOf("jig1.gif") < 0)
    {
        ...
```

Of course, we don't want to rotate the grid, so we'll check that the filename does not contain the name of the grid image, **jig1.gif**. If it doesn't, the **indexOf** method returns **-1**, and we can start the process of rotating our image.

177

Building Up the New Image Filename

The first step is to strip off the beginning of the filename (which includes the path), up to and including the **gogh** part. This leaves us with just the number and the **.gif** file extension. By looking for the period, we can strip this extension part off the end of the string as well. In both cases, we're using the **substr** method, which takes the index of the start and end characters for the new string as arguments:

```
String.substr(start_index, [end_index])
```

```
...
// extract just the image number as a string
intStart = strSrc.indexOf("/gogh");
if (intStart != -1) strSrc = strSrc.substr(intStart + 5);
intEnd = strSrc.indexOf(".");
if (intEnd != -1) strSrc = strSrc.substr(0, intEnd);
...
```

In the first case in our code, we've omitted the second (optional) argument. In this case, the function will return the remainder of the string.

Once we've got the image number, we can increment it. We've opted to split the string into two, and convert the last digit into a **Number** type variable so we can increment it mathematically. Then, we set it back to 1 if it exceeds 4. Finally, we need to convert it back to a string again, using the **toString** method:

```
...
//split into image and attitude numbers
strImgNum = strSrc.substr(0, strSrc.length - 1);
strAttNum = strSrc.substr(strSrc.length - 1, strSrc.length - 1);

// calculate the new image attitude number
intAttNum = strAttNum.valueOf();
intAttNum ++;
if (intAttNum > 4) intAttNum = 1;
strAttNum = intAttNum.toString();
...
```

At last, we're ready to go. We can build up the new image filename from the image number and attitude number strings, then assign it to the **src** property of our image element. The final line just routes the event back up the object hierarchy, although there is no real need because we aren't handling it again anywhere else:

```
...
// create and assign the new image name
e.target.src = "gogh" + strImgNum + strAttNum + ".gif";
document.routeEvent(e);
}
}
```

Why Not Drag and Drop?

This example demonstrates how one event handler can be used to manipulate several elements in a page. However, you may be wondering why we chose to have the user click on a jigsaw piece to select it, then click again to place it—

178

rather than implementing the more usual left-button drag that is seen in *Windows* and other operating systems. In our case, it's due to the fact the **Event** object doesn't return a value for the **which** property (that indicates which button is pressed) for an **onMouseMove** event.

It's possible work round this, by reacting to the **onMouseDown** and **onMouseUp** events. However, the method we've chosen is probably simpler—both to code and understand—while demonstrating the benefits of layers and event capturing.

The Book List Example Page

The second sample page, Book List, also demonstrates layers in use—but this time taking advantage of more of their capabilities. When first opened, it displays five of our books and the invitation to click on one to get more information:

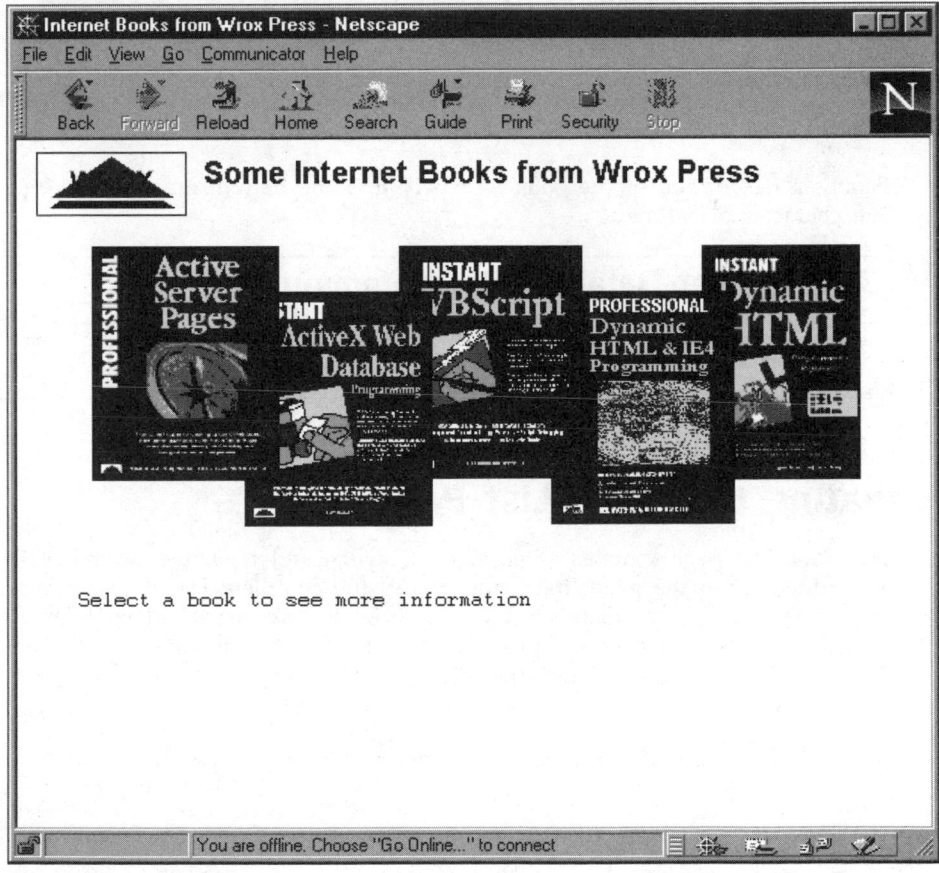

You can run this page directly, or download it, from our Web site at
http://rapid.wrox.co.uk/books/1193/

Selecting a Book

Selecting one of the books starts off a series of actions. First, the book is brought to the front of the stack and its color changes to make it stand out, although this may not be very visible from the screenshots. (It goes from dark to bright red—try the sample yourself to see.) Next, the book title scrolls in from the right:

Finally, a description of the book is 'typed' into the bottom area of the page, one character at a time:

ActiveX Web Database Programming

```
The major task every business faces when they start to build a Web
site or Intranet is to link the data in their databases to the
pages on their Web site.
```

Creating the Book List Page

The Book List page contains a selection of layers, and this time several of them are hidden when the page first loads. Here's the complete HTML section of the page. You can see that there are layers to hold the five dark red book cover images, the description of the book, the five book titles, and then five layers that are all hidden and contain the highlighted (or selected) bright red book cover images:

```
<!DOCTYPE HTML PUBLIC "-//IETF//DTD HTML//EN">
<HTML>
<HEAD>
<STYLE TYPE="text/javascript">
  tags.H3.fontFamily="Arial"
  tags.H3.fontSize="20"
  tags.H3.color="blue"
  tags.H2.fontFamily="Arial"
  tags.H2.fontSize="20"
  tags.H2.color="darkred"
  tags.P.fontFamily="Courier"
  tags.P.fontSize="14"
```

```
      tags.P.fontWeight="normal"
</STYLE>
<TITLE>Internet Books from Wrox Press</TITLE>
</HEAD>
<BODY BGCOLOR=FFFFFF>
<H3><IMG SRC="wrox0.gif" HSPACE=5 WIDTH=100 HEIGHT=42 ALT="Wrox Press"
ALIGN="MIDDLE">
Some Internet Books from Wrox Press</H3>

<!-- Define the layers to hold the book cover images -->
<LAYER NAME="C0685" TOP=70 LEFT=450><IMG SRC="B0685.gif" BORDER=2
ONMOUSEDOWN="SelectTitle('0685', 2);"></LAYER>
<LAYER NAME="C0707" TOP=100 LEFT=350><IMG SRC="B0707.gif" BORDER=2
ONMOUSEDOWN="SelectTitle('0707', 1);"></LAYER>
<LAYER NAME="C0448" TOP=70 LEFT=250><IMG SRC="B0448.gif" BORDER=2
ONMOUSEDOWN="SelectTitle('0448', 3);"></LAYER>
<LAYER NAME="C0464" TOP=100 LEFT=150><IMG SRC="B0464.gif" BORDER=2
ONMOUSEDOWN="SelectTitle('0464', 4);"></LAYER>
<LAYER NAME="C0723" TOP=70 LEFT=50><IMG SRC="B0723.gif" BORDER=2
ONMOUSEDOWN="SelectTitle('0723', 0);"></LAYER>

<!-- Define the layer to hold the description of the book -->
<LAYER NAME="TEXT" TOP=295 LEFT=40><P>Select a book to see more information</P></
LAYER>

<!-- Define the layers to hold the book titles -->
<LAYER NAME="T0723" TOP=275 LEFT=50 VISIBILITY=HIDDEN><H2>Professional Active
Server Pages</H2></LAYER>
<LAYER NAME="T0707" TOP=300 LEFT=50 VISIBILITY=HIDDEN><H2>Professional Dynamic
HTML and IE4 Programming</H2></LAYER>
<LAYER NAME="T0685" TOP=300 LEFT=50 VISIBILITY=HIDDEN><H2>Instant Dynamic HTML
Programmer's Reference</H2></LAYER>
<LAYER NAME="T0448" TOP=300 LEFT=50 VISIBILITY=HIDDEN><H2>Instant VBScript
Programming</H2></LAYER>
<LAYER NAME="T0464" TOP=300 LEFT=50 VISIBILITY=HIDDEN><H2>ActiveX Web Database
Programming</H2></LAYER>

<!-- Define non-visible layers to pre-load the highlighted book cover images -->
<LAYER NAME="Z0685" TOP=0 LEFT=0 VISIBILITY=HIDDEN><IMG SRC="F0685.gif"></LAYER>
<LAYER NAME="Z0707" TOP=0 LEFT=0 VISIBILITY=HIDDEN><IMG SRC="F0707.gif"></LAYER>
<LAYER NAME="Z0448" TOP=0 LEFT=0 VISIBILITY=HIDDEN><IMG SRC="F0448.gif"></LAYER>
<LAYER NAME="Z0464" TOP=0 LEFT=0 VISIBILITY=HIDDEN><IMG SRC="F0464.gif"></LAYER>
<LAYER NAME="Z0723" TOP=0 LEFT=0 VISIBILITY=HIDDEN><IMG SRC="F0723.gif"></LAYER>

</BODY>
```

You can see that we have an image inside each of the first five layers, holding the dark colored version of the book cover (with filenames starting with "**B**"). Each of these images has an **onMouseDown** event handler defined. The function they call is **SelectedTitle()**, and they provide it with the appropriate book ID number and a second argument that corresponds to the description of the book. You'll see how this works in the next section.

Following the cover image layers is a single layer that will hold the book description. When the page first loads, it displays the text Select a book to see more information. After that there are the five title layers. Each of these has the **VISIBILITY** attribute set to **HIDDEN**, so that they are not visible on the page.

Pre-Loading Images using Layers

Finally come five more layers containing images. These are the bright red book covers, with filenames starting "**F**". The layers all have their **VISIBILITY** attribute set to **HIDDEN** as well. However, this still forces the browser to load and cache the images. When we come to display them, they'll be loaded from the user's cache, instead of having to be fetched across the 'Net. This will, of course, speed up the process, and make the page appear more responsive.

How the Script Section Works

The working parts of the page, in the **<SCRIPT>** section, consist of several global variables and five functions. The first part defines the variables we'll be using, and the descriptions of each book. These descriptions are stored in an array, so that they can be retrieved as required by our code:

```
<SCRIPT LANGUAGE=JAVASCRIPT>

// create a new array to hold the description strings for the books
strDesc = new Array;
strDesc[0] = "Active Server Pages is simply the ... etc. ";
strDesc[1] = "There's no doubt that a lot people ... etc. ";
strDesc[2] = "If you want to produce really stunning ... etc. ";
strDesc[3] = "Learn VBScript Programming fast, with ... etc. ";
strDesc[4] = "The major task every business faces when ... etc. ";

// declare and preset the values of the global variables
intPos = 0;          // position in string when typing description to TEXT layer
strText = "";        // the text description retrieved from the array
strTitle = "";       // the title of the book and index to the title layers
strPrevTitle = "";   // the previous title layer, so it can be hidden
...
```

Resizing the Browser Window

It's important that the user can see all the elements when they view our page, but it uses absolute positioning, which means that the contents won't move about, to fit neatly into the browser window. This situation is similar to the previous example, where you might not have been able to see all the jigsaw pieces when you first loaded the page. In this page, we're reacting to the window object's **onLoad** event, and using it to change the size of the browser window to suit our page:

```
...
window.onLoad = SizeWindow();

function SizeWindow()
// set the browser window to the correct size for our page
{
  window.resizeTo(600,450);
}
...
```

This is a useful technique, and you can even move the browser window on the screen if required so that all of it is visible. However, take care when moving the window, as your viewers probably won't appreciate having to chase their browser around the screen to click on links in your pages.

Selecting a Book

The second function in the page runs when the user clicks on a book. This is the **SelectTitle()** function we mentioned earlier. It expects to receive a string that is the ID of the book, and a number that indicates which entry it should retrieve from the global array of book descriptions:

```
function SelectTitle(strBookID, intDesc)
// runs when a book cover is clicked by the user
{
   // create a reference to the selected layer
   strSelectLayer = "C" + strBookID;
   objSelectLayer = document.layers[strSelectLayer];

   // change the image source to the foreground picture
   objSelectLayer.document.images[0].src = "F" + strBookID + ".gif";
   ...
```

Given the book ID, it can create a reference to the layer containing that cover image—these layer names all start with "**C**". This reference is stored in the variable **objSelectLayer**. Then, it's a simple matter to change the image in that layer to the bright red foreground picture. To get to the image, we use the **images** array of the document in that layer, for which we stored a reference in the variable **objSelectlayer** earlier.

Changing the Stacking Order

We've now got a foreground-style image in the layer, but it could well still be stacked behind other layers. To bring it to the front, we can use the **moveAbove** method of the **layer** object. We need to call this method for all the other cover image layers, using our new 'front' layer. To do this, we'll loop through the **layers** array of the main document:

```
...
// loop through all the book cover layers
for (intLay = 0; intLay < document.layers.length; intLay++)
{
   // get the layer name
   strLayerName = document.layers[intLay].name;

   // if it's a cover layer with name like 'Cxxx'
   if (strLayerName.substr(0, 1) == "C")
   {
      // see if it's the selected layer
      if (strLayerName != strSelectLayer)
      {
         // if not, change source of it's cover image to the background one
         strNewSource = "B" + strLayerName.substr(1, 4) + ".gif";
         document.layers[intLay].document.images[0].src = strNewSource;

         // and move it below the selected layer
         objSelectLayer.moveAbove(document.layers[intLay]);
      }
   }
}
...
```

Within the **for** loop, we extract the layer's **name** property from the **layers** array using the index, and see if it's a cover array. Remember there are several other layers in the document as well, and we only want to pull our selected cover in front of the four other cover layers. If it is a cover layer, but not the selected layer, we use the **moveAbove** method of the selected layer, providing the layer we want to move in front of as the argument.

183

But before we can actually do this, there's something else we have to do. We need to make sure that any previously selected cover is returned to its original dark red cover image. If we change the stacking order of the array first, the layer index we saved in **intLay** will refer to the wrong layer. So, we create the background cover image filename, and assign it to the image's **src** property, before we call the **moveAbove** method.

Preparing to Show the Title and Description

Before we can finish the **SelectedTitle()** function, we have a few more things to do. We need to zero the variable that holds the current length of the 'typed' string of characters that form the book description, and set the global **strText** and **strTitle** variable ready for other functions to display them. We also need to hide any title layer that might be visible from a previous book selection, and stop the interval timer that will be running if there was a previous selection. The variable **strPrevTitle** will hold the name of the title layer that was made visible last time, if there was one:

```
...
// zero the 'typed string' length pointer
intPos = 0;

// get the description string and name of title layer
strText = strDesc[intDesc];
strTitle = "T" + strBookID;

// if we've got a selection at the moment, we need to remove it
if (strPrevTitle.length > 0)
{
  // hide the title layer, and stop the interval timer
  document.layers[strPrevTitle].visibility = "hidden";
  window.clearInterval(timTyping);
}
...
```

Finally, we can clear the contents of the description layer (named **TEXT**) by opening and closing its document, then call the next function in the chain—**SetTitle()**:

```
...
// clear the contents of the description layer
document.layers["TEXT"].document.open();
document.layers["TEXT"].document.close();

// finally, we set the process going for the selected title
SetTitle();
}
```

Setting Up and Scrolling the Book Title into View

The **SetTitle()** function has the task of preparing the page to display the book title, then starting off the process of scrolling it into view. The first step is to position the appropriate layer off to the right of the page, and make it visible. Notice that this time we've used the **moveToAbsolute** method of the layer, rather than setting its **top** and **left** properties directly. Then we save this title in the variable **strPrevTitle**, so that we can hide it again when the user makes a different selection:

```
function SetTitle()
// positions and makes the relevant title layer visible
{
  document.layers[strTitle].moveToAbsolute(600, 270);
  document.layers[strTitle].visibility = "show";

  // save the title ready for the next user selection
  strPrevTitle = strTitle;

  // and start the scroll timer running
  timTyping = window.setInterval("ScrollTitle()", 50);
}
```

The final line starts an interval timer running, with an interval of 50ms. This will execute our **ScrollTitle()** function each time it fires. The **ScrollTitle()** function has a simple enough task. It just moves the appropriate title layer to the left 10 pixels each time it is executed. Remember, we stored the name of the selected title layer in the global variable **strTitle** back in the **SelectTitle()** function:

```
function ScrollTitle()
// scrolls the title into view across the screen
{
  // move the layer ten pixels to the left
  document.layers[strTitle].pageX = document.layers[strTitle].pageX - 10;

  // stop when the layer is near the left edge of the page
  if (document.layers[strTitle].pageX < 50)
  {
    // clear the timer, and reset it to start typing the description
    window.clearInterval(timTyping);
    timTyping = window.setInterval("TypeText()", 100);
  }
}
```

Once the title layer gets within 50 pixels of the left edge of the document, we stop the interval timer and set a new one going (there's no problem with using the same reference **timTyping** for it). This interval timer will now run the **TypeText()** function every 100 ms.

Typing the Description into the Page

So, we're nearly there. The final function in our page, **TypeText()**, just displays the description of the book by adding one character at a time to the layer named **TEXT**. It does this using the **write** method of the layer's **document** object. However, each time we open the document to write to it, the existing content is lost—so we actually write the entire new content each time.

The global variable **intPos** has been previously set to zero in the **SelectTitle()** function. Each time our function is executed, we write that many characters from the description string we placed in the global variable **strText** (again in the **SelectTitle()** function) to the layer, then increment **intPos**. Once it exceeds the length of the string, **strText.length**, we can stop the interval timer running, and our page is complete:

```
function TypeText()
// types the text of the book description into the bottom layer
{
```

```
   // open the layer's document, and write the text to it
   document.layers["TEXT"].document.open();
   document.layers["TEXT"].document.write("<P>" + strText.substr(0, intPos) + "</
P>");
   document.layers["TEXT"].document.close();

   // increment the length of the string to show in the layer
   intPos ++;

   // stop when the string is all displayed
   if (intPos > strText.length) window.clearInterval(timTyping);
}

</SCRIPT>
</HTML>
```

Notice that we surround the text we write into the layer with the `<P>` and `</P>` tags. This is because we defined the style for this tag in the `<HEAD>` section of the page to represent typed monospace characters.

Using Signed Scripts

In earlier chapters, we discovered that quite a few of the features available through script and the object model can only be used when the script has been **signed**. In essence, we must be able to convince the browser (and ultimately the user) that the code they are about to run will not harm their system or provoke a security risk. This applies not only to scripts written in JavaScript, of course, but also to any other code that we include in our pages. This could be a Java Applet, or other component.

In this book, we're interested in the language Dynamic HTML, and don't have the space to provide a full discussion of security in the browser. For most of the things we want to do, it will not be an issue anyway. However, it's worth knowing something about the subject—and in this final section of the chapter, we'll take a look at how signed scripts are integrated into our pages.

What Is Object Signing?

One of the problems with using any communication system that can transfer and execute code on the client (your browser) is that a malicious author could use these capabilities to do damage to your machine, or compromise security and steal information. As browsers become more complicated and feature-laden, and as the languages they understand grow in capabilities, the potential for this kind of damage increases.

To help minimize the dangers, browser manufacturers have developed the concept of signing code, so that the original author can be identified and any unauthorised changes to the code can be detected. To sign code for use in Communicator, we can use a special utility that is available from Netscape's Web site. Follow the Security link from `http://developer.netscape.com/library/documentation/index.html`

Object signing involves converting the code into a package that cannot be changed without the browser detecting the changes. Users will be warned that the code has been tampered with, and that they should be wary of running it unless they can confirm that it is safe. In many cases, the browser will prevent them from running the code at all.

Of course, as you saw back in Chapter 4, editing the Preferences file can turn off this feature. The browser will then allow you to run unsigned code.

The JAR Packager Tool

The tool that allows us to sign code, and produce the packages we need to send to our viewers, is called the **JAR Packager**. It gets its name from the filename of the packages—they have the file extension **.jar** (Java Archive). The resulting package is examined by the browser before being unpacked and installed or executed.

To be able to sign scripts or code, we obviously need a signature. This is generally termed a **digital certificate**, and can be obtained from an appropriate Certificate Authority (CA) such as Verisign. This certificate identifies you or your organization, and allows code to be traced back to you.

The JAR Packager automatically compresses the code, then encrypts it using your certificate information. This is in effect your 'private key', and only this can be used to create the JAR package. However, your 'public key', which can be used to unencrypt it, is freely available. This means that anyone can use the code by applying the public key, but only you can create the package in the first place.

A JAR package can contain more than one digital signature, and several scripts can be included. However, as the code is delivered in a separate package, it means that you can't use it to create signed scripts that are part of a page, or 'in-line' code. Instead, this is the job of the Page Signer tool.

The Page Signer Tool

Netscape is developing a tool that will allow in-line code within a page to be signed, without having to download it as a separate file. The **Page Signer** is an interim solution, using a Perl script, and can be downloaded from Netscape's Documentation site as well. In time, a complete tool will be available to make the task easier. Until then, you may prefer to use the JAR Packager directly to package up scripts, and insert them into the page using the **ARCHIVE**, **SRC** and **ID** attributes of the **<SCRIPT>** tag—the subject of the next section.

Using Signed Scripts in Pages

Once we have created a signature for our script, we need to be able to define it in our pages. This is done with the **ARCHIVE** attribute, and optionally the **ID** attribute, in the **<SCRIPT>** tag. The **ARCHIVE** attribute defines the JAR file that contains the signature, and the **ID** attribute connects the script to that signature. In this example, the code has been signed with the digital signature in the JAR file identified with the **ID** of **1**:

```
<SCRIPT ARCHIVE="MyJarFile.jar" ID="1">
   // script code goes here
</SCRIPT>
```

If the script is loaded from a separate file, we define the JAR file that contains the signature in the **ARCHIVE** attribute, and use the **SRC** attribute, instead of **ID**, to indicate where the script is to be loaded from:

```
<SCRIPT ARCHIVE="MyJarFile.jar" SRC="MyScript.js">
</SCRIPT>
```

When there is more than one script in a page, we only need to define the **ARCHIVE** attribute in the first **<SCRIPT>** tag. In this case, each **ID** attribute defines the signature that applies to that script:

```
<SCRIPT ARCHIVE="MyJarFile.jar" ID="1">
   // first script code goes here
</SCRIPT>
...
<SCRIPT ID="2">
   // second script code goes here
</SCRIPT>
```

Signed In-line Event Handlers

The **ARCHIVE** attribute can only be used in a **<SCRIPT>** tag, so when we use in-line scripts, we have to define the JAR file separately first. We can't define it within the in-line code. This means that a 'dummy' script must precede the in-line code:

```
<SCRIPT ARCHIVE="MyJarFile.jar" ID="1">
   // some dummy code here
</SCRIPT>
...
<IMPUT TYPE=BUTTON ONCLICK="alert('You clicked me');" ID="2">
```

Why Use Signed Scripts?

One of the reasons for signing script code, rather than applets or plug-ins, is to allow the script to access areas of the browser that are normally 'off-limits'. Within a signed script, we can request extended privileges using the Netscape **PrivilegeManager** object:

netscape.security.PrivilegeManager.enablePrivilege("*privilege_required*"**)**

There are four privilege levels we can request, **UniversalBrowserWrite**, **UniversalBrowserRead**, **UniversalFileRead** and **UniversalSendMail**.

The Expanded Privileges

UniversalBrowserWrite allows our scripts to:

 Add or remove a window's title bar, directory bar, location bar, menu bar, personal bar, scroll bars and toolbar, either directly or with the **window.open** method.

- Move a window off screen with the **MoveBy** or **MoveTo** methods or position properties, or make it smaller that 100 pixels square or larger than the screen using **resizeTo** and **resizeBy** or size properties.

- Make a window appear 'always on top' (**alwaysRaised**) or 'always underneath' (**alwaysLowered**) other windows, or set its **z-lock**.

- Close a window other than the current one, or enable external event capturing in other windows.

- Change the **Event** object's properties, or the **History** object's **preferences** property.

UniversalBrowserRead allows our scripts to:

- Read the **History** object's properties

- Read the **data** property of the **Event** object for a **DragDrop** event

- Use a URL starting with **about:** (The URL **about:blank**, which just displays a blank page, is available without the expanded privilege).

UniversalFileRead allows our scripts to set the file name when using a **FileUpload** control element.

UniversalSendMail allows our scripts to submit the contents of a form to a URL which starts with **mailto:** or **news:**.

Summary

In this chapter, we've examined in more detail the way that one of the important additions to Netscape Communicator and Dynamic HTML works. By using **layers**, we can add a whole set of new features to our pages to make them 'come alive'—and provide all kinds of effects that were not previously possible unless embedded applets or other controls were used.

We've seen how we can:

- Change the stacking order of layers, using their properties and methods

- Hide or show layers, by changing their **visibility** property

- Move and resize layers, by changing their **top**, **left**, **pageX**, **pageY**, and clipping properties

- Change the background color or picture in a layer, or make it transparent again

- Change the entire contents of a layer, either by loading a different page or writing new content to it from script with the **document.write** method

Finally, we finished up by looking at how we can use signed scripts, both to protect our users from malicious code and to access extra features within the browser. Object and script signing are complex subjects, which we can't do justice to in their entirety in this book. For more information, and a complete guide to Netscape's implementation of security in the browser, visit **http://developer.netscape.com/library/documentation/index.html** and follow the Security link.

We've now completed our tour of Dynamic HTML as far as describing how it is used. In the final chapter, we'll take a look at the upcoming standards for the new version of HTML, and see how they compare to Netscape's current implementation. We'll also investigate how we can make our Dynamic HTML pages compatible with the other new mainline browser—Microsoft's Internet Explorer 4.0.

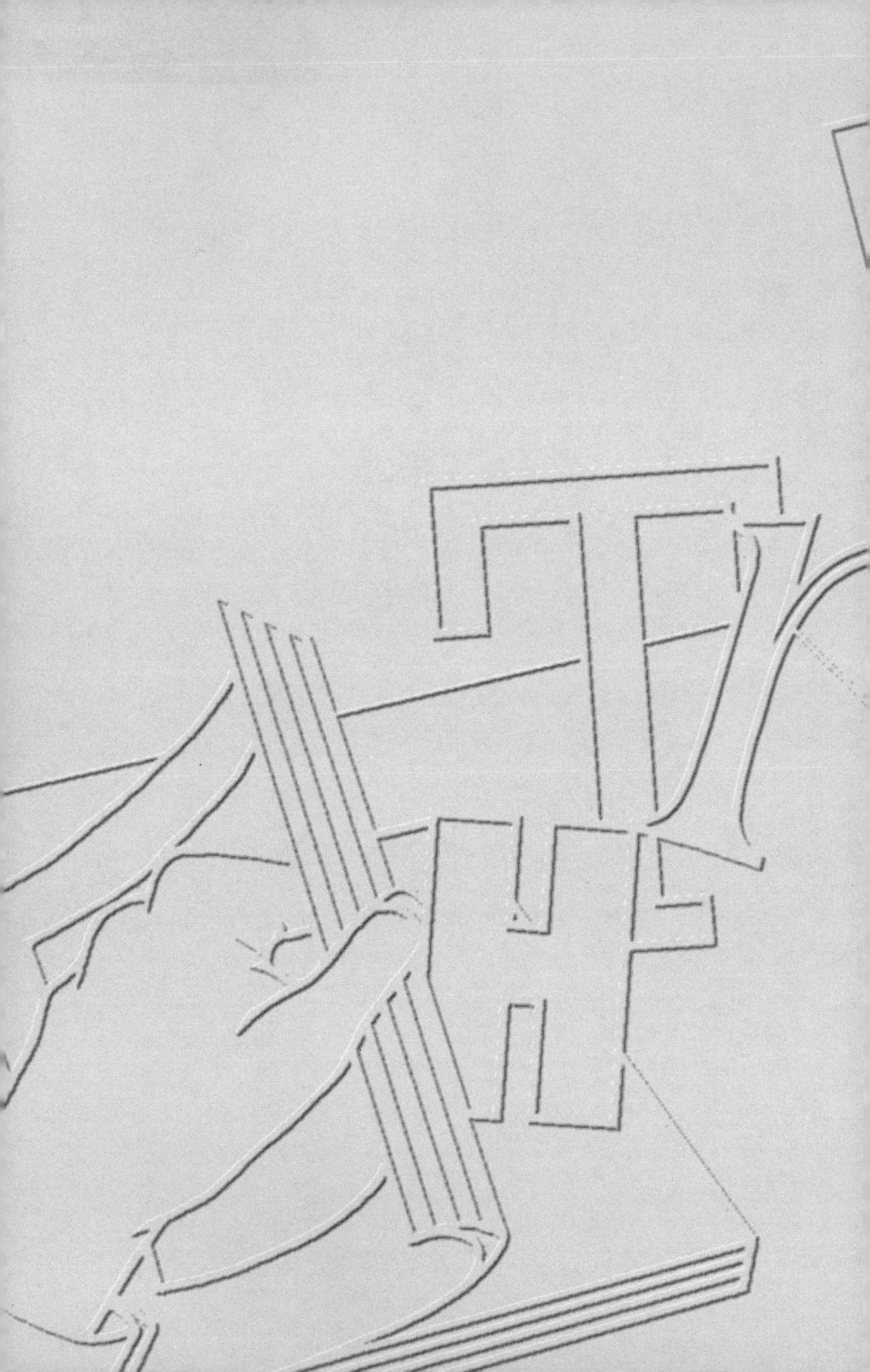

Browser Compatibility and the Future of HTML

In the introduction to this book, we talked about the World Wide Web Consortium (W3C) Project Cougar proposals, ultimately paving the way for HTML 4.0. At the time of writing, W3C had just published the first working drafts of HTML 4.0, to cover the tags and attributes that they expect to be part of the final ratification. However, what we haven't done is to look at what Project Cougar actually encompasses. We avoided a dry and technical discussion of the current proposals in favor of showing you what Dynamic HTML can do, and how you can use it to make your web pages more interactive—and more dynamic.

We also mentioned the problems that always arise when HTML standards change or are updated. At the time of writing, both the major players in the game (Microsoft and Netscape) have released versions of their browser with support for Dynamic HTML. In this final chapter, we'll look at how each of them compares to the current proposals.

We also need to consider the issue of compatibility between these two browsers, not only how they compare in support for Dynamic HTML, but how compatible they are with existing standards as well. Unless you are working in the confined environment of an Intranet, where you can control which browser is used and which pages are available for viewing, you must consider how you go about supporting existing pages out there on the Internet as a whole.

So, this chapter will cover:

- The outline proposals for Project Cougar and HTML 4.0 (or Dynamic HTML as it has been christened by the two main browser manufacturers)

- The compatibility of these two main browsers with the proposals, and with each other

- The compatibility of the two new browsers with existing pages

- How we can create pages that are compatible with both of the new browsers

We'll start with a look at what W3C are currently discussing as the new version of HTML.

Project Cougar - HTML for the Future

Some would say that HTML standards are a mess. Different browsers support different feature sets, and we still await the final ratification of the most recently agreed standard—HTML 3.2. However, W3C have a huge task to accomplish, and progress in the software industry doesn't take time off to wait for them. As fast as they can agree on new standards for one generation of HTML, the mainline manufacturers are bringing out new browsers with even more new and product-specific features.

However, none of this is the reason for the upheaval that Project Cougar (or HTML 4.0) will bring to the whole game. The problem is that in other areas of development, such as word processing, document management, presentation systems and desktop publishing, the ability to produce ever more complex and dynamic results means that the Web browser is being left behind. On top of this, the Web browser is fast becoming a tool for running application interfaces for Web-based client/server programs—a task that sorely stretches its current abilities to provide a visually appealing and interactive front end for this kind of task.

The Evolving of HTML Standards

But, of course, the explosive growth of the Internet for all kinds of activities has taken most people by surprise. The fundamental way that HTML and the Web work means that the page is still constructed with a very basic structure. Essentially, the HTML source and any other content is flowed into a single column window—although it is possible to control the position of elements to some extent through the use of alignment attributes, tables and relative spacing between elements. In more complex pages, the window may be divided up into frames or use layers—but each of these is, again, just a simple single-column page.

As we explained in Chapter 1, the way that the HTML tags and attributes actually define the elements of the page is laid down in a series of Document Type Definitions (DTDs), written using a language called Standard Generalized Markup Language (SGML). These lay down the syntax requirements and provide browser manufacturers with a detailed guide to how the elements should behave. As we've seen, however, it's often the browser manufacturers who add the tag to their products first, leaving W3C to decide if, and how, to adopt it as part of the HTML standards.

The Traditional Structure of the Document

The inclusion of scripting in the browser has also produced a new area of compatibility problems. As long as the appearance of the page is mainly due to the elements it contains, the browser just has to accept them in the HTML stream coming from the server and render them visibly on screen. Provided that everything is in the right place, in theory at least, you've done the job.

All this falls apart when you add programmability to the browser, where scripts written in the page—or within an external plug-in component—can access the page elements and change their contents. To do this, the browser has to organize the elements into a structural hierarchy that provides the scripting language with clearly defined access to them. And for pages to be compatible between different browsers, they must all implement this structure in exactly the same way.

W3C refers to this structure as the **Document Object Model**, though—as you've seen in this book—that isn't the whole story. The browser will actually implement an object model that contains another layer of objects 'above' the document itself, the **window** object and associated objects and collections (or object arrays). These allow the script to access the browser itself, as well as the document(s) it is displaying. Project Cougar aims to define the Document Object Model as well as the tags and attributes that are available.

> *The current documentation, proposals and working drafts for Project Cougar and HTML 4.0 are available from the W3C Web site at* **http:// www.w3.org/pub/www/TR/**. *At the time this book was being written, the first working draft of HTML 4.0 had just been released. The manufacturers who are listed as part of the Cougar development team are Adobe, Hewlett Packard, IBM, Microsoft, Netscape Communications, Novell, SoftQuad and Sun Microsystems.*

Project Cougar in Outline

Back in Chapter 1, we listed the new features of Dynamic HTML that we've concentrated on in this book. They were:

- **Cascading and JavaScript style sheets** which give the developer a lot more control over the positioning and formatting of elements on a page. They provide hooks to the page elements from scripting code

- **Absolute positioning of elements**, including **control of the z-order**, allows a desktop publishing style of authoring, and 'two-and-a-half-D' appearance

- **The Document Object Model** provides more programmability for JavaScript used in the pages

- **Dynamic re-drawing** of any or all parts of the page allows changes to a loaded page to be made visible. Pages no longer need to be reloaded to show the updated version

- **New event-handling techniques** are supported, including the ability to capture events and route them through the object hierarchy

- **Dynamic Fonts** which allow the developer to create new fonts for others to download, as they would do with image files

- **Canvas Mode** lets the developer view the window or HTML page in "full screen" mode, which takes up the entire screen

While these are part of a whole raft of the Project Cougar proposals, they are by no means the only new features. It's just that these are the ones that represent the real advances as far as the web page author is concerned. We'll go back a little, and see where the initial proposals for Cougar came from.

The Background to Project Cougar

The main motivation behind the search for a new approach to web page design is the problem of keeping up with both the changing methods of document production and the continual evolution of document appearance. The challenge is to provide a language that can produce these ever more complex and dynamic pages, while maintaining backward compatibility with existing HTML standards.

All the changes to HTML are controlled by the **HTML Working Group** at W3C. This is made up of the leading software and hardware manufacturers in the industry, and individuals who have helped to develop the technology of the Web so far. Their target is to provide a language that supports:

- Interactive Documents and Rich Forms
- Dynamic Pages Driven by Script Code
- More Flexible Frames and Subsidiary Windows
- Better Multimedia Object Handling
- Improved Access for People with Disabilities

We've seen how many of these aims are being met in earlier chapters. The complete proposal will also go on to tackle tasks such as:

- Support for different fonts and other internationalization issues
- Security in scripts through digital signatures
- An improved mechanism for providing information about the page to both web search engines and 'viewing control programs' that monitor pages for the type of content

The New Document Object Model

The current "work in progress" documentation describes the overall structure of a document object model that is language neutral and platform independent. It includes the proposal that *all* elements, their attributes, their style properties and their contents will be:

- Part of a defined object structure within the user agent (i.e. the browser). This will include 'implied' elements, such as `<HTML>`, `<HEAD>` and `<BODY>`
- Accessible from within the document by scripting code embedded there, and by external agents (such as components, plug-ins or embedded controls)
- Able to generate events that bubble up through the document structure

In essence, these three statements describe the kinds of things we've been looking at throughout the book. It's clear that either the browser manufacturers have worked quickly to implement the proposals, or that (and of course this is the most likely) the proposals were drawn up based on original developments by the browser manufacturers themselves. Whichever is the case, the outline drafts of the project already provide a good guide to what the language will have to offer in the long term.

Browser Compatibility with Cougar

As we've suggested earlier, the two mainline browsers aren't completely in line with all the current proposals being discussed as part of Project Cougar. This isn't surprising, as the proposals themselves are open to change—W3C describes them as 'work in progress'. In particular, the current release of Netscape Communicator (4.0) suffers from being first to market. The range of tags it supports is quite different from those described in the working drafts of HTML 4.0. However, Netscape have assured the industry that they will be adopting the recommendations as soon as they are ratified.

Microsoft's Internet Explorer 4 is, in many ways, a much more wide-ranging project than Netscape has taken on with Communicator. It aims to link directly into the core of the Windows operating system to provide a seamless Web/Internet/Desktop environment. This will of course mean that the Active Desktop features of Internet Explorer will be locked into the Windows operating system. Communicator, on the other hand, has always been available for a wide range of platforms—including Unix and its derivatives. Unix is still at the heart of the Internet as a whole, so cross-platform compatibility remains very high on their agenda. However, the Communicator project does include features that can use the desktop as a browser window.

> To learn more about Internet Explorer 4, and the entire Active Desktop environment, look out for **Professional Dynamic HTML and IE4 Programming (ISBN 1-861000-70-7)**, from Wrox Press.

So, it's possible that everything could change in the months to come, as the standard gets closer to ratification. In the meantime, it means that you, the web page author, need to be aware of which way the HTML ship is sailing, and how close each browser is likely to be to its destination port.

Netscape Communicator 4

In this book, we've based our exploration of Dynamic HTML on Netscape's new browser, Communicator 4 (NC4). As we said earlier, its current incarnation does not follow the working drafts for HTML 4.0 as closely as Netscape probably would have preferred. However, in most areas, it does provide much of the functionality that Project Cougar is attempting to bring to the language.

Structure Navigation, Document and Content Manipulation

The first thing to note is that NC4 doesn't attempt to provide access to *all* the elements in the page. The element object arrays that were part of the previous

197

browser object model— such as **plugins**, **embeds**, **applets**, **forms**, **elements**, etc—are still available through JavaScript, but there is no universal array of all the element tags. The **tags** and **ids** arrays only provide access to the styles that have been applied to individual elements. These arrays are not 'true' document object arrays either, in that they have no **length** property and cannot be iterated through like the other element arrays.

The major new system for providing dynamic content is based on two new tags, **<LAYER>** and **<ILAYER>**. These can be positioned (absolutely in the case of the **<LAYER>** tag), moved, hidden, and their content and z-order changed, while the main document is displayed in the browser. They also provide a parent/child navigation system through special properties. However, few of the other existing elements have these kinds of abilities. For example, it isn't possible to absolutely position headings, images, or other block elements, without placing them within a **<LAYER>** element.

NC4 can retrieve the contents of the current user's selection in the document, as a simple string, using the **getSelection** method. It can search for text in the page using the new **find** method. There is no system for changing the displayed content outside a layer, although this is not generally a problem. Layers are flexible enough to allow a page to be created where the contents can be changed dynamically by code running in the browser.

The Event Model

The Project Cougar proposals include the requirement for the browser to provide a rich selection of events for all objects, which can be bound to script code in order to allow the construction of completely interactive documents.

NC4 implements a new **Event** object that provides information about all the scriptable events that are occurring in the browser. Instead of providing event bubbling as the default, as discussed by W3C, Communicator implements a system called **event capturing**. The **document** or **window** can be instructed, with the **captureEvents** method, to capture events originally destined for a contained element. The event can then be handled or routed to the original element with a **routeEvent** method call. This system also allows events to be captured in other documents loaded into a **<FRAMESET>**, depending on the security settings in those documents.

Project Cougar specifies a 'rich set of events for all elements', and NC4 doesn't fully deliver at present. New events are available, but the range of elements to which they apply is very limited. For example, the new **mouse** and **key-press** events provide a lot of opportunity to make pages more reactive to the viewer. However, they are generally restricted to elements like the document, links, and in some cases images.

Styles and Style Sheet Object Model Support

Netscape were early adopters of the use of styles and style sheets, and NC4 is documented as offering 'full support for the CSS1 standards'. This includes the recommendations for the new positioning properties and—once defined—the styles can be accessed using JavaScript to provide dynamic pages.

Netscape have also developed a separate style language called **JavaScript Style Sheets** (JSS). We've seen this in use throughout this book. It works in a similar way to CSS, but uses JavaScript methods to assign the styles to elements. It provides absolute positioning to some elements, and access to the style properties of most of the elements in the page.

NC4 now contains a JavaScript **delete** method that can remove objects, properties or elements from the page. Finally, NC4 provides support for the two tags **<SPAN>** and **<DIV>**, in a way that is documented to be compatible with the current proposals. Remember, however, that the **<DIV>** tag in NC4 does not provide any events, and so is not compatible with dynamic pages that use events generated from a **<DIV>** tag.

Document and Error Information

The Project Cougar proposals require the browser to expose information about the document, its embedded objects, the user agent (browser) itself and any cookies available for the current document. This is done using the **window** and **document** objects, plus their subsidiary objects (such as **navigator**), and the various arrays of contained objects (such as **images**, **links**, **forms**, etc.)

Project Cougar also requires a document-wide error reporting and logging system to be in place. Through JavaScript, NC4 provides an **onerror** event for images and the script in the page. There is no indication of how it will support other document-based errors at present.

Scripting Languages

The Project Cougar Scripting proposals include the requirement for support of the **SRC** and **TYPE** attributes in a **<SCRIPT>** tag, allowing a script to be downloaded separately from the initial document.

NC4 implements an interpreter for JavaScript, and the **<SCRIPT>** tag supports the **SRC** attribute in order to allow signed (secure) scripts to be imported into a page. However, this is not completely in line with current Project Cougar proposals, although it is closer than Internet Explorer 4 at present.

Changes are also proposed in the HTML 4.0 working drafts to replace the **LANGUAGE** attribute with **TYPE**, i.e. **TYPE="script/javascript"**. This is not supported at present.

Enhanced HTML Forms

Project Cougar, and the HTML 4.0 working draft, talk about providing better access to elements on a form. This is with new attributes such as **DISABLED**, **READONLY**, **ACCESSKEY** and **TABINDEX**. There are also new tags proposed— **<BUTTON>**, **<FIELDSET>**, **<LEGEND>** and **<LABEL>**. There are even indications of future direction in the provision of more intrinsic controls such as scroll bars, tabular entry fields and multiple page layouts.

In Communicator version 4.0, there is no support for these enhanced HTML forms. As enhanced forms were originally a Microsoft proposal, it's perhaps not surprising that this feature is yet to be implemented in NC4. It's likely that there will be some considerable changes to the working drafts in this area before final ratification.

Communicator and the <OBJECT> Tag

Communicator does not support the **<OBJECT>** tag at present, despite rumors circulating during its development. In general, executable objects are inserted using an **<APPLET>** tag, and embedded documents and other files with an **<EMBED>** tag. The proposals for HTML 4.0 suggest that both these tags will disappear, to be replaced with **<OBJECT>**. In fact, even the **<IMG>** tag is destined to be replaced by extensions to the **<OBJECT>** tag. We'll take a look at these proposals later in this chapter.

Internet Explorer 4

Internet Explorer 4 provides support for almost the entire set of current Project Cougar Document Object Model proposals. This isn't to say that the final specification of HTML 4.0 will use the same object model, properties, methods and events as Internet Explorer—but there is a strong case to be made that IE4 is the more compatible of the two contenders at the moment. However Microsoft have had a poor track record where HTML standards compatibility is concerned and it's likely that, since many of the proposals for HTML 4.0 are originating from Microsoft, this is the main reason that IE4 is currently very closely compliant to Project Cougar proposals.

> *At the time of writing, the Platform Preview (beta 2) version of Internet Explorer 4 had just been released, and it will no doubt change again before final release as part of the Memphis project to create an integrated Web desktop/browser metaphor. However, as with all things Internet-related, it's difficult to define any product as being a 'final' version. Sometimes it's almost like we live in a permanent cycle of beta software!*

We'll look at the new features of Internet Explorer 4 in relation to Project Cougar and HTML 4.0 as it stands today. It provides the conditions necessary for the three main requirements—a defined object structure accessible from JavaScript and VBScript (and other scripting languages that may become available), access to all the elements in the page, and event bubbling by default throughout the object hierarchy.

Structure Navigation, Document and Content Manipulation

IE4 contains methods and properties that meet the laid down requirements for structure navigation and document and content manipulation. Each element has a **parentElement** property, and the object model provides a collection (or array) named **all**—as well as the usual **images**, **links**, **anchors**, **forms**, **elements** etc. It also provides a **contains** method for each element, enabling script to track which elements are contained within others.

New methods such as **innerText** and **outerText** allow script to access, determine and change any of the contents of the document—including the

HTML source—without it having to be within a separate container such as a **<LAYER>** or **<DIV>**. (IE4 does not support layers in the same way as NC4). Properties of any element can be accessed and changed using the **getAttribute**, **setAttribute** and **removeAttribute** methods. In certain cases, new elements can be created and existing ones removed.

IE4 can retrieve the contents of the current user's selection in the document using the new **Selection** object, and provide a range of properties—including the selection type and content—and can also search for text within the page.

The Event Model

IE4 does provide a rich selection of events for all objects, with a raft of new events. All visible elements provide at least a subset of these. For example, even simple text tags like **<H1>** and **<B>** support the **onclick** and **ondblclick** events, plus a full range of mouse events.

On top of this, the event model allows events to bubble up through the object hierarchy by default, and a new **Event** object provides global access to extra parameters of each event—allowing control of this event bubbling. The workings are fundamentally different from Communicator, however, and even the names of the **Event** object's properties are not the same.

Styles and Style Sheet Object Model Support

IE4 supports the CSS1 cascading style sheet standards in general. It also implements an internal **style** object for each element—as required by Project Cougar. This provides script code with access to the style properties for all the elements in the page, and the ability to change them as required. However, IE4 doesn't support the full range of style properties that CSS1 currently includes, such as **padding**, **list-style** and **white-space**. These may appear in subsequent releases.

There are also additions to the existing style sheet standards proposed by Project Cougar, which will allow frames to be created in a document and content to be piped to different frames. Currently this is done using a **<FRAMESET>** and by loading different pages into each frame. Using the new method, a single page will be able to create the frames and divide its content between them. This is not supported in IE4 or Communicator at present.

IE4 does not provide layers, or support the **<LAYER>** and **<ILAYER>** tags. Instead, it uses the two tags, **<SPAN>** and **<DIV>**, in a way that is compatible with the current proposals. The **<DIV>** tag can create document divisions (rather like layers) which can be manipulated from script. They can be sized, moved, absolutely positioned, hidden and the content and z-order changed dynamically.

Document and Error Information

The requirement to expose information about the document, it's embedded objects, the user agent (browser) itself and any cookies is met in the same way in IE4 as it is in NC4. The existing parts of the **window** and **document** object model, plus the subsidiary objects and collections (or arrays), have been generally compatible over previous versions of the two browsers (especially in version 3) and can provide this information.

201

The document-wide error reporting and logging system required by Project Cougar is not fully implemented in IE4, though new objects within the object model now provide properties to indicate the status of various objects, and the scripting languages can provide an object that records and reports scripting errors.

Scripting Languages

At present, IE4 doesn't support the new proposals for the **<SCRIPT>** tag, including the **SRC** and **TYPE** attributes. However, it does contain updated versions of the JScript (compatible with JavaScript 1.1) and VBScript languages.

Enhanced HTML Forms

One area we haven't really explored in detail is the construction of forms in Dynamic HTML. In Communicator 4, not much has changed in this respect. However, the Project Cougar proposals for enhanced forms are either supported or under development in Internet Explorer 4. This includes the new **<LABEL>** and **<BUTTON>** tags.

Improvements to the <OBJECT> Tag

It is proposed in HTML 4.0 to make the **<OBJECT>** tag a generic tag for inserting all kinds of content into a web page. Internet Explorer introduced this tag with support for ActiveX controls, and Microsoft has continued to develop around it. At present, it doesn't fully support all the new recommendations, although Microsoft has stated that the 'final' release version will.

The Future of the <OBJECT> Tag

The **<OBJECT>** tag was introduced by Microsoft to provide a way to insert ActiveX controls into a web page, but is also proposed as a generic tag to be used to insert any kind of object—including Java applets. For that reason, it supports the **CODE** attribute, so that the Java **class** file can be specified. In Netscape Communicator, this is still done using the **<APPLET>** tag because the **<OBJECT>** tag is not supported.

However, the W3C working discussion documents propose to go even further than that. They envisage the **<OBJECT>** tag being used to insert any kind of object, be it Java applets, ActiveX controls or other components, plug-ins, images, audio, video and rich-text formatted files, and embedded documents. In other words, the **<OBJECT>** tag is cited to supercede the **<APPLET>**, **<EMBED>** and **<IMG>** tags, and Microsoft's existing **DYNASRC** attribute. This will provide a single means of embedding a whole range of objects into web documents, and is designed to offer more universal, cross-platform support for our pages.

New Ways to Use the <OBJECT> Tag Attributes

In order to cope with all the different types of content, the **CODETYPE** and **TYPE** attributes of the **<OBJECT>** tag are used to indicate the type of data that the object comprises. **TYPE** is a string description of the content, such as

"application/java-vm" for a Java applet requiring a virtual machine to run, or **"application/avi"** for an AVI file. In general terms, the application that is required is defined by **"application/<**document_type**>"**. The **CODETYPE** argument can be a standard **mime type**, in much the same way as the **TYPE** attribute.

The **DATA** attribute provides the data for the object, either as a URL from where it can be downloaded, or in-line as a string of values. This is much the same way as ActiveX controls work at present. As an example, this code will display an AVI file named **MyVideo.avi**. If the browser can't support the object, it will display the text My Video:

```
<OBJECT DATA="http://mysite.com/video/MyVideo.avi" TYPE="application/avi" ALT="My
Video">
</OBJECT>
```

Here's an example that embeds a local Microsoft Word document into the page. When activated, Word will be used to allow it to be edited:

```
<OBJECT DATA="BankLetter.doc" TYPE="application/msword" ALT="Letter to the bank">
</OBJECT>
```

> *A list of the mime types supported by your machine can be found in Windows registry under HKEY_CLASSES_ROOT\MIME\Database\ContentType\.*

If the data content is reasonably small, the object can be defined by including the data itself in the **<OBJECT>** tag. This is called an **in-line** definition:

```
<OBJECT CLASSID="clsid:663CA835-1E82-3BB2-4112-66FF428C18E3"
    DATA="data:application/x-oleobject;3300,FF00,2756,E5A0,E3A0,22F6, ... etc">
</OBJECT>
```

As you can see from the last example, the **TYPE** and **CODETYPE** attributes are optional. However, in this case, the only way that the browser can be sure of knowing if it can handle the file is by downloading it first—not all files can be uniquely identified from, say, a file extension, and not all systems use file extensions anyway. By including the **TYPE** or **CODETYPE** attribute, we can tell the browser exactly what type of file it is. Then, if the browser can't handle it, it won't waste time and bandwidth downloading it.

Fall Back in Browsers That Don't Support an Object

If the browser can't display the object, it will usually provide some text alternative—as defined either by the **ALT** or **STANDBY** attributes of the **<OBJECT>** tag. However, we can do better than this. We can include text and other elements that are only visible on browsers that either don't recognize the **<OBJECT>** tag, or that can't handle the content type of the data it specifies. This is done by placing it between the opening and closing **<OBJECT>** tags, and outside any parameter tags:

```
<OBJECT DATA="http://mysite.com/video/MyVideo.avi" TYPE="application/avi" ALT="My
Video">
  Sorry, you browser can't support video files, you should upgrade.
</OBJECT>
```

203

We can also use other elements here, perhaps a still image as a **gif** file:

```
<OBJECT DATA="http://mysite.com/video/MyVideo.avi" TYPE="application/avi" ALT="My
Video">
  <IMG SRC="http://mysite.com/stills/MyPicture.gif">
</OBJECT>
```

Inserting Images with an <OBJECT> Tag

One of the most intriguing proposals is the use of the **<OBJECT>** tag to embed ordinary graphics files, such as **gif** and **jpg** files. This is also likely to extend the kinds of graphic files that are supported, possibly to include Windows **bmp** files and **wmf** or other graphics meta files. In its most basic form the use is simple:

```
<OBJECT DATA="MyPicture.gif">
</OBJECT>
```

The **DATA** attribute works just like the **SRC** attribute, but can also accept in-line data where the image is small. This can reduce the time needed to view a page, by reducing the number of server connections required.

```
<OBJECT TYPE="image/jpeg"
  DATA="data:image/jpeg;3300,FF00,2756,E5A0,E3A0,22F6, ... etc">
</OBJECT>
```

And finally, by adding the usual **WIDTH**, **HEIGHT**, **ALT** and **ALIGN** attributes, we have a system that can emulate all the usual **<IMG>** attributes:

```
<OBJECT DATA="MyDog.gif" WIDTH=120 HEIGHT=100 ALIGN=LEFT ALT="A picture of my
dog">
</OBJECT>
```

There are occasions, however, when we use an image to provide a set of clickable hot spots, such as in a graphical menu. These are called **image maps**, and the **<OBJECT>** tag will provide these as well.

Server-side Image Maps

If we include the **SHAPES** attribute in the opening **<OBJECT>** tag any **<A>** tags between this and the closing **<OBJECT>** tag which themselves contain the **SHAPE** attribute, are considered to be definitions of hot-spots in the image. In Dynamic HTML-terminology, these are called **areas**—all image maps expose this set of areas through their **areas** collections.

If the **<A>** tag contains the attribute **ISMAP**, with the **SHAPE** definition of **DEFAULT**, the browser will access the URL in the **<A>** tag and send it the x and y offsets of the mouse pointer within the image as parameters. These can be decoded at the server end in the usual way, and the appropriate page sent back to the browser:

```
<OBJECT TYPE="image/gif" DATA=MyMenu.gif SHAPES>
  <A HREF="/scripts/imagemap.pl" ISMAP SHAPE=DEFAULT> Click here </A>
</OBJECT>
```

Client-side Image Maps

Instead of a round trip to the server to find out which page to load, recent browsers have implemented client-side image maps. The `<OBJECT>` tag can create these as well, by simply adding the list of `<A>` tags inside the `<OBJECT>` tag:

```
<OBJECT TYPE="image/gif" DATA=MyMenu.gif SHAPES>
    <A HREF="page1.htm" SHAPE=RECT    COORDS=5,5,50,35> Page 1</A>
    <A HREF="page2.htm" SHAPE=CIRCLE COORDS=25,50,50>  Page 2</A>
    <A HREF="page3.htm" SHAPE=POLY    COORDS=50,60,125,200,20,200>
        Page 3 </A>
</OBJECT>
```

However, if you are converting existing pages that contain client-side image maps, you may prefer to leave the existing `<MAP>` section intact and reference it separately. This too is possible with the `<OBJECT>` tag and a `USEMAP` attribute:

```
<OBJECT TYPE="image/gif" DATA=MyMenu.gif USEMAP="#MyMap">
</OBJECT>
  ...
  ...
<MAP NAME="MyMap">
  <AREA HREF="page1.htm" SHAPE=RECT
        COORDS=10,10,50,35 ALT="Page 1">
  <AREA HREF="page2.htm" SHAPE=CIRCLE
        COORDS=150,150,50  ALT="Page 2">
  <AREA HREF="page3.htm" SHAPE=POLY
        COORDS=40,60,125,200,20,200 ALT="Page 3">
</MAP>
```

To learn more about client-side image maps, and other HTML 3.2 tags, look out for Instant HTML Programmers Reference, *ISBN 1-861000-76-6, from Wrox Press.*

The Declare Attribute

The new proposals under discussion at the time of writing also suggest a new attribute named **DECLARE**. This will allow the browser to download the object, and embed a container for it in the page, but not actually instantiate it. In other words, its own internal code will not start to run when downloading completes, as is the case with objects at present. This means that you can download and install objects on the users' systems, and set references to them in the page, without having them executing immediately.

Backward Compatibility Issues

Just because a new version of HTML is starting to appear, and new browsers are available to support it, doesn't mean that everyone will be rewriting their site just to take advantage of this. All software (and hardware for that matter) has to cope with issues of backward compatibility.

This is something that is perhaps more important on the Web than in most other situations. The geographical and technical spread of the source documents, and the already confusing mixture of HTML versions and browser-specific language extensions in use, means that any new browser must make every effort to support a huge range of tags and attributes.

It also needs to be forgiving, and cope with pages that may not follow the exact syntactical rules of HTML wherever possible (such as missing `</BODY>` tags, for example), as well as those containing tags it can't handle or doesn't recognize.

Netscape Communicator 4

Netscape's new browser, Communicator 4, is designed to be fully compatible with pages designed for all earlier versions of the Navigator browser. As you'd expect, all the tags and attributes from Navigator 3 and earlier are fully supported and handled in a way that produces the same effect.

Communicator with Old Navigator Pages

Although Communicator 4 contains some changes to the core JavaScript scripting language, these have cleverly been hidden from existing pages. When `LANGUAGE="JavaScript1.2"` is included in the `<SCRIPT>` tag, the browser 'turns on' the new features in the JavaScript interpreter. With any other `LANGUAGE` attribute they are not activated, so existing scripts will work without being changed. Likewise, you can specify `"JavaScript1.1"` or `"JavaScript1.0"` if scripts are written to a particular version of JavaScript.

Communicator with Old Internet Explorer Pages

However, Netscape have made no move towards supporting the features that Microsoft added to version 3 of their browser. Up until then, Microsoft were playing a catch-up game with Navigator, as well as adding their own proprietary tags and attributes. This diversity has been only too clear in the number of sites that display messages such as Designed for Netscape Navigator or Best viewed with Internet Explorer.

In particular, Netscape have not added support for things like the `<MARQUEE>` tag, the `DYNASRC` image attribute, or ActiveX controls. VBScript still requires a separate plug-in to work in Communicator. And Communicator still handles Java Applets using the LiveConnect mechanism, while Internet Explorer wraps them up in an ActiveX/COM interface.

Microsoft Internet Explorer 4

Just as Netscape have made it a priority to support all existing Navigator pages, Microsoft have made sure that Internet Explorer 4 will support all existing pages designed for earlier versions of Internet Explorer. However, they have also 'extended the olive branch' to some extent, by adding features which provide more support for old Navigator-specific pages.

Internet Explorer with Old IE Pages

Internet Explorer 4 supports all the existing tags and attributes from earlier versions of this browser, such as the `<MARQUEE>` tag, and the `DYNASRC` image attribute. This is despite the fact that these will be superceded by the ability of Dynamic HTML to create the same kinds of effects with the core language and the extensions proposed to the `<OBJECT>` tag.

Internet Explorer 4 also brings with it new versions of JScript and VBScript. These are fully compatible with earlier versions of the interpreter, and existing scripts will still work without being changed. However, if pages take advantage of the new features of these languages, while running on the older version, errors will occur. Unlike NC4, IE4 does not support the scripting version number as part of the **LANGUAGE** attribute. However, it does provide the new **ScriptEngine**, **ScriptEngineMajorVersion**, **ScriptEngineMinorVersion** and **ScriptEngineBuildVersion** properties. At the time of writing, in Platform Preview 2, the current version was **VBScript 3.0.1810**.

Internet Explorer with Old Navigator Pages

Microsoft have also added new tags, attributes and integral browser objects to make Internet Explorer 4 better able to handle pages that were aimed at Netscape Navigator 3 and earlier. These are not part of the proposals for Dynamic HTML, but are included simply to widen the browser's appeal, and allow it to do a better job with sites that pronounce themselves Designed for Netscape Navigator.

These additions include new collections of **applets**, **embeds** and **plugins** and support for a wider range of **ALIGN** attribute values and named colors. In general, pages aimed at Navigator should display more intelligently in Internet Explorer 4 than in previous versions of Internet Explorer.

Pages that Work in All Older Browsers

Of course, compatibility issues become even more of a headache if we have to support a range of older browsers. In this case, we can create pages that only use the new features of Dynamic HTML for non-core tasks and effects.

For example, we can create a page that uses the ordinary HTML elements, and works in older browsers; then add extra effects using Dynamic HTML-specific **STYLE** attributes and event code to react to the events that are supported in newer browsers. In an old browser, these new style properties will not be recognized or applied, and the new events will not be fired. However, the page will behave well on most systems.

In general, we can always add **STYLE** and other new attributes to existing tags, and handlers for events that might not be available, without upsetting the older browser. The problem is that there is only so much 'decorative' work you can do in a page without affecting the usability. By trying to maintain backward compatibility, even to the version 3 browsers, all the real advantages of Dynamic HTML must be abandoned.

Creating Compatible Sites and Pages

As you'll have gathered from the previous discussions, we have some difficulties to face if we need to build a web page, or a complete web site, which performs properly for all our visitors. It's pretty obvious that anything designed specifically for a browser that supports Dynamic HTML is not going to look good on an earlier browser unless we go to some lengths to make this happen—it's never going to be an automatic process.

So, let's consider the issues we have to face. At the moment, we could aim to produce pages that:

- Are specific to one Dynamic HTML browser, either Netscape Communicator 4 or Internet Explorer 4, or

- Are designed to produce a similar output on both Dynamic HTML browsers, or

- Work on Dynamic HTML browsers, but still work on version 3 browsers as well, or

- Look OK on all kinds of browsers, on any platform

Of these options, of course, only the first two make sense when using the new features of Dynamic HTML. At the end of the day, the only real answer is to maintain at least two different versions of your complete Web site. An alternative is to have one site with different sections for the areas where you want to exploit the features offered by Dynamic HTML.

Maintaining Separate Sets of Pages

Maintaining two separate sets of pages for a site seems a crazy idea, though it is done already where sites still need to support very old browsers—or specialist browsers that are text-only or designed for people with disabilities. How much extra effort this involves is hard to say, and depends on the size and complexity of the site. Perhaps only a section of it needs to be duplicated, anyway.

Of course, it's safe to assume that in time the majority of visitors will be using the new browsers. You may even make a decision to build a new copy of your site using Dynamic HTML to full effect and abandon development of the existing site, or a section of its pages.

Navigating by Browser Type

To be able to offer separate sites, depending on the browser version, means that we must be able to differentiate between the browsers when they hit our index, or 'welcome' page. We could offer the two separate sets of pages as different choices on the main menu, but this can produce a negative effect. People with old browsers may feel like second-class citizens and may still select the new pages anyway. Instead, we need to make the choice for them in the background. There are different ways of doing this; we'll show you some examples.

Redirecting Visitors Automatically

The easiest way to automatically load a different page, depending on the browser that is accessing our site, is to create a **redirector page**. It is loaded as the default page for the whole site, and uses the different properties or capabilities of each browser to load another page. This second page will be the home page, or index, of the set of pages appropriate for that browser.

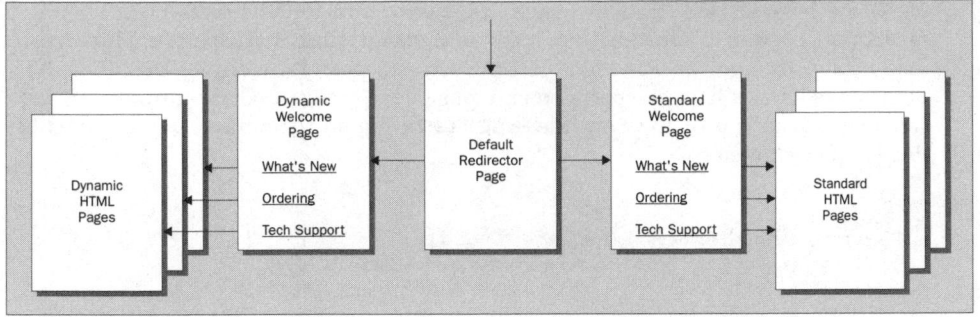

The default redirector page appears as a blank document, and the code in it loads the appropriate home page, a menu for a set of other pages or a single page that is browser specific. All the viewer sees is the browser window clearing followed by the new page loading.

We could include a welcome message, and even a logo or graphic. However, this slows down loading of the page, and—depending on how we load the next page—may disappear again as soon as it's finished loading. Visitors might not get time to read it. Instead, we can give the redirector page a **<TITLE>** of Loading, please wait, which is displayed in the title bar while the next page loads.

Redirection with a META HTTP-EQUIV Tag

One of the most reliable ways to redirect the user is to include a **meta-refresh instruction** in the **<HEAD>** section of the page. This tells the browser to fetch a different page, and we can specify a delay before it does so:

```
<HTML>
<HEAD>
  <TITLE> Loading, please wait </TITLE>
  <META HTTP-EQUIV=REFRESH CONTENT="2;URL=http://mysite.com/std_menu.htm">
</HEAD>
<BODY>
</BODY>
</HTML>
```

This waits 2 seconds (the first part of the **CONTENT** attribute), then loads the URL specified. However, this will always load the *same* new page. We want to be able to load a different page if the browser can support it. This is done by adding some script that redirects the browser before the 2 second delay has expired:

```
  ...
  <META HTTP-EQUIV=REFRESH CONTENT="2;URL=http://mysite.com/std_menu.htm">
</HEAD>
<BODY>
  <SCRIPT LANGUAGE=JAVASCRIPT>
    location.href = "http://www.mysite.com/js_menu.htm";
  </SCRIPT>
</BODY>
  ...
```

Now, the browser will load the page **js_menu.htm** if the browser supports JavaScript, or wait 2 seconds and load **std_menu.htm** if it doesn't. This doesn't really help, though, because lots of browsers support JavaScript—including the older ones. If we have a special menu page for Netscape Communicator 4, we can take advantage of the way the **<SCRIPT>** tag in Communicator can identify the language version:

```
...
<BODY>
  <SCRIPT LANGUAGE="JavaScript1.2">
    location.href = "http://www.mysite.com/nc4_menu.htm";
  </SCRIPT>
  <SCRIPT LANGUAGE=JAVASCRIPT>
    location.href = "http://www.mysite.com/js_menu.htm";
  </SCRIPT>
</BODY>
...
```

This loads the page **nc4_menu.htm** only if the browser can execute JavaScipt version 1.2. Other browsers will get **js_menu.htm** if they support JavaScript at all, or **std_menu.htm** (via the **HTTP-EQUIV** tag) if they don't support JavaScript. Notice that we place the JavaScript 1.2 section before the 'vanilla' JavaScript section, so that it will execute first if the browser supports it.

Of course, we can do the same if we have a section of the site that supports Microsoft-based browsers, or at least those that recognize VBScript:

```
...
<BODY>
  <SCRIPT LANGUAGE="JavaScript1.2">
    location.href = "http://www.mysite.com/nc4_menu.htm";
  </SCRIPT>
  <SCRIPT LANGUAGE=VBSCRIPT>
    location.href = "http://www.mysite.com/vbs_menu.htm"
  </SCRIPT>
  <SCRIPT LANGUAGE=JAVASCRIPT>
    location.href = "http://www.mysite.com/js_menu.htm";
  </SCRIPT>
</BODY>
...
```

Again, we place the JavaScript 1.2 section before the VBScript section, so that it will execute first if the browser supports it. Otherwise, if a VBScript plug-in were available, the browser would execute the jump to the VBScript page instead. As only Communicator 4 can interpret JavaScript version 1.2 (at present), only this browser will execute the code in the first script section. We can even extend this by using the other versions of JavaScript, if we want to redirect older Netscape browsers to specific pages.

The only problem with redirecting using VBScript is that we can't detect which version of the browser it is just from this. Both IE3 and IE4 support the 'vanilla' VBScript. To get round this, we need to use some other properties of the browser.

Redirection Using the Browser's Properties

All browsers that support scripting should make available one or more properties that contain the name and version of the browser. These will generally be properties of the **navigator** object:

Property	Description
appCodeName	The code name of the browser.
appName	The product name of the browser.
appVersion	The version of the browser.
userAgent	The user-agent (browser name) header sent as part of the HTTP protocol.

If we use the **appName** and **appVersion** properties, we can easily identify the manufacturer and the actual version number string. This code displays both in an **alert** dialog:

```
...
<SCRIPT LANGUAGE="JavaScript">
  alert(navigator.appName + ' : ' + navigator.appVersion);
</SCRIPT>
...
```

The results with Communicator 4, Internet Explorer 3.01 and Internet Explorer 4 are shown below:

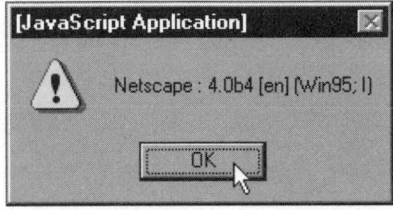

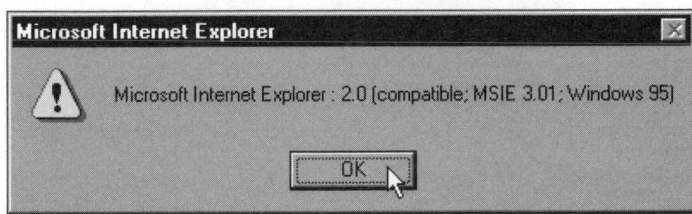

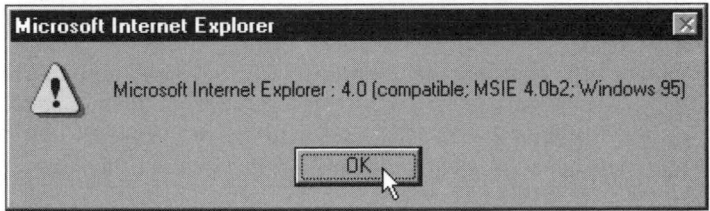

So, our code can read these properties, and decide what to do next. Here's an example—it's written in 'generic' JavaScript, so that it will work on any script-enabled browser. We've also used a **<NOSCRIPT>** tag to provide a message for users whose browser doesn't support scripting at all. They can click on the link we place in the page in this case, and it means that the page can still be used in browsers that don't support the **META HTTP-EQUIV** method either:

211

```
<HTML>
<HEAD>
<TITLE> Loading, please wait </TITLE>
<META HTTP-EQUIV=REFRESH CONTENT="2;URL=http://mysite.com/std_menu.htm">
</HEAD>
<BODY>
<SCRIPT LANGUAGE="JavaScript">

  // Get the manufacturer and version information
  manufacturer=navigator.appName;
  version=navigator.appVersion;

  // Look for Communicator 4
  if (manufacturer.indexOf('Netscape')>=0 && version.indexOf('4.0')>=0)
    location.href='http://mysite.com/nc4_menu.htm';

  // Look for Internet Explorer 4
  if (manufacturer.indexOf('Microsoft')>=0 && version.indexOf('4.0')>=0)
    location.href='http://mysite.com/ie4_menu.htm';

  // Look for some version 3.0x browser
  if (version.indexOf('3.0')>=0)
    location.href='http://mysite.com/v3_menu.htm';

</SCRIPT>

<NOSCRIPT>
  Your browser doesn't support scripting. However, we do
  have a special area of our site for you to visit.
  <A HREF="http://mysite.com/std_menu.htm"> Click here to continue </A>
</NOSCRIPT>

</BODY>
</HTML>
```

You can see an example of automatic redirection, based on the browser version, by visiting the site **http://www.stonebroom.com.**

Cross-Browser Compatible Pages

Having seen how we can offer different pages for different browsers, let's move on to look at what is probably the major topic of concern as the two newest browsers are being developed. We've already seen that each browser is not fully compatible with pages written for the other, but we would like to be able to create Dynamic HTML pages that will work in both of them.

How easy this is depends on the complexity of the page, and the actual effects we are trying to achieve. We'll look at three general situations, static 2.5-D pages using style and font properties, pages that simply access the browser object model in script, and pages that use more complex mixtures of scripting and event handling techniques.

Compatible Style and Font Properties

One of the simplest pages we looked at back in Chapter 2 used the new absolute positioning properties of Dynamic HTML Cascading Style Sheets, in conjunction with some font style properties, to create a simple 3-D title. Loading it into Internet Explorer as it stands doesn't look very encouraging at first:

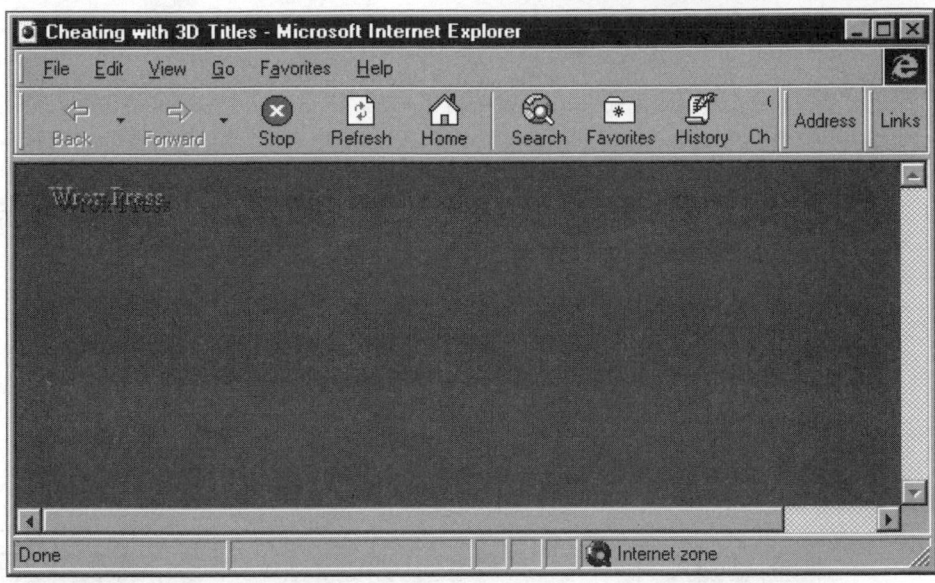

Obviously, we've lost the font family and font size properties somewhere. Here's the original code for the page:

```
<HTML>
<HEAD><TITLE> Cheating with 3D Titles </TITLE></HEAD>

<STYLE TYPE="text/css">
  P { color:red; fontfamily:"Impact", "sans-serif"; fontsize:96 }
  P.highlight { color:silver }
  P.shadow { color:darkred }
</STYLE>

<BODY BGCOLOR=408080>

<DIV STYLE="position:absolute; top:5; left:5; width:600; height:100; margin:10">
<P CLASS=shadow>Wrox Press</P>
</DIV>

<DIV STYLE="position:absolute; top:0; left:0; width:600; height:100; margin:10">
<P CLASS=highlight>Wrox Press</P>
</DIV>

<DIV STYLE="position:absolute; top:2; left:2; width:600; height:100; margin:10">
<P>Wrox Press</P>
</DIV>

</BODY>
</HTML>
```

Managing Incompatible Style Property Names

We know that IE4 supports the **<DIV>** tag, and absolute positioning of the divisions through CSS style sheets. This much is obvious from the screen shot. It also recognizes the color property for the font. The problem is those two style properties, **fontfamily** and **fontsize**. Internet Explorer expects the property names to have a non-standard hyphen like **font-family** and **font-size**, and prefers both the font names to be in the same set of quotation marks—like this:

```
P { color:red; font-family:"Impact, sans-serif"; font-size:96 }
```

The problem now is that Communicator won't recognize the font family and size properties. However, browsers will ignore style properties that they don't support, so we can make our page work on both browsers by including both sets of styles. Here, we've separated the original P definition into three separate ones. The first works for both browsers, and sets the font color. The next one applies the properties appropriate to Communicator, and the one after that the properties appropriate for Internet Explorer:

```
<STYLE TYPE="text/css">
  P { color:red }
  P { fontfamily:"Impact", "sans-serif"; fontsize:96 }
  P { font-family:"Impact, sans-serif"; font-size:96 }
  P.highlight { color:silver }
  P.shadow { color:darkred }
</STYLE>
```

Now the page works fine on both browsers:

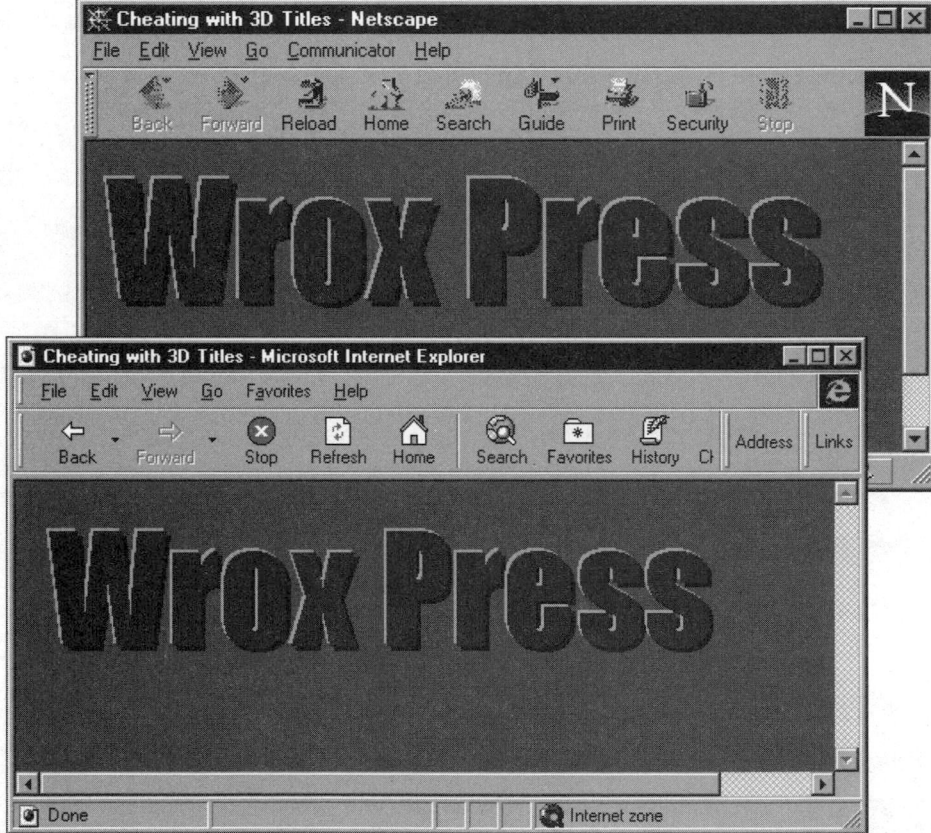

*Notice that placing the different browser-specific properties all in the **same** definition does not work. You need to split them into separate definitions, even though they are applied to the same element type.*

Accessing the Browser Object Model

In Chapter 5, we used a simple page to demonstrate some of the properties that are available from the browser's `location`, `history`, `navigator` and `screen` objects. It worked by creating the complete HTML for the table and the contents in a string variable, then using the `write` method of the `document` object to display it. The page also contained two buttons which, when clicked, used methods of the `history` object to load a different page.

Both of these tasks rely on a common object model, and in these areas the two browsers are reasonably compatible. They both provide the `document.write` and `history.go` methods, and (in the main) the same object properties to include in our table. So we might expect it to work in Internet Explorer.

In this example, we have removed some of the properties originally included in the example in Chapter 5. First, this is what it looks like in Netscape Communicator 4:

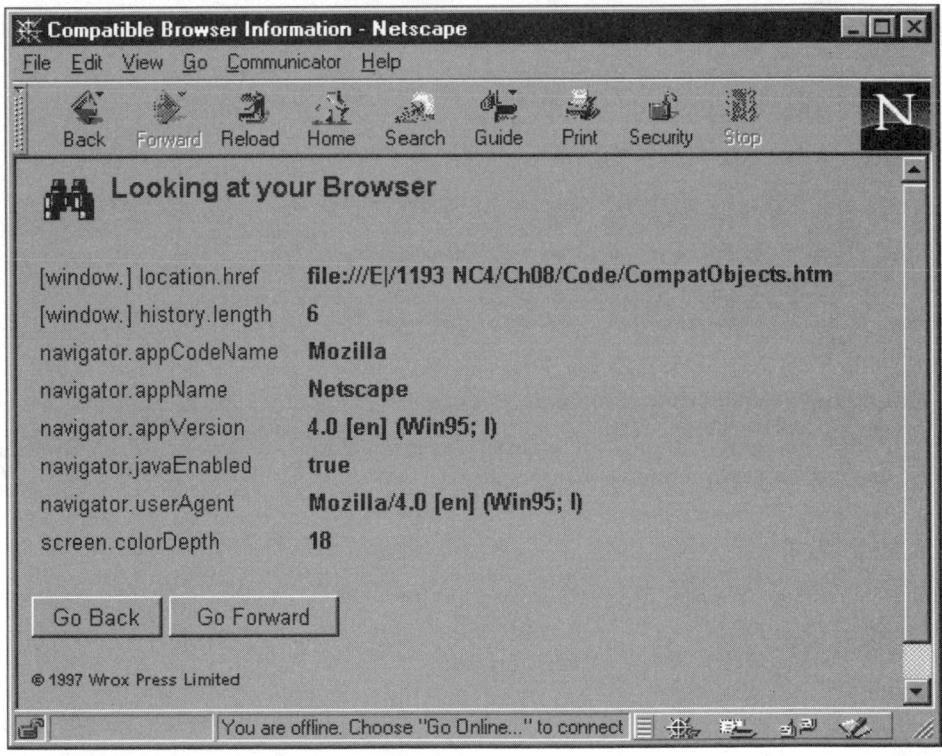

Here's the script section of the document, which creates the string containing the table that you see in the page. It uses values from several of the intrinsic browser objects. You can also see the form section containing the buttons at the bottom of the page:

```
<SCRIPT LANGUAGE="JAVASCRIPT">

var strInfo = "<CENTER><TABLE WIDTH=100%>" +
              "<TR><TD>[window.] location.href</TD>\n" +
              "<TD><B>" + window.location.href + "</TD></TR>\n" +
              "<TR><TD>[window.] history.length</TD>\n" +
              "<TD><B>" + window.history.length + "</TD></TR>\n" +
              "<TR><TD>navigator.appCodeName</TD>\n" +
              "<TD><B>" + navigator.appCodeName + "</TD></TR>\n" +
              "<TR><TD>navigator.appName</TD>\n" +
              "<TD><B>" + navigator.appName + "</TD></TR>\n" +
              "<TR><TD>navigator.appVersion</TD>\n" +
              "<TD><B>" + navigator.appVersion + "</TD></TR>\n" +
              "<TR><TD>navigator.javaEnabled</TD>\n" +
              "<TD><B>" + navigator.javaEnabled() + "</TD></TR>\n" +
              "<TR><TD>navigator.userAgent</TD>\n" +
              "<TD><B>" + navigator.userAgent + "</TD></TR>\n" +
              "<TR><TD>screen.colorDepth</TD>\n" +
              "<TD><B>" + screen.colorDepth + "</TD></TR>\n" +
              "</TABLE></CENTER><P>\n";
document.write(strInfo);

function history_OnClick(dir, dirs) {
  var intPlaces;
  intPlaces = Math.floor((Math.random() * 3) + 1);
  alert("Trying to go " + dirs + " " + intPlaces + " places.");
  window.history.go(dir * intPlaces);
}

</SCRIPT>

<FORM>
  <INPUT TYPE=button VALUE="Go Back" NAME="cmdBack"
         onClick="history_OnClick(-1, 'back')">
  <INPUT TYPE=button VALUE="Go Forward" NAME="cmdForward"
         onClick="history_OnClick(1, 'forward')">
</FORM>
```

Managing Incompatible Browser Objects

When we open this page in Internet Explorer, things at first appear to be fine—the next screenshot shows the results:

216

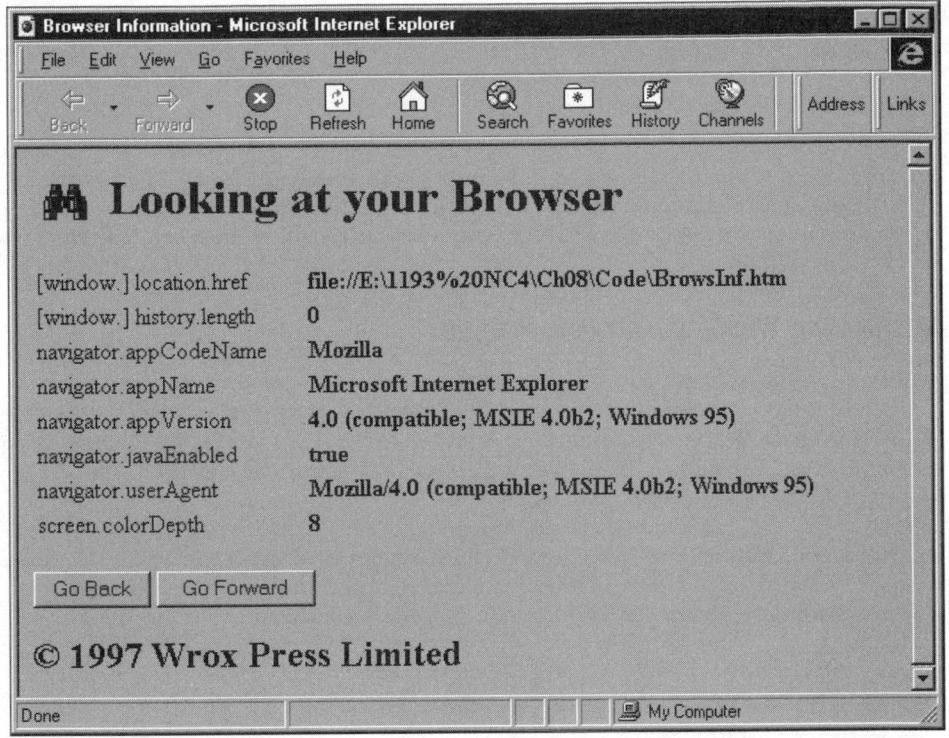

Of course, we've lost the style formatting of the text, because the **STYLE** properties we defined are Communicator-specific. However, the more worrying problem is in the last line in the table. It uses the **screen** object to retrieve the color depth setting. In Communicator, this is the number of colors used, but in Internet Explorer 4 this property returns the number of bits per pixel. Both the screenshots were taken with the system set to 256 colors, but Communicator returns **18** while Internet Explorer returns **8**. To return the 'bits per pixel' in Communicator, we need to refer to the **pixelDepth** property and not the **colorDepth** property.

To get round this, we can use the technique we saw earlier of examining the **navigator.appName** and **navigator.appVersion** to see which browser we're running under, then create the appropriate code in the string that defines the table. Here are the modifications to the code:

```
    . . .
manufacturer = navigator.appName
version = navigator.appVersion;
if (manufacturer.indexOf('Netscape')>=0 && version.indexOf('4.0')>=0)
   tablerow = "<TR><TD>screen.pixelDepth</TD>\n" +
              "<TD><B>" + screen.pixelDepth + "</TD></TR>\n";
if (manufacturer.indexOf('Microsoft')>=0 && version.indexOf('4.0')>=0)
   tablerow = "<TR><TD>screen.colorDepth</TD>\n" +
              "<TD><B>" + screen.colorDepth + "</TD></TR>\n";
var strInfo = "<CENTER><TABLE WIDTH=100%>" +
    . . .
```

```
        ...
        "<TD><B>" + navigator.userAgent + "</TD></TR>\n" +
        tablerow +
        "</TABLE></CENTER><P>\n";
  document.write(strInfo);
  ...
```

Now, we get the correct answer, 8, under both browsers. You can load the finished page, **CompatObjects.htm**, from our Web site at **http://rapid.wrox.co.uk/books/1193**, and view it in either Internet Explorer 4 or Netscape Communicator 4.

Managing More Complex Pages

When we have pages that are more complex than those you've seen so far in this chapter, we have to do a great deal more work to make them compatible with both Netscape Communicator 4 and Internet Explorer 4. We'll demonstrate some of the techniques available, and offer you some tips on how you can adapt them to suit your own pages

In general, we can use a mixture of the techniques we've seen so far to create a page where parts of the content are either ignored by one of the browsers or an appropriate section of HTML code is generated dynamically as the page loads.

Coping with <LAYER> and <DIV> Compatibility

Communicator supports the **<LAYER>** tag to create dynamic document divisions and adds the **<NOLAYER>** tag for use when browsers don't support layers. Internet Explorer uses the **<DIV>** tag to create dynamic document divisions and doesn't recognize the **<LAYER>** or **<NOLAYER>** tags. However, Communicator also recognizes the **<DIV>** tag, though it doesn't behave in quite the same way when we use events in our page.

So, if we need to create an area in the page that responds to mouse events, we have to use a **<LAYER>** tag in Communicator, and a **<DIV>** tag in Internet Explorer. The trick is to get the browser to react correctly in both cases.

By enclosing the **<DIV>** tags inside **<NOLAYER>** and **</NOLAYER>** tags, we prevent Communicator from seeing them, while Internet Explorer will—but it won't recognize the **<LAYER>** tags. However, we have to do this with the opening and closing **<DIV>** tags separately, so that the content of the layer/division is only included once.

```
<LAYER ... >          <- start of layer in NC4

  <NOLAYER>
   <DIV ... >          <- start of division in IE4
  </NOLAYER>

   Content             <- the contents of the layer or division

  <NOLAYER>
   </DIV>              <- end of division in IE4
  </NOLAYER>

</LAYER>               <- end of layer in NC4
```

Here's the body section of our page, **CompatLayers.htm**. You can load this from our Web site at **http://rapid.wrox.co.uk/books/1193**:

```
<LAYER NAME=MyLayer BGCOLOR="white" TOP=50 LEFT=50
  ONMOUSEOVER="colorlayer('red')" ONMOUSEOUT="colorlayer('white')" >

  <NOLAYER>
    <DIV ID=MyDiv STYLE="position:absolute; top:50; left:50">
  </NOLAYER>

    <P>Wrox Press</P>

  <NOLAYER>
    </DIV>
  </NOLAYER>

  <SCRIPT LANGUAGE=JavaScript1.2>
    function colorlayer(changeto)
      { bgColor=changeto }
  </SCRIPT>
</LAYER>

<SCRIPT LANGUAGE=VBSCRIPT>
  Sub MyDiv_onmouseover()
    document.all.MyDiv.style.backgroundColor = "red"
  End Sub
  Sub MyDiv_onmouseout()
    document.all.MyDiv.style.backgroundColor = "white"
  End Sub
</SCRIPT>
```

In Communicator, we can include a script section inside a layer, and it then applies to that layer only. This is what we've done in the code above, using **LANGUAGE=JavaScript1.2** so that Internet Explorer won't see it. Outside the layer, we've placed a section of code that uses VBScript. The subroutines here are directly linked to the **<DIV>** element **MyDiv** through the event names and the **ID** of the element. Even if Communicator has a VBScript interpreter installed, it can't execute these routines because it can't see the division tag with the **ID** of **MyDiv**.

The result in both cases is that the area around the text changes color when the mouse pointer is moved over it. OK, so there are other ways of doing the same thing, but this serves to demonstrate the way we can use layers and document divisions to provide compatible pages.

A Compatible 3D Title - Netscape
File Edit View Go Communicator Help
Back Forward Reload Home Search Guide Print Security Stop
Wrox Press
You are offline. Choose "Go Online..." to connect

A Compatible 3D Title - Microsoft Internet Explorer
File Edit View Go Favorites Help
Back Forward Stop Refresh Home Search Favorites History Channels
Address Links
Wrox Press
Internet zone

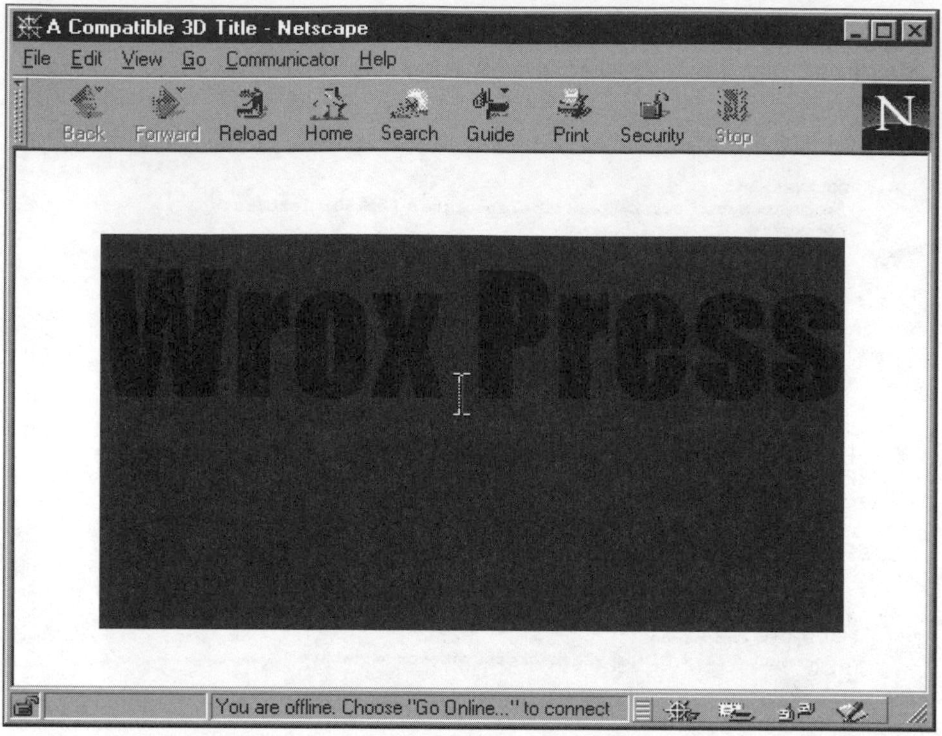

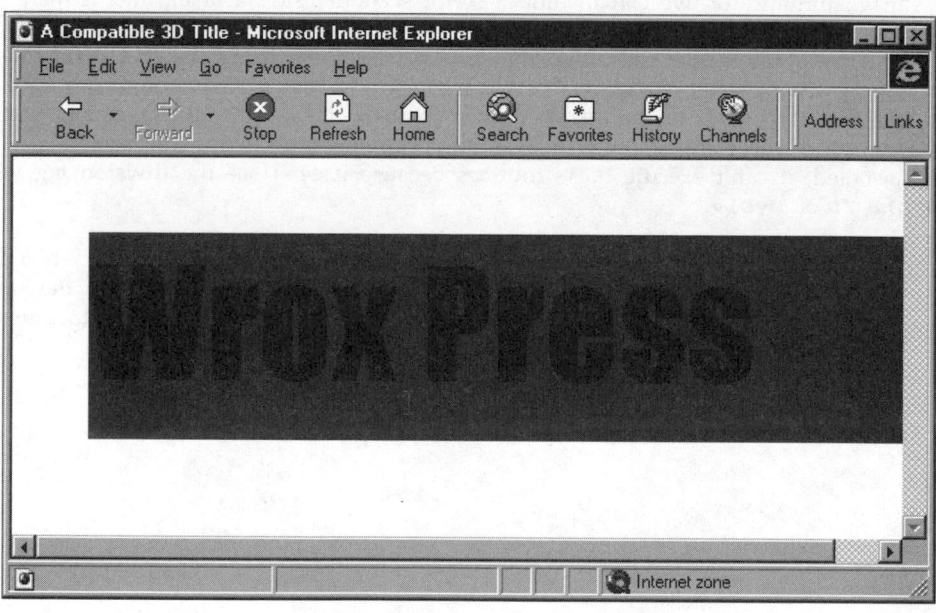

Including Two Script Sections

As you've just seen again in the previous example, we can use the trick we saw earlier of creating two script sections in the page, only one of which is executed in either browser. This provides us with a way of writing content dynamically to the page. Here's a compatible version of the code for the keypress example we first used in Chapter 5. You can load it from our Web site at `http://rapid.wrox.co.uk/books/1193` as `CompatKeys.htm`:

```
<HTML>
<HEAD>
<TITLE> A Compatible Keypress Page </TITLE>

<SCRIPT LANGUAGE="JavaScript1.2">
function stringify_event(e) {
   strMesg = "You pressed the " + String.fromCharCode(e.which) + " key, "
           + "which has an ASCII value of " + String(e.which);
   strMesg = strMesg + String.fromCharCode(10) + "while holding down the ";
   if (e.modifiers & Event.SHIFT_MASK)    strMesg = strMesg + "Shift key ";
   if (e.modifiers & Event.CONTROL_MASK)     strMesg = strMesg + "Ctrl key ";
   if (e.modifiers & Event.ALT_MASK)    strMesg = strMesg + "Alt key ";
   strMesg = strMesg + String.fromCharCode(10)
      + "The mouse pointer is at position " + "x = " + e.x + ", y = " + e.y;
   return strMesg;
}
function report_key1(e) {
   var strMesg = stringify_event(e);
   alert(strMesg);
}
document.onkeyup=report_key1;
</SCRIPT>

<SCRIPT LANGUAGE=VBSCRIPT>
Sub document_onkeypress()
   If InStr(navigator.appName, "Microsoft") Then
      strMesg = "You pressed the " & Chr(window.event.keyCode) & " key, " _
              & "which has an ASCII value of " & window.event.keyCode
      strMesg = strMesg & Chr(10) & "while holding down the "
      If window.event.shiftKey Then strMesg = strMesg & "Shift key "
      If window.event.ctrlKey Then strMesg = strMesg & "Ctrl key "
      If window.event.altKey Then strMesg = strMesg & "Alt key "
      strMesg = strMesg & Chr(10) & "The mouse pointer is at position " _
              & "x = " & window.event.x & ", y = " & window.event.y
      MsgBox strMesg, vbInformation, "The Event object parameters"
   End If
End Sub
</SCRIPT>

</HEAD>
<BODY >
      <H2>Press a key, holding down Shift, Ctrl, Alt if you like... </H2>
</BODY>
</HTML>
```

Notice that we have a script section that will only be executed when the browser supports JavaScript version 1.2 (i.e. Communicator), and a VBScript section that will be executed in Internet Explorer. The only catch is if Communicator has a VBScript interpreter plug-in installed. To prevent any problems in this case, we check that the browser is in fact a Microsoft product before we carry out the action in the **onkeypress** event handler.

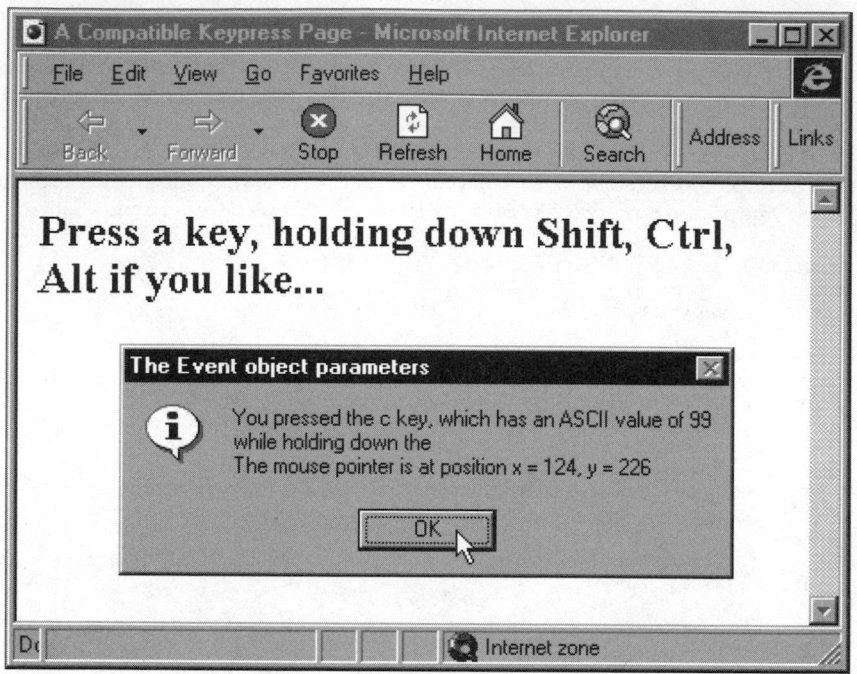

Of course, we can always just use a single script section written in 'vanilla' JavaScript. Within it we can then determine what actions to take depending on the values of the **appName** and **appVersion** properties of the **navigator** object—much as we did with the properties of the browser earlier in this chapter.

Doing It on the Server

Finally, we might decide to do all the work on the server instead. Technologies like Active Server Pages, or other CGI programming methods, can create pages dynamically. We simply need to read the user agent details from the HTTP header that the browser sends to the server when it requests a page, and dynamically create a fully compatible page to send back.

> This topic is outside the scope of the book, but you can learn more about server-side programming techniques from other books in our range:
>
> Professional Active Server Pages Programming, ISBN 1-861000-766
>
> Professional NT C++ ISAPI Programming, ISBN 1-8614416-66-4

Going Your Own Way

Of course, when it comes down to your own site, you don't *have* to do any of this. If you want to get the best out of your chosen browser, you might decide to program it all in one scripting language, and not worry about backwards compatibility. After all, getting your page to display correctly in one browser is often enough of a task. In this case, you just stick the 'Best viewed in Internet Explorer / Netscape Communicator' logo at the foot of your page. But while your pages will look much better if you just exploit all the latest features of your preferred browser, you'll be well on the way to admitting that the intense rivalry of the two market-leader browser vendors is destroying the heart of the Web as an inherently cross-platform medium.

Summary

This completes our tour of browser compatibility. We looked at the main Project Cougar proposals, and tried to see to what extent they have been adopted by Netscape and Microsoft. We looked at how you can make your pages backward compatible over previous releases of the same browser. Finally we looked at how you could make your pages function on both Communicator 4 and IE4.

Having read this book, and this chapter, you may feel that it is slanted unduly towards one or other of the two main *Windows*-based browsers. Previously, HTML had been a truly cross-platform language, and Microsoft's non-compliance with proposals and standards (interpreted as setting future guidelines) was as confounding as Netscape's current stance. This is a book about Dynamic HTML, and isn't intended to favor either browser. However, you want to know more about it than just the concepts, as documented in the W3C proposals and discussed in this chapter. To do that we had to choose a browser to work with—trying to cover both together is not an option, due to the totally different way most of the new features are implemented.

Despite the recent release of the HTML 4.0 working draft, Dynamic HTML isn't a finished language, and will undoubtedly evolve over future browser releases and future standards upgrades. We've tried to capture the main concepts at the heart of the proposals. We would like to have seen a language that was supported by both browsers, but instead we've ended up with two editions of what should have been one book. If you wish to know more about Microsoft's implementation of Dynamic HTML, look out for the 'IE4' edition of this book. And if that book makes you want to learn more about the whole concept of Internet Explorer 4 and the Active Desktop, look out for Professional Dynamic HTML and IE4 Programming – ISBN 1-861000-70-7.

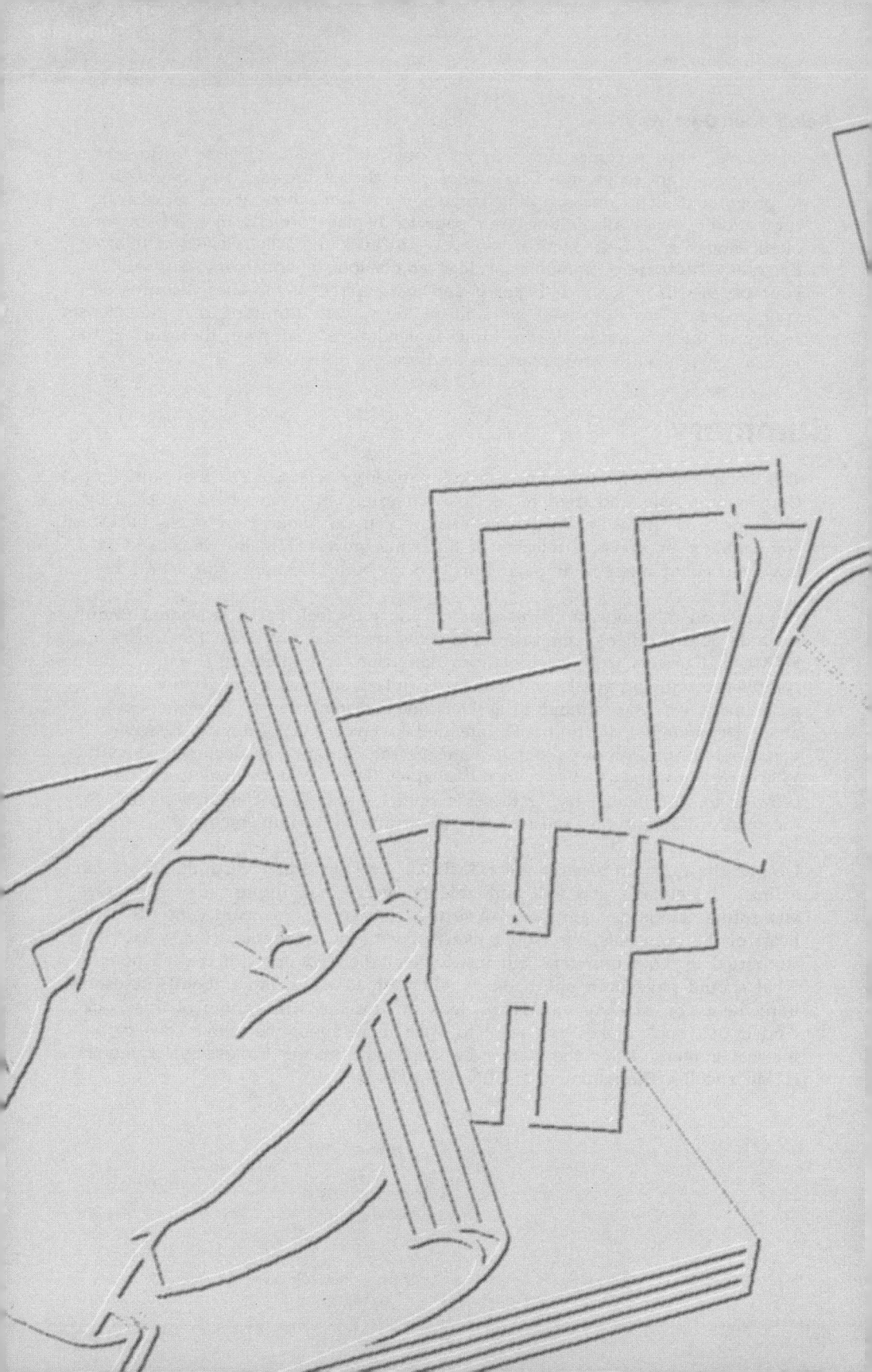

Reference Section

This section of the book is designed to help you to quickly and efficiently find the information you need while working with Dynamic HTML. To achieve this, we've split it up into separate, but inter-related, sections.

For example, when working with a **<LAYER>** tag, you can look in Section **B** to find a full list of the Properties, Methods and Events it supports, plus the Attributes you can include in the tag itself and a list of the equivalent Style properties.

Then, to get a description of what each of these actually do, you can use the lists of Properties, Methods and Events in Section **A**. If you then need to know how to reference the layer, using the browser's Object Model, you can see the overall structure, and look up individual objects within the hierarchy, in Section **E**.

Section A - Lists of Properties, Methods and Events

The list of **Properties** includes the equivalent HTML **Attributes** and **JavaScript Styles**, plus the type of data or individual values you can use with each one.

Section B - List of Dynamic HTML Tags

An alphabetical list of all the **HTML Tags** that can be used in Dynamic HTML files. The entry for each tag provides the following information: a short description of the tag, tables of the Properties, Methods and Events it provides, the Attributes it accepts and the data types or values that can be used with them, the equivalent Style values, and some sample code, where appropriate, to show you how it is used.

Section C - Style Sheet Properties Reference

This listing contains all the attributes and values that can be used in **JavaScript Style Sheets**, **STYLE** sections of a page, and in-line HTML **STYLE** tags.

Section D - List of HTML Tags by Category

This section will help you to find which tag you need. It lists all the HTML tags by name, divided into **categories** like **Tables**, **Graphics**, **Forms**, etc.

Reference Section

Section E - The Browser Object Model Reference

This section covers the **object model** that is available in the browser through Dynamic HTML.

It contains a view of the overall structure, and a list of all the **objects** and **collections** that are provided. It goes on to show the Properties, Methods and Events which each object and collection supports.

Section F - HTML Color Names and Values

Many Dynamic HTML properties and methods expect you to provide a **color value**. This can be one of the accepted color names, or a numeric value that indicates the red green and blue (RGB) components of the color (also known as the hexadecimal value). This appendix lists all the color names, and shows the equivalent RGB values.

Section G - Special HTML Characters

Many of the **common symbols** we use in web pages cannot be transmitted as ASCII code because HTTP only supports 7-bit characters. Instead we use special codes in the page to indicate which of the **special characters** we want the browser to display. This section lists all the available characters and their equivalent codes.

Section H - JavaScript Quick Reference

The one language that most browsers, including Netscape Navigator and Communicator, and Microsoft's Internet Explorer, support is JavaScript. This section contains a quick reference to the **JavaScript language**, including functions, keywords and constants.

Section I - Support and Errata

Explains in detail how to contact us for support on this book, and how to log any errata that you may find in it.

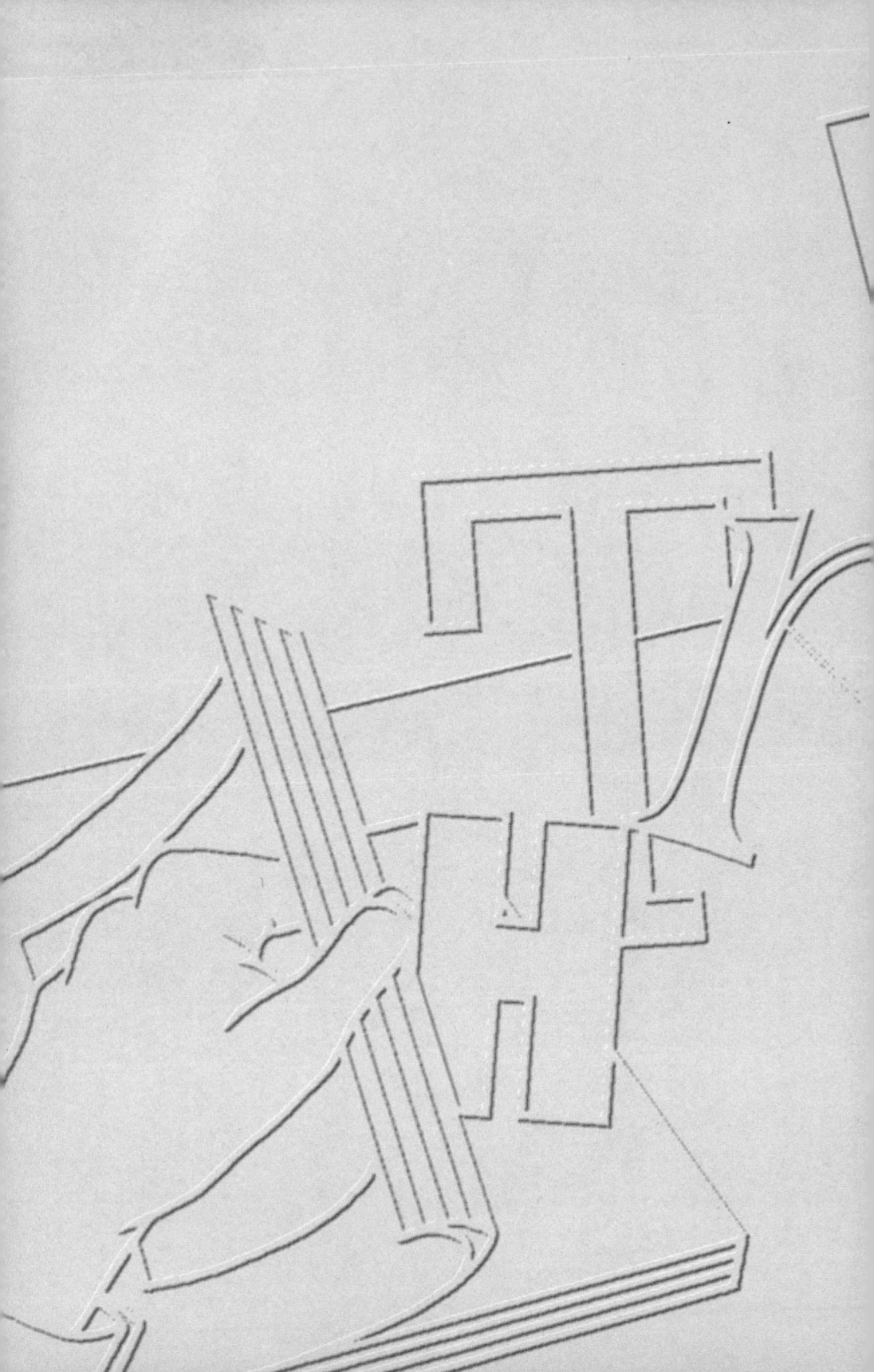

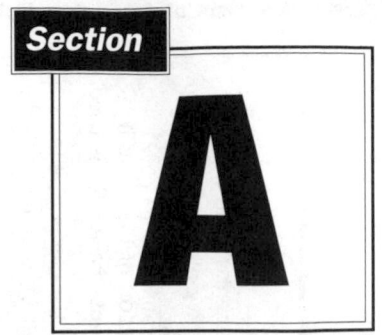

Section

A

Lists of Properties, Methods and Events

This section consists of three tables; a listing of Properties, Attributes and CSS Equivalents, a listing of Dynamic HTML Methods and a listing of Dynamic HTML Events. Where there is more than one possible use/description for an item there will sometimes be more than one entry for it in the table. To find out more about any of the items listed here, check out the Netscape Dynamic HTML reference section at

http://developer.netscape.com/library/documentation

The notation for the tables is as follows:

- One vertical bar means *either/or*—that is, only one of the items is allowed

- Two vertical bars mean *either/both/any*—that is, any number of the items are allowed

- {} denotes each style sheet within the **STYLE** tag, which have to be enclosed between braces

- [] means the item is optional

- <> means the actual value of the items needs to be substituted, for example **#FFCC00** for **<color>**

Listing of the Dynamic HTML Properties

Property	Attribute	Attribute Values	Style Name	Style Values	Description
above	ABOVE	<object_id>			Indicates that the element should be above another one within the z-order of the page, or returns the element above it.
action	ACTION	<string>			The URL for the ACTION of the form. If not specified, document's base URL is used.
	ALIGN	CENTER | LEFT | RIGHT | TOP | TEXTTOP | MIDDLE | ABSMIDDLE | BASELINE | BOTTOM | ABSBOTTOM	align	none | left | right	Sets the alignment of the element with respect to the page or its container, and the text wrapping.
alinkColor	ALINK	<color>			Color of the active links on the page, i.e. those where the mouse button is held down.
	ALT	<string>			Text to be displayed while the element contents are downloading or if not available.
appCodeName					The code name of the browser.
appName					The product name of the browser.
appVersion					The version of the browser.
arity					Indicates number of arguments expected by a function when the language is JavaScript 1.2.
	ARCHIVE	<url>			URL of the file holding the digital signature for a script or applet.

Property	Syntax/Value	Description
`availHeight`		Height of the available screen space in pixels (excluding screen furniture).
`availWidth`		Width of the available screen space in pixels (excluding screen furniture).
`background`	`BACKGROUND` *<url>*	The location of an image to be rendered behind the elements on the page.
`below`	*<object_id>*	Indicates that the element should be below another one within the z-order of the page, or returns the element below it.
`bgColor`	`BGCOLOR` *<color>*	Specifies the background color to be used for an element.
`border`	`BORDER` *<number>*	Specifies the border to be drawn around the element.
	`borderWidths()` (*<top_number>*, *<right_number>*, *<bottom_number>*, *<left_number>*)	
	`borderBottomWidth` *<number>*	The width of the border displayed at the bottom of an element.
	`BORDERCOLOR` `borderColor` *<color>*	Defines the color of the border for the element.
	`borderLeftWidth` *<number>*	The width of the border displayed at the left of an element.
	`borderRightWidth` *<number>*	The width of the border displayed at the right of an element.
	`borderStyle` `none	solid	3D`	Used to specify the style of one or more borders of an element.
	`borderTopWidth` *<number>*	The width of the border displayed at the top of an element.
`caller`		Returns the name of the function that called the current function.

Property	Attribute	Attribute Values	Style Name	Style Values	Description
	CELLPADDING	CELLPADDING *<number>*			Defines the distance in pixels between the contents and the edge of a cell in a table.
		CELLSPACING *<number>*			Defines the distance in pixels between cells in a table.
	CHALLENGE	CHALLENGE *<string>*			A string to be packaged with the public key value into for a <KEYGEN> tag.
checked	CHECKED	CHECKED			For check boxes and radio buttons, indicates that they are selected.
classes	CLASS	*<string>*			Identifies the class of the element for reference in a style sheet.
	CLEAR	LEFT | RIGHT | ALL	clear	none | left | right | both	Indicates that the next element will be rendered underneath (below) this element.
clip.bottom	CLIP	[*<number>,*] [*<number>,*] *<number>*			Defines the *y* coordinate of the bottom of the clipping rectangle around an element. Use the CLIP attribute in HTML with two or four numbers to define the entire clipping area.
clip.height					Defines the height of the clipping rectangle around an element.
clip.left	CLIP	[*<number>,*] [*<number>,*] *<number>, <number>*			Defines the *x* coordinate of the left of the clipping rectangle around an element. Use the CLIP attribute in HTML with two or four numbers to define the entire clipping area.
clip.right	CLIP	[*<number>,*] [*<number>,*] *<number>, <number>*			Defines the *x* coordinate of the right of the clipping rectangle around an element. Use the CLIP attribute in HTML with two or four numbers to define the entire clipping area.

Term	Syntax	Description
clip.top	CLIP [<number>,] [<number>,] <number>, <number>	Defines the y coordinate of the top of the clipping rectangle around an element. Use the CLIP attribute in HTML with two or four numbers to define the entire clipping area.
clip.width		Defines the width of the clipping rectangle around an element.
closed		Indicates if a window is closed.
	CODE <string>	The name of a class file to be used to instantiate the object.
	CODEBASE <string>	A URL where the code for an object can be downloaded from.
	COLOR <color> color <color>	Defines the color to be used for the element, by name or as a number.
colorDepth		Returns the maximum number of colors that are supported by the user's display system.
	COLS <string> | <number>	Defines the number and size of the columns used for a frameset, table, or text area.
	COLSPAN <number>	Number of columns to span a table cell across without dividing it into separate cells.
	COMPACT COMPACT	Displays a list in compact form, using less page area.
complete		Denotes whether the specified element has completed loading.
constructor		Reference to the constructor function for this object.

Property	Attribute	Attribute Values	Style Name	Style Values	Description
	CONTENT	*\<string\>*			Information in a \<META\> tag to be associated with the given name or HTTP response header.
cookie					The string value of a cookie stored by the browser.
	COORDS	*\<string\>*			Defines the coordinates of an area in an image map.
current					The current item in the browser's history list.
data					The URLs of the objects dropped onto the Navigator window, as an array of strings.
defaultChecked					Denotes if an element is checked by default.
defaultSelected					Denotes if a list item is selected by default.
defaultStatus					The default message displayed in the status bar at the bottom of the window.
defaultValue					The text displayed as the initial contents of a control.
description					Returns a description of a MIME type or plug-in.
	DISABLED	DISABLED			Prevents the user from being able to react with a control or element.
			display	none | block | inline | list-item	Indicates if the element is inline, block-level, or a block-level list item.
document					A reference to the document object from a contained element or object.

domain			Sets or returns the domain of the document for use in cookies and security.
E	event_name	<name of event>	Constant value of the mathematical symbol e. Name of the event handler to be called when the specified event occurs.
enabledPlugin			Returns the plug-in that can handle the specified MIME type.
encoding	ENC_TYPE	<string>	Defines the type of encoding to be used when submitting a form.
	FACE	<string>	Sets the family name of the font used to render the text.
fontFamily	serif | sans-serif | cursive | monospace | fantasy | <string>		
fgColor	TEXT	<color>	Sets the color of the document foreground text.
filename			The name of a plugin file.
fontStyle	normal | italic | italic small-caps | oblique | oblique small-caps | small-caps		Defines the style (normal, italic, small-caps) etc. for the text.
fontWeight	normal | bold | bolder | lighter | <number>		Defines the weight of the font used to render the text.
	WEIGHT		
form			Reference to the form object that contains the element.

235

Property	Attribute	Attribute Values	Style Name	Style Values	Description
	FRAMEBORDER	1 | 0			Indicates if the frame displays a border.
	GUTTER	<number>			Spacing in pixels between the columns in a table.
hash					The string following the # symbol in the URL.
height	HEIGHT	<string> | <number>	height	<length> | auto	Height at which the element is to be drawn, or returns the height of the screen in pixels.
	HIDDEN	<string>			Forces the embedded element to be invisible.
host					The hostname:port part of the location or URL.
hostname					The host name part of the location or URL.
href	HREF	<string>			The entire URL as a string.
hspace	HSPACE	<number>			Specifies the horizontal spacing or margin between an element and its neighbors.
	HTTP-EQUIV	<string>			Used to bind the CONTENT of the element to an HTTP response header.
ids	ID	<string>			Identifier of the object or element, same as the NAME. Also used to relate script to a JAR file.

index		Returns the ordinal position of the option in a list box.
innerHeight		Height of the window or object excluding the window or object borders.
innerWidth		Width of the window or object excluding the window or object borders.
ISMAP	ISMAP	Indicates that the element is an image map.
java		A read-only reference to the **java** package name hierarchy.
language	LANGUAGE JAVASCRIPT | JAVASCRIPT1.1 | JAVASCRIPT1.2 | VBSCRIPT	Defines the scripting language used in a **<SCRIPT>** block.
lastModified		A string containing the last-modified date of the page, where available.
layerX		Horizontal position of the mouse pointer in layer co-ordinates.
layerY		Vertical position of the mouse pointer in layer co-ordinates.
left	LEFT *<number>*	Position in pixels of the left-hand side of the object in relation to its container.
length		Specifies a length-related feature of the calling object or array.
lineHeight	*<number>* | *<length>* | **<percentage>**	The height of individual lines of text in the page.
linkColor	LINK *<color>*	The color of the unvisited links in the page.

Property	Attribute	Attribute Values	Style Name	Style Values	Description
LN10					Constant definition of the natural logarithm of 10.
LN2					Constant definition of the natural logarithm of 2.
location					The full URL of the document.
locationbar					Defines whether the address bar will be displayed in the browser window.
LOG10E					Constant definition of the base-10 logarithm of e.
LOG2E					Constant definition of the base-2 logarithm of e.
lowsrc	LOWSRC	<url>			Specifies the URL of a lower resolution image to display.
	MARGINHEIGHT	<number>	margins( )	(<top_length>, <right_length>, <bottom_length>, <left_length>) | (<top_percentage>, <right_percentage>, <bottom_percentage>, <left_percentage>)	Size of the margin above and below (or surrounding) an element.
	MARGINWIDTH	<number>	margins( )	(<top_length>, <right_length>, <bottom_length>, <left_length>) | (<top_percentage>, <right_percentage>, <bottom_percentage>, <left_percentage>)	Size (either relative or in pixels) of all four margins of the page.

marginBottom	*<length>* | *<percentage>*	Size (either relative or in pixels) of the bottom margin of the page.
marginLeft	*<length>* | *<percentage>*	Size (either relative or in pixels) of the left margin of the page.
marginRight	*<length>* | *<percentage>*	Size (either relative or in pixels) of the right margin of the page.
marginTop	*<length>* | *<percentage>*	Size (either relative or in pixels) of the top margin of the page.
MAXLENGTH	*<number>*	Defines the maximum number of characters a user can enter into a control.
MAX_VALUE		The maximum numeric value representable in JavaScript.
MAYSCRIPT	YES | NO	Indicates if an applet can accept instructions from script code in the page.
menubar		Defines whether the menu bar will be displayed in the browser window.
method	GET | POST	Indicates how the form data should be sent to the server; either GET or POST.
MIN_VALUE		The smallest positive numeric value representable in JavaScript.
modifiers		String containing the names of the keys held down for a key-press event.
MULTIPLE	MULTIPLE	Indicates that a <SELECT> list will allow more than one item to be selected concurrently.
name	*<string>*	Specifies the name of the element, control, or applet.

Property	Attribute	Attribute Values	Style Name	Style Values	Description
NaN					Constant value returned when a mathematical operation or value is not a valid number.
NEGATIVE_INFINITY					Constant value returned from an operation that creates a number smaller than MIN_VALUE.
netscape					A read-only reference to the netscape package name hierarchy.
next					Refers to the next item in the browser's history list.
	NOHREF	NOHREF			Indicates that this <AREA> of an image map does not reference another page.
	NORESIZE	NORESIZE			Indicates that a frame cannot be resized by the viewer.
	NOSHADE	NOSHADE			Indicates that the object should be rendered without 3D shading effects.
	NOWRAP	NOWRAP			Indicates that text and content should not be wrapped inside the element.
opener					Returns a reference to the window that created the current window.
outerHeight					Height of the window or object including the window or object borders.
outerWidth					Width of the window or object including the window or object borders.

Name	Syntax/Value	Description
paddings( )	(<top_length>, <right_length>, <bottom_length>, <left_length>) | (<top_percentage>, <right_percentage>, <bottom_percentage>, <left_percentage>)	Defines the space in pixels between the borders and the content of an element.
paddingBottom	<length> | <percentage>	Defines the space in pixels between the bottom border and the content of an element.
paddingLeft	<length> | <percentage>	Defines the space in pixels between the left border and the content of an element.
paddingRight	<length> | <percentage>	Defines the space in pixels between the right border and the content of an element.
paddingTop	<length> | <percentage>	Defines the space in pixels between the top border and the content of an element.
pageX	PAGEX <number>	Horizontal position in pixels of the mouse pointer or a layer, with respect to the document's window.
pageXOffset		Horizontal offset of the top left of the visible part of the page within the window in pixels.
pageY	PAGEY <number>	Vertical position in pixels of the mouse pointer or a layer, with respect to the document's window.
pageYOffset		Vertical offset of the top left of the visible part of the page within the window in pixels.

Property	Attribute	Attribute Values	Style Name	Style Values	Description
	PALETTE	FOREGROUND | BACKGROUND			Defines which client system color palette an embedded document or control should use.
parent					Returns the parent object in the object hierarchy.
parentLayer					Returns a reference to the layer that contains the current layer.
pathname					The file or object path name following the third slash in a URL.
personalbar					Defines whether the user's personal button bar will be displayed in the browser window.
PI					Constant value approximating to the mathematical symbol *pi*.
pixelDepth					Returns the number of bits used per pixel by the system display hardware.
	PLAIN	PLAIN			Indicates that the element is to be displayed without formatting.
platform					Indicates the machine type the browser was compiled for.
	PLUGINSPAGE	<string>			Defines the plug-in to be used with an embedded document.
	POINT-SIZE	<string> | <number>			The absolute or relative size of the font used for the text.
port					The port number in a URL.

POSITIVE_INFINITY		Constant value returned from an operation that creates a number larger than MAX_VALUE.
previous		Refers to the previous item in the browser's history list.
PROMPT	*<string>*	The message to be displayed in a query text input field as a prompt.
protocol		The initial sub-string up to and including the first colon, indicating the URL's access method.
prototype		A reference to the base function or object used to construct the function or object.
referrer		The URL of the page that referenced the current page.
REL	*<string>*	Indicates how the target file is related to the current file in a **<LINK>** tag.
REV	*<string>*	Indicates how the current file is related to the target file in a **<LINK>** tag.
ROWS	*<string>* | *<number>*	Defines the number and size of the rows used for a frameset, table, or text area.
ROWSPAN	*<number>*	Number of rows to span a table cell over without dividing it into separate cells.
screenX		Horizontal position in pixels of the mouse pointer on the screen for an event.
screenY		Vertical position in pixels of the mouse pointer on the screen for an event.
scrollbars	SCROLLING YES | NO | AUTO	Defines whether a frame or window will provide scrollbars if all the content cannot be displayed.

Property	Attribute	Attribute Values	Style Name	Style Values	Description
search					The contents of the query string, or form data, following the **?** in the complete URL.
selected	SELECTED	SELECTED			Indicates that this item in a list is the default. If not present the first item is selected by default.
selectedIndex					An integer specifying the index of the selected option in a **<SELECT>** element.
self					A reference to the current window.
	SHAPE	RECT | POLY | CIRCLE			Defines the type of shape that an **<AREA>** in an image map definition represents.
siblingAbove					A reference to the layer above the current layer if they share the same parent layer.
siblingBelow					A reference to the layer below the current layer if they share the same parent layer.
	SIZE	*<string>* | *<number>*	fontSize	**x-small** | **small** | **medium** | **large** | **x-large** | **xx-large** | **larger** | **smaller** | *<percentage>*	Defines the size of an element, such as a control, or the size of the font in a **<FONT>** tag.
SQRT1_2					Constant value representing one divided by the square root of two.
SQRT2					Constant value representing the square root of two.
src	SRC	*<url>*			Specifies an external file that contains the source data for the element.

START	*<number>*	Defines the number used for the first item in an ordered list.
status		The text displayed in the current window's status bar.
statusbar		Defines whether the status bar will be displayed in the browser window.
style **STYLE**	*<string>*	Specifies an in-line style sheet (or set of style properties) for the element.
suffixes		A comma separated list of filename suffixes that are used with the specified MIME type.
sun		A read-only reference to the **sun** package name hierarchy.
target **TARGET**	**_blank	_parent	_self	_top**	*<string>*	Specifies the window or frame where the new page will be loaded.
text **TEXT**	*<string>*	The plain text contained within an element, such as an **<OPTION>** tag.
textAlign	**left	right	center	justify**	Defines how the text is aligned within an element.
textDecoration	**none	underline	overline	line-through	blink**	Defines the decoration added to text, such as underlines or blinking.
textIndent	*<length>*	*<percentage>*	Specifies how the first line of the text will be indented.

Property	Attribute	Attribute Values	Style Name	Style Values	Description
			textTransform	none | capitalize | uppercase | lowercase	Indicates the way that the text is transformed, i.e. to upper or lower case or capitalized.
title	TITLE	<string>			String representing the title of the document.
toolbar					Defines whether the toolbar will be displayed in the browser window.
top	TOP	<number>			Position of the top of the element. Also can return the topmost window object.
type	TYPE	<string>	listStyleType	<string> | none | disc | circle | square | decimal | lower-roman | upper-roman | lower-alpha | upper-alpha	Either provides information regarding the type of an object or element, or specifically the kind of bullets used for a list.
	UNITS	EN | PIXELS			Defines how the size units of the contents should be used in the containing document.
	USEMAP	<mapname>			Name of the <MAP> to be used with an image map.
URL	URL	<string>			Returns the Uniform Resource Locator (address) for the current document.
userAgent					The user-agent (browser name) header sent in the HTTP protocol from the client to the server.

Property	HTML Attribute	Attribute values	JS Property	JS values	Description
value	VALUE	`<string>` | `<number>`			The default value of text/numeric controls, or the value when control is 'on' for Boolean controls.
	VALIGN	TOP | MIDDLE | BOTTOM | BASELINE	verticalalign	baseline | sub | super | top | text-top | middle | bottom | text-bottom	Defines the way the element is aligned with its neighbors.
visibility	VISIBILITY	SHOW | HIDDEN | INHERIT	visibility		Defines whether the element should be displayed on the page.
vlinkColor	VLINK	`<color>`			Color of the visited links in the page.
vspace	VSPACE	`<string>` | `<number>`			Specifies the vertical spacing or margin between an element and its neighbors.
which					Returns the ASCII value of a key that was pressed, or indicates which mouse button was clicked.
			whiteSpace	normal | pre	Indicates whether white space in an element should be collapsed or retained, as in text formatting.
width	WIDTH	`<string>` | `<number>`	width	`<length>` | `<percentage>` | auto	Width at which the element is to be drawn, or returns the width of the screen in pixels.
window					Reference to the window object that contains the element.
	WRAP	OFF | HARD | SOFT			Indicates that the contents of an element should be wrapped to match the element width.
zIndex	Z-INDEX	`<number>`			Position in the z-order or stacking order of the page, i.e. the z coordinate.
$n>					Slot for an expression in a **RegExp** object.

Listing of the Dynamic HTML Methods

MethodName	Syntax	Description
abs	*Number* = *object*.**abs**(*x*)	Returns the absolute (positive) value of a number *x*.
acos	*Number* = *object*.**acos**(*x*)	Returns the arc cosine value of a number *x* in radians.
alert	*object*.**alert**([*message*])	Displays an Alert dialog box with a *message* and an OK button.
anchor	*String* = *object*.**anchor**(*name*)	Returns a string with the name surrounded in **<A NAME="***name***">** and **</A>** tags.
asin	*Number* = *object*.**asin**(*x*)	Returns the arc sine value of a number *x* in radians.
assign	*object*.**assign**(*value*)	Used to provide overloading of *value* assignments to an object.
atan	*Number* = *object*.**atan**(*x*)	Returns the arc tangent value of a number *x* in radians.
atan2	*Number* = *object*.**atan2**(*x*, *y*)	Returns the angle in radians from the X-axis to a point.
back	*object*.**back**()	Loads the previous URL in the browser's history list, or the previously viewed page.
big	*String* = *object*.**big**()	Cause the string to be displayed as if surrounded by **<BIG>** and **</BIG>** tags.
blink	*String* = *object*.**blink**()	Causes the string to be displayed as if surrounded by **<BLINK>** and **</BLINK>** tags.
blur	*object*.**blur**	Causes a control to lose focus and fire its **onblur** event.
bold	*String* = *object*.**bold**()	Causes the string to be displayed as if surrounded by **<B>** and **</B>** tags.
captureEvents	*object*.**captureEvents**(*event_type*)	Instructs the window or document to capture all events of the specified type.
ceil	*Number* = *object*.**ceil**(*x*)	Returns the nearest whole number equal to or greater than a number *x*
charAt	*Character* = *object*.**charAt**(*position*)	Returns the single character at the index *position* within a string.

charCodeAt	*Number = object*.**charAt**(*position*)	Returns the ordinal codeset value of the character at the index *position* within a string.
clear	*object*.**clear**	Clears the contents of the selection. Not usually required, use **write** or **writeln** directly.
clearInterval	*object*.**clearTimeout**(*interval_ID*)	Cancels a timeout set with the **setInterval** method.
clearTimeout	*object*.**clearTimeout**(*timeout_ID*)	Cancels a timeout set with the **setTimeout** method.
click	*object*.**click**	Simulates a click on an element, and fires its **onclick** event.
close	*object*.**close**	Closes an output stream forcing data to be displayed, or closes the current browser window.
compile	*object*.**compile**(*expression*)	Compiles an expression in a **RegExp** object.
confirm	*object*.**confirm**([*message*])	Displays a Confirm dialog box with a *message* and OK and Cancel buttons.
cos	*Number = object*.**cos**(*x*)	Returns the cosine value of a number *x* in radians.
disableExternalCapture	*object*.**disableExternalCapture**()	Prevents a window that includes frames from capturing events in documents loaded from different locations.
enableExternalCapture	*object*.**enableExternalCapture**()	Allows a window that includes frames to capture events in documents loaded from different locations.
eval	*Value = object*.**eval**(*code*)	Evaluates the *code* and returns a representation of its value
exec	*object*.**exec**(*expression*)	Executes an *expression* in a **RegExp** object.
exp	*Number = object*.**exp**(*x*)	Returns a number equal to *e* to the power of another number *x*.
find	*Boolean = object*.**find**(*string* [, *case_sensitive, backwards]*)	Returns **true** if the *string* is found in the text in the current window. Search can be case-sensitive or backwards.
fixed	*String = object*.**fixed**()	Causes a string to be displayed as if surrounded by **<TT>** and **</TT>** tags.
floor	*Number = object*.**floor**(*x*)	Returns the nearest whole number equal to or less than a number *x*.
focus	*object*.**focus**()	Causes a control to receive the focus, and fires its **onfocus** event.

MethodName	Syntax	Description
fontcolor	String = object.fontcolor(color)	Causes a string to be displayed as if surrounded by `<FONT COLOR="`color`">` and `</FONT>` tags.
fontsize	String = object.fontsize(size)	Causes a string to be displayed as if surrounded by `<FONT SIZE="`size`">` and `</FONT>` tags.
forward	object.forward()	Loads the next URL in the browser's history list.
fromCharCode	String = fromCharCode(n1, n2, .., nn)	Constructs a string from a series of ordinal codeset values.
getDate	Number = object.getDate()	Returns the day of the month as a number between 1 and 31.
getDay	Number = object.getDay()	Returns the day of the week as a number between 0 (*Sunday*) and 6 (*Saturday*).
getHours	Number = object.getHours()	Returns the hours part of the date as a number between 0 and 23.
getMinutes	Number = object.getMinutes()	Returns the minutes part of the date as a number between 0 and 59.
getMonth	Number = object.getMonth()	Returns the month of the year as a number between 0 and 11.
getSeconds	Number = object.getSeconds()	Returns the seconds part of the date as a number between 0 and 59.
getSelection	String = object.getSelection()	Returns a string containing the text currently selected in the document.
getTime	object.getTime()	Returns the date as a number of milliseconds since 1st Jan 1970 at midnight GMT.
getTimezoneOffset	object.getTimezoneOffset()	Returns the difference in minutes between the object date and time, and GMT.
getYear	Number = object.getYear()	Returns the year as a number. This can be two or four digits, depending on the year.
go	object.go(relative | location)	Loads the specified URL from the browser's history list.
handleEvent	object.handleEvent(event)	Invokes the appropriate *event* handling code of the object for this event.
home	object.home()	Loads the user's Home page into the window referred to by object.
indexof	Number = object.indexOf(substring [, start])	Returns the index of the first occurrence of *substring* within a string, optionally starting from *start*.

Method	Syntax	Description
`italics`	`String = object.italics()`	Displays the string as if surrounded by `<I>` and `</I>` tags.
`javaEnabled`	`Boolean = object.JavaEnabled()`	Returns `true` only if the browser supports Java, and it is enabled.
`join`	`String = object.join([separator])`	Joins the elements of an array into a string, incorporating *separator* to separate them.
`lastIndexOf`	`Number = object.lastIndexOf(substring [, start])`	Returns the index of the last occurrence of *substring* within a string, optionally starting from *start*.
`link`	`String = object.link(href)`	Returns a copy of the string surrounded in `<A HREF="`*href*`">` and `</A>` tags.
`load`	`object.load(url, width)`	Loads the file specified in *url* into the object, and changes the width of the object to *width* pixels.
`log`	`Number = object.log(x)`	Returns the natural logarithm of a number *x*.
`match`	`Boolean = String.match(substring)`	Returns `true` if a regular expression *substring* matches the contents of the string.
`max`	`Number = object.max(a, b)`	Returns the larger of two numbers *a* and *b*.
`min`	`Number = object.min(a, b)`	Returns the smaller of two numbers *a* and *b*.
`moveAbove`	`object.moveAbove(object)`	Changes the z-order so that the object is rendered above (overlaps) the specified *object*.
`moveBelow`	`object.moveBelow(object)`	Changes the z-order so that the object is rendered below (overlapped by) the specified *object*.
`moveBy`	`object.moveBy(horizontal, vertical)`	Moves the object horizontally and vertically by a specified number of pixels.
`moveTo`	`object.moveTo(x, y)`	Moves the object so that the top left is at a position *x*, *y* (in pixels) within its container.
`moveToAbsolute`	`object.moveToAbsolute(x, y)`	Moves the object to a position specified in *x* and *y* with respect to the page and not the container.
`open`	`object.open([mimetype])`	Opens a stream to collect output of `write` or `writeln` methods, or opens a new browser window.

MethodName	Syntax	Description
parse	*Number* = *object*.**parse**(*date*)	Returns the date as a number of milliseconds since 1st Jan 1970 at midnight GMT.
pow	*Number* = *object*.**pow**(*a*, *b*)	Returns the value of the number *a* to the power *b*.
preference	*object*.**preference**(*prefname*)	Allows a signed script to get and set certain Navigator preferences.
print	*object*.**print**()	Prints the contents of a frame or window, equivalent to pressing the Print button.
prompt	*object*.**prompt**(*message* , [*inputDefault*])	Displays a Prompt dialog box with a *message* and an input field.
random	*Number* = *object*.**random**()	Returns a pseudo-random number between 0 and 1.
refresh	*object*.**refresh**()	Updates the contents of an object array to reflect changes to its source.
releaseEvents	*object*.**releaseEvents**(*event_type*)	Instructs the window or document to stop capturing events of a particular type.
reload	*object*.**reload**([*force*])	Reloads the current page. Setting *force* to true forces a reload from the server instead of the cache.
replace	*object*.**replace**(*URL*)	Loads a document, replacing the current document's session history entry with its *URL*.
reset	*object*.**reset**()	Simulates a mouse click on a **RESET** button in a form.
resizeBy	*object*.**resizeBy**(*horizontal*, *vertical*)	Resizes the object horizontally and vertically by a specified number of pixels.
resizeTo	*object*.**resizeTo**(*x*, *y*)	Resizes the object to a size specified in *x* and *y* (in pixels).
reverse	*object*.**reverse**()	Reverses the order of the elements in an array.
round	*Number* = *object*.**round**(*x*)	Returns the nearest whole number (larger or smaller) to a number *x*.
routeEvent	*object*.**handleEvent**(*event*)	Passes an *event* that has been captured back up through the normal event hierarchy.
scroll	*object*.**scroll**(*x*, *y*)	Scrolls the document within the window so that the point *x*, *y* is at the top left corner.

Method	Syntax	Description
`scrollBy`	*object*.`scrollBy`(*horizontal*, *vertical*)	Scrolls the document within the window by a *horizontal* and *vertical* number of pixels.
`scrollTo`	*object*.`scrollTo`(*x*, *y*)	Scrolls the document within the window so that the point *x*, *y* is at the top left corner.
`select`	*object*.`select`()	Makes the active selection equal to the current object, or highlights the input area of a form element.
`setDate`	*object*.`setDate`(*day*)	Sets the *day* of the month for a **Date** object.
`setHours`	*object*.`setHours`(*hour*)	Sets the *hours* part of the time in a **Date** object.
`setInterval`	*interval_ID* = *object*.`setInterval`(*routinename*, *msec* , [*args*])	Denotes a code routine to execute every specified number of milliseconds.
`setMinutes`	*object*.`setMinutes`(*minutes*)	Sets the *minutes* part of the time in a **Date** object.
`setMonth`	*object*.`setMonth`(*month*)	Sets the *month* of the year for a **Date** object.
`setSeconds`	*object*.`setSeconds`(*seconds*)	Sets the *seconds* part of the time in a **Date** object.
`setTime`	*object*.`setTime`(*milliseconds*)	Sets the *milliseconds* part of the time in a **Date** object.
`setTimeout`	*timeout_ID* = *object*.`setTimeout`(*routinename*, *msec* [, *args*])	Denotes a code routine to execute once only, a specified number of milliseconds after loading the page.
`setYear`	*object*.`setYear`(*year*)	Sets the *year* for a **Date** object.
`sin`	*Number* = *object*.`sin`(*x*)	Returns the value of the sine of a number *x* in radians.
`small`	*String* = *object*.`small`()	Causes the string to be displayed as if surrounded by `<SMALL>` and `</SMALL>` tags.
`sort`	*object*.`sort`([*order_function*])	Sorts an array, using an optional *order_function* to define the ordering.
`split`	*Array* = *object*.`split`(*delimiter*)	Returns an array of strings from a single string, using *delimiter* as the point to break the string into components.
`sqrt`	*Number* = *object*.`sqrt`(*x*)	Returns the value of the square root of a positive number *x*.
`stop`	*object*.`stop`()	Stops the current download, equivalent to pressing the Stop button.
`strike`	*String* = *object*.`strike`()	Causes the string to be displayed as if surrounded by `<STRIKE>` and `</STRIKE>` tags.

MethodName	Syntax	Description
sub	String = object.sub()	Causes the string to be displayed as if surrounded by _{and} tags.
submit	object.submit()	Submits a form, as when the SUBMIT button is clicked.
substr	String = object.substring(from [, count])	Returns a section of the original string starting at from and including the next count characters or the rest of the string.
substring	String = object.substring(from [, to])	Returns a section of the original string starting at from and ending one character before to, or the rest of the string.
sup	String = object.sup()	Causes the string to be displayed as if surrounded by ^{and} tags.
taintEnabled	object.taintEnabled()	Specifies whether data tainting is enabled.
tan	Number = object.tan(x)	Returns the value of the tangent of a number x in radians.
toGMTString	String = object.toGMTString()	Returns a string representation of a Date object as a converted GMT time and date.
toLocaleString	String = object.toLocaleString()	Returns a string representation of a Date object using the local time zone.
toLowerCase	String = object.toLowerCase()	Returns a string with all of the letters of the original string in lower case.
toString	object.toString()	Returns a string containing a textual representation of the object's value.
toUpperCase	String = object.toUpperCase()	Returns a string with all of the letters of the original string in upper case.
UTC	Number = object.UTC(year, month, day [, hours, minutes, seconds])	Returns the date as a number of milliseconds since 1st Jan 1970 at midnight GMT.
valueOf	Value = object.valueOf()	Returns the primitive value of an object, or the name of the object itself.
write	object.write([text])	Writes text (including HTML) to a document in the specified window or to a layer.
writeln	object.writeln([text])	Writes text (including HTML) to a document or layer, followed by a carriage return.

Listing of the Dynamic HTML Events

EventName	Description
onAbort	Occurs if the downloading of the image is aborted by the user.
onBlur	Occurs when the control loses the focus.
onChange	Occurs when the contents of the element are changed.
onClick	Occurs when the user clicks the mouse button on an element.
onDblClick	Occurs when the user double-clicks on an element.
onDragDrop	Occurs when the user drops a file or object onto the Navigator window.
onError	Occurs when an error loading the image arises.
onFocus	Occurs when the control receives the focus.
onKeyDown	Occurs when the user presses a key.
onKeyPress	Occurs when the user presses a key.
onKeyUp	Occurs when the user releases a key.
onLoad	Occurs immediately after the contents of the page, element or document have been loaded.
onMouseDown	Occurs when the user presses a mouse button.
onMouseMove	Occurs only when event capturing is on and the user moves the mouse pointer.
onMouseOut	Occurs when the mouse pointer leaves the element.
onMouseOver	Occurs when the mouse pointer first enters the element.
onMouseUp	Occurs when the user releases a mouse button.
onMove	Occurs when the Navigator window or a frame within it is moved.
onReset	Occurs when the RESET button on a form is clicked or a form is reset.
onResize	Occurs when the Navigator window or a frame within it is resized.

EventName	Description
onSelect	Occurs when the current selection in an element is changed.
onSubmit	Occurs when the **SUBMIT** button on a form is clicked or a form is submitted.
onUnload	Occurs immediately prior to the page being unloaded.

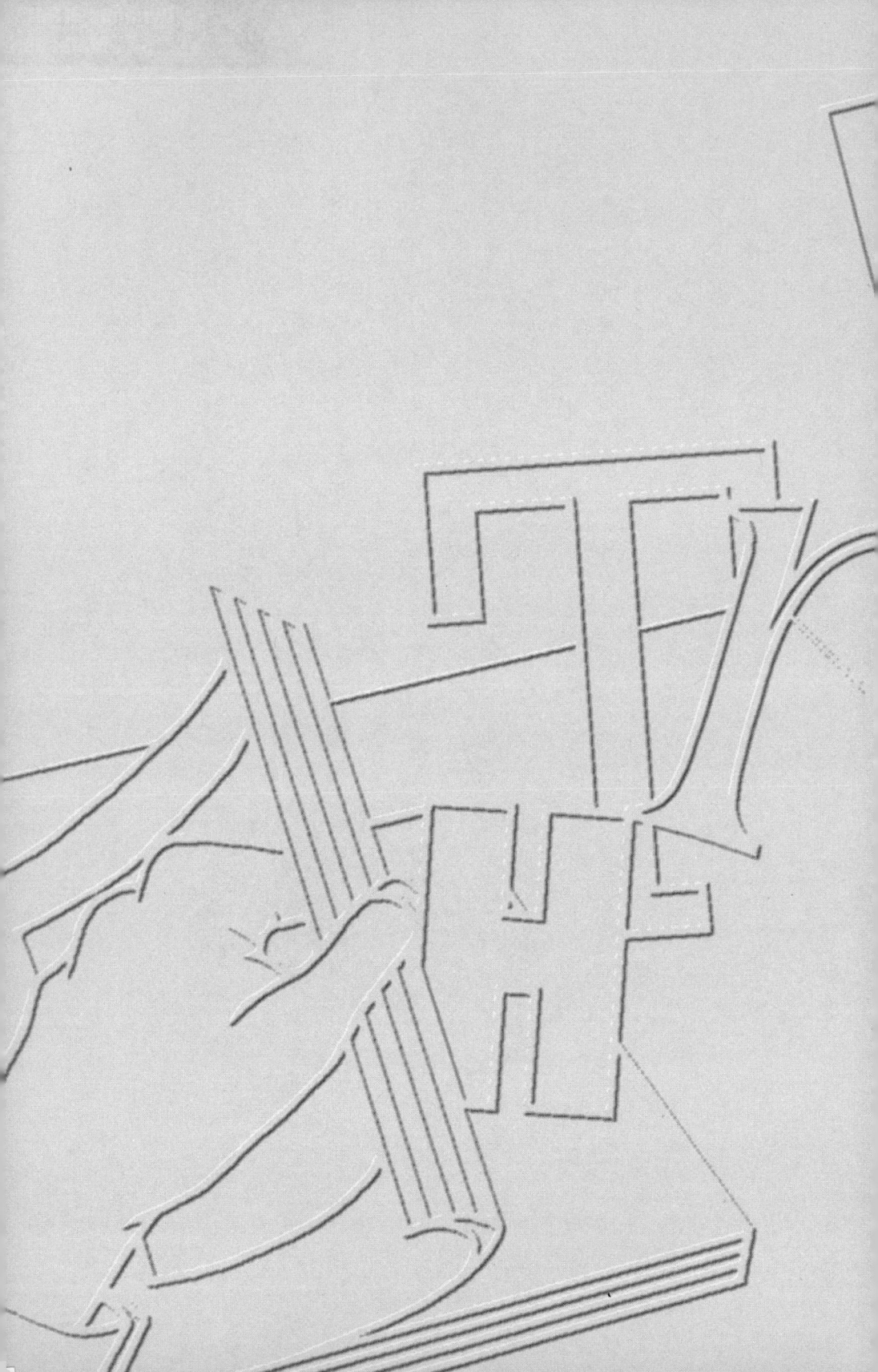

Section

B

List of Dynamic HTML Tags

This section provides an alphabetical list of all the **HTML Tags** which can be used in Dynamic HTML files. The entry for each tag provides the following information; a short description of the tag, tables of the Properties, Methods and Events it provides, the Attributes it accepts and the data types or values that can be used with them, the equivalent CSS values and some sample code, where appropriate, to show you how it is used.

!--

Denotes a comment that is ignored by the HTML parser.

There are no properties, methods or events for this element.

The comment tag can be used to insert individual comments, or to hide things like script code from older browsers that do not support scripting:

```
<!-- This is a comment that won't be visible -->

<SCRIPT LANGUAGE=JAVASCRIPT1.2>
<!--   start hiding the script from older browsers
  function MeaningOfLife() {return 42};
-->
</SCRIPT>
```

!DOCTYPE

Declares the type and content format of the document.

There are no properties, methods or events for this element.

A rigorous HTML-checking program will reject any document that does not contain this tag. However, most browsers are not so particular, and most documents on the Web do not use it.

It is required by the HTML 3.2 standard, and this is the format to be used in this case:

```
<DOCTYPE HTML PUBLIC "-//W3C//DTD HTML 3.2 Draft// EN">
```

There is no standard yet for HTML 4.0, so this is the current acceptable format for Dynamic HTML pages.

Defines a hypertext link. The **HREF** or the **NAME** attribute must be specified.

Properties	Attributes	Attribute Values	Style Equivalents
classes	CLASS	*<string>*	
hash			
host			
hostname			
href	HREF	*<string>*	
ids	ID	*<string>*	
name	NAME	*<string>*	
pathname			
port			
protocol			
search			
style	STYLE	*<string>*	
target	TARGET	_blank | _parent | _self | _top | *<string>*	

Methods

eval	handleEvent	toString	valueOf

Events

onClick	onDblClick	onKeyDown
onKeyPress	onKeyUp	onMouseDown
onMouseOut	onMouseOver	onMouseUp

```
<A HREF="http://www.wrox.com" onclick="MsgBox 'Switching to the Wrox web site'">
Click here to go to Wrox!</A>
```

```
<A NAME="MyAnchor">
...
<A HREF="#MyAnchor"> Jump to MyAnchor </A>
```

ADDRESS

Specifies information such as address, signature and authorship.

Properties	Attributes	Attribute Values	Style Equivalents
classes	CLASS	*<string>*	
ids	ID	*<string>*	
style	STYLE	*<string>*	

There are no methods or events for this element.

```
Produced by:
<ADDRESS>
  Wrox Press Inc
  1512 North Fremont Suite 103
  Chicago
  IL 60622
</ADDRESS>
```

APPLET

Places a Java applet or other executable content in the page.

Properties	Attributes	Attribute Values	Style Equivalents
	`ALIGN`	`CENTER` | `LEFT` | `RIGHT` | `TOP` | `TEXTTOP` | `MIDDLE` | `ABSMIDDLE` | `BASELINE` | `BOTTOM` | `ABSBOTTOM`	`align`
	`ALT`	*<string>*	
	`ARCHIVE`	*<url>*	
`classes`	`CLASS`	*<string>*	
	`CODE`	*<string>*	
	`CODEBASE`	*<string>*	
`height`	`HEIGHT`	*<string>* | *<number>*	`height`
`hspace`	`HSPACE`	*<number>*	
`ids`	`ID`	*<string>*	
	`MAYSCRIPT`	`YES` | `NO`	
`style`	`STYLE`	*<string>*	
`vspace`	`VSPACE`	*<number>*	
`width`	`WIDTH`	*<string>* | *<number>*	`width`

There are no methods or events for this element.

```
<APPLET CODEBASE="http://mysite.com/applets/samples/" CODE="myapp.class"
  WIDTH=250 HEIGHT=150 NAME="MyApp">
  <PARAM NAME="PropertyValue" VALUE="17438">
  <PARAM NAME="AnotherProperty" VALUE="StatusRed">
</APPLET>
```

AREA

Specifies the shape of a "hot spot" in a client-side image map.

Properties	Attributes	Attribute Values	Style Equivalents
classes	CLASS	*<string>*	
	COORDS	*<string>*	
hash			
host			
hostname			
href	HREF	*<string>*	
ids	ID	*<string>*	
name	NAME	*<string>*	
	NOHREF	NOHREF	
pathname			
port			
protocol			
search			
	SHAPE	RECT | POLY | CIRCLE	
style	STYLE	*<string>*	
target	TARGET	_blank | _parent | _self | _top | *<string>*	

Methods

eval   **handleEvent**   **toString**   **valueOf**

Events

onDblClick   **onMouseOut**   **onMouseOver**

```
<MAP NAME="toolbar">
  <AREA SHAPE="RECT" COORDS="12,216,68,267" HREF="wrox.html">
  <AREA SHAPE="CIRCLE" COORDS="100,200,50" HREF="index.html">
</MAP>
```

See also **MAP**

Renders text in boldface where available.

Properties	Attributes	Attribute Values	Style Equivalents
classes	CLASS	*\<string\>*	
ids	ID	*\<string\>*	
style	STYLE	*\<string\>*	

There are no methods or events for this element. This example will produce the word **BOLD** in bold font:

```
<B>BOLD</B>
```

See also **STRONG**.

BASE

Specifies the document's base URL.

Properties	Attributes	Attribute Values	Style Equivalents
classes	CLASS	*\<string\>*	
href	HREF	*\<string\>*	
ids	ID	*\<string\>*	
style	STYLE	*\<string\>*	
target	TARGET	**_blank** | **_parent** | **_self** | **_top** | *\<string\>*	

There are no methods or events for this element.

This is the address used to reference other resources, such as documents, graphics, etc., which do not specify a full URL. For example:

```
<IMG SRC="MyGraphic.gif">
```

If you have set up a **\<BASE\>** tag defining the base directory, **MyGraphic.gif** will be loaded from the directory defined by the **\<BASE\>** tag.

BASEFONT

Sets a base font value to be used as the default font when rendering text.

Properties	Attributes	Attribute Values	Style Equivalents
classes	CLASS	*<string>*	
ids	ID	*<string>*	
style	STYLE	*<string>*	
	SIZE	*<string>* | *<number>*	fontSize

There are no methods or events for this tag.

Once the **BASEFONT** for a document has been set, you can use relative sizes for the font in different places, or specify individual sizes as required:

```
<BASEFONT SIZE=4 FACE="Arial,Tahoma,sans-serif">
<FONT SIZE=-1> A bit smaller font than the base </FONT>
<FONT SIZE=-3> A larger font than the base will be used here </FONT>
<FONT SIZE=2> This is small and not related to BASEFONT </FONT>
```

See also **FONT**.

BIG

Renders text in a relatively larger font than the current font.

Properties	Attributes	Attribute Values	Style Equivalents
classes	CLASS	*<string>*	
ids	ID	*<string>*	
style	STYLE	*<string>*	

There are no methods or events for this tag.

```
<BIG> This text will be one size larger than the rest. </BIG>
```

BLINK

Causes the text to flash on and off.

Properties	Attributes	Attribute Values	Style Equivalents
classes	CLASS	*<string>*	
ids	ID	*<string>*	
style	STYLE	*<string>*	

There are no methods or events for this tag.

```
<BLINK> This text will flash on and off once the page has loaded. </BLINK>
```

BLOCKQUOTE

Denotes a quotation in text.

Properties	Attributes	Attribute Values	Style Equivalents
classes	CLASS	*<string>*	
ids	ID	*<string>*	
style	STYLE	*<string>*	

There are no methods or events for this tag.

Normally displays text indented:

```
<HTML>
  <HEAD>
  </HEAD>
  <BODY>
    This is normal text
    <BR>
    <BLOCKQUOTE>
      This is a blockquote which will produce indented text
    </BLOCKQUOTE>
  </BODY>
</HTML>
```

BODY

Defines the beginning and end of the body section of the page.

Properties	Attributes	Attribute Values	Style Equivalents
alinkColor	ALINK	*\<color\>*	
background	BACKGROUND	*\<url\>*	backgroundImage
bgColor	BGCOLOR	*\<color\>*	backgroundColor
classes	CLASS	*\<string\>*	
ids	ID	*\<string\>*	
linkColor	LINK	*\<color\>*	
style	STYLE	*\<string\>*	
text	TEXT	*\<string\>*	
vlinkColor	VLINK	*\<color\>*	

There are no methods or events for this tag.

To set the colors of the links in the page, we include the **ALINK**, **LINK** and **VLINK** attributes in the **BODY** tag. To set the color of the page itself, and the color of the text, we use the **BGCOLOR** and **TEXT** attributes:

```
<BODY BGCOLOR="red" TEXT="white" LINK="blue" ALINK="maroon">
```

Alternatively, we can specify the colors using their RGB values:

```
<BODY BGCOLOR="#ff0000" TEXT="#ffffff" LINK="#ff" ALINK="#ff00ff">
```

To display a picture on the page as a background, we use the **BACKGROUND** attribute:

```
<BODY BACKGROUND="bgpattern.gif">
```

Inserts a line break.

Properties	Attributes	Attribute Values	Style Equivalents
classes	CLASS	*<string>*	
	CLEAR	LEFT | RIGHT | ALL	clear
ids	ID	*<string>*	
style	STYLE	*<string>*	

There are no methods or events for this tag. If we want the line break to move following text or elements down past another element, such as an image which is left or right aligned, we use the **CLEAR** attribute. Without it, the following text or elements would continue to wrap around the other element. To move the following elements below a left-aligned image, for example, we can use:

```
<BR CLEAR=LEFT>
```

CAPTION

Specifies a caption for a table.

Properties	Attributes	Attribute Values	Style Equivalents
	ALIGN	CENTER | LEFT | RIGHT	align
classes	CLASS	*<string>*	
ids	ID	*<string>*	
style	STYLE	*<string>*	
	VALIGN	TOP | BOTTOM	verticalAlign

There are no methods or events for this tag.

```
<TABLE>
  <CAPTION ALIGN=LEFT> This is the table caption </CAPTION>
  <TR><TD> table content </TD></TR>
</TABLE>
```

See also **TABLE**.

CENTER

Causes subsequent text and other elements to be centred on the page.

Properties	Attributes	Attribute Values	Style Equivalents
classes	CLASS	*<string>*	
ids	ID	*<string>*	
style	STYLE	*<string>*	

There are no methods or events for this tag.

```
<CENTER>
  This text will be centered on the page.
  <H1> So will this heading </H1>
  <IMG SRC="MyImage.gif"> <P>
  And so will the image above.
</CENTER>
```

The **<CENTER>** tag is still available for backward compatibility purposes, but the W3C recommendation is that you use **ALIGN** instead.

CITE

Renders text in italics, as a citation. Often used for copyright statements.

Properties	Attributes	Attribute Values	Style Equivalents
classes	CLASS	*<string>*	
ids	ID	*<string>*	
style	STYLE	*<string>*	

There are no methods or events for this tag.

```
<CITE> &copy;1997 Wrox Press Limited, UK </CITE>
```

270

CODE

Renders text as a code sample in a fixed width font.

Properties	Attributes	Attribute Values	Style Equivalents
classes	CLASS	*string*	
ids	ID	*string*	
style	STYLE	*string*	

There are no methods or events for this tag.

```
<CODE>  <!-- following is rendered as a code listing on the screen -->
   function MyRoutine(datToday)
     { if (datToday == 'Saturday')  strDestination = 'The beach.'
       else strDestination = 'The office again.' };
</CODE>
```

DD

The definition for a definition list, and is usually indented from the other text.

Properties	Attributes	Attribute Values	Style Equivalents
classes	CLASS	*string*	
ids	ID	*string*	
style	STYLE	*string*	

There are no methods or events for this tag.

The **DD** tag is used inside a definition list to provide the definition of the text in the **DT** tag. It may contain block elements, but also plain text and markup. The end tag is optional, as it's always clear from the context where the tag's contents end.

```
<DL>
<DT>Wrox</DT>
<DD>The publisher of Instant Dynamic HTML Programming</DD>
</DL>
```

See also **DL** and **DT**.

DFN

Indicates that text should be rendered as a definition.

Properties	Attributes	Attribute Values	Style Equivalents
classes	CLASS	*<string>*	
ids	ID	*<string>*	
style	STYLE	*<string>*	

There are no methods or events for this tag.

```
<DFN>
  This text will be treated as though it were a definition of some term.
</DFN>
```

DIR

Renders text as a directory listing.

Properties	Attributes	Attribute Values	Style Equivalents
classes	CLASS	*<string>*	
	COMPACT	COMPACT	
ids	ID	*<string>*	
style	STYLE	*<string>*	
type	TYPE	CIRCLE | DISC | SQUARE	

There are no methods or events for this tag.

```
<DIR TYPE="DISC" COMPACT>
  <LI><CODE> properties.doc    421,564 </CODE>
  <LI><CODE> methods.doc        23,518 </CODE>
</DIR>
```

Defines a container section in the page, or logical division within a document.

Properties	Attributes	Attribute Values	Style Equivalents
	ALIGN	CENTER | LEFT | RIGHT | TOP | TEXTTOP | MIDDLE | ABSMIDDLE | BASELINE | BOTTOM | ABSBOTTOM	align
classes	CLASS	*string*	
ids	ID	*string*	
	NOWRAP	NOWRAP	
style	STYLE	*string*	

There are no methods or events for this tag.

```
<DIV>
   This text is inside a document division.
</DIV>
```

For formatting documents using containers, see **SPAN**, **LAYER** and **ILAYER**.

DL

Denotes a definition list.

Properties	Attributes	Attribute Values	Style Equivalents
classes	CLASS	*string*	
	COMPACT	COMPACT	
ids	ID	*string*	
style	STYLE	*string*	

There are no methods or events for this tag.

```
<DL>
<DT>Wrox</DT>
<DD>The publisher of Instant Dynamic HTML Programming</DD>
</DL>
```

DT

Denotes a definition term within a definition list.

Properties	Attributes	Attribute Values	Style Equivalents
classes	CLASS	*<string>*	
ids	ID	*<string>*	
style	STYLE	*<string>*	

There are no methods or events for this tag.

```
<DL>
<DT>Wrox</DT>
<DD>The publisher of Instant Dynamic HTML Programming</DD>
</DL>
```

The **DT** tag is used inside a list created with **DL**. It marks a term whose definition is provided by the next **DD**. The **DT** tag may only contain text-level markup. See also **DD**, **DL**.

EM

Renders text as emphasised, usually in italics.

Properties	Attributes	Attribute Values	Style Equivalents
classes	CLASS	*<string>*	
ids	ID	*<string>*	
style	STYLE	*<string>*	

There are no methods or events for this tag.

```
<EM> This text will be emphasized, by being rendered in italics </EM>
```

EMBED

Embeds documents of any type in the page, to be viewed in another suitable application.

Properties	Attributes	Attribute Values	Style Equivalents
	ALIGN	TOP | BOTTOM | LEFT | RIGHT	align
border	BORDER	*<number>*	borderWidths()
classes	CLASS	*<string>*	
height	HEIGHT	*<string>* | *<number>*	height
	HIDDEN	HIDDEN	
hspace	HSPACE	*<number>*	
ids	ID	*<string>*	
name	NAME	*<string>*	
	PALETTE	BACKGROUND | FOREGROUND	
	PLUGINSPAGE	*<url>*	
src	SRC	*<url>*	
style	STYLE	*<string>*	
type	TYPE	*<string>*	
	UNITS	EN | PIXELS	
vspace	VSPACE	*<number>*	
width	WIDTH	*<string>* | *<number>*	width

There are no methods or events for this tag.

```
<EMBED SRC="MyMovie.mov" WIDTH=300 HEIGHT=200>
<EMBED SRC="Letter.doc" WIDTH=600 HEIGHT=400>
```

See also **NOEMBED**.

FONT

Specifies the font face, size, and color for rendering the text.

Properties	Attributes	Attribute Values	Style Equivalents
classes	CLASS	*<string>*	
	COLOR	*<color>*	color
	FACE	*<string>*	fontFamily
ids	ID	*<string>*	
	POINT-SIZE	*<string>* | *<number>*	
	SIZE	*<string>* | *<number>*	fontSize
style	STYLE	*<string>*	
	WEIGHT	*<string>* | *<number>*	fontWeight

There are no methods or events for this tag.

We can change the size in relation to the current **BASEFONT** setting. This will render the word font as slightly bigger than the other text:

```
<FONT SIZE="+1">font</FONT>
```

We can also specify the font face (font name) and color. This will render the word font in slightly larger, white Arial font:

```
<FONT FACE="ARIAL" SIZE=""+1" COLOR="#FFFFFF">font</FONT>
```

Alternatively, we can use the **POINT-SIZE** and **WEIGHT** attributes. The **WEIGHT** is set using a number between **100** and **900**:

```
<FONT POINT-SIZE="18px" WEIGHT=900>some large and very bold text</FONT>
```

Denotes a form on the page that can contain other controls and elements.

Properties	Attributes	Attribute Values	Style Equivalents
action	ACTION	*<string>*	
classes	CLASS	*<string>*	
encoding	ENC_TYPE	*<string>*	
ids	ID	*<string>*	
length			
method	METHOD	GET | POST	
name	NAME	*<string>*	
style	STYLE	*<string>*	
target	TARGET	_blank | _parent | _self | _top | *<string>*	

Methods

eval	handleEvent	reset
submit	toString	valueOf

Events

onReset	onSubmit

```
<FORM NAME="MyForm" ACTION="http://mysite.com/scripts/handler.pl">
  This is a form which can be submitted to the server.
  Enter Your Opinion: <INPUT TYPE="TEXT" NAME="txtOpinion">
  <INPUT TYPE="SUBMIT" VALUE="Send Opinion">
  <INPUT TYPE="RESET" VALUE="Clear Form">
</FORM>
```

FRAME

Specifies an individual frame within a frameset.

Properties	Attributes	Attribute Values	Style Equivalents
	ALIGN	CENTER | LEFT | RIGHT | TOP | TEXTTOP | MIDDLE | ABSMIDDLE | BASELINE | BOTTOM | ABSBOTTOM	align
	BORDERCOLOR		borderColor
classes	CLASS	<string>	
	FRAMEBORDER	YES | NO | 1 | 0	
ids	ID	<string>	
length			
	MARGINWIDTH	<number>	margins()
	MARGINHEIGHT	<number>	margins()
name	NAME	<string>	
	NORESIZE	NORESIZE	
parent			
scrollbars	SCROLLING	YES | NO | AUTO	
self			
src	SRC	<url>	
style	STYLE	<string>	
window			

Methods

blur	clearInterval	clearTimeout	eval
focus	handleEvent	print	
setInterval	setTimeout	toString	valueOf

Events

onBlur	onFocus	onMove	onResize

See also FRAMESET, NOFRAMES.

278

FRAMESET

Specifies a frameset containing multiple frames and other nested framesets.

Properties	Attributes	Attribute Values	Style Equivalents
border	BORDER	*<number>*	borderWidths()
	BORDERCOLOR		borderColor
classes	CLASS	*<string>*	
	COLS	*<string>* | *<number>*	
	FRAMEBORDER	1 | 0	
ids	ID	*<string>*	
	ROWS	*<string>* | *<number>*	
style	STYLE	*<string>*	

Methods

handleEvent

Events

onBlur   onFocus

Array	Description
frames	Array of all the frames defined within a **<FRAMESET>** tag.

```
<FRAMESET FRAMESPACING=0 COLS="140,*" BORDER=1>
   <FRAME SRC="menu.htm" NAME="menuframe" MARGINWIDTH=0 SCROLLING=NO NORESIZE>
   <FRAME SRC="main.htm" NAME="mainframe" MARGINWIDTH=10 MARGINHEIGHT=10>
</FRAMESET>
```

See also **FRAME**, **NOFRAMES**.

HEAD

Contains tags holding un-viewed information about the document.

Properties	Attributes	Attribute Values	Style Equivalents
classes	CLASS	*<string>*	
ids	ID	*<string>*	
style	STYLE	*<string>*	

There are no methods or events for this tag.

```
<HTML>
  <HEAD>

    <META NAME="Updated" CONTENT="25th Aug 1997">

    <LINK REL="stylesheet" HREF="MyStyle.css">

    <TITLE> Wrox Prress Home Page </TITLE>

    <SCRIPT>
      function MyRoutine(datToday)
        { if (datToday == 'Saturday')  strDestination = 'The beach.'
          else strDestination = 'The office again.' };
    </SCRIPT>

    <STYLE TYPE="text/javascript">
      classes.thisone.all.color = "green";
    </STYLE>

  </HEAD>

  <BODY>
    This is body of the document
  </BODY>

</HTML>
```

Usually only contains **TITLE**, **META**, **BASE**, **ISINDEX**, **LINK**, **SCRIPT** and **STYLE** tags.

Render text as a heading style (**<H1>** to **<H6>**).

Properties	Attributes	Attribute Values	Style Equivalents
	ALIGN	**CENTER** | **LEFT** | **RIGHT**	align
classes	**CLASS**	*<string>*	
ids	**ID**	*<string>*	
style	**STYLE**	*<string>*	

There are no methods or events for this tag.

```
<H1> This is the largest size of heading </H1>
<H6> This is the smallest size of heading </H6>
<H4> And this is somewhere in between </H4>
```

Places a horizontal rule in the page.

Properties	Attributes	Attribute Values	Style Equivalents
	ALIGN	**CENTER** | **LEFT** | **RIGHT**	align
classes	**CLASS**	*<string>*	
ids	**ID**	*<string>*	
	NOSHADE	**NOSHADE**	
	SIZE	*<string>* | *<number>*	
style	**STYLE**	*<string>*	
width	**WIDTH**	*<string>* | *<number>*	width

There are no methods or events for this tag.

For a red horizontal rule half the page width, 5 pixels deep, and with no 3-D effect, we can use:

```
<HR SIZE=5 WIDTH=50% COLOR="#ff0000" NOSHADE>
```

HTML

Identifies the document as containing HTML elements.

Properties	Attributes	Attribute Values	Style Equivalents
classes	CLASS	*<string>*	
ids	ID	*<string>*	
style	STYLE	*<string>*	

There are no methods or events for this tag.

A standard HTML document MUST BE enclosed by the **HTML** tags. Inside these, the **HEAD** and **BODY** tags are used to divide the document up into sections. The **HEAD** section contains information about the document, specifies how it should be displayed, and issues other instructions to the browser. The **BODY** section contains the elements of the document designed to be displayed by the browser:

```
<HTML>
  <HEAD>
    <TITLE> Page title goes here </TITLE>
  </HEAD>
  <BODY>
    This is the main visible part of the page
  </BODY>
</HTML>
```

I

Renders text in an italic font where available.

Properties	Attributes	Attribute Values	Style Equivalents
classes	CLASS	*<string>*	
ids	ID	*<string>*	
style	STYLE	*<string>*	

There are no methods or events for this tag.

```
<I> This text will be displayed in italic font style. </I>
```

Creates an inline layer to act as a container.

Properties	Attributes	Attribute Values	Style Equivalents
above	ABOVE	*\<object_id>*	
background	BACKGROUND	*\<url>*	backgroundImage
below	BELOW	*\<object_id>*	
bgColor	BGCOLOR	*\<color>*	backgroundColor
classes	CLASS	*\<string>*	
clip.bottom	CLIP	[*\<number>*,] [*\<number>*,] *\<number>*, *\<number>*	
clip.height			
clip.left	CLIP	[*\<number>*,] [*\<number>*,] *\<number>*, *\<number>*	
clip.right	CLIP	[*\<number>*,] [*\<number>*,] *\<number>*, *\<number>*	
clip.top	CLIP	[*\<number>*,] [*\<number>*,] *\<number>*, *\<number>*	
clip.width			
ids	ID	*\<string>*	
left	LEFT	*\<number>*	
name	NAME	*\<string>*	
pageX	PAGEX	*\<number>*	
pageY	PAGEY	*\<number>*	
parentLayer			
siblingAbove			
siblingBelow			
src	SRC	*\<url>*	
style	STYLE	*\<string>*	
top	TOP	*\<number>*	
visibility	VISIBILITY	SHOW | HIDDEN | INHERIT	
width	WIDTH	*\<number>*	width
zIndex	Z-INDEX	*\<number>*	

Continued on next page

...ILAYER

Methods

captureEvents	eval	handleEvent	load
moveAbove	moveBelow	moveBy	moveTo
moveToAbsolute		releaseEvents	resizeBy
resizeTo	routeEvent	toString	valueOf

Events

onBlur	onFocus	onLoad
onMouseOut	onMouseOver	

Layers allow us to create a separate section of the document that can be moved, shown, hidden or updated without affecting the rest of the page. Inline layers are used where the contents are required to follow the flow of the rest of the HTML in the page.

```
<ILAYER SRC="http://mysite.com/layerfiles/thislayer.htm">
</ILAYER>
```

```
<ILAYER ID=mylayer WIDTH=75% HEIGHT=100 BGCOLOR="aliceblue">
  This is some text within an inline layer.
  <HR>
  <CENTER><IMG SRC="http://mysite.com/images/thisimage.gif"></CENTER>
  It can contain any HTML to create the contents. We can even use
  separate script sections within a layer, like this:
  <SCRIPT LANGUAGE=JAVASCRIPT1.2>
    function meaningOfLife() {return 42};
  </SCRIPT>
</ILAYER>
```

See also **LAYER, NOLAYERS**.

Embeds an image or a video clip in the document. Most browsers only support GIF and JPEG file types for inline images. Video clips are more usually handled by the **EMBED** tag.

Properties	Attributes	Attribute Values	Style Equivalents
	ALIGN	**CENTER** | **LEFT** | **RIGHT** | **TOP** | **TEXTTOP** | **MIDDLE** | **ABSMIDDLE** | **BASELINE** | **BOTTOM** | **ABSBOTTOM**	**align**
	ALT	*<string>*	
border	**BORDER**	*<number>*	**borderWidths()**
classes	**CLASS**	*<string>*	
complete			
height	**HEIGHT**	*<string>* | *<number>*	**height**
hspace	**HSPACE**	*<number>*	
ids	**ID**	*<string>*	
	ISMAP	**ISMAP**	
lowsrc	**LOWSRC**	*<url>*	
name	**NAME**	*<string>*	
prototype			
src	**SRC**	*<url>*	
style	**STYLE**	*<string>*	
	USEMAP	*<mapname>*	
vspace	**VSPACE**	*<string>* | *<number>*	
width	**WIDTH**	*<string>* | *<number>*	**width**

Methods

eval   handleEvent   toString   valueOf

Events

onAbort	onBlur	onError	onFocus
onKeyDown	onKeyPress	onKeyUp	onLoad

INPUT

Specifies a form input control.

Properties	Attributes	Attribute Values	Style Equivalents
	ALIGN	**TOP | MIDDLE | BOTTOM**	**align**
checked (1)	**CHECKED**	**CHECKED**	
classes	**CLASS**	*<string>*	
defaultChecked (1)			
defaultValue (2)			
form			
ids	**ID**	*<string>*	
length (2)			
	MAXLENGTH	*<number>* (2)	
name	**NAME**	*<string>*	
	SIZE	*<number>*	
style	**STYLE**	*<string>*	
type	**TYPE**	**BUTTON | CHECKBOX | HIDDEN | IMAGE | PASSWORD | RADIO | RESET | SELECT-ONE| SELECT-MULTIPLE| SUBMIT | TEXT | TEXTAREA**	
value	**VALUE**	*string*	

(1) Applies to **CHECKBOX** and **RADIO** types only.
(2) Applies to **TEXT** types only.

Methods

blur (2)	**click**	**eval**	**focus**
handleEvent	**select** (2)	**toString**	**valueOf**

(2) Applies to **TEXT** types only.

Events

onblur (2)	**onchange** (2)	**onclick**	**onfocus**
onkeydown	**onkeypress**	**onkeyup**	**onmousedown**
onmouseup	**onselect** (2)		

(2) Applies to **TEXT** types only.

The **INPUT** tag is used to create a range of HTML controls, depending on the setting of the **TYPE** attribute:

```
<INPUT TYPE="TEXT" NAME="txtFavorite" VALUE="Enter Your Favorite" SIZE=30>
<INPUT TYPE="BUTTON" NAME="btnOK" VALUE="OK" ONCLICK="MyClickCode()">
<INPUT TYPE="CHECKBOX" NAME="chkYes" CHECKED>
<INPUT TYPE="SUBMIT" NAME="btnSubmit" VALUE="Send Details">
<INPUT TYPE="RESET" NAME="btnReset" VALUE="Clear Form">
<INPUT TYPE="HIDDEN" NAME="hidMyValue" VALUE="Hidden from view">
<INPUT TYPE="PASSWORD" NAME="txtPassword">
```

ISINDEX

Defines the text input field for entering a query.

Properties	Attributes	Attribute Values	Style Equivalents
	ACTION	*url*	
classes	**CLASS**	*<string>*	
ids	**ID**	*<string>*	
	PROMPT	*string*	
style	**STYLE**	*<string>*	

There are no methods or events for this tag.

The **ISINDEX** tag was used before **FORM** became more popular. When inserted in a document it allows users to enter keywords which are then sent to the server. The server executes a search and returns the results. The **PROMPT** attribute can be used to override the default text in the dialog box ("Enter search keywords:").

KBD

Renders text in fixed-width font.

Properties	Attributes	Attribute Values	Style Equivalents
classes	CLASS	*<string>*	
ids	ID	*<string>*	
style	STYLE	*<string>*	

There are no methods or events for this tag.

KBD is used to indicate text which should be entered by the user. It is often drawn in a mono-spaced font, although this is not required. It differs from **CODE** in that **CODE** indicates code fragments and **KBD** indicates input.

```
This tag is useful to indicate that <KBD> something </KBD> is to be typed.
```

KEYGEN

Used to generate key information in a form.

Properties	Attributes	Attribute Values	Style Equivalents
	CHALLENGE	*<string>*	
classes	CLASS	*<string>*	
ids	ID	*<string>*	
	NAME	*<string>*	
style	STYLE	*<string>*	

There are no methods or events for this tag.

This tag is used to provide a challenge string into which the key to be used by the server is packed:

```
<KEYGEN CHALLENGE="h29tsi73meu8sgh3kdh7sgns" NAME=MyKey>
```

288

Creates a layer that can be absolutely positioned.

Properties	Attributes	Attribute Values	Style Equivalents
above	ABOVE	*<object_id>*	
background	BACKGROUND	*<url>*	backgroundImage
below	BELOW	*<object_id>*	
bgColor	BGCOLOR	*<color>*	backgroundColor
classes	CLASS	*<string>*	
clip.bottom	CLIP	[*<number>*,] [*<number>*,] *<number>*, *<number>*	
clip.height			
clip.left	CLIP	[*<number>*,] [*<number>*,] *<number>*, *<number>*	
clip.right	CLIP	[*<number>*,] [*<number>*,] *<number>*, *<number>*	
clip.top	CLIP	[*<number>*,] [*<number>*,] *<number>*, *<number>*	
clip.width			
ids	ID	*<string>*	
left	LEFT	*<number>*	
name	NAME	*<string>*	
pageX	PAGEX	*<number>*	
pageY	PAGEY	*<number>*	
parentLayer			
siblingAbove			
siblingBelow			
src	SRC	*<url>*	
style	STYLE	*<string>*	
top	TOP	*<number>*	
visibility	VISIBILITY	SHOW | HIDDEN | INHERIT	
width	WIDTH	*<number>*	width
zIndex	Z-INDEX	*<number>*	

Continued on next page

...LAYER

Methods

captureEvents	eval	handleEvent	load
moveAbove	moveBelow	moveBy	moveTo
moveToAbsolute		releaseEvents	resizeBy
resizeTo	routeEvent	toString	valueOf

Events

onBlur	onFocus	onLoad
onMouseOut	onMouseOver	

Layers allow us to create a separate section of the document that can be moved, shown, hidden or updated without affecting the rest of the page. Layers created with the **LAYER** tag are used where the contents need to be placed at an absolute position within the page, outside the flow of the rest of the HTML.

```
<LAYER SRC="http://mysite.com/layerfiles/thislayer.htm">
</LAYER>
```

```
<LAYER ID=mylayer TOP=200 LEFT=50 HEIGHT=100 WIDTH=200>
  This is some text within an absolute positioned layer.
  <HR>
  <CENTER><IMG SRC="http://mysite.com/images/thisimage.gif"></CENTER>
  It can contain any HTML to create the contents. We can even use
  separate script sections within a layer, like this:
  <SCRIPT LANGUAGE=JAVASCRIPT1.2>
    function meaningOfLife() {return 42};
  </SCRIPT>
</LAYER>
```

See also **ILAYER, NOLAYERS**.

Denotes one item within an ordered or unordered list.

Properties	Attributes	Attribute Values	Style Equivalents
classes	CLASS	*<string>*	
ids	ID	*<string>*	
style	STYLE	*<string>*	
type	TYPE	A | a | I | i | 1	listStyleType
value	VALUE	*<string>* | *<number>*	

There are no methods or events for this tag.

Used to create indented lists of items, either in an ordered or unordered list. Tags can be nested to provide sub-lists:

```
<OL>
  <LI> This is item one in an ordered list
  <LI> This is item two in an ordered list
  <OL>
    <LI> This is item one in a nested list, inside the first list
    <LI> This is item two in a nested list, inside the first list
  </OL>
  <UL>
    <LI> Plus, we can nest unordered lists inside ordered lists
    <LI> And vice-versa. This is an unordered list containing
    <LI> Three items.
  </UL>
</OL>
```

In an ordered list, we can also specify different types of numbering, and start the numbers where we like:

```
<OL START=5 TYPE=1>
  <LI> This item will be numbered 5
  <LI> This item will be numbered 6
</OL>
```

See also **UL**, **OL**.

LINK

Defines a hyperlink between the document and some other resource.

Properties	Attributes	Attribute Values	Style Equivalents
classes	CLASS	*<string>*	
href	HREF	*<url>*	
ids	ID	*<string>*	
	REV	*<string>*	
	REL	*<string>*	
style	STYLE	*<string>*	
			textAlign
title	TITLE	*<string>*	
type	TYPE	*<string>*	

There are no methods or events for this tag.

LINK is used to indicate relationships between documents. There are two possible relationships: **REL** indicates a normal relationship to the document specified in the **URL**. **REV** indicates a reverse relationship. In other words, the *other* document has the indicated relationship with this one. The **TITLE** attribute can be used to suggest a title for the referenced **URL** or relation.

Some possible values for **REL** and **REV** are:

REV="made"   Indicates the creator of the document. Usually the URL is a **mailto:** URL with the creator's e-mail address. Advanced browsers will now let the reader comment on the page with just one button or keystroke.

REL="stylesheet" This indicates the location of the appropriate style sheet for the current document.

```
<LINK REL="stylesheet" HREF="http://mysite.com/styles/mystyle.css">
```

```
<LINK REL="subdocument" HREF="http://mysite.com/docs/subdoc.htm">
<LINK REV="maindocument" HREF="http://mysite.com/styles/maindoc.htm">
```

Specifies a collection of hot spots for a client-side image map

Properties	Attributes	Attribute Values	Style Equivalents
classes	CLASS	*<string>*	
ids	ID	*<string>*	
name	NAME	*<string>*	
style	STYLE	*<string>*	

Array	Description
areas	Array of all the areas that make up the image map.

```
<MAP NAME="toolbar">
  <AREA SHAPE="RECT" COORDS="12,216,68,267" HREF="wrox.html">
  <AREA SHAPE="CIRCLE" COORDS="100,200,50" HREF="index.html">
</MAP>
```

There are no methods or events for this tag. See also **AREA**.

Renders text as in a menu list.

Properties	Attributes	Attribute Values	Style Equivalents
classes	CLASS	*<string>*	
	COMPACT	COMPACT	
ids	ID	*<string>*	
style	STYLE	*<string>*	

There are no methods or events for this tag.

```
<MENU>
  <LI> This is an item in a menu
  <LI> This is another item in a menu
</MENU>
```

META

Provides various types of un-viewed information or instructions to the browser.

Properties	Attributes	Attribute Values	Style Equivalents
classes	CLASS	*<string>*	
	CONTENT	*<string>*	
	HTTP-EQUIV	*<string>*	
ids	ID	*<string>*	
name	NAME	*<string>*	
style	STYLE	*<string>*	

There are no methods or events for this tag.

```
<META NAME="Updated" CONTENT="05-Aug-97">
<META NAME="Author" CONTENT="Wrox Press Limited">
<META NAME="Keywords" CONTENT="HTML Dynamic Web Internet">
<META NAME="Description" CONTENT="A page about Dynamic HTML">
```

A popular use for the **META** tag is to set HTTP values, and redirect the browser to another page:

```
<META HTTP-EQUIV="REFRESH" CONTENT="10;URL=http://www.wrox.com">
<META HTTP-EQUIV="EXPIRES" CONTENT="Fri, 06 Jun 1997 12:00:00 GMT">
```

MULTICOL

Used to define formatting information for multiple columns.

Properties	Attributes	Attribute Values	Style Equivalents
classes	CLASS	*<string>*	
	COLS	*<number>*	
	GUTTER	*<number>*	
ids	ID	*<string>*	
style	STYLE	*<string>*	
	WIDTH	*<number>*	

There are no methods or events for this tag.

NOEMBED

Defines the HTML to be displayed by browsers that do not support embeds.

Properties	Attributes	Attribute Values	Style Equivalents
classes	CLASS	*<string>*	
ids	ID	*<string>*	
style	STYLE	*<string>*	

There are no methods or events for this tag.

```
<EMBED SRC="MyMovie.mov" WIDTH=300 HEIGHT=200>

<NOEMBED>
  Sorry, your browser cannot display the embedded document.
</NOEMBED>
```

NOFRAMES

Defines the HTML to be displayed by browsers that do not support frames.

Properties	Attributes	Attribute Values	Style Equivalents
classes	CLASS	*<string>*	
ids	ID	*<string>*	
style	STYLE	*<string>*	

There are no methods or events for this tag.

```
<FRAMESET FRAMESPACING=0 COLS="140,*" BORDER=1>
  <FRAME SRC="menu.htm" NAME="menuframe" MARGINWIDTH=0 SCROLLING=NO >
  <FRAME SRC="main.htm" NAME="mainframe" MARGINWIDTH=10 MARGINHEIGHT=10>
</FRAMESET>

<NOFRAMES>
  Sorry, your browser does not support frames.
</NOFRAMES>
```

NOLAYER

Defines the HTML to be displayed by browsers that do not support layers.

Properties	Attributes	Attribute Values	Style Equivalents
classes	CLASS	*<string>*	
ids	ID	*<string>*	
style	STYLE	*<string>*	

There are no methods or events for this tag. See also **ILAYER**, **LAYER**.

```
<LAYER SRC="http://mysite.com/mylayers/layerone.htm>
</LAYER>

<NOLAYERS>
  Sorry, your browser does not support document layers.
</NOLAYERS>
```

NOSCRIPT

Defines the HTML to be displayed in browsers that do not support scripting.

Properties	Attributes	Attribute Values	Style Equivalents
classes	CLASS	*<string>*	
ids	ID	*<string>*	
style	STYLE	*<string>*	

There are no methods or events for this tag. See also **SCRIPT**.

```
<SCRIPT LANGUAGE=JAVASCRIPT>
  function MeaningOfLife() {return 42};
</SCRIPT>

<NOSCRIPT>
  Sorry, your browser does not support scripting.
</NOSCRIPT>
```

Renders lines of text with `<LI>` tags as an ordered list.

Properties	Attributes	Attribute Values	Style Equivalents
classes	CLASS	*<string>*	
	COMPACT	COMPACT	
ids	ID	*<string>*	
	START	*<number>*	
style	STYLE	*<string>*	
type	TYPE	A | a | I | i | 1	listStyleType

There are no methods or events for this tag.

Used to create indented lists of items, either in an ordered or unordered list. Tags can be nested to provide sub-lists:

```
<OL>
  <LI> This is item one in an ordered list
  <LI> This is item two in an ordered list
  <OL>
    <LI> This is item one in a nested list, inside the first list
    <LI> This is item two in a nested list, inside the first list
  </OL>
  <UL>
    <LI> Plus, we can nest unordered lists inside ordered lists
    <LI> And vice-versa. This is an unordered list containing
    <LI> Three items.
  </UL>
</OL>
```

In an ordered list, we can also specify different types of numbering, and start the numbers where we like:

```
<OL START=5 TYPE=1>
  <LI> This item will be numbered 5
  <LI> This item will be numbered 6
</OL>
```

See also **UL**, **LI**.

OPTION

Denotes one choice in a **<SELECT>** element.

Properties	Attributes	Attribute Values	Style Equivalents
classes	CLASS	*<string>*	
defaultSelected			
	DISABLED	DISABLED	
ids	ID	*<string>*	
index			
length			
	PLAIN	PLAIN	
selected	SELECTED	SELECTED	
style	STYLE	*<string>*	
text	TEXT	*<string>*	
value	VALUE	*<string>* | *<number>*	

Methods

eval	toString	valueOf

There are no events for this element. The **VALUE** attribute is the value returned when that item is selected. The text after the **OPTION** is displayed in the list:

```
<SELECT SIZE=1 ID="MyDropList">
   <OPTION VALUE="0.25"> 1/4 inch thick
   <OPTION VALUE="0.5"> 1/2 inch thick
   <OPTION VALUE="0.75" SELECTED> 3/4 inch thick
   <OPTION VALUE="1"> 1 inch thick
</SELECT>

<SELECT SIZE=12 ID="MySelectList" MULTIPLE>
   <OPTION VALUE="0723"> Active Server Pages
   <OPTION VALUE="1002"> HTML Help Systems
   <OPTION VALUE="0448"> VBScript Programming
   <OPTION VALUE="0464"> ActiveX Web Databases
   <OPTION VALUE="0707"> IE4 Programming
</SELECT>
```

Denotes a paragraph.

Properties	Attributes	Attribute Values	Style Equivalents
	ALIGN	Left | CENTER | RIGHT	align
classes	CLASS	*<string>*	
ids	ID	*<string>*	
style	STYLE	*<string>*	

There are no methods or events for this tag. The **P** tag can be used on its own or to enclose the text in a paragraph:

```
This sentence is separated from the next.<P> This is another paragraph.

<P> This is one paragraph. </P> <P>This is another paragraph. </P>
```

PARAM

Used in an **<APPLET>** tag to set the applet's properties.

Properties	Attributes	Attribute Values	Style Equivalents
name	NAME	*<string>*	
classes	CLASS	*<string>*	
ids	ID	*<string>*	
style	STYLE	*<string>*	
value	VALUE	*<string>* | *<number>*	

There are no methods or events for this tag.

```
<APPLET CODEBASE="http://mysite.com/applets/samples/" CODE="myapp.class"
  WIDTH=250 HEIGHT=150 NAME="MyApp">
  <PARAM NAME="PropertyValue" VALUE="17438">
  <PARAM NAME="AnotherProperty" VALUE="StatusRed">
</APPLET>
```

See also **APPLET**.

PRE

Renders text in fixed-width type without processing tags.

Properties	Attributes	Attribute Values	Style Equivalents
classes	CLASS	*<string>*	
ids	ID	*<string>*	
style	STYLE	*<string>*	
width	WIDTH	*<string>* | *<number>*	width

There are no methods or events for this tag.

```
<PRE>
  Text here will be rendered in a fixed width font and the line breaks
  will be maintained, so this part will be on the second line.
</PRE>
```

S

Renders text in strikethrough type.

Properties	Attributes	Attribute Values	Style Equivalents
classes	CLASS	*<string>*	
ids	ID	*<string>*	
style	STYLE	*<string>*	

There are no methods or events for this tag.

```
We can show a word in <S>strikethrough</S> format like this.
```

See also **STRIKE**.

SAMP

Renders text as a code sample listing.

Properties	Attributes	Attribute Values	Style Equivalents
classes	CLASS	*<string>*	
ids	ID	*<string>*	
style	STYLE	*<string>*	

There are no methods or events for this tag.

```
<SAMP>
  ...
  x = sqr(y + b) * 2^e
  result = (x + y) / cos(t)
  ...
</SAMP>
```

SCRIPT

Specifies a script for the page that will be interpreted by a script engine.

Properties	Attributes	Attribute Values	Style Equivalents
	ARCHIVE	*<url>*	
classes	CLASS	*<string>*	
ids	ID	*<string>*	
language	LANGUAGE	JAVASCRIPT | JAVASCRIPT1.1 | JAVASCRIPT1.2 | VBSCRIPT	
src	SRC	*<url>*	
style	STYLE	*<string>*	

There are no methods or events for this tag.

```
<SCRIPT LANGUAGE=JavaScript1.2>
  function MyRoutine(datToday)
    { if (datToday == 'Saturday')  strDestination = 'The beach.'
      else strDestination = 'The office again.' };
</SCRIPT>
```

SELECT

Defines a list box or dropdown list.

Properties	Attributes	Attribute Values	Style Equivalents
classes	CLASS	*<string>*	
form			
ids	ID	*<string>*	
length			
	MULTIPLE	MULTIPLE	
name	NAME	*<string>*	
selectedIndex			
	SIZE	*<number>*	
style	STYLE	*<string>*	
text	TEXT	*<string>*	
type			

Methods

blur	eval	focus
handleEvent	toString	valueOf

Events

onblur	onchange	onfocus

The **VALUE** attribute can be used to provide a different value to scripting code from the text displayed in the list:

```
<SELECT SIZE=12 ID="MySelectList" MULTIPLE>
  <OPTION VALUE="0723"> Active Server Pages
  <OPTION VALUE="1002"> HTML Help Systems
  <OPTION VALUE="0448"> VBScript Programming
  <OPTION VALUE="0464"> ActiveX Web Databases
  <OPTION VALUE="0707"> IE4 Programming
</SELECT>
```

SERVER

Used to execute a LiveWire script.

Properties	Attributes	Attribute Values	Style Equivalents
classes	CLASS	*<string>*	
ids	ID	*<string>*	
style	STYLE	*<string>*	

There are no methods or events for this tag.

```
<SERVER>
  ...
  any code placed here will be executed on the server, not in the browser
  ...
</SERVER>
```

SMALL

Specifies that text should be displayed with a relatively smaller font than the current font.

Properties	Attributes	Attribute Values	Style Equivalents
classes	CLASS	*<string>*	
ids	ID	*<string>*	
style	STYLE	*<string>*	

There are no methods or events for this tag.

```
We can show <SMALL>some of the text</SMALL> in a smaller font.
```

SPACER

Defines horizontal and vertical spacing.

Properties	Attributes	Attribute Values	Style Equivalents
	ALIGN	LEFT | RIGHT | TOP | TEXTTOP | MIDDLE | ABSMIDDLE | BASELINE | BOTTOM | ABSBOTTOM	
classes	CLASS	*<string>*	
	HEIGHT	*<number>*	
ids	ID	*<string>*	
	SIZE	*<number>*	
style	STYLE	*<string>*	
	TYPE	BLOCK | HORIZONTAL | VERTICAL	
	WIDTH	*<number>*	

There are no methods or events for this tag.

SPAN

Used with a style sheet to define non-standard attributes for text on the page.

Properties	Attributes	Attribute Values	Style Equivalents
classes	CLASS	*<string>*	
ids	ID	*<string>*	
style	STYLE	*<string>*	

There are no methods or events for this tag.

```
<STYLE>
  classes.myformat.color = "red";
</STYLE>

<P STYLE="color=green"> In a green paragraph, we can change
<SPAN CLASS="myformat">some of the text to red</SPAN>
without changing anything else. </P>
```

304

Renders text in strikethrough type.

Properties	Attributes	Attribute Values	Style Equivalents
classes	CLASS	*<string>*	
ids	ID	*<string>*	
style	STYLE	*<string>*	

There are no methods or events for this tag.

```
We can show a word in <STRIKE>strikethrough</STRIKE> format like this.
```

See also **S**.

Renders text in boldface.

Properties	Attributes	Attribute Values	Style Equivalents
classes	CLASS	*<string>*	
ids	ID	*<string>*	
style	STYLE	*<string>*	

There are no methods or events for this tag.

```
<STRONG>BOLD</STRONG>
```

This example will produce the word **BOLD** in bold font.

See also **B**.

STYLE

Specifies the style sheet for the page.

Properties	Attributes	Attribute Values	Style Equivalents
classes	CLASS	*<string>*	
ids	ID	*<string>*	
src	SRC	*<url>*	
style	STYLE	*<string>*	
type	TYPE	*<string>*	

There are no methods or events for this tag.

Styles for a document can be specified by using a separate style sheet file, a style section in the **HEAD** section of the document, or by using an inline style attribute:

```
<STYLE SRC="http://www.mysite.com/styles/thisone.css">
```

```
<STYLE TYPE="text/javascript">
  tags.H3.textDecoration = "blink";
  classes.mystyle.color="green";
</STYLE>
...
<H3>This is some text that will blink</H3>
<P CLASS="mystyle"> This is some green text</P>
```

```
<P STYLE="color=red"> This is a red paragraph</P>
```

You can also use the **SPAN** tag with styles to over-ride the inherited styles:

```
<STYLE>
  classes.myformat.color = "red";
</STYLE>

<P STYLE="color=green"> In a green paragraph, we can change
<SPAN CLASS="myformat">some of the text to red</SPAN>
without changing anything else. </P>
```

Renders text as a subscript using a smaller font than the current font.

Properties	Attributes	Attribute Values	Style Equivalents
classes	CLASS	*<string>*	
ids	ID	*<string>*	
style	STYLE	*<string>*	

There are no methods or events for this tag.

```
To calculate the result multiply x<SUB>1</SUB> by x<SUB>2</SUB>.
```

SUP

Renders text as a superscript using a smaller font than the current font.

Properties	Attributes	Attribute Values	Style Equivalents
classes	CLASS	*<string>*	
ids	ID	*<string>*	
style	STYLE	*<string>*	

There are no methods or events for this tag.

```
To calculate the result use x<SUP>3</SUP> - y<SUP>2</SUP>.
```

TABLE

Denotes a section of **<TR>** **<TD>** and **<TH>** tags organized into rows and columns.

Properties	Attributes	Attribute Values	Style Equivalents
	ALIGN	CENTER | LEFT | RIGHT	align
bgColor	BGCOLOR	*<color>*	backgroundColor
border	BORDER	*<number>*	borderWidths()
	CELLSPACING	*<number>*	
	CELLPADDING	*<number>*	
classes	CLASS	*<string>*	
	COLS	*<number>*	
height	HEIGHT	*<number>*	height
hspace	HSPACE	*<number>*	
ids	ID	*<string>*	
style	STYLE	*<string>*	
vspace	VSPACE	*<number>*	
width	WIDTH	*<string>* | *<number>*	width

There are no methods or events for this tag.

```
<TABLE BACKGROUND="wrox.gif" BORDER=1 WIDTH=100%>
  <TR>
    <TH COLSPAN=2>This is a heading cell</TH>
  </TR>
  <TR BGCOLOR=aliceblue>
    <TD>This is a body detail cell</TD>
    <TD>And so is this one</TD>
  </TR>
  <TR>
    <TD NOWRAP>This is a detail cell that won't wrap</TD>
    <TD>And so is this one</TD>
  </TR>
</TABLE>
```

Specifies a cell in a table.

Properties	Attributes	Attribute Values	Style Equivalents
	ALIGN	CENTER | LEFT | RIGHT	align
bgColor	BGCOLOR	*<color>*	backgroundColor
classes	CLASS	*<string>*	
	COLSPAN	*<number>*	
height	HEIGHT	*<number>*	height
ids	ID	*<string>*	
	NOWRAP	NOWRAP	
	ROWSPAN	*<number>*	
style	STYLE	*<string>*	
	VALIGN	TOP | MIDDLE | BOTTOM | BASELINE	verticalAlign
width	WIDTH	*<string>* | *<number>*	width

There are no methods or events for this tag.

```
<TABLE BACKGROUND="wrox.gif" BORDER=1 WIDTH=100%>
  <TR>
    <TH COLSPAN=2>This is a heading cell</TH>
  </TR>
  <TR BGCOLOR=aliceblue>
    <TD>This is a body detail cell</TD>
    <TD>And so is this one</TD>
  </TR>
  <TR>
    <TD NOWRAP>This is a detail cell that won't wrap</TD>
    <TD>And so is this one</TD>
  </TR>
</TABLE>
```

TEXTAREA

Specifies a multi-line text input control.

Properties	Attributes	Attribute Values	Style Equivalents
classes	CLASS	*<string>*	
	COLS	*<string>* | *<number>*	
defaultValue			
form			
ids	ID	*<string>*	
name	NAME	*<string>*	
	ROWS	*<string>* | *<number>*	
style	STYLE	*<string>*	
type			
value	VALUE	*string*	
	WRAP	OFF | HARD | SOFT	

Methods

blur	eval	focus	handleEvent
select	toString	valueOf	

Events

onblur	onchange	onfocus
onkeydown	onkeypress	onkeyup
onselect		

```
<TEXTAREA NAME=mytext ROWs=5 COLS=30>
  Enter your comments here.
</TEXTAREA>
```

Denotes a header row in a table. Contents are centred within each cell and are bold.

Properties	Attributes	Attribute Values	Style Equivalents
	ALIGN	CENTER | LEFT | RIGHT	align
bgColor	BGCOLOR	*<color>*	backgroundColor
classes	CLASS	*<string>*	
	COLSPAN	*<number>*	
height	HEIGHT	*<number>*	height
ids	ID	*<string>*	
	NOWRAP	NOWRAP	
	ROWSPAN	*<number>*	
style	STYLE	*<string>*	
	VALIGN	TOP | MIDDLE | BOTTOM | BASELINE	verticalAlign
width	WIDTH	*<string>* | *<number>*	width

There are no methods or events for this tag.

```
<TABLE BACKGROUND="wrox.gif" BORDER=1 WIDTH=100%>
  <TR>
    <TH COLSPAN=2>This is a heading cell</TH>
  </TR>
  <TR BGCOLOR=aliceblue>
    <TD>This is a body detail cell</TD>
    <TD>And so is this one</TD>
  </TR>
  <TR>
    <TD NOWRAP>This is a detail cell that won't wrap</TD>
    <TD>And so is this one</TD>
  </TR>
</TABLE>
```

TITLE

Denotes the title of the document, and used in the browser's window title bar.

Properties	Attributes	Attribute Values	Style Equivalents
classes	CLASS	*<string>*	
ids	ID	*<string>*	
style	STYLE	*<string>*	

There are no methods or events for this tag.

```
<HTML>
  <HEAD>
    <TITLE> My new Web page </TITLE>
  </HEAD>
  <BODY>
    Page contents
  </BODY>
</HTML>
```

TR

Specifies a row in a table.

Properties	Attributes	Attribute Values	Style Equivalents
	ALIGN	CENTER | LEFT | RIGHT	align
bgColor	BGCOLOR	*<color>*	backgroundColor
classes	CLASS	*<string>*	
ids	ID	*<string>*	
style	STYLE	*<string>*	
	VALIGN	TOP | MIDDLE | BOTTOM | BASELINE	verticalAlign

There are no methods or events for this tag.

Renders text in fixed-width type.

Properties	Attributes	Attribute Values	Style Equivalents
classes	CLASS	*<string>*	
ids	ID	*<string>*	
style	STYLE	*<string>*	

There are no methods or events for this tag.

```
<TT>
This text will be shown in a fixed width font.
It comes from when documents were usually sent
from place to place on a teletype machine.
</TT>
```

Renders text underlined.

Properties	Attributes	Attribute Values	Style Equivalents
classes	CLASS	*<string>*	
ids	ID	*<string>*	
style	STYLE	*<string>*	

There are no methods or events for this tag.

```
We can use this tag to <U>underline</U> some words.
```

UL

Renders lines of text with `<LI>` tags as a bulleted list.

Properties	Attributes	Attribute Values	Style Equivalents
classes	CLASS	*<string>*	
	COMPACT	COMPACT	
ids	ID	*<string>*	
style	STYLE	*<string>*	
type	TYPE	disc | circle | square	listStyleType

There are no methods or events for this tag.

Used to create indented lists of items, either in an ordered or unordered list. Tags can be nested to provide sub-lists:

```
<UL>
  <LI> This is an item in an un-ordered list
  <LI> This is another item in an un-ordered list
  <OL>
    <LI> This is item one in a nested ordered list, inside the first list
    <LI> This is item two in a nested ordered list, inside the first list
  </OL>
</UL>
```

In an unordered list, we can also specify different types of bullet to be used:

```
<UL TYPE=square>
  <LI> This is an item in a list that uses square bullets
  <LI> This is also an item in a list that uses square bullets
</UL>
```

See also **OL**, **LI**.

VAR

Properties	Attributes	Attribute Values	Style Equivalents
classes	CLASS	*<string>*	
ids	ID	*<string>*	
style	STYLE	*<string>*	

There are no methods or events for this tag.

```
Used to show the name of a variable like <VAR>MyVariable</VAR>
```

Inserts a soft line break in a block of NOBR text.

Properties	Attributes	Attribute Values	Style Equivalents
classes	CLASS	*<string>*	
ids	ID	*<string>*	
style	STYLE	*<string>*	

There are no methods or events for this tag.

```
<NOBR>
  This text will not break onto two lines in the browser window.
  This text will only break here<WBR>, and only if it won't fit on one line.
</NOBR>
```

Renders text as example code, usually in a mono-spaced font.

Properties	Attributes	Attribute Values	Style Equivalents
classes	CLASS	*<string>*	
ids	ID	*<string>*	
style	STYLE	*<string>*	

There are no methods or events for this tag.

```
<XMP>
  ...
  x = sqr(y + b) * 2^e
  result = (x + y) / cos(t)
  ...
</XMP>
```

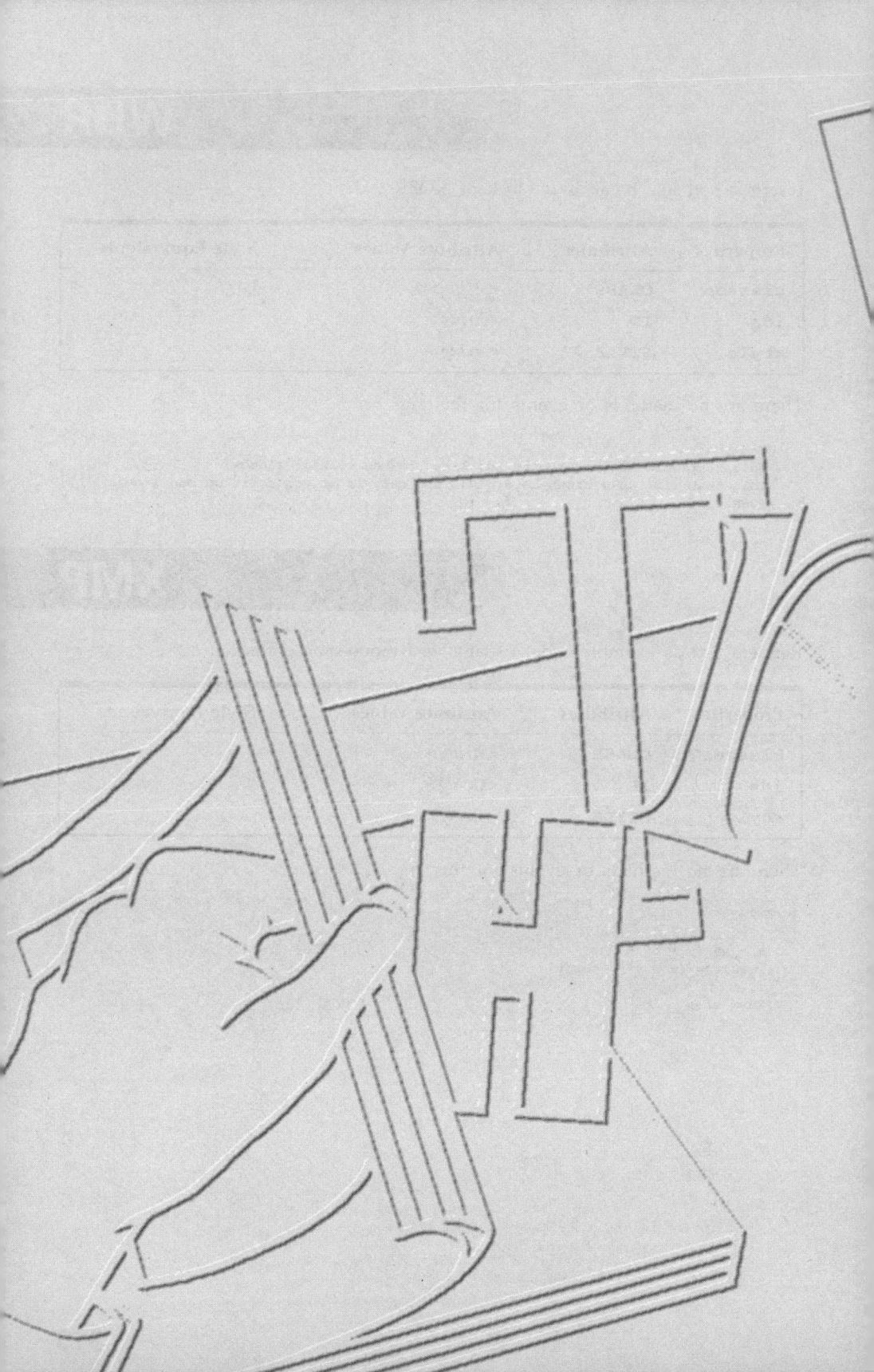

Section

C

Style Sheet Properties

There are almost fifty properties defined for the standard implementation of CSS, and most are used in Dynamic HTML. They are broken up into several major 'groups'. We've listed all of the properties below (by group), with some of the crucial information for each. Note that not all browsers support all the properties. We've marked the points at which Communicator diverges, where possible, and also included the equivalent **JavaScript Style Sheet (JSS)** properties where appropriate. There are also the six new properties that have been introduced in HTML 4.0, and don't form part of the CSS1 recommendations. These new properties have all been clearly marked as well. We start with a summary of the units of measurement that can be used in the properties.

Units of Measurement

There are two basic categories of unit: relative and absolute (plus percentages). As a general rule, relative measures are preferred, as using absolute measures requires familiarity with the actual mechanism of display (e.g. what kind of printer, what sort of monitor, etc.).

Relative Units

Values: **em, en, ex, px**

em, en and **ex** are typographic terms, and refer to the sizes of other characters on display.
px refers to a measurement in screen pixels, which is generally only meaningful for display on computer monitors and depends on the user's display resolution setting.

*Note that Netscape Communicator 4 does not support **en**.*

Absolute Units

Values: in, cm, mm, pt, pc

in gives the measurement in inches, **cm** gives it in centimetres, **mm** in millimetres, **pt** is in typeface points (72 to an inch), and **pc** is in picas (1 pica equals 12 points). These units are generally only useful when you know what the output medium is going to be, since browsers are allowed to approximate if they must.

> Note that Netscape Communicator 4 only supports **pt** and **pi** (the equivalent to **px**).

Percentage

Values: Numeric

This is given as a number (with or without a decimal point), and is relative to a length unit (which is usually the font size of the current element). You should note that child elements will inherit the computed value, not the percentage value (so a child will not be 20% of the parent, it will be the same size as the parent).

Listing of Properties

There follows a listing of all the properties for use in Dynamic HTML, together with the possible values, defaults and other useful information. The properties are divided up into categories—**font** properties, **color** and **background** properties, **text** properties and **size** and **position** properties.

Font Properties

font

JSS Equivalent:	not supported
Values:	<font-size>, [/<line-height>], <font-family>
Default:	Not defined
Applies to:	All elements
Inherited:	Yes
Percentage?:	Only on <font-size> and <line-height>

This allows you to set several font properties all at once, with the initial **Values** being determined by the properties being used (e.g. the default for **font-size** is different to the default for **font-family**). This property should be used with multiple values separated by spaces, or a comma if specifying multiple font-families.

font-family

JSS Equivalent:	fontFamily
Values:	Name of a font family (e.g. New York) or a generic family (e.g. Serif)
Default:	Set by browser
Applies to:	All elements
Inherited:	Yes
Percentage?:	No

You can specify multiple values in order of preference (in case the browser doesn't have the font you want). To do so, simply specify them and separate multiple values with commas. You should end with a generic font-family (allowable values would then be **serif, sans-serif, cursive, fantasy** or **monospace**). If the font name has spaces in it, you should enclose the name in quotation marks.

font-size

JSS Equivalent:	fontSize
Values:	\<absolute\>, \<relative\>, \<length\>, \<percentage\>
Default:	medium
Applies to:	All elements
Inherited:	Yes
Percentage?:	Yes, relative to parent font size

The values for this property can be expressed in several ways:

- Absolute size: legal values are **xx-small, x-small, small, medium, large, x-large, xx-large**

- Relative size: values are **larger, smaller**

- Length: values are in any unit of measurement, as described at the beginning of this Section.

- Percentage: values are a percentage of the parent font size

font-style

JSS Equivalent:	fontStyle
Values:	normal, italic, oblique
Default:	normal
Applies to:	All elements
Inherited:	Yes
Percentage?:	No

This is used to apply styling to your font—if a pre-rendered font is available (e.g. New York Oblique) then that will be used if possible. If not, the styling will be applied electronically. In JavaScript Style Sheets, you can also use the values **small-caps, italic small-caps** and **oblique small-caps**.

font-variant

JSS Equivalent: not supported
Values: `normal, small-caps`
Default: `normal`
Applies to: All elements
Inherited: Yes
Percentage?:   No

`Normal` is the standard appearance, and is therefore set as the default. `Small-caps` uses capital letters that are the same size as normal lowercase letters. In JavaScript you can use the `fontStyle` property to get this effect, which supports extra values over and above those of CSS.

font-weight

JSS Equivalent: `fontWeight`
Values: `normal`, `bold`, `bolder`, `lighter`, <number from 100 to 900>
Default: `normal`
Applies to: All elements
Inherited: Yes
Percentage?:   No

Specifies the 'boldness' of text, which is usually expressed by stroke thickness. If numeric values are used, they must proceed in 100-unit increments (e.g. 250 isn't legal). `400` is the same as `normal`, and `700` is the same as `bold`.

Color and Background Properties

color

JSS Equivalent: `color`
Values: Color name or RGB value
Default: Depends on browser
Applies to: All elements
Inherited: Yes
Percentage?:   No

Sets the text color of any element. The color can be specified by name (e.g. green) or by RGB-value. The RGB value can be expressed in several ways; in hex—"#FFFFFF", by percentage—"80%, 20%, 0%", or by value—"255,0,0".

background

JSS Equivalent: not supported
Values: `transparent`, <color>, <URL>, <repeat>, <scroll>, <position>
Default: `transparent`
Applies to: All elements
Inherited: No
Percentage?:   Yes, will refer to the dimension of the element itself

Specifies the background of the document. `Transparent` is the same as having no defined background. You can use a solid color, or you can specify the URL for an image to be used. The URL can be absolute or relative, but must be enclosed in parentheses and immediately preceded by **url**:

```
BODY { background: url(http://foo.bar.com/image/small.gif) }
```

It is possible to use a color and an image, in which case the image will be overlaid on top of the color. The color can be a single color, or two colors that will be blended together. Images can have several properties set:

- <repeat> can be **repeat**, **repeat-x** (where **x** is a number), **repeat-y** (where **y** is a number) and **no-repeat**. If no repeat value is given, then **repeat** is assumed

- <scroll> determines whether the background image will remain fixed, or scroll when the page does. Possible values are **fixed** or **scroll**

- <position> specifies the location of the image on the page. Values are by percentage (horizontal, vertical), by absolute distance (in a unit of measurement, horizontal then vertical), or by keyword (values are **top**, **middle**, **bottom**, **left**, **center**, **right**)

In CSS, it is also possible to specify different parts of the background properties separately using these next five properties. In JavaScript, you can use some of these instead of the **background** property, which is not supported.

background-attachment

JSS Equivalent:	not supported
Values:	**fixed**, **scroll**
Default:	**scroll**
Applies to:	Background image
Inherited:	No
Percentage?:	No

Determines whether the background will remain fixed, or scroll when the page does.

background-color

JSS Equivalent:	**backgroundColor**
Values:	**transparent**, <color>
Default:	**transparent**
Applies to:	Background color
Inherited:	No
Percentage?:	No

Sets a color for the background. This can be a single color, or two colors blended together. The colors can be specified by name (e.g. green) or by RGB-value (which can be stated in hex "#FFFFFF", by percentage "80%, 20%, 0%", or by value "255,0,0"). The syntax for using two colors is:

```
BODY { background-color: red / blue }
```

321

background-image

JSS Equivalent: **backgroundImage**
Values: **none**, <URL>
Default: **none**
Applies to: Background image
Inherited: No
Percentage?: No

You can specify the URL for an image to be used as the background. The URL can be absolute or relative, but must be enclosed in parentheses and immediately preceded by **url**. See **background** for example syntax.

background-position

JSS Equivalent: not supported
Values: <position> <length> **top**, **center**, **bottom**, **left**, **right**.
Default: **top, left**
Applies to: Background image
Inherited: No
Percentage?: No

Specifies the initial location of the background image on the page using two values, which are defined as a percentage (horizontal, vertical), an absolute distance (in a unit of measurement, horizontal then vertical), or using two of the available keywords.

background-repeat

JSS Equivalent: not supported
Values: **repeat**, **repeat-x**, **repeat-y**, **no-repeat**.
Default: **repeat**
Applies to: Background image
Inherited: No
Percentage?: No

Determines whether the image is repeated to fill the page or element. If **repeat-x** or **repeat-y** are used, the image is repeated in only one direction. The default is to repeat the image in both directions.

Text Properties

letter-spacing

JSS Equivalent: not supported
Values: **normal**, <length>
Default: **normal**
Applies to: All elements
Inherited: Yes
Percentage?: No

Sets the distance between letters. The length unit indicates an addition to the default space between characters. Values, if given, should be in units of measurement.

line-height

JSS Equivalent:	`lineHeight`
Values:	**normal**, <number>, <length>, <percentage>
Default:	Depends on browser
Applies to:	All elements
Inherited:	Yes
Percentage?:	Yes, relative to the font-size of the current element

Sets the height of the current line. Numerical values are expressed as the font size of the current element multiplied by the value given (for example, 1.2 would be valid). If given by length, a unit of measurement must be used. Percentages are based on the font-size of the current font, and should normally be more than 100%.

list-style

JSS Equivalent:	not supported
Values:	<image>, <position>, <type>
Default:	Depends on browser
Applies to:	List elements
Inherited:	No
Percentage?:	No

Defines how list items are displayed. Can be used to set all the properties, or the individual styles can be set independently using the following styles.

list-style-image

JSS Equivalent:	not supported
Values:	**none**, <image>
Default:	**none**
Applies to:	List elements
Inherited:	No
Percentage?:	No

Defines the URL of an image to be used as the 'bullet' or list marker for each item in a list.

list-style-position

JSS Equivalent:	not supported
Values:	**inside**, **outside**
Default:	**outside**
Applies to:	List elements
Inherited:	No
Percentage?:	No

Indicates if the list marker should be placed indented or extended in relation to the list body.

323

list-style-type

JSS Equivalent:	`listStyleType`
Values:	`none`, `circle`, `disc`, `square`, `decimal`, `lower-alpha`, `upper-alpha`, `lower-roman`, `upper-roman`
Default:	`disc`
Applies to:	List elements
Inherited:	No
Percentage?:	No

Defines the type of 'bullet' or list marker used to precede each item in the list.

text-align

JSS Equivalent:	`textAlign`
Values:	`left`, `right`, `center`, `justify`
Default:	Depends on browser
Applies to:	Block-level elements
Inherited:	Yes
Percentage?:	No

Describes how text is aligned within the element. Essentially replicates the `<DIV ALIGN=>` tag.

text-decoration

JSS Equivalent:	`textDecoration`
Values:	`none`, `underline`, `overline`, `line-through`, `blink`
Default:	`none`
Applies to:	All elements
Inherited:	No
Percentage?:	No

Specifies any special appearance of the text. Open to extension by vendors, with unidentified extensions rendered as an underline. This property is not inherited, but will usually span across any 'child' elements.

text-indent

JSS Equivalent:	`textIndent`
Values:	`normal`, <length>, <percentage>
Default:	Zero
Applies to:	Block-level elements
Inherited:	Yes
Percentage?:	Yes, refers to width of parent element

Sets the indentation values in units of measurement, or as a percentage of the parent element's width.

text-transform

JSS Equivalent: `textTransform`
Values: `capitalize`, `uppercase`, `lowercase`, `none`
Default: none
Applies to: All elements
Inherited: Yes
Percentage?:   No

- **capitalize** will set the first character of each word in the element as uppercase
- **uppercase** will set every character in the element in uppercase
- **lowercase** will place every character in lowercase
- **none** will neutralize any inherited settings

vertical-align

JSS Equivalent: `verticalAlign`
Values: `baseline`, `sub`, `super`, `top`, `text-top`, `middle`, `bottom`
                  `text-bottom`, <percentage>
Default: `baseline`
Applies to: Inline elements
Inherited: No
Percentage?:   Yes, will refer to the line-height itself

Controls the vertical positioning of any affected element.

- **baseline** sets the alignment with the base of the parent
- **middle** aligns the vertical midpoint of the element with the baseline of the parent plus half of the vertical height of the parent
- **sub** makes the element a subscript
- **super** makes the element a superscript
- **text-top** aligns the element with the top of text in the parent element's font
- **text-bottom** aligns with the bottom of text in the parent element's font
- **top** aligns the top of the element with the top of the tallest element on the current line
- **bottom** aligns with the bottom of the lowest element on the current line

325

word-spacing

JSS Equivalent:	not supported
Values:	<length>, <percentage>
Default:	Zero
Applies to:	Text elements
Inherited:	Yes
Percentage?:	Yes, refers to parent's width

Sets the spacing between words in the text. Using a <percentage> value will base the spacing on the parent element or default spacing for that element.

Size and Border Properties

These values are used to set the characteristics of the layout 'box' that exists around elements. They can apply to characters, images and so on.

border-color

JSS Equivalent:	**borderColor**
Values:	<color>
Default:	<none>
Applies to:	All elements
Inherited:	No
Percentage?:	No

Sets the color of the four borders. By supplying the URL of an image instead, the image itself is repeated to create the border.

border-style

JSS Equivalent:	**borderStyle**
Values:	**none, solid, dashed, dotted, double, groove, inset, outset, ridge**
Default:	**none**
Applies to:	All elements
Inherited:	No
Percentage?:	No

Sets the style of the four borders.

border-top, border-right, border-bottom, border-left, border

JSS Equivalent:	not supported
Values:	<border-width>, <border-style>, <color>
Default:	**medium, none**, <none>
Applies to:	All elements
Inherited:	No
Percentage?:	No

Sets the properties of the border element (box drawn around the affected element). Works roughly the same as the margin settings, except that it can be made visible.

326

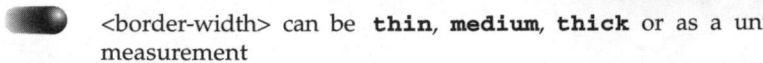

● <border-width> can be **thin, medium, thick** or as a unit of measurement

● <border-style> can be **none, solid**

The color argument is used to fill both the background of the element while it loads, and any transparent parts of the element. By supplying the URL of an image instead, the image itself is repeated to create the border. It is also possible to specify values for attributes of the border property separately using the **border-width, border-style** and **border-color** properties.

border-top-width, border-right-width, border-bottom-width, border-left-width, border-width

JSS Equivalents:	**borderTopWidth, borderRightWidth, borderBottomWidth, borderLeftWidth, borderWidths()**
Values:	**thin, medium, thick**, <length>
Default:	**medium**
Applies to:	All elements
Inherited:	No
Percentage?:	No

Sets the width of the border for the element. Each side can be set individually, or the **border-width** property can be used to set all of the sides. You can also supply up to four arguments for the **border-width** property to set individual sides, in the same way as you can with the **margin** property. In JavaScript Style Sheets, you must specify all four values for the **borderWidths()** property.

clear

JSS Equivalent:	**clear**
Values:	**none, both, left, right**
Default:	**none**
Applies to:	Block-level elements
Inherited:	No
Percentage?:	No

Forces the following elements to be displayed below an element which is aligned. Normally, they would wrap around it.

display

JSS Equivalent:	**display**
Values:	**block, in-line, list-item, none**
Default:	According to HTML
Applies to:	All elements
Inherited:	No
Percentage?:	No

This property indicates whether an element is in-line (e.g. **<EM>**), block-level (e.g. **<H1>**), or a list item (e.g. **<LI>**).

float

JSS Equivalent:	**align**
Values:	**none**, **left**, **right**
Default:	**none**
Applies to:	Block elements
Inherited:	No
Percentage?:	No

Causes following elements to be wrapped to the left or right of the element, rather than being placed below it. Notice that, because **float** is a reserved word in JavaScript, the JSS Equivalent is named **align**.

height

JSS Equivalent:	**height**
Values:	**auto**, <length>
Default:	**auto**
Applies to:	Block-level elements
Inherited:	No
Percentage?:	No

Sets the vertical size of an element, and will scale the element if necessary. The value is returned as an integer.

left

Not supported in CSS1 - NEW IN HTML 4.0	
JSS Equivalent:	not supported
Values:	**auto**, <length>, <percentage>
Default:	**auto**
Applies to:	**Block-level elements**
Inherited:	No
Percentage?:	Yes, refers to parent's width

Sets or returns the left position of an element when displayed in 2-D canvas mode, allowing accurate placement and animation of individual elements. The value is returned as an integer.

margin-top, margin-right, margin-bottom, margin-left, margin

JSS Equivalents:	**marginTop**, **marginRight**, **marginBottom**, **marginLeft**, **margins()**
Values:	**auto**, <length>, <percentage>
Default:	**Zero**
Applies to:	All elements
Inherited:	No
Percentage?:	Yes, refers to parent element's width

Sets the size of margins around any given element. You can use **margin** as shorthand for setting all of the other values (as it applies to all four sides). If you use multiple values in **margin** but use less than four, opposing sides will try to be equal. These values all set the effective minimum distance between the current element and others. In JavaScript Style Sheets, you must specify all four values for the `margins()` property.

overflow

Not supported in CSS1 - NEW in HTML 4.0

JSS Equivalent:	not supported
Values:	`none, clip, scroll`
Default:	none
Applies to:	Block-level elements
Inherited:	No
Percentage?:	No

This controls how a container element will display its content if this is not the same size as the container.

- `none` means that the container will use the **Default** method. For example, as in an image element, the content may be resized to fit the container

- `clip` means that the contents will not be resized, and only a part will be visible

- `scroll` will cause the container to display scroll bars so that the entire contents can be viewed by scrolling

padding-top, padding-right, padding-bottom, padding-left, padding

JSS Equivalents:	`paddingTop, paddingRight, paddingBottom, paddingLeft, paddings()`
Values:	`auto`, <length>, <percentage>
Default:	`Zero`
Applies to:	All elements
Inherited:	No
Percentage?:	Yes, refers to parent element's width

Sets the distance between the content and border of an element. You can use `padding` as shorthand for setting all of the other values (as it applies to all four sides). If you use multiple values in `padding` but use less than four, opposing sides will try to be equal. These values all set the effective minimum distance between the current element and others. In JavaScript Style Sheets, you must specify all four values for the `paddings()` property.

position

Not supported in CSS1 - NEW IN HTML 4.0

JSS Equivalent:	not supported
Values:	`absolute, relative, static`
Default:	`relative`
Applies to:	All elements
Inherited:	No
Percentage?:	No

Specifies if the element can be positioned directly on the 2-D canvas.

- **absolute** means it can be fixed on the background of the page at a specified location, and move with it

- **static** means it can be fixed on the background of the page at a specified location, but not move when the page is scrolled

- **relative** means that it will be positioned normally, depending on the preceding elements

top

Not supported in CSS1 - NEW IN HTML 4.0
JSS Equivalent: not supported
Values: **auto**, <percentage>, <length>
Default: **auto**
Applies to: Block-level elements
Inherited: No
Percentage?: Yes, refers to parent's width

Sets or returns the vertical position of an element when displayed in 2-D canvas mode, allowing accurate placement and animation of individual elements. Value is returned as an integer.

visibility

Not supported in CSS1 - NEW IN HTML 4.0
JSS Equivalent: not supported
Values: **visible, hidden, inherit**
Default: **inherit**
Applies to: All elements
Inherited: If value is **inherit**
Percentage?: No

Allows the element to be displayed or hidden on the page. Elements which are hidden still take up the same amount of space, but are rendered transparently. Can be used to dynamically display only one of several overlapping elements

- **visible** means that the element will be visible

- **hidden** means that the element will not be visible

- **inherit** means that the element will only be visible when its parent or container element is visible

white-space

JSS Equivalent:	whiteSpace
Values:	<length>, <percentage>
Default:	zero
Applies to:	Block-level elements
Inherited:	No
Percentage?:	Yes, refers to parent's width

Sets the spacing between elements. Using a <percentage> value will base the spacing on the parent element or default spacing for that element.

width

JSS Equivalent:	width
Values:	auto, <length>, <percentage>
Default:	auto, except for any element with an intrinsic dimension
Applies to:	Block-level elements
Inherited:	No
Percentage?:	Yes, refers to parent's width

Sets the horizontal size of an element, and will scale the element if necessary. The value is returned as an integer.

z-index

Not supported in CSS1 - NEW IN HTML 4.0	
JSS Equivalent:	not supported
Values:	<number>
Default:	Depends on the HTML source
Applies to:	Block-level elements
Inherited:	No
Percentage?:	No

Controls the ordering of overlapping elements, and defines which will be displayed 'on top'. Positive numbers are above the normal text on the page, and negative numbers are below. Allows a 2.5-D appearance by controlling the layering of the page's contents.

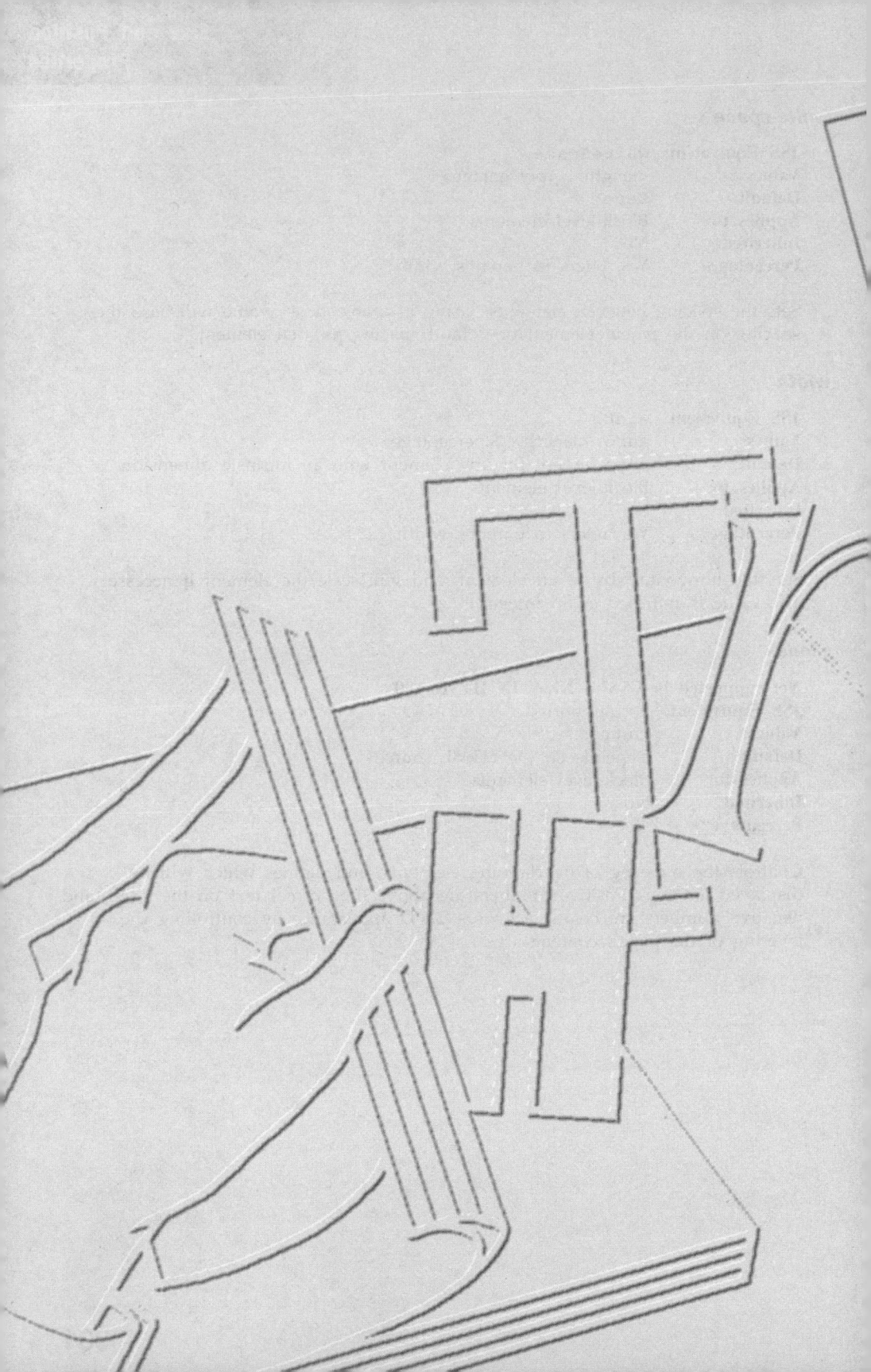

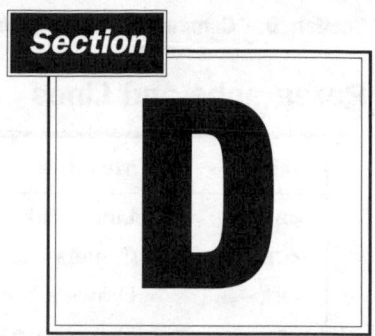

Common HTML Tags by Category

Here we have listed some of the most commonly used tags by category. When you know what you want to do, but you're not sure which tag will achieve the desired effect, use the reference tables below to put you on the right track.

Document Structure

Tag	Meaning
`<!-- -->`	Allows authors to add comments to code.
`<!DOCTYPE>`	Defines the document type. This is required by all HTML documents.
`<BASE>`	Specifies the document's base URL—its original location. It's not normally necessary to include this tag. It may only be used in `<HEAD>` section.
`<BODY>`	Contains the main part of the HTML document.
`<DIV>`	Defines a block division of the `<BODY>`.
`<HEAD>`	Contains information about the document itself.
`<HTML>`	Signals the beginning and end of an HTML document.
`<LINK>`	Defines the current document's relationship with other resources. Used in `<HEAD>` section only.
`<META>`	Describes the content of a document.

Titles and Headings

Tag	Meaning	Tag	Meaning
`<H1>`	Heading level 1	`<H5>`	Heading level 5
`<H2>`	Heading level 2	`<H6>`	Heading level 6
`<H3>`	Heading level 3	`<TITLE>`	Defines the title of the document.
`<H4>`	Heading level 4		

Paragraphs and Lines

Tag	Meaning
**\ **	Line break.
\<CENTER>	Centers subsequent text/images
\<HR>	Draws a horizontal rule.
\<P>	Defines a paragraph.
\<SPACER>	Defines horizontal and vertical spacing.
\<WBR>	Inserts a soft line break in a block of **\<NOBR>** text.

Text Styles

Tag	Meaning
\<ADDRESS>	Indicates an address. The address is typically displayed in italics.
\<B>	Emboldens text.
\<BASEFONT>	Sets font size to be used as default.
\<BIG>	Changes the physical rendering of the font to one size larger.
\<BLINK>	Causes the text to flash on and off.
\<BLOCKQUOTE>	Formats a quote—typically by indentation
\<CITE>	Renders text in italics.
\<CODE>	Renders text in a font resembling computer code.
\<DFN>	Indicates the first instance of a term or important word.
\<EM>	Emphasized text—usually italic.
\<FONT>	Changes font properties.
\<I>	Defines italic text.
\<KBD>	Indicates typed text. Useful for instruction manuals etc.
\<PRE>	Pre-formatted text. Renders text exactly how it is typed, i.e. carriage returns, styles etc., *will* be recognized.
\<S> \<STRIKE>	Strike through. Renders the text as 'deleted' (crossed out).
\<SAMP>	Specifies sample code.
\<SMALL>	Changes the physical rendering of a font to one size smaller.
\<SPAN>	Defines an area for reference by a style sheet
\<STRONG>	Strong emphasis—usually bold.
\<STYLE>	Specifies the style sheet for the page.
\<SUB>	Subscript.
\<SUP>	Superscript.
\<TT>	Renders text in fixed width, typewriter style font.

334

Tag	Meaning
<U>	Underlines text. Not widely supported at present, and not recommended, as it can cause confusion with hyperlinks, which also normally appear underlined.
<VAR>	Indicates a variable.
<XMP>	Renders text in fixed width type, used for example text.

Lists

Tag	Meaning
<DD>	Definition description. Used in definition lists with <DT> to define the term.
<DIR>	Denotes a directory list by indenting the text.
<DL>	Defines a definition list.
<DT>	Defines a definition term. Used with definition lists.
<LI>	Defines a list item in any type of list other than a definition list.
<MENU>	Defines a menu list.
<OL>	Defines an ordered (numbered) list.
<UL>	Defines an unordered (bulleted) list.

Tables

Tag	Meaning
<CAPTION>	Puts a title above a table.
<MULTICOL>	Used to define formatting information for multiple columns.
<TABLE>	Defines a series of columns and rows to form a table.
<TD>	Specifies a cell in a table.
<TH>	Specifies a header column. Text will be centered and bold.
<TR>	Defines the start of a table row.

Links

Tag	Meaning
<A>	Used to insert an anchor, which can be either a local reference point or a hyperlink to another URL.
<A HREF="url">	Hyperlink to another document.
<A NAME="name">	Link to a local reference point.

Graphics, Objects, Multimedia and Scripts

Tag	Meaning
`<APPLET>`	Inserts an applet.
`<AREA>`	Specifies the shape of a "hot spot" in a client-side image map.
`<EMBED>`	Defines an embedded object in an HTML document.
`<IMG>`	Embeds an image or a video clip in a document.
`<MAP>`	Specifies a collection of hot spots for a client-side image map.
`<NOEMBED>`	Defines the HTML to be displayed by browsers that do not support embeds.
`<NOSCRIPT>`	Specifies HTML to be displayed in browsers which don't support scripting.
`<PARAM>`	Defines parameters for a Java applet.
`<SCRIPT>`	Inserts a script.
`<SERVER>`	Used to execute a LiveWire script.

Forms

Tag	Meaning
`<FORM>`	Defines part of the document as a user fill-out form.
`<INPUT>`	Defines a user input box.
`<KEYGEN>`	Used to generate key material.
`<OPTION>`	Used within the **SELECT** tag to present the user with a number of options.
`<SELECT>`	Denotes a list box or drop-down list.
`<TEXTAREA>`	Defines a text area inside a **FORM** element.

Frames and Layers

Tag	Meaning
`<FRAME>`	Defines a single frame in a frameset.
`<FRAMESET>`	Defines the main container for a frame.
`<ILAYER>`	Creates an inline layer to act as a container.
`<ISINDEX>`	Defines a text input field for entering a query.
`<LAYER>`	Creates a layer that can be absolutely positioned.
`<NOFRAMES>`	Allows for backward compatibility with non-frame compliant browsers.
`<NOLAYER>`	Defines the HTML to be displayed by browsers that do not support layers.

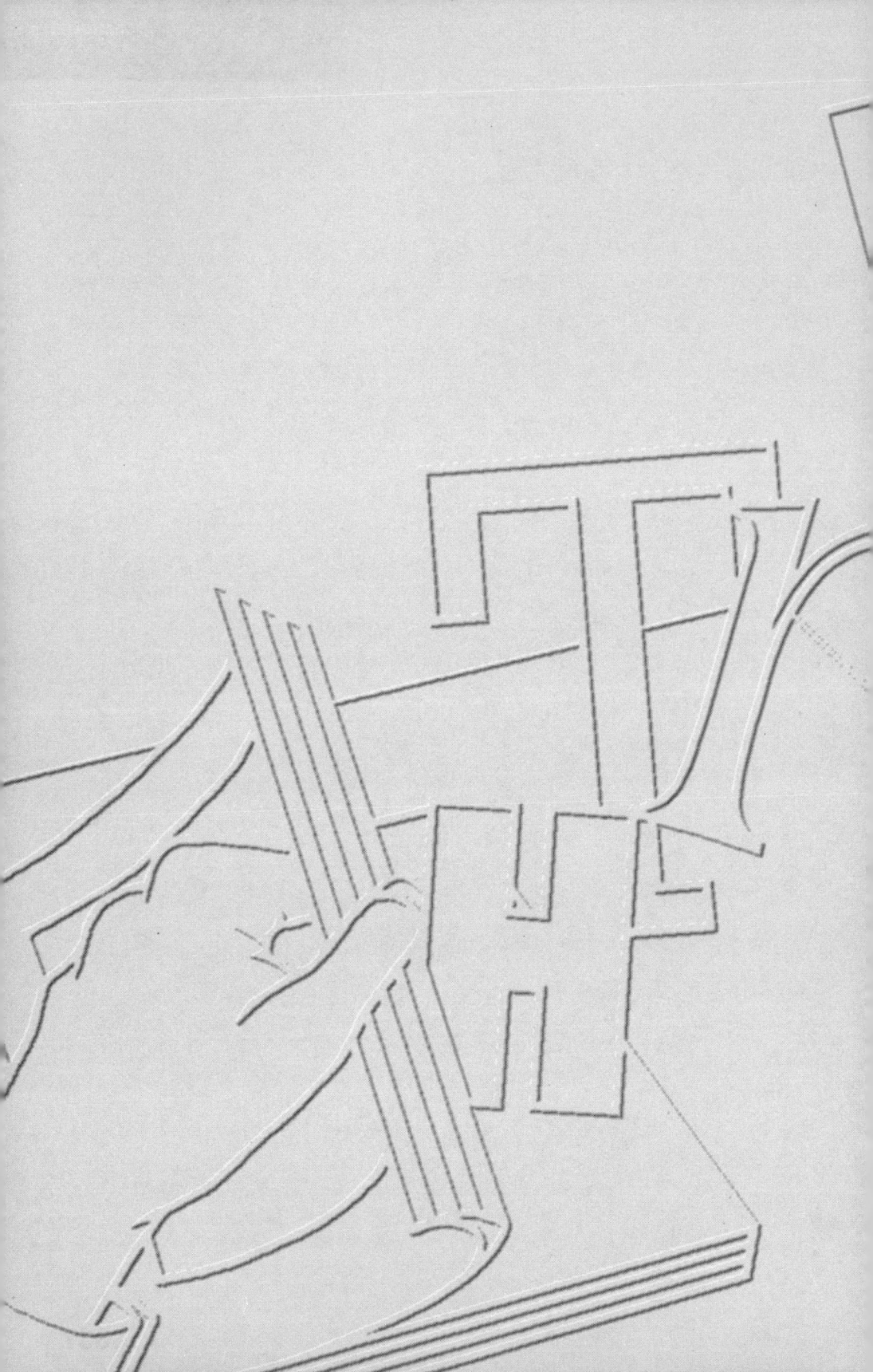

The Browser Object Model

The Dynamic HTML Object Model contains 38 **objects** and 17 **arrays**. Most of these are organized into a strict hierarchy that allows HTML authors to access all the parts of the browser, and the pages that are loaded, from a scripting language like JavaScript.

The Object Model In Outline

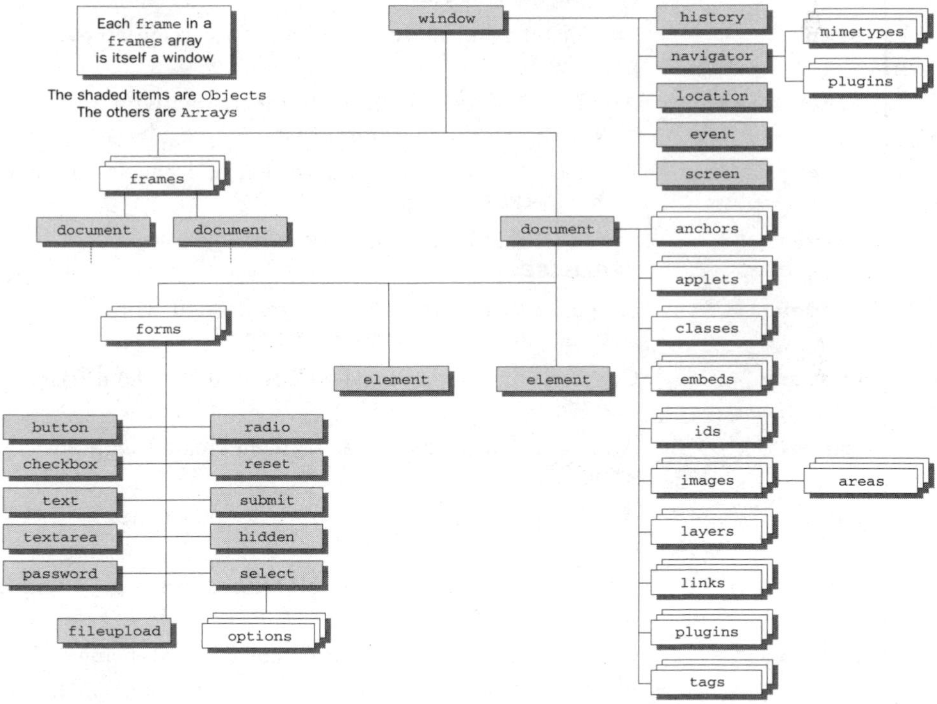

Each frame in a frames array is itself a window

The shaded items are Objects
The others are Arrays

window

history

mimetypes

navigator

plugins

location

event

screen

frames

document

document

document

anchors

applets

classes

forms

element

element

embeds

ids

button

radio

checkbox

reset

images

areas

text

submit

layers

textarea

hidden

links

password

select

plugins

fileupload

options

tags

The diagram shows the object hierarchy in graphical form. It is followed by a list of the objects and arrays, with a brief description. Then, each object is documented in detail, showing the properties, methods, and events it supports.

Note that not all the objects and arrays are included in the diagram. Some are not part of the overall object model, but are used to access other items such as dialogs or HTML elements. Others are objects used in JavaScript when writing scripts in a page. We've listed the browser objects and the JavaScript objects separately.

The Browser Objects

Objects	Description
anchor	An object that represents an anchor created with `<A NAME="..">` in the document.
area	An area created within a `<MAP>` element by an `<AREA>` tag.
button	An object that represents a control created with an `<INPUT>` tag where `TYPE=BUTTON`.
checkbox	An object that represents a control created with an `<INPUT>` tag where `TYPE=CHECKBOX`.
document	Exposes the contents of the HTML document through a number of arrays and properties.
element	An object that represents a control in the array of all the controls on a `<FORM>`.
event	The global event object exposed for accessing an event's parameters.
fileUpload	An object that represents a control created with an `<INPUT>` tag where `TYPE=FILE`.
form	An object that represents the section of a page contained within a `<FORM>` tag.
frame	An object that represents a `<FRAME>` within a `<FRAMESET>`.
hidden	An object that represents a control created with an `<INPUT>` tag where `TYPE=HIDDEN`.
history	Contains information on the URLs that the client has visited.
image	An object that represents an element created with an `<IMG>` tag.
layer	An object that represents a `<LAYER>` or `<ILAYER>` in a document.
link	An object that represents a link created in the page with an `<A HREF="..">` tag.
location	Contains information about the current URL being displayed.
mimeType	Contains information about the MIME types supported by the browser.
navigator	An object representing the browser itself, and its properties.

340

Objects	Description
option	An individual **<OPTION>** item in a list created by a **<SELECT>** tag.
password	An object that represents a control created with an **<INPUT>** tag where **TYPE=PASSWORD**.
plugin	An object that represents the features of an installed plugin component.
radio	An object that represents a control created with an **<INPUT>** tag where **TYPE=RADIO**.
reset	An object that represents a control created with an **<INPUT>** tag where **TYPE=RESET**.
screen	Contains information about the client's screen and rendering abilities.
select	An object that represents a list control created with a **<SELECT>** tag.
submit	An object that represents a control created with an **<INPUT>** tag where **TYPE=SUBMIT**.
text	An object that represents a control created with an **<INPUT>** tag where **TYPE=TEXT**.
textarea	An object that represents a text area control created with a **<TEXTAREA>** tag.
window	An object that provides information about the current browser window.

The Browser Object Arrays

Arrays	Description
anchors	Array of all the anchors in the document.
applets	Array of all the objects in the document, including intrinsic controls, images, applets, embeds and other objects.
areas	Array of all the areas that make up an image map.
arguments	Array of all the arguments supplied to a function.
classes	Array of all the style classes defined in the document.
elements	Array of all controls and elements in the form.
embeds	Array of all the embed tags in the document.
forms	Array of all the forms in the page.
frames	Array of all the frames defined within a **<FRAMESET>** tag.
ids	Array of all the individual element styles defined in the document.
images	Array of all the images in the page.

Table continued on following page

341

Arrays	Description
layers	Array of all the layers in a document or another layer.
links	Array of all the links and **<AREA>** blocks in the page.
mimeTypes	Array of all the supported MIME types.
options	Array of all the items in a **<SELECT>** list.
plugins	Array of all the plugins available.
tags	Array of all the elements in the document.

The JavaScript Objects

Objects	Description
array	An object that is used in script to manipulate the contents of an array.
boolean	An object that is used in script to represent a Boolean (**true** or **false**) value.
date	An object that is used in script to represent a date.
function	An object that represents a script function written within the page.
math	An object that is used in script to manipulate numbers and perform calculations.
number	An object that is used in script to represent a number.
packages	An object that represents the classes of a Java package embedded in the document.
regExp	An object that is used in script to represent a regular expression.
string	An object that is used in script to represent a string of characters.

The Browser Objects in Detail

This section documents all the properties, arrays, methods and events available for each object in the browser hierarchy. The JavaScript objects are covered at the end of this reference section.

The Anchor Object

An object that represents an anchor created with **<A NAME="..">** in the document.

Property	Attribute	Description
name	NAME	Specifies the name to use to refer to the anchor.

Methods	Description
eval	Evaluates the object and returns a representation of its value
toString	Returns a string containing a textual representation of the object's value.
valueOf	Returns the primitive value of an object, or the name of the object itself.

The Area Object

An area created within a `<MAP>` element by an `<AREA>` tag.

Properties	Attribute	Description
hash		The string following the # symbol, the anchor name, in the HREF value.
host		The hostname:port part of the location or URL.
hostname		The hostname part of the location or URL.
href	HREF	The destination URL or anchor point.
pathname		The file or object path name following the third slash in a URL.
port		The port number in a URL.
protocol		The initial sub-string indicating the URL's access method.
search		Any query string or form data following the ? in the complete URL.
target	TARGET	Specifies the window or frame where the new page will be loaded.

Methods	Description
eval	Evaluates the object and returns a representation of its value
handleEvent	Invokes the appropriate event handling code of the object for this event.
toString	Returns a string containing a textual representation of the object's value.
valueOf	Returns the primitive value of an object, or the name of the object itself.

Events	Description
onDblClick	Occurs when the user double-clicks on the area.

Table continued on following page

Events	Description
onMouseOut	Occurs when the mouse pointer leaves the area.
onMouseOver	Occurs when the mouse pointer first enters the area.

The Button Object

An object that represents a control created with an **<INPUT>** tag where **TYPE=BUTTON**.

Properties	Attribute	Description
form		Reference to the form object that contains the element.
name	NAME	Specifies the name to use to refer to the button.
type	TYPE	Must be **"BUTTON"** for a Button element.
value	VALUE	The caption of the button.

Methods	Description
blur	Causes the element to lose the focus, and fire its **onBlur** event.
click	Simulates a click on the element, and fires its **onClick** event.
eval	Evaluates the object and returns a representation of its value
focus	Causes the element to receive the focus, and fire its **onFocus** event.
handleEvent	Invokes the appropriate event handling code of object for this event.
toString	Returns a string containing a textual representation of the object's value.
valueOf	Returns the primitive value of an object, or the name of the object itself.

Events	Description
onBlur	Occurs when the button control loses the focus.
onClick	Occurs when the button control is clicked or 'pressed'.
onFocus	Occurs when the button control receives the focus.
onMouseDown	Occurs when the user presses a mouse button.
onMouseUp	Occurs when the user releases a mouse button.

The CheckBox Object

An object that represents a control created with an **<INPUT>** tag where **TYPE=CHECKBOX**.

Properties	Attribute	Description
checked	**CHECKED**	Indicates that the checkbox is selected (i.e. 'on' or ticked).
defaultChecked		Denotes if the checkbox is checked by default.
form		Reference to the form object that contains the element.
name	**NAME**	Specifies the name to use to refer to the checkbox.
type	**TYPE**	Must be **"CHECKBOX"** for a Checkbox element.
value	**VALUE**	The value of the control when checked.

Methods	Description
blur	Causes the control to lose the focus, and fire its **onBlur** event.
click	Simulates a click on the control, and fires its **onClick** event.
eval	Evaluates the object and returns a representation of its value
focus	Causes the control to receive the focus, and fire its **onFocus** event.
handleEvent	Invokes the appropriate event handling code of the object for this event.
toString	Returns a string containing a textual representation of the object's value.
valueOf	Returns the primitive value of an object, or the name of the object itself.

Events	Description
onBlur	Occurs when the checkbox loses the focus.
onClick	Occurs when the mouse button is clicked on the checkbox.
onFocus	Occurs when the checkbox receives the focus.

345

The Document Object

Exposes the entire HTML content through its own arrays and properties, and provides a range of events and methods to work with documents.

Properties	Attribute	JSS Equivalent	Description
alinkColor	ALINK	color	Color of the active links on the page, i.e. those where the mouse button is held down.
bgColor	BGCOLOR	background -color	Background color of the page.
cookie			String value of a cookie stored by the browser.
domain			Security domain of the document.
fgColor	TEXT	color	Color of the document foreground text.
lastModified			Date the document was last modified.
linkColor	LINK	color	The color of the unvisited links in the page.
referrer			URL of the page containing the link that loaded this page, if available.
title	TITLE		The title of the document as defined in the <TITLE> tag
URL	URL		Uniform Resource Locator of the page.
vlinkColor	VLINK	color	Color of the visited links in the page.

Arrays	Description
anchors	Array of all the anchors defined in the document.
applets	Array of all the objects in the document, including intrinsic controls, images, applets, embeds and other objects.
classes	Array of all the style classes defined in the document.
embeds	Array of all the <EMBED> tags in the document.
forms	Array of all the forms defined in the document.

Arrays	Description
`ids`	Array of all the individual element styles defined in the document.
`images`	Array of all the images defined on the document.
`layers`	Array of all the layers defined in the document.
`links`	Array of all the links and `<AREA>` blocks defined in the document.
`plugins`	An alias for array of all the embeds defined in the document.
`tags`	Array of all the elements defined in the document.

Methods	Description
`captureEvents`	Instructs the document to capture events of a particular type.
`close`	Closes an output stream to a document and updates the display.
`eval`	Evaluates the object and returns a representation of its value
`getSelection`	Returns a string containing the text currently selected in the document.
`handleEvent`	Invokes the appropriate event handling code of the object for this event.
`open`	Opens a new browser window.
`releaseEvents`	Instructs the document to stop capturing events of a particular type.
`routeEvent`	Passes an event that has been captured back up through the normal event hierarchy.
`toString`	Returns a string containing a textual representation of the object's value.
`valueOf`	Returns the primitive value of an object, or the name of the object itself.
`write`	Writes text and HTML to a document in the specified window.
`writeln`	Writes text and HTML followed by a carriage return.

Events	Description
`onClick`	Occurs when the mouse button is clicked on the document.

Table continued on following page

Events	Description
onDblClick	Occurs when the user double-clicks on the document.
onKeyDown	Occurs when the user presses a key.
onKeyPress	Occurs when the user presses and releases a key.
onKeyUp	Occurs when the user releases a key.
onMouseDown	Occurs when the user presses a mouse button.
onMouseMove	Occurs when the user moves the mouse pointer.
onMouseUp	Occurs when the user releases a mouse button.

The Element Object

An object that represents a control in the array of all the controls on a **<FORM>**.

Properties	Attribute	Description
checked	CHECKED	Indicates that a checkbox or radio element is selected (i.e. 'on' or ticked).
defaultChecked		Denotes if a checkbox or radio element is checked by default.
defaultValue		The text displayed as the initial contents of a text-based control.
form		Reference to the form object that contains the element.
length		Returns the number of elements in an element sub-array.
name	NAME	Specifies the name to use to refer to the element.
selectedIndex		An integer specifying the index of the selected option in a **<SELECT>** element.
type	TYPE	The type of the element, such as **TEXT**, **BUTTON** or **RADIO**.
value	VALUE	The default value of text/numeric controls, or the value when the control is 'on' for Boolean controls.

Methods	Description
blur	Causes the element to lose the focus, and fire its **onBlur** event.
click	Simulates a click on the element, and fires its **onClick** event.

348

Methods	Description
eval	Evaluates the object and returns a representation of its value
focus	Causes the element to receive the focus, and fire its onFocus event.
handleEvent	Invokes the appropriate event handling code of object for this event.
select	Highlights the input area of a text-based element.
toString	Returns a string containing a textual representation of the object's value.
valueOf	Returns the primitive value of an object, or the name of the object itself.

Events	Description
onBlur	Occurs when the control loses the focus.
onChange	Occurs when the contents of the control are changed.
onClick	Occurs when the mouse button is clicked on the control.
onFocus	Occurs when the control receives the focus.
onKeyDown	Occurs when the user presses a key.
onKeyPress	Occurs when the user presses and releases a key.
onKeyUp	Occurs when the user releases a key.
onMouseDown	Occurs when the user presses a mouse button.
onMouseUp	Occurs when the user releases a mouse button.
onSelect	Occurs when the current selection in the control is changed.

The Event Object

The global object provided to allow the scripting language to access an event's parameters. It provides the following properties, and the three standard methods:

Properties	Description
data	The URLs of the objects dropped onto the Navigator window, as an array of strings.
layerX	Horizontal position of the mouse pointer in pixels in relation to the containing layer.

Table continued on following page

349

Properties	Description
layerY	Vertical position of the mouse pointer in pixels in relation to the containing layer.
modifiers	String containing the names of the keys held down for a key-press event.
pageX	Horizontal position in pixels of the mouse pointer or a layer in relation to the document's window.
pageY	Vertical position in pixels of the mouse pointer or a layer in relation to the document's window.
screenX	Horizontal position in pixels of the mouse pointer on the screen for an event.
screenY	Vertical position in pixels of the mouse pointer on the screen for an event.
target	The name of the object where the event was originally sent.
type	The type of event, as a string.
which	ASCII value of a key that was pressed, or indicates which mouse button was clicked.

Methods	Description
eval	Evaluates the object and returns a representation of its value
toString	Returns a string containing a textual representation of the object's value.
valueOf	Returns the primitive value of an object, or the name of the object itself.

The FileUpload Object

An object that represents a control created with an **<INPUT>** tag where **TYPE=FILE**.

Properties	Attribute	Description
form		Reference to the form object that contains the element.
name	NAME	Specifies the name to use to refer to the element.
type	TYPE	Must be **"FILE"** for a FileUpload element.
value	VALUE	The text value of the control.

Methods	Description
`blur`	Causes the element to lose the focus, and fire its **onBlur** event.
`eval`	Evaluates the object and returns a representation of its value
`focus`	Causes the element to receive the focus, and fire its **onFocus** event.
`handleEvent`	Invokes the appropriate event handling code of object for this event.
`toString`	Returns a string containing a textual representation of the object's value.
`valueOf`	Returns the primitive value of an object, or the name of the object itself.

Events	Description
`onBlur`	Occurs when the control loses the focus.
`onChange`	Occurs when the contents of the control are changed.
`onFocus`	Occurs when the control receives the focus.

The Form Object

An object that represents the section of a page contained within a `<FORM>` tag.

Properties	Attribute	Description
`action`	**ACTION**	The URL where the form is to be sent.
`encoding`	**ENC_TYPE**	Defines the type of encoding to be used when submitting the form.
`length`		Returns the number of elements in the form.
`method`	**METHOD**	How the form data should be sent to the server; either **GET** or **POST**.
`name`	**NAME**	Specifies the name to use to refer to the form.
`target`	**TARGET**	Specifies the window or frame where the return page will be loaded.

Array	Description
`elements`	Array of all controls and elements in the form.

Methods	Description
eval	Evaluates the object and returns a representation of its value
handleEvent	Invokes the appropriate event handling code of object for this event.
reset	Simulates a mouse click on a RESET button in the form.
submit	Submits the form, as when the SUBMIT button is clicked.
toString	Returns a string containing a textual representation of the object's value.
valueOf	Returns the primitive value of an object, or the name of the object itself.

Events	Description
onReset	Occurs when the RESET button on the form is clicked, or the form is reset.
onSubmit	Occurs when the SUBMIT button on the form is clicked, or the form is submitted.

The Frame Object

An object that represents a <FRAME> within a <FRAMESET>.

Properties	Attribute	Description
length		Returns the number of frames in a frames sub-array for the frame.
name	NAME	Specifies the name to use to refer to the frame.
parent		Returns the parent frame or window in the hierarchy.
self		A reference to the current frame.
window		Reference to the window object that contains the frame.

Array	Description
frames	Array of all the frames defined within a <FRAMESET> tag.

Methods	Description
blur	Causes the frame to lose the focus, and fire its **onBlur** event.
clearInterval	Cancels a timeout that was set with the **setInterval** method.
clearTimeout	Cancels a timeout that was set with the **setTimeout** method.
eval	Evaluates the object and returns a representation of its value
focus	Causes the frame to receive the focus, and fire its **onFocus** event.
handleEvent	Invokes the appropriate event handling code of object for this event.
print	Prints the contents of the frame, equivalent to pressing the Print button.
setInterval	Denotes a code routine to execute every specified number of milliseconds.
setTimeout	Denotes a code routine to execute once only, a specified number of milliseconds after loading a page.
toString	Returns a string containing a textual representation of the object's value.
valueOf	Returns the primitive value of an object, or the name of the object itself.

Events	Description
onBlur	Occurs when the frame loses the focus.
onFocus	Occurs when the frame receives the focus.
onMove	Occurs when the frame is moved.
onResize	Occurs when the frame is resized.

The Hidden Object

An object that represents a control created with an **<INPUT>** tag where **TYPE=HIDDEN**.

Properties	Attribute	Description
name	NAME	Specifies the name to use to refer to the element.
type	TYPE	Must be **"HIDDEN"** for a Hidden element.
value	VALUE	The text value of the control.

Methods	Description
eval	Evaluates the object and returns a representation of its value.
toString	Returns a string containing a textual representation of the object's value.
valueOf	Returns the primitive value of an object, or the name of the object itself.

The History Object

Contains information about the URLs that the client has visited, as stored in the browser's History list, and allows the script to move through the list.

Properties	Description
current	The current item in the browser's history list.
length	Returns the number of items in the browser's history list.
next	Refers to the next item in the browser's history list.
previous	Refers to the previous item in the browser's history list.

Methods	Description
back	Loads the previous URL in the browser's history list.
eval	Evaluates the object and returns a representation of its value.
forward	Loads the next URL in the browser's history list.
go	Loads a specified URL from the browser's history list.
toString	Returns a string containing a textual representation of the object's value.
valueOf	Returns the primitive value of an object, or the name of the object itself.

The Image Object

An object that represents an element created with an <IMG> tag.

Properties	Attribute	JSS Equivalents	Description
border	BORDER	borderWidths( )	Specifies the border to be drawn around the image.
complete			Indicates if the image has completed loading.

Properties	Attribute	JSS Equivalents	Description
height	HEIGHT	height	Sets the height for the image in pixels.
hspace	HSPACE		The horizontal spacing between the image and its neighbors.
lowsrc	LOWSRC		Specifies the URL of a lower resolution image to display.
name	NAME		Specifies the name to use to refer to the image.
prototype			A reference to the base object used to construct the object.
src	SRC		An external file that contains the source data for the image.
vspace	VSPACE		The vertical spacing between the image and its neighbors.
width	WIDTH	width	Sets the width for the image in pixels.

Array	Description
areas	Array of all the `<AREA>` tags defined within an image map's `<MAP>` tag.

Methods	Description
eval	Evaluates the object and returns a representation of its value
handleEvent	Invokes the appropriate event handling code of object for this event.
toString	Returns a string containing a textual representation of the object's value.
valueOf	Returns the primitive value of an object, or the name of the object itself.

355

Events	Description
onAbort	Occurs if the downloading of the image is aborted by the user.
onError	Occurs when an error arises while the image is loading.
onKeyDown	Occurs when the user presses a key.
onKeyPress	Occurs when the user presses and releases a key.
onKeyUp	Occurs when the user releases a key.
onLoad	Occurs immediately after the image has been loaded.

The Layer Object

An object that represents a **<LAYER>** or **<ILAYER>** element in a document.

Properties	Attribute	JSS Equivalents	Description
above	ABOVE		Indicates that the layer should be above another element in the z-order of the page, or returns the element above it.
background	BACKGROUND	background Image	URL of an image to display behind the elements in the layer.
below	BELOW		Indicates that the layer should be below another element in the z-order of the page, or returns the element below it.
bgColor	BGCOLOR	background Color	Specifies the background color to be used for the layer.
clip.bottom	CLIP		Y co-ordinate of the bottom of the clipping rectangle for the layer.
clip.height			Height of the clipping rectangle for the layer.
clip.left	CLIP		X co-ordinate of the left of the clipping rectangle for the layer.
clip.right	CLIP		X co-ordinate of the right of the clipping rectangle for the layer.

356

Properties	Attribute	JSS Equivalents	Description
clip.top	CLIP		Y co-ordinate of the top of the clipping rectangle for the layer.
clip.width			Width of the clipping for the layer.
left	LEFT		Position in pixels of the left-hand side of the layer in relation to its containing layer or the document.
name	NAME		Specifies the name to use to refer to the layer.
pageX	PAGEX		Horizontal position of the mouse pointer in pixels with respect to the layer.
pageY	PAGEY		Vertical position of the mouse pointer in pixels with respect to the layer.
parentLayer			Reference to the layer that contains the current layer.
siblingAbove			Reference to the layer above the current layer if they share the same parent layer.
siblingBelow			Reference to the layer below the current layer if they share the same parent layer.
src	SRC		An external file that contains the source data for the layer.
top	TOP		Position of the top of the layer.
visibility	VISIBILITY		Defines whether the layer should be displayed on the page.
zIndex	Z-INDEX		Position in the z-order or stacking order of the page, i.e. the z co-ordinate.

Methods	Description
captureEvents	Instructs the layer to capture events of a particular type.
eval	Evaluates the element and returns a representation of its value
handleEvent	Invokes the appropriate event handling code of the object for this event.
load	Loads a file into the layer, and can change the width of the layer.
moveAbove	Changes the z-order so that the layer is rendered above (overlaps) another element.
moveBelow	Changes the z-order so that the layer is rendered below (overlapped by) another element.
moveBy	Moves the layer horizontally and vertically by a specified number of pixels.
moveTo	Moves the layer so that the top left is at a position x, y (in pixels) within its container.
moveToAbsolute	Moves the layer to a position specified in x and y with respect to the page and not the container.
releaseEvents	Instructs the layer to stop capturing events of a particular type.
resizeBy	Resizes the layer horizontally and vertically by a specified number of pixels.
resizeTo	Resizes the layer to a size specified in x and y (in pixels).
routeEvent	Passes an event that has been captured back up through the normal event hierarchy.
toString	Returns a string containing a textual representation of the object's value.
valueOf	Returns the primitive value of an object, or the name of the object itself.

Events	Description
onBlur	Occurs when the layer loses the focus.
onFocus	Occurs when the layer receives the focus.
onLoad	Occurs immediately after the layer's contents have been loaded.
onMouseOut	Occurs when the mouse pointer leaves the layer.
onMouseOver	Occurs when the mouse pointer first enters the layer.

The Link Object

An object that represents a hyperlink created in the page with an **<A HREF="..">** tag.

Properties	Attribute	Description
hash		The string following the **#** symbol, the anchor name, in the **HREF** value.
host		The **hostname:port** part of the location or URL.
hostname		The **hostname** part of the location or URL.
href	**HREF**	The destination URL or anchor point.
pathname		The file or object path name following the third slash in a URL.
port		The **port** number in a URL.
protocol		The initial sub-string indicating the URL's access method.
search		Any query string or form data following the **?** in the complete URL.
target	**TARGET**	Specifies the window or frame where the new page will be loaded.

Methods	Description
eval	Evaluates the object and returns a representation of its value
handleEvent	Invokes the appropriate event handling code of object for this event.
toString	Returns a string containing a textual representation of the object's value.
valueOf	Returns the primitive value of an object, or the name of the object itself.

Events	Description
onClick	Occurs when the mouse button is clicked on the link.
onDblClick	Occurs when the user double-clicks on the link.
onKeyDown	Occurs when the user presses a key.
onKeyPress	Occurs when the user presses and releases a key.

Table continued on following page

Events	Description
onKeyUp	Occurs when the user releases a key.
onMouseDown	Occurs when the user presses a mouse button.
onMouseOut	Occurs when the mouse pointer leaves the link.
onMouseOver	Occurs when the mouse pointer first enters the link.
onMouseUp	Occurs when the user releases a mouse button.

The Location Object

Contains information on the current URL. It also provides methods that will reload a page.

Properties	Attribute	Description
hash		The string following the # symbol, the anchor name, in the HREF value.
host		The hostname:port part of the location or URL.
hostname		The hostname part of the location or URL.
href	HREF	The destination URL or anchor point.
pathname		The file or object path name following the third slash in a URL.
port		The port number in a URL.
protocol		The initial sub-string indicating the URL's access method.
search		Any query string or form data following the ? in the complete URL.

Methods	Description
eval	Evaluates the object and returns a representation of its value
reload	Reloads the current page.
replace	Loads a page replacing the current page's session history entry with its URL.
toString	Returns a string containing a textual representation of the object's value.
valueOf	Returns the primitive value of an object, or the name of the object itself.

The MimeType Object

Provides information about the page's **MIME** data type.

Properties	Description
`description`	Returns a description of the MimeType.
`enabledPlugin`	Returns the plug-in that can handle the specified MimeType.
`name`	Specifies the name of the MimeType.
`suffixes`	A list of filename suffixes suitable for use with the specified MimeType.

Methods	Description
`eval`	Evaluates the object and returns a representation of its value.
`toString`	Returns a string containing a textual representation of the object's value.
`valueOf`	Returns the primitive value of an object, or the name of the object itself.

The Navigator Object

This object represents the browser application itself, providing information about its manufacturer, version, and capabilities.

Properties	Description
`appCodeName`	The code name of the browser.
`appName`	The product name of the browser.
`appVersion`	The version of the browser.
`language`	Returns the language the browser was compiled for.
`platform`	Returns the name of the operating system the browser was compiled for.
`userAgent`	The user-agent (browser name) header sent as part of the HTTP protocol.

Array	Description
`mimeTypes`	Array of all the MIME types supported by the browser.
`plugins`	Array of all the plugins that are installed.

361

Methods	Description
eval	Evaluates the object and returns a representation of its value.
javaEnabled	Indicates if execution of Java code is enabled by the browser.
toString	Returns a string containing a textual representation of the object's value.
valueOf	Returns the primitive value of an object, or the name of the object itself.

The Option Object

An individual **<OPTION>** item in a list created by a **<SELECT>** tag.

Properties	Attribute	Description
default	Selected	Denotes if a list item is selected by default.
index		Returns the ordinal position of the option in a list.
length		Returns the number of elements in an element sub-array.
selected	SELECTED	Indicates that this item in a list is the default.
selectedIndex		An integer specifying the index of the selected option in a list.
text	TEXT	The text displayed in the list.
value	VALUE	The text value of the option when selected.

Methods	Description
eval	Evaluates the object and returns a representation of its value.
toString	Returns a string containing a textual representation of the object's value.
valueOf	Returns the primitive value of an object, or the name of the object itself.

The Password Object

An object that represents a control created with an **<INPUT>** tag where
TYPE=PASSWORD.

Properties	Attribute	Description
defaultValue		The text displayed as the initial contents of the control.
form		Reference to the form object that contains the control.
name	NAME	Specifies the name to use to refer to the control.
type	TYPE	Must be **"PASSWORD"** for a Password control.
value	VALUE	The text value of the control.

Methods	Description
blur	Causes the control to lose the focus, and fire its **onBlur** event.
eval	Evaluates the object and returns a representation of its value.
focus	Causes the control to receive the focus, and fire its **onFocus** event.
handleEvent	Invokes the appropriate event handling code of object for this event.
select	Highlights the input area of the control.
toString	Returns a string containing a textual representation of the object's value.
valueOf	Returns the primitive value of an object, or the name of the object itself.

Events	Description
onBlur	Occurs when the control loses the focus.
onFocus	Occurs when the control receives the focus.

The Plugin Object

An object that represents the features of an installed plugin component.

Properties	Attribute	Description
description		Returns a description of the MIME type.
filename		The name of the file that implements the plugin.

Table continued on following page

Properties	Attribute	Description
length		Returns the number of plugins.
name	NAME	Specifies the name to use to refer to the plugin.

Methods	Description
eval	Evaluates the object and returns a representation of its value.
refresh	Updates the information to reflect changes to installed plugins.
toString	Returns a string containing a textual representation of the object's value.
valueOf	Returns the primitive value of an object, or the name of the object itself.

The Radio Object

An object that represents a control created with an **<INPUT>** tag where **TYPE=RADIO**.

Properties	Attribute	Description
checked	CHECKED	Indicates that the radio button is selected (i.e. 'on').
defaultChecked		Denotes if the radio button is checked by default.
form		Reference to the form object that contains the element.
length		Returns the number of controls in a sub-array.
name	NAME	Specifies the name to use to refer to the radio button.
type	TYPE	Must be **"RADIO"** for a Radio element.
value	VALUE	The value of the control when checked.

Methods	Description
blur	Causes the control to lose the focus, and fire its **onBlur** event.
click	Simulates a click on the control, and fires its **onClick** event.
eval	Evaluates the object and returns a representation of its value.

Methods	Description
`focus`	Causes the control to receive the focus, and fire its `onFocus` event.
`handleEvent`	Invokes the appropriate event handling code of the object for this event.
`toString`	Returns a string containing a textual representation of the object's value.
`valueOf`	Returns the primitive value of an object, or the name of the object itself.

Events	Description
`onBlur`	Occurs when the radio button loses the focus.
`onClick`	Occurs when the mouse button is clicked on the radio button.
`onFocus`	Occurs when the radio button receives the focus.

The Reset Object

An object that represents a control created with an `<INPUT>` tag where `TYPE=RESET`.

Properties	Attribute	Description
`form`		Reference to the form object that contains the element.
`name`	`NAME`	Specifies the name to use to refer to the element.
`type`	`TYPE`	Must be `"RESET"` for a Reset element.
`value`	`VALUE`	The text used for the reset button's caption.

Methods	Description
`blur`	Causes the control to lose the focus, and fire its `onBlur` event.
`click`	Simulates a click on the control, and fires its `onClick` event.
`eval`	Evaluates the object and returns a representation of its value.

Table continued on following page

Methods	Description
focus	Causes the control to receive the focus, and fire its **onFocus** event.
handleEvent	Invokes the appropriate event handling code of the object for this event.
toString	Returns a string containing a textual representation of the object's value.
valueOf	Returns the primitive value of an object, or the name of the object itself.

Events	Description
onBlur	Occurs when the control loses the focus.
onClick	Occurs when the mouse button is clicked on the control.
onFocus	Occurs when the control receives the focus.

The Screen Object

The **Screen** object provides the scripting language with information about the client's screen resolution and rendering abilities.

Properties	Description
availHeight	Height of the available screen space in pixels (excluding screen furniture).
availWidth	Width of the available screen space in pixels (excluding screen furniture).
colorDepth	Maximum number of colors that are supported by the user's display system.
height	Overall height of the user's screen in pixels.
pixelDepth	Returns the number of bits used per pixel by the system display hardware.
width	Overall width of the user's screen in pixels.

Methods	Description
eval	Evaluates the object and returns a representation of its value.
toString	Returns a string containing a textual representation of the object's value.
valueOf	Returns the primitive value of an object, or the name of the object itself.

The Select Object

An object that represents a list control created with a `<SELECT>` tag.

Properties	Attribute	Description
form		Reference to the form object that contains the list element.
length		Number of items in the list.
name	NAME	Specifies the name to use to refer to the list element.
selectedIndex		The numeric position within the list of the selected item.
type		Indicates the type of list, i.e. SELECT-ONE, SELECT-MULTI, etc.
text		The text of the currently selected item.

Methods	Description
blur	Causes the control to lose the focus, and fire its onBlur event.
eval	Evaluates the object and returns a representation of its value.
focus	Causes the control to receive the focus, and fire its onFocus event.
handleEvent	Invokes the appropriate event handling code of the object for this event.
toString	Returns a string containing a textual representation of the object's value.
valueOf	Returns the primitive value of an object, or the name of the object itself.

Events	Description
onBlur	Occurs when the control loses the focus.
onChange	Occurs when an item in the list is selected so that the selection is changed.
onFocus	Occurs when the control receives the focus.

The Submit Object

An object that represents a control created with an **<INPUT>** tag where
TYPE=SUBMIT.

Properties	Attribute	Description
form		Reference to the form object that contains the element.
name	NAME	Specifies the name to use to refer to the element.
type	TYPE	Must be **"SUBMIT"** for a Submit element.
value	VALUE	The text for the submit button's caption.

Methods	Description
blur	Causes the control to lose the focus, and fire its **onBlur** event.
click	Simulates a click on the control, and fires its **onClick** event.
eval	Evaluates the object and returns a representation of its value.
focus	Causes the control to receive the focus, and fire its **onFocus** event.
handleEvent	Invokes the appropriate event handling code of the object for this event.
toString	Returns a string containing a textual representation of the object's value.
valueOf	Returns the primitive value of an object, or the name of the object itself.

Events	Description
onBlur	Occurs when the control loses the focus.
onClick	Occurs when the mouse button is clicked on the control.
onFocus	Occurs when the control receives the focus.

The Text Object

An object that represents a control created with an **<INPUT>** tag where
TYPE=TEXT.

Properties	Attribute	Description
defaultValue		The text displayed as the initial contents of the control.
form		Reference to the form object that contains the element.
name	NAME	Specifies the name to use to refer to the element.
type	TYPE	Must be **"TEXT"** (or omitted) for a text element.
value	VALUE	The text currently within the text box.

Methods	Description
blur	Causes the control to lose the focus, and fire its **onBlur** event.
click	Simulates a click on the control, and fires its **onClick** event.
eval	Evaluates the object and returns a representation of its value.
focus	Causes the control to receive the focus, and fire its **onFocus** event.
handleEvent	Invokes the appropriate event handling code of the object for this event.
select	Highlights the input area of the control.
toString	Returns a string containing a textual representation of the object's value.
valueOf	Returns the primitive value of an object, or the name of the object itself.

Events	Description
onBlur	Occurs when the control loses the focus.
onChange	Occurs when the contents of the element are changed.
onFocus	Occurs when the control receives the focus.
onSelect	Occurs when the current selection in the control is changed.

The TextArea Object

An object that represents a text area control created with a **<TEXTAREA>** tag.

Properties	Attribute	Description
defaultValue		The text displayed as the initial contents of the control.
form		Reference to the form object that contains the element.
name	NAME	Specifies the name to use to refer to the element.
type		Information about the type of the control.
value	VALUE	The text currently within the text box.

Methods	Description
blur	Causes the control to lose the focus, and fire its **onBlur** event.
eval	Evaluates the object and returns a representation of its value.
focus	Causes the control to receive the focus, and fire its **onFocus** event.
handleEvent	Invokes the appropriate event handling code of the object for this event.
select	Highlights the input area of a form element.
toString	Returns a string containing a textual representation of the object's value.
valueOf	Returns the primitive value of an object, or the name of the object itself.

Events	Description
onBlur	Occurs when the control loses the focus.
onClick	Occurs when the mouse button is clicked on the control.
onFocus	Occurs when the control receives the focus.
onKeyDown	Occurs when the user presses a key.
onKeyPress	Occurs when the user presses and releases a key.
onKeyUp	Occurs when the user releases a key.

The Window Object

The **window** object refers to the current window. This can be a top-level window, or a window that is within a frame created by a **<FRAMESET>** in another document.

Properties	Attribute	Description
closed		Indicates if a window is closed.
defaultStatus		The default message displayed in the status bar at the bottom of the window.
document		A reference to the document object from a contained element or object.
innerHeight		Height of the window excluding the window borders.
innerWidth		Width of the window excluding the window borders.
length		Returns the number of frames in a window.
location		The full URL of the document being displayed.
locationbar		Defines whether the address bar will be displayed in the browser window.
menubar		Defines whether the menu bar will be displayed in the browser window.
name	**NAME**	Specifies the name to use to refer to the window.
opener		Returns a reference to the window that created the current window.
outerHeight		Height of the window including the window borders.
outerWidth		Width of the window including the window borders.
pageXOffset		Horizontal offset of the top left of the visible part of the page within the window in pixels.
pageYOffset		Vertical offset of the top left of the visible part of the page within the window in pixels.
parent		Returns a reference to the parent window.
personalbar		Defines whether the user's personal button bar will be displayed in the browser window.
scrollbars	**SCROLLING**	Defines whether the window will provide scrollbars if all the content cannot be displayed.
self		A reference to the current window.
status		The text displayed in the current window's status bar.

Table continued on following page

Properties	Attribute	Description
statusbar		Defines whether the status bar will be displayed in the browser window.
toolbar		Defines whether the toolbar will be displayed in the browser window.
top		Returns a reference to the topmost window object.
window		Reference to the window object that contains the window.

Array	Description
frames	Array of all the frames defined within a **<FRAMESET>** tag.

MethodName	Description
alert	Displays an Alert dialog box with a message and an OK button.
back	Loads the previous URL in the browser's history list.
blur	Causes the window to lose the focus, and fire its **onBlur** event.
captureEvents	Instructs the window to capture events of a particular type.
clearInterval	Cancels a timeout that was set with the **setInterval** method.
clearTimeout	Cancels a timeout that was set with the **setTimeout** method.
close	Closes the current browser window.
confirm	Displays a Confirm dialog box with a message and OK and Cancel buttons.
disableExternalCapture	Prevents a window that includes frames from capturing events in documents loaded from different locations.
enableExternalCapture	Allows a window that includes frames to capture events in documents loaded from different locations.
eval	Evaluates the code and returns a representation of its value.
find	Returns **true** if a specified string is found in the text in the current window.

MethodName	Description
focus	Causes the window to receive the focus, and fire its onFocus event.
forward	Loads the next URL in the browser's history list.
handleEvent	Invokes the appropriate event handling code of the object for this event.
home	Loads the user's Home page into the window.
moveBy	Moves the window horizontally and vertically.
moveTo	Moves the window so that the top left is at a position x, y (in pixels).
open	Opens a new browser window.
print	Prints the contents of the window, equivalent to pressing the Print button.
prompt	Displays a Prompt dialog box with a message and an input field.
releaseEvents	Instructs the window to stop capturing events of a particular type.
resizeBy	Resizes the window horizontally and vertically.
resizeTo	Resizes the window to a size x, y specified in pixels.
routeEvent	Passes an event that has been captured up through the normal event hierarchy.
scrollBy	Scrolls the document horizontally and vertically within the window by a number of pixels.
scrollTo	Scrolls the document within the window so that the point x, y is at the top left corner.
setInterval	Denotes a code routine to execute every specified number of milliseconds.
setTimeout	Denotes a code routine to execute once only, a specified number of milliseconds after loading the page.
stop	Stops the current download, equivalent to pressing the Stop button.
toString	Returns a string containing a textual representation of the object's value.
valueOf	Returns the primitive value of an object, or the name of the object itself.

EventName	Description
onBlur	Occurs when the window loses the focus.
onDragDrop	Occurs when the user drops a file or object onto the Navigator window.
onError	Occurs when an error loading a document arises.
onFocus	Occurs when the window receives the focus.
onLoad	Occurs when a document has completed loading.
onMouseMove	Occurs only when event capturing is on and the user moves the mouse pointer.
onMove	Occurs when the window is moved.
onResize	Occurs when the window is resized.
onUnload	Occurs immediately prior to the current document being unloaded.

HTML Controls Cross Reference

Dynamic HTML provides the same integral control types as HTML 3.2. However, there are more properties, methods and events available now for all the controls.

The following tables show those that are relevant to controls. For a full description of the properties, methods and events for each element, check out Sections **A** and **B**.

Control Properties	checked	defaultChecked	defaultSelected	defaultValue	form	index	length	name	selected	selectedIndex	text	type	value
Button	✗	✗	✗	✗	✓	✗	✗	✓	✗	✗	✗	✓	✓
Checkbox	✓	✓	✗	✗	✓	✗	✗	✓	✗	✗	✗	✓	✓
FileUpload	✗	✗	✗	✗	✓	✗	✗	✓	✗	✗	✗	✓	✓
Hidden	✗	✗	✗	✗	✗	✗	✗	✓	✗	✗	✗	✓	✓
Option	✗	✗	✓	✗	✗	✓	✓	✗	✓	✓	✓	✗	✓
Password	✗	✗	✗	✓	✓	✗	✗	✓	✗	✗	✗	✓	✓
Radio	✓	✓	✗	✗	✓	✗	✓	✓	✗	✗	✗	✓	✓
Reset	✗	✗	✗	✗	✓	✗	✗	✓	✗	✗	✗	✓	✓
Select	✗	✗	✗	✗	✓	✗	✓	✓	✗	✓	✓	✓	✗
Submit	✗	✗	✗	✗	✓	✗	✗	✓	✗	✗	✗	✓	✓
Text	✗	✗	✗	✓	✓	✗	✗	✓	✗	✗	✗	✓	✓
Textarea	✗	✗	✗	✓	✓	✗	✗	✓	✗	✗	✗	✓	✓

Control Methods	blur	click	eval	focus	handleEvent	select	toString	valueOf
Button	✓	✓	✓	✓	✓	✗	✓	✓
Checkbox	✓	✓	✓	✓	✓	✗	✓	✓
FileUpload	✓	✗	✓	✓	✓	✗	✓	✓
Hidden	✗	✗	✓	✗	✗	✗	✓	✓
Option	✗	✗	✓	✗	✗	✗	✓	✓
Password	✓	✗	✓	✓	✓	✓	✓	✓
Radio	✓	✓	✓	✓	✓	✗	✓	✓
Reset	✓	✓	✓	✓	✓	✗	✓	✓
Select	✓	✗	✓	✓	✓	✗	✓	✓
Submit	✓	✓	✓	✓	✓	✗	✓	✓
Text	✓	✓	✓	✓	✓	✓	✓	✓
Textarea	✓	✗	✓	✓	✓	✓	✓	✓

Control Events	onBlur	onChange	onClick	onFocus	onKeyDown	onKeyPress	onKeyUp	onMouseDown	onMouseUp	onSelect
Button	✓	✗	✓	✓	✗	✗	✗	✓	✓	✗
Checkbox	✓	✗	✓	✓	✗	✗	✗	✗	✗	✗
FileUpload	✓	✗	✓	✓	✗	✗	✗	✗	✗	✗
Hidden	✗	✗	✗	✗	✗	✗	✗	✗	✗	✗
Option	✗	✗	✗	✗	✗	✗	✗	✗	✗	✗
Password	✓	✗	✗	✓	✗	✗	✗	✗	✗	✗
Radio	✓	✗	✓	✓	✗	✗	✗	✗	✗	✗
Reset	✓	✗	✓	✓	✗	✗	✗	✗	✗	✗
Select	✓	✓	✗	✓	✗	✗	✗	✗	✗	✗
Submit	✓	✗	✓	✓	✗	✗	✗	✗	✗	✗
Text	✓	✓	✗	✓	✗	✗	✗	✗	✗	✓
Textarea	✓	✗	✓	✓	✓	✓	✓	✗	✗	✗

JavaScript Style Properties

These properties provide access to the individual styles of an element. They could have been previously set by a style sheet, or by an inline style tag within the page. The equivalent HTML attributes are shown where appropriate.

JavaScript Style Property	Attribute	CSS Equiv.
align	ALIGN	float
Specifies the alignment of the element on the page		
backgroundColor	BGCOLOR	background-color
Specifies the background color of the page.		
backgroundImage	BACKGROUND	background-image
Specifies a URL for the background image for the page.		
borderColor	BORDERCOLOR	
The color of the bottom border for an element.		
borderBottomWidth	MARGINHEIGHT	border-bottom-width
The width of the bottom border for an element.		
borderLeftWidth	MARGINWIDTH	border-left-width
The width of the left border for an element.		
borderRightWidth	MARGINWIDTH	border-right-width
The width of the right border for an element.		
borderStyle		border-style
Used to specify the style of one or more borders of an element.		
borderTopWidth	MARGINHEIGHT	border-top-width
The width of the top border for an element.		
borderWidths()	BORDER	border
Allows all four of the borders for an element to be specified with one attribute.		
clear	CLEAR	clear
Causes the next element or text to be displayed below left-aligned or right-aligned images.		
color	COLOR	color
Defines the color to be used for the element, by name or as a number.		
display		display
Specifies if the element will be visible (displayed) in the page.		
fontFamily	FACE	font-family
Specifies the name of the typeface, or 'font family'.		
fontSize	SIZE	font-size
Specifies the font size.		
fontStyle		font-style
Specifies the style of the font, i.e. normal or italic.		
fontWeight	WEIGHT	font-weight
Sets the weight (boldness) of the text.		

JavaScript Style Property	Attribute	CSS Equiv.

height   **HEIGHT**   **height**
Specifies the height at which the element is to be rendered on the page.

lineHeight   **line-height**
The distance between the baselines of two adjacent lines of text.

listStyleType   **TYPE**   **list-style-type**
The type of bullets to be used for a list.

marginBottom   **margin-bottom**
Specifies the bottom margin for the page or text block.

marginLeft   **margin-left**
Specifies the left margin for the page or text block.

marginRight   **margin-right**
Specifies the right margin for the page or text block.

marginTop   **margin-top**
Specifies the top margin for the page or text block.

margins()   **margin**
Allows all four margins to be specified with a single attribute.

paddingBottom   **padding-bottom**
Specifies the spacing between an element's contents and the bottom border of the element.

paddingLeft   **padding-left**
Specifies the spacing between an element's contents and the left border of the element.

paddingRight   **padding-right**
Specifies the spacing between an element's contents and the right border of the element.

paddingTop   **padding-top**
Specifies the spacing between an element's contents and the top border of the element.

paddings()   **padding**
Allows all four paddings to be specified with a single attribute.

textAlign   **ALIGN**   **text-align**
Indicates how text should be aligned within the element.

textDecoration   **text-decoration**
Font decorations (underline, overline, strikethrough) added to the text of an element.

textIndent   **text-indent**
The indent for the first line of text in an element, may be negative.

textTransform   **text-transform**
Transforms the text for the element.

Table continued on following page

JavaScript Style Property	Attribute	CSS Equiv.
`verticalAlign`	`VALIGN`	`vertical-align`
Sets or returns the vertical alignment of the element on the page.		
`whiteSpace`		`white-space`
Indicates whether white space in an element should be collapsed or retained, as in text formatting.		
`width`	`WIDTH`	`width`
Specifies the width at which the element is to be rendered on the page.		

The JavaScript Objects in Detail

The JavaScript interpreter within the browser provides a set of objects that we can use in our code to carry out calculations, and access other objects. Unlike the browser objects, they are not related to parts of the browser itself, or the page(s) currently being displayed.

The JavaScript Array Object

An object that is used in script to manipulate the contents of an array.

Properties	Description
`length`	Returns the number of objects or elements in an array.
`prototype`	A reference to the base object used to construct the object.

Methods	Description
`eval`	Evaluates the object and returns a representation of its value.
`join`	Concatenates the elements of an array into a string.
`reverse`	Reverses the order of the elements in an array.
`sort`	Sorts an array, using an optional function to define the ordering.
`toString`	Returns a string containing a textual representation of the object's value.
`valueOf`	Returns the primitive value of an object, or the name of the object itself.

380

The JavaScript Boolean Object

An object that is used in script to represent a Boolean (**true** or **false**) value.

Methods	Description
eval	Evaluates the object and returns a representation of its value.
toString	Returns a string containing a textual representation of the object's value.
valueOf	Returns the primitive value of an object, or the name of the object itself.

The JavaScript Date Object

An object that is used in script to represent a date.

Property	Description
prototype	A reference to the base object used to construct the object.

Methods	Description
eval	Evaluates the code and returns a representation of its value.
getDate	Returns the day of the month as a number between 1 and 31.
getDay	Returns the day of the week as a number between 0 (Sunday) and 6 (Saturday).
getHours	Returns the hours part of the date as a number between 0 and 23.
getMinutes	Returns the minutes part of the date as a number between 0 and 59.
getMonth	Returns the month of the year as a number between 0 and 11.
getSeconds	Returns the seconds part of the date as a number between 0 and 59.
getTime	Returns the date as a number of milliseconds since 1st Jan 1970 at midnight GMT.
getTimezone Offset	Returns the difference in minutes between the object date and time, and GMT.

Table continued on following page

Methods	Description
getYear	Returns the year as a number. This can be two or four digits, depending on the year.
parse	Returns the date as a number of milliseconds since 1st Jan 1970 at midnight GMT.
setDate	Sets the day of the month for a Date object.
setHours	Sets the hours part of the time in a Date object.
setInterval	Denotes a code routine to execute every specified number of milliseconds.
setMinutes	Sets the minutes part of the time in a Date object.
setMonth	Sets the month of the year for a Date object.
setSeconds	Sets the seconds part of the time in a Date object.
setTime	Sets the day of the month for a Date object.
toGMTString	Returns a string representation of a Date object as a converted GMT time and date.
toLocaleString	Returns a string representation of a Date object using the local time zone.
toString	Returns a string containing a textual representation of the object's value.
UTC	Returns the date as a number of milliseconds since 1st Jan 1970 at midnight GMT.
valueOf	Returns the primitive value of an object, or the name of the object itself.

The JavaScript Function Object

An object that represents a script function written within the page.

Property	Description
caller	A reference to the function that called the current function.
prototype	A reference to the base object used to construct the object.

Array	Description
arguments	Array of all the arguments supplied to a function.

382

Methods	Description
`eval`	Evaluates the object and returns a representation of its value.
`toString`	Returns a string containing a textual representation of the object's value.
`valueOf`	Returns the primitive value of an object, or the name of the object itself.

The JavaScript Math Object

An object that is used in script to manipulate numbers and perform calculations.

PropertyName	Description
`E`	Constant value of the mathematical symbol e.
`LN10`	Constant definition of the natural logarithm of 10.
`LN2`	Constant definition of the natural logarithm of 2.
`LOG10E`	Constant definition of the base-10 logarithm of e.
`LOG2E`	Constant definition of the base-2 logarithm of e.
`PI`	Constant value approximating to the mathematical symbol pi.
`SQRT1_2`	Constant value representing one divided by the square root of two.
`SQRT2`	Constant value representing the square root of two.

MethodName	Description
`abs`	Returns the absolute (positive) value of a number x.
`acos`	Returns the arc cosine value of a number x in radians.
`asin`	Returns the arc sine value of a number x in radians.
`atan`	Returns the arc tangent value of a number x in radians.
`atan2`	Returns the distance between a point x, y and the X-axis.
`ceil`	Returns the nearest whole number equal to or greater than a number x.
`cos`	Returns the cosine value of a number x in radians.
`eval`	Evaluates the code and returns a representation of its value.
`exp`	Returns a number equal to e to the power of another number x.

Table continued on following page

MethodName	Description
floor	Returns the nearest whole number equal to or less than a number x.
log	Returns the natural logarithm of a number x.
max	Returns the larger of two numbers a and b.
min	Returns the smaller of two numbers a and b.
pow	Returns the value of the number a to the power b.
random	Returns a pseudo-random number between 0 and 1.
round	Returns the nearest whole number (larger or smaller) to a number x.
sin	Returns the value of the sine of a number x in radians.
sqrt	Returns the value of the square root of a positive number x.
tan	Returns the value of the tangent of a number x in radians.
toString	Returns a string containing a textual representation of the object's value.
valueOf	Returns the primitive value of an object, or the name of the object itself.

The JavaScript Number Object

An object that is used in script to represent a number.

PropertyName	Description
MAX_VALUE	Constant representing the largest value that can be stored.
MIN_VALUE	Constant representing the smallest value that can be stored.
NaN	Constant value returned when a mathematical operation or value is not a valid number.
NEGATIVE_INFINITY	Constant value returned from an operation that creates a number smaller than MIN_VALUE.
POSITIVE_INFINITY	Constant value returned from an operation that creates a number larger than MAX_VALUE.

Methods	Description
eval	Evaluates the object and returns a representation of its value.

Methods	Description
toString	Returns a string containing a textual representation of the object's value.
valueOf	Returns the primitive value of an object, or the name of the object itself.

The JavaScript Packages Object

An object that represents the classes of a Java package embedded in the document.

PropertyName	Description
java	A read-only reference to the java package name hierarchy.
netscape	A read-only reference to the netscape package name hierarchy.
sun	A read-only reference to the sun package name hierarchy.

Methods	Description
eval	Evaluates the object and returns a representation of its value.
toString	Returns a string containing a textual representation of the object's value.
valueOf	Returns the primitive value of an object, or the name of the object itself.

The JavaScript RegExp Object

An object that is used in script to represent a regular expression.

PropertyName	Description
$<n>	Each of nine slots available for an expression in a RegExp object.

MethodName	Description
compile	Compiles an expression in a RegExp object.

Table continued on following page

385

MethodName	Description
eval	Evaluates the code and returns a representation of its value
exec	Executes an expression in a RegExp object.
toString	Returns a string containing a textual representation of the object's value.
valueOf	Returns the primitive value of an object, or the name of the object itself.

The JavaScript String Object

An object that is used in script to represent a string.

Properties	Description
length	Returns the number of objects or elements in an array.
prototype	A reference to the base object used to construct the object.

MethodName	Description
anchor	Returns a string with the name surrounded in **<A NAME="***name***">** and **</A>** tags.
big	Displays the string as if surrounded by **<BIG>** and **</BIG>** tags.
blink	Displays the string as if surrounded by **<BLINK>** and **</BLINK>** tags.
bold	Displays the string as if surrounded by **<B>** and **</B>** tags.
charAt	Returns the single character at the index position within a string.
charCodeAt	Returns the ordinal code-set value of the character at the index position within a string.
eval	Evaluates the code and returns a representation of its value.
fixed	Displays the string as if surrounded by **<TT>** and **</TT>** tags.
fontcolor	Displays the string as if surrounded by **<FONT COLOR="***color***">** and **</FONT>** tags.
fontsize	Displays the string as if surrounded by **<FONT COLOR="***size***">** and **</FONT>** tags.
fromCharCode	Constructs a string from a series of ordinal code-set values.

MethodName	Description
`indexOf`	Returns the index of the first occurrence of sub-string within a string, optionally starting from start.
`italics`	Displays the string as if surrounded by `<I>` and `</I>` tags.
`lastIndexOf`	Returns the index of the last occurrence of sub-string within a string, optionally starting from start.
`link`	Displays the string as if surrounded by `<A HREF="`*href*`">` and `</A>` tags.
`match`	Returns true if a regular expression sub-string matches the contents of the string.
`replace`	Loads a document, replacing the current document's session history entry with its URL.
`small`	Displays the string as if surrounded by `<SMALL>` and `</SMALL>` tags.
`split`	Returns an array of strings from a single string, using delimiter as the point to break the string into components.
`strike`	Displays the string as if surrounded by `<STRIKE>` and `</STRIKE>` tags.
`sub`	Displays the string as if surrounded by `<SUB>` and `</SUB>` tags.
`substr`	Returns a section of the original string starting at from and including the next count characters or the rest of the string.
`substring`	Returns a section of the original string starting at from and ending one character before to, or the rest of the string.
`sup`	Displays the string as if surrounded by `<SUP>` and `</SUP>` tags.
`toLowerCase`	Returns a string with all of the letters of the original string in lower case.
`toString`	Returns a string containing a textual representation of the object's value.
`toUpperCase`	Returns a string with all of the letters of the original string in upper case.
`valueOf`	Returns the primitive value of an object, or the name of the object itself.

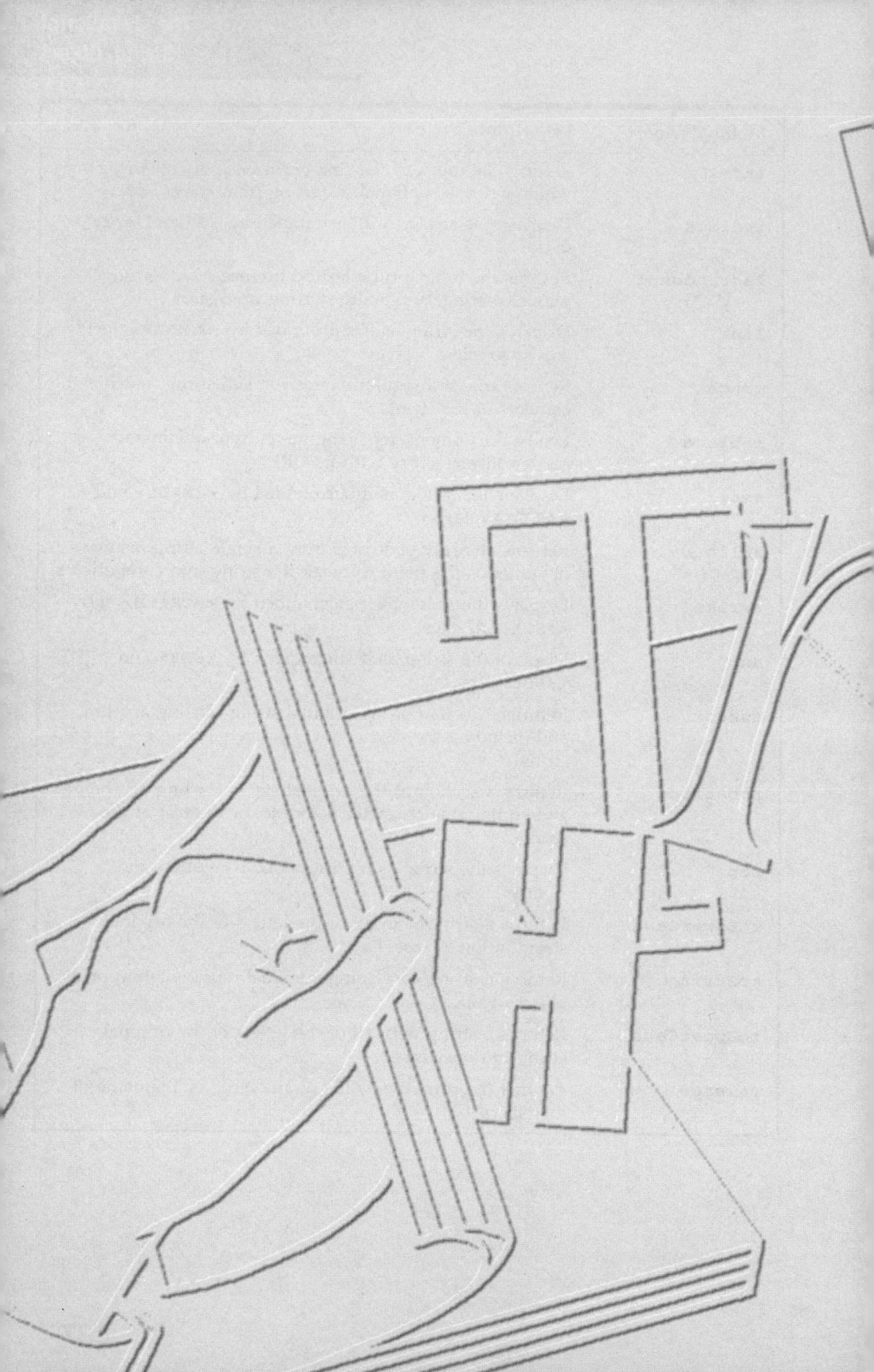

HTML Color Names and Values

Colors Sorted by Name

Color Name	Value	Color Name	Value
aliceblue	F0F8FF	darkgreen	006400
antiquewhite	FAEBD7	darkkhaki	BDB76B
aqua	00FFFF	darkmagenta	8B008B
aquamarine	7FFFD4	darkolivegreen	556B2F
azure	F0FFFF	darkorange	FF8C00
beige	F5F5DC	darkorchid	9932CC
bisque	FFE4C4	darkred	8B0000
black	000000	darksalmon	E9967A
blanchedalmond	FFEBCD	darkseagreen	8FBC8F
blue	0000FF	darkslateblue	483D8B
blueviolet	8A2BE2	darkslategray	2F4F4F
brown	A52A2A	darkturquoise	00CED1
burlywood	DEB887	darkviolet	9400D3
cadetblue	5F9EA0	deeppink	FF1493
chartreuse	7FFF00	deepskyblue	00BFFF
chocolate	D2691E	dimgray	696969
coral	FF7F50	dodgerblue	1E90FF
cornflowerblue	6495ED	firebrick	B22222
cornsilk	FFF8DC	floralwhite	FFFAF0
crimson	DC143C	forestgreen	228B22
cyan	00FFFF	fuchsia	FF00FF
darkblue	00008B	gainsboro	DCDCDC
darkcyan	008B8B	ghostwhite	F8F8FF
darkgoldenrod	B8860B	gold	FFD700
darkgray	A9A9A9	goldenrod	DAA520

Color Name	Value	Color Name	Value
gray	808080	midnightblue	191970
green	008000	mintcream	F5FFFA
greenyellow	ADFF2F	mistyrose	FFE4E1
honeydew	F0FFF0	moccasin	FFE4B5
hotpink	FF69B4	navajowhite	FFDEAD
indianred	CD5C5C	navy	000080
indigo	4B0082	oldlace	FDF5E6
ivory	FFFFF0	olive	808000
khaki	F0E68C	olivedrab	6B8E23
lavender	E6E6FA	orange	FFA500
lavenderblush	FFF0F5	orangered	FF4500
lawngreen	7CFC00	orchid	DA70D6
lemonchiffon	FFFACD	palegoldenrod	EEE8AA
lightblue	ADD8E6	palegreen	98FB98
lightcoral	F08080	paleturquoise	AFEEEE
lightcyan	E0FFFF	palevioletred	DB7093
lightgray	D3D3D3	papayawhip	FFEFD5
lightgreen	90EE90	peachpuff	FFDAB9
lightpink	FFB6C1	peru	CD853F
lightsalmon	FFA07A	pink	FFC0CB
lightseagreen	20B2AA	plum	DDA0DD
lightskyblue	87CEFA	powderblue	B0E0E6
lightslategray	778899	purple	800080
lightsteelblue	B0C4DE	red	FF0000
lightyellow	FFFFE0	rosybrown	BC8F8F
lime	00FF00	royalblue	4169E1
limegreen	32CD32	saddlebrown	8B4513
linen	FAF0E6	salmon	FA8072
magenta	FF00FF	sandybrown	F4A460
maroon	800000	seagreen	2E8B57
mediumaquamarine	66CDAA	seashell	FFF5EE
mediumblue	0000CD	sienna	A0522D
mediumorchid	BA55D3	silver	C0C0C0
mediumpurple	9370DB	skyblue	87CEEB
mediumseagreen	3CB371	slateblue	6A5ACD
mediumslateblue	7B68EE	slategray	708090
mediumspringgreen	00FA9A	snow	FFFAFA
mediumturquoise	48D1CC	springgreen	00FF7F
mediumvioletred	C71585	steelblue	4682B4

Color Name	Value	Color Name	Value
tan	D2B48C	wheat	F5DEB3
teal	008080	white	FFFFFF
thistle	D8BFD8	whitesmoke	F5F5F5
tomato	FF6347	yellow	FFFF00
turquoise	40E0D0	yellowgreen	9ACD32
violet	EE82EE		

Colors Sorted by Group

Color Name	Value	Color Name	Value
Blues		deepskyblue	00BFFF
azure	F0FFFF	darkcyan	008B8B
aliceblue	F0F8FF	blue	0000FF
lavender	E6E6FA	mediumblue	0000CD
lightcyan	E0FFFF	darkblue	00008B
powderblue	B0E0E6	navy	000080
lightsteelblue	B0C4DE		
paleturquoise	AFEEEE	Greens	
lightblue	ADD8E6		
blueviolet	8A2BE2	mintcream	F5FFFA
lightskyblue	87CEFA	honeydew	F0FFF0
skyblue	87CEEB	greenyellow	ADFF2F
mediumslateblue	7B68EE	yellowgreen	9ACD32
slateblue	6A5ACD	palegreen	98FB98
cornflowerblue	6495ED	lightgreen	90EE90
cadetblue	5F9EA0	darkseagreen	8FBC8F
indigo	4B0082	olive	808000
mediumturquoise	48D1CC	aquamarine	7FFFD4
darkslateblue	483D8B	chartreuse	7FFF00
steelblue	4682B4	lawngreen	7CFC00
royalblue	4169E1	olivedrab	6B8E23
turquoise	40E0D0	mediumaquamarine	66CDAA
dodgerblue	1E90FF	darkolivegreen	556B2F
midnightblue	191970	mediumseagreen	3CB371
aqua	00FFFF	limegreen	32CD32
cyan	00FFFF	seagreen	2E8B57
darkturquoise	00CED1	forestgreen	228B22

391

Color Name	Value	Color Name	Value
lightseagreen	20B2AA	darkviolet	9400D3
springgreen	00FF7F	mediumpurple	9370DB
lime	00FF00	darkmagenta	8B008B
mediumspringgreen	00FA9A	darkred	8B0000
teal	008080	purple	800080
green	008000	maroon	800000
darkgreen	006400		

Pinks and Reds

Yellows

Color Name	Value	Color Name	Value
		ivory	FFFFF0
lavenderblush	FFF0F5	lightyellow	FFFFE0
mistyrose	FFE4E1	yellow	FFFF00
pink	FFC0CB	floralwhite	FFFAF0
lightpink	FFB6C1	lemonchiffon	FFFACD
orange	FFA500	cornsilk	FFF8DC
lightsalmon	FFA07A	gold	FFD700
darkorange	FF8C00	khaki	F0E68C
coral	FF7F50	darkkhaki	BDB76B
hotpink	FF69B4		
tomato	FF6347	Beiges and Browns	
orangered	FF4500		
deeppink	FF1493	snow	FFFAFA
fuchsia	FF00FF	seashell	FFF5EE
magenta	FF00FF	papayawhite	FFEFD5
red	FF0000	blanchedalmond	FFEBCD
salmon	FA8072	bisque	FFE4C4
lightcoral	F08080	moccasin	FFE4B5
violet	EE82EE	navajowhite	FFDEAD
darksalmon	E9967A	peachpuff	FFDAB9
plum	DDA0DD	oldlace	FDF5E6
crimson	DC143C	linen	FAF0E6
palevioletred	DB7093	antiquewhite	FAEBD7
orchid	DA70D6	beige	F5F5DC
thistle	D8BFD8	wheat	F5DEB3
indianred	CD5C5C	sandybrown	F4A460
mediumvioletred	C71585	palegoldenrod	EEE8AA
mediumorchid	BA55D3	burlywood	DEB887
firebrick	B22222	goldenrod	DAA520
darkorchid	9932CC	tan	D2B48C

Color Name	Value	Color Name	Value
chocolate	D2691E	whitesmoke	F5F5F5
peru	CD853F	gainsboro	DCDCDC
rosybrown	BC8F8F	lightgray	D3D3D3
darkgoldenrod	B8860B	silver	C0C0C0
brown	A52A2A	darkgray	A9A9A9
sienna	A0522D	gray	808080
saddlebrown	8B4513	lightslategray	778899
		slategray	708090
Whites and Grays		dimgray	696969
		darkslategray	2F4F4F
white	FFFFFF	black	000000
ghostwhite	F8F8FF		

Colors Sorted by Depth

Color Name	Value	Color Name	Value
white	FFFFFF	darkorange	FF8C00
ivory	FFFFF0	coral	FF7F50
lightyellow	FFFFE0	hotpink	FF69B4
yellow	FFFF00	tomato	FF6347
snow	FFFAFA	orangered	FF4500
floralwhite	FFFAF0	deeppink	FF1493
lemonchiffon	FFFACD	fuchsia	FF00FF
cornsilk	FFF8DC	magenta	FF00FF
seashell	FFF5EE	red	FF0000
lavenderblush	FFF0F5	oldlace	FDF5E6
papayawhip	FFEFD5	linen	FAF0E6
blanchedalmond	FFEBCD	antiquewhite	FAEBD7
mistyrose	FFE4E1	salmon	FA8072
bisque	FFE4C4	ghostwhite	F8F8FF
moccasin	FFE4B5	mintcream	F5FFFA
navajowhite	FFDEAD	whitesmoke	F5F5F5
peachpuff	FFDAB9	beige	F5F5DC
gold	FFD700	wheat	F5DEB3
pink	FFC0CB	sandybrown	F4A460
lightpink	FFB6C1	azure	F0FFFF
orange	FFA500	honeydew	F0FFF0
lightsalmon	FFA07A	aliceblue	F0F8FF

Color Name	Value	Color Name	Value
khaki	F0E68C	mediumpurple	9370DB
lightcoral	F08080	lightgreen	90EE90
palegoldenrod	EEE8AA	darkseagreen	8FBC8F
violet	EE82EE	saddlebrown	8B4513
darksalmon	E9967A	darkmagenta	8B008B
lavender	E6E6FA	darkred	8B0000
lightcyan	E0FFFF	blueviolet	8A2BE2
burlywood	DEB887	lightskyblue	87CEFA
plum	DDA0DD	skyblue	87CEEB
gainsboro	DCDCDC	gray	808080
crimson	DC143C	olive	808000
palevioletred	DB7093	purple	800080
goldenrod	DAA520	maroon	800000
orchid	DA70D6	aquamarine	7FFFD4
thistle	D8BFD8	chartreuse	7FFF00
lightgray	D3D3D3	lawngreen	7CFC00
tan	D2B48C	mediumslateblue	7B68EE
chocolate	D2691E	lightslategray	778899
peru	CD853F	slategray	708090
indianred	CD5C5C	olivedrab	6B8E23
mediumvioletred	C71585	slateblue	6A5ACD
silver	C0C0C0	dimgray	696969
darkkhaki	BDB76B	mediumaquamarine	66CDAA
rosybrown	BC8F8F	cornflowerblue	6495ED
mediumorchid	BA55D3	cadetblue	5F9EA0
darkgoldenrod	B8860B	darkolivegreen	556B2F
firebrick	B22222	indigo	4B0082
powderblue	B0E0E6	mediumturquoise	48D1CC
lightsteelblue	B0C4DE	darkslateblue	483D8B
paleturquoise	AFEEEE	steelblue	4682B4
greenyellow	ADFF2F	royalblue	4169E1
lightblue	ADD8E6	turquoise	40E0D0
darkgray	A9A9A9	mediumseagreen	3CB371
brown	A52A2A	limegreen	32CD32
sienna	A0522D	darkslategray	2F4F4F
yellowgreen	9ACD32	seagreen	2E8B57
darkorchid	9932CC	forestgreen	228B22
palegreen	98FB98	lightseagreen	20B2AA
darkviolet	9400D3	dodgerblue	1E90FF

Color Name	Value	Color Name	Value
midnightblue	191970	teal	008080
aqua	00FFFF	green	008000
cyan	00FFFF	darkgreen	006400
springgreen	00FF7F	blue	0000FF
lime	00FF00	mediumblue	0000CD
mediumspringgreen	00FA9A	darkblue	00008B
darkturquoise	00CED1	navy	000080
deepskyblue	00BFFF	black	000000
darkcyan	008B8B		

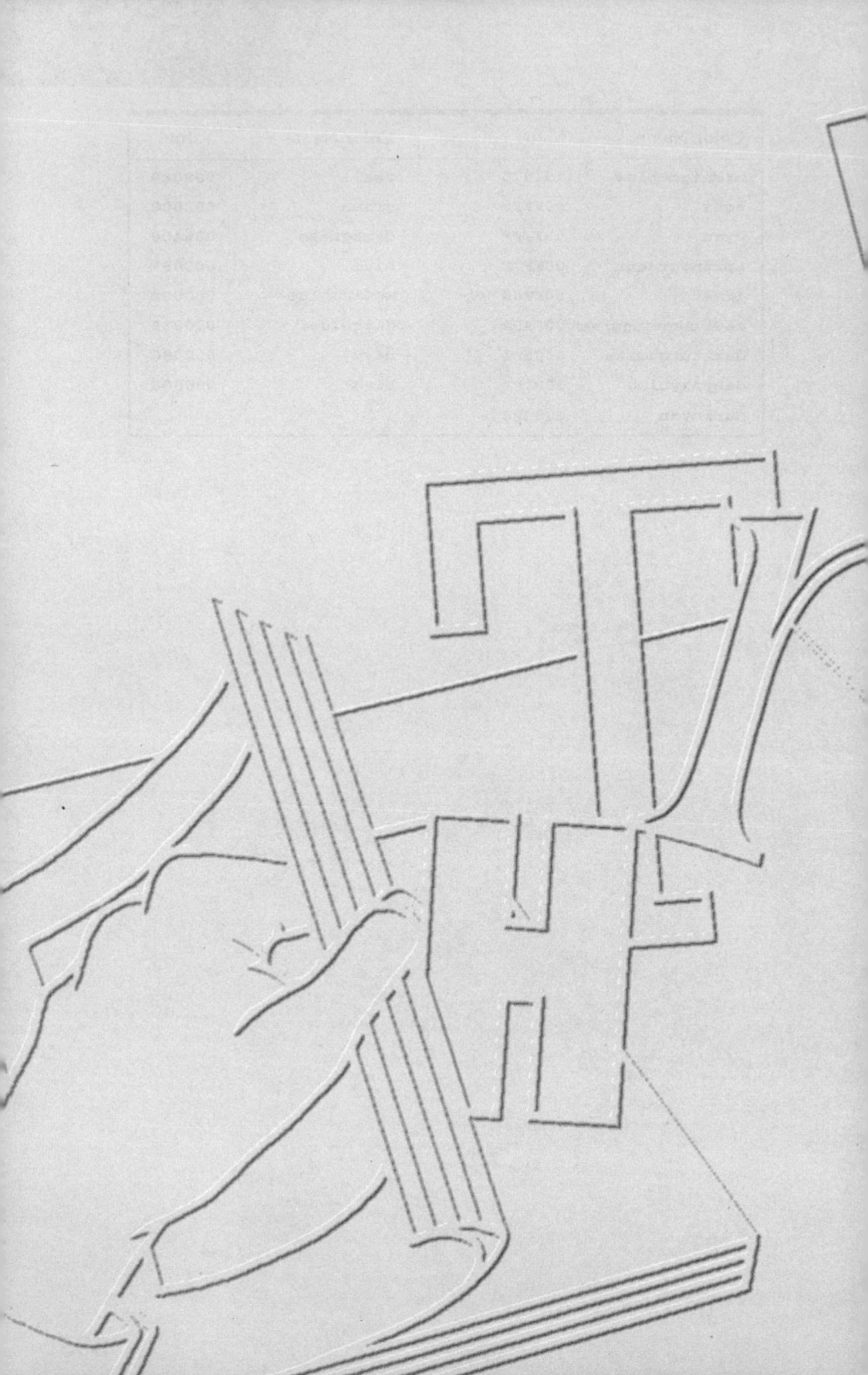

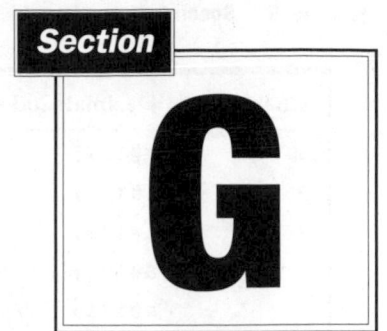

Section

G

Special Characters in HTML

The following table gives you the codes you need to insert special characters into your HTML documents. Some characters have their own mnemonic names—for example, the registered trademark character can be written in HTML as **&reg**. Where there is no mnemonic name, you can insert the character simply by including its decimal code.

Character	Decimal Code	HTML	Description
"	&#34;	&quot;	Quotation mark
&	&#38;	&amp;	Ampersand
<	&#60;	&lt;	Less than
>	&#62;	&gt;	Greater than
			Non-breaking space
¡	&#161;	&iexcl;	Inverted exclamation
¢	&#162;	&cent;	Cent sign
£	&#163;	&pound;	Pound sterling
¤	&#164;	&curren;	General currency sign
¥	&#165;	&yen;	Yen sign
¦	&#166;	&brvbar;	Broken vertical bar
§	&#167;	&sect;	Section sign
¨	&#168;	&uml;	Diæresis/umlaut
©	&#169;	&copy;	Copyright
ª	&#170;	&ordf;	Feminine ordinal
«	&#171;	&laquo;	Left angle quote,
¬	&#172;	&not;	Not sign
–	&#173;	&shy;	Soft hyphen
®	&#174;	&reg;	Registered trademark
¯	&#175;	&macr;	Macron accent
°	&#176;	&deg;	Degree sign

Section G - Special Characters in HTML

Character	Decimal Code	HTML	Description
±	&#177;	&plusmn;	Plus or minus
²	&#178;	&sup2;	Superscript two
³	&#179;	&sup3;	Superscript three
´	&#180;	&acute;	Acute accent
µ	&#181;	&micro;	Micro sign
¶	&#182;	&para;	Paragraph sign
·	&#183;	&middot;	Middle dot
¸	&#184;	&cedil;	Cedilla
¹	&#185;	&sup1;	Superscript one
º	&#186;	&ordm;	Masculine ordinal
»	&#187;	&raquo;	Right angle quote
¼	&#188;	&frac14;	Fraction one quarter
½	&#189;	&frac12;	Fraction one half
¾	&#190;	&frac34;	Fraction three-quarters
¿	&#191;	&iquest;	Inverted question mark
À	&#192;	&Agrave;	Capital A, grave accent
Á	&#193;	&Aacute;	Capital A, acute accent
Â	&#194;	&Acirc;	Capital A, circumflex
Ã	&#195;	&Atilde;	Capital A, tilde
Ä	&#196;	&Auml;	Capital A, diæresis / umlaut
Å	&#197;	&Aring;	Capital A, ring
Æ	&#198;	&AElig;	Capital AE, ligature
Ç	&#199;	&Ccedil;	Capital C, cedilla
È	&#200;	&Egrave;	Capital E, grave accent
É	&#201;	&Eacute;	Capital E, acute accent
Ê	&#202;	&Ecirc;	Capital E, circumflex
Ë	&#203;	&Euml;	Capital E, diæresis / umlaut
Ì	&#204;	&Igrave;	Capital I, grave accent
Í	&#205;	&Iacute;	Capital I, acute accent
Î	&#206;	&Icirc;	Capital I, circumflex
Ï	&#207;	&Iuml;	Capital I, diæresis /umlaut
Ð	&#208;	&ETH;	Capital Eth, Icelandic
Ñ	&#209;	&Ntilde;	Capital N, tilde
Ò	&#210;	&Ograve;	Capital O, grave accent
Ó	&#211;	&Oacute;	Capital O, acute accent
Ô	&#212;	&Ocirc;	Capital O, circumflex
Õ	&#213;	&Otilde;	Capital O, tilde

Character	Decimal Code	HTML	Description
Ö	&#214;	&Ouml;	Capital O, diæresis / umlaut
×	&#215;	&times;	Multiplication sign
Ø	&#216;	&Oslash;	Capital O, slash
Ù	&#217;	&Ugrave;	Capital U, grave accent
Ú	&#218;	&Uacute;	Capital U, acute accent
Û	&#219;	&Ucirc;	Capital U, circumflex
Ü	&#220;	&Uuml;	Capital U, diæresis / umlaut
Ý	&#221;	&Yacute;	Capital Y, acute accent
Þ	&#222;	&THORN;	Capital Thorn, Icelandic
ß	&#223;	&szlig;	German sz
à	&#224;	&agrave;	Small a, grave accent
á	&#225;	&aacute;	Small a, acute accent
â	&#226;	&acirc;	Small a, circumflex
ã	&#227;	&atilde;	Small a, tilde
ä	&#228;	&auml;	Small a, diæresis / umlaut
å	&#229;	&aring;	Small a, ring
æ	&#230;	&aelig;	Small ae ligature
ç	&#231;	&ccedil;	Small c, cedilla
è	&#232;	&egrave;	Small e, grave accent
é	&#233;	&eacute;	Small e, acute accent
ê	&#234;	&ecirc;	Small e, circumflex
ë	&#235;	&euml;	Small e, diæresis / umlaut
ì	&#236;	&igrave;	Small i, grave accent
í	&#237;	&iacute;	Small i, acute accent
î	&#238;	&icirc;	Small i, circumflex
ï	&#239;	&iuml;	Small i, diæresis / umlaut
ð	&#240;	&eth;	Small eth, Icelandic
ñ	&#241;	&ntilde;	Small n, tilde
ò	&#242;	&ograve;	Small o, grave accent
ó	&#243;	&oacute;	Small o, acute accent
ô	&#244;	&ocirc;	Small o, circumflex
õ	&#245;	&otilde;	Small o, tilde
ö	&#246;	&ouml;	Small o, diæresis / umlaut
÷	&#247;	&divide;	Division sign
ø	&#248;	&oslash;	Small o, slash
ù	&#249;	&ugrave;	Small u, grave accent
ú	&#250;	&uacute;	Small u, acute accent

Character	Decimal Code	HTML	Description
û	û	û	Small u, circumflex
ü	ü	ü	Small u, diæresis / umlaut
ý	ý	ý	Small y, acute accent
þ	þ	þ	Small thorn, Icelandic
ÿ	ÿ	ÿ	Small y, diæresis / umlaut

Remember, if you want to show HTML code in a browser, you have to use the special character codes for the angled brackets in order to avoid the browser interpreting them as start and end of tags.

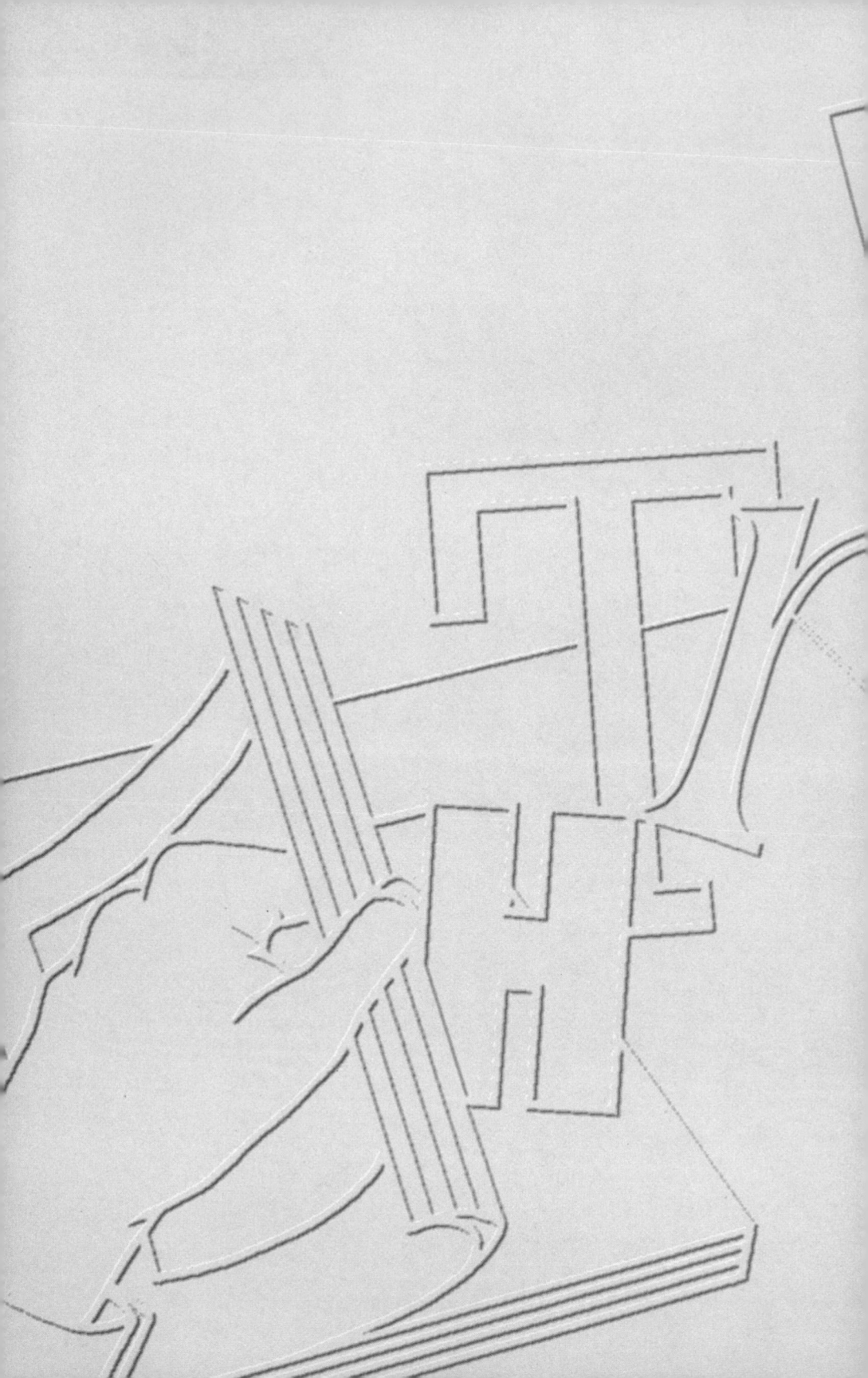

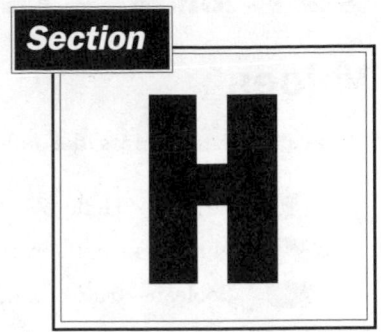
JavaScript Quick Reference

This is a very quick overview of all of the main programming constructs in JavaScript. If you need more than a very quick refresher, then we suggest you look out for Instant JavaScript – ISBN 1-861001-274.

General Information

JavaScript is included in an HTML document with the **<SCRIPT>** tag. Here's an example:

```
<HTML>
<HEAD>

<!-- wrap script in comments
<script language = "JavaScript">
script code would be here
</SCRIPT>
-->

</HEAD>
<BODY>
    HTML document would be here
</BODY>
</HTML>
```

The following points should be kept in mind:

- All JavaScript code should be put in the **<HEAD>** section of the document. This ensures that all the code has been loaded before an attempt is made to execute it.

- The script code should be wrapped in a comment, as this stops older (non-JavaScript) browsers from trying to read the code.

- JavaScript is case-sensitive.

Values

JavaScript recognizes the following data types:

- Strings—"Hello World"
- Numbers—both integers(86) and decimal values(86.235)
- Boolean—true or false

A null (or nil) value is assigned with the keyword **null**.

JavaScript also makes use of 'special characters' similar to other programming languages:

Character	Function
\n	newline
\t	tab
\f	form feed
\b	backspace
\r	carriage return

You may escape other characters by preceding them with a backslash (\). This is most commonly used for quotes and backslashes.

```
document.write("I want to \"quote\" this without terminating my string.");
document.write("The following is a backslash: \\");
```

Variables

JavaScript is a *loosely typed language*. This means that variables do not have an explicitly defined variable type. Instead, every variable can hold values of various types. Conversions between types are done automatically when needed, as this example demonstrates:

```
x = 55;      // x is assigned to be the integer 55;
y = "55";    // y is assigned to be the string "55";

z = 1 + y;
<!-- even though y is a string, it will be automatically converted to the
appropriate integer value so that 1 may be added to it. -->

<!-- the number 55 will be written to the screen. Even though x is an integer and
not a string, Javascript will make the  necessary conversion for you. -->
document.write(x);
```

Variable names must start with either a letter or an underscore. Beyond the first letter, variables may contain any combination of letters, underscores, and digits. JavaScript is case-sensitive, so **this_variable** is not the same as **This_Variable**.

Variables do not need to be declared before they are used. However, you may use the **Var** keyword to explicitly define a variable. This is especially useful when there is the possibility of conflicting variable names. When in doubt, use **Var**.

```
Var x = "55";
```

Arrays

Currently, JavaScript has no explicit array structure. However, JavaScript's object mechanisms allow for easy creation of arrays.

The following is the standard 'array-creation' code taken from Netscape's documentation:

```
function MakeArray(n) {
   this.length = n;
   for (var i = 1; i <= n; i++) {
     this[i] = 0 }
     return this
 }
```

Once this code is included in your script, you may create arrays by doing the following:

```
cats = new MakeArray(20);
```

You can then populate the array like this:

```
cats[1] = "Boo Boo"
cats[2] = "Purrcila"
cats[3] = "Sam"
cats[4] = "Lucky"
```

Assignment Operators

The following operators are used to make assignments in JavaScript:

Operator	Example	Result
=	x=y	x equals y
+=	x+=y	x equals x +y
-=	x-=y	x equals x-y
*=	x*=y	x equals x multiplied by y
/=	x/=y	x equals x divided by y
%=	x%=y	x equals x modulus y

Each operator assigns the value on the right to the variable on the left.

```
x = 100;
y = 10;

x += y;
// x now is equal to 110
```

Equality Operators

Operator	Result
==	Equal
!=	Not equal
>	Greater than
>=	Greater than or equal to
<	Less than
<=	Less than or equal to

Other Operators

Operator	Result
+	Addition
-	Subtraction
*	Multiplication
/	Division
%	Modulus
++	Increment
--	Decrement
-	Unary Negation
& or AND	Bitwise AND
| or OR	Bitwise OR
^ or XOR	Bitwise XOR
<<	Bitwise Left Shift
>>	Bitwise Right Shift
>>>	Zero-fill Right Shift
&&	Logical AND
||	Logical OR
!	Not

Comments

Operator	Result
//	A single line comment
/* ... */	A multiline comment; the comment text replaces the ...

Control Flow

There are two ways of controlling the flow of a program in JavaScript. The first way involves conditional statements, which follow either one branch of the program or another. The second way is to use a repeated iteration of a set of statements.

Conditional Statements

JavaScript has one conditional statement:

if...then...else—used to run various blocks of code—depending on conditions. **if...then...else** statements have the following general form in JavaScript:

```
if  (condition)  {
    code  to  be  executed  if  condition  is  true;
}
else  {
    code  to  be  executed  if  condition  is  false;
}
```

In addition:

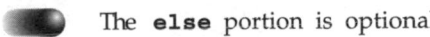 The **else** portion is optional

 **if** statements may be nested

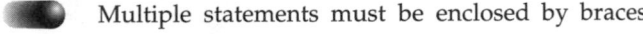 Multiple statements must be enclosed by braces

Here is an example:

```
person_type = prompt("what are ya?", "");
if (person_type == "cat") {
  alert("Here, have some cat food");
  }
    else {
      if (person_type == "dog") {
        alert("Here, have some dog food");
        }
        else {
          if (person_type == "human") {
              alert("Here have some, er, human food!");
              }
}
```

Loop Statements

for—executes a block of code a specified number of times.

```
for (i = 0; i = 10; i++) {
        document.write(i);
        }
```

while—executes a block of code while a condition is true.

```
while (condition) {
    statements...
}
```

break— will cause an exit from a loop regardless of the condition statement.

```
x = 0;
while (x != 10) {
    x = prompt("Enter a number or q to quit", "");
    if (x == "q") {
            alert("See ya");
            break;
            }
    }
```

continue— will cause the loop to jump immediately back to the condition statement.

```
x = 0;
while (x != 1) {

    if (!(confirm("Should I add 1 to x?"))) {
            continue;
            // the following x++ is never executed
            x++;
            }
    x++;
    }

alert("Bye");
```

Input/Output

In JavaScript, there are three different methods of providing information to the user, and getting a response back.

Alert

This displays a message with an OK button.

```
alert("Hello World!");
```

408

Confirm

Displays a message with both an OK and a Cancel button. True is returned if the OK button is pressed, and false is returned if the Cancel button is pressed.

```
confirm("Are you sure you want to quit?");
```

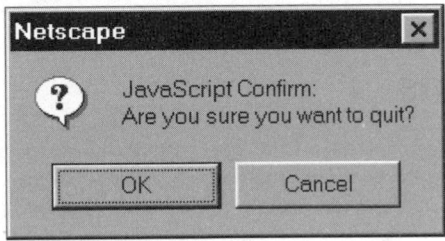

Prompt

Displays a message and a text box for user input. The first string argument forms the text that is to be displayed above the text box. The second argument is a string, integer, or property of an existing object, which represents the default value to display inside the box. If the second argument is not specified, "**<undefined>**" is displayed inside the text box.

The string typed into the box is returned if the OK button is pressed. False is returned if the Cancel button is pressed

```
prompt("What is your name?", "");
```

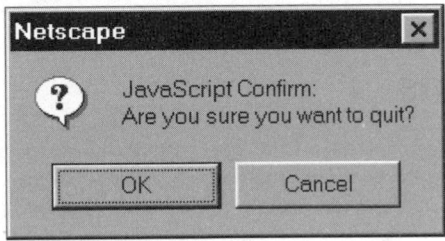

Built-in Functions

JavaScript provides a number of built-in functions which can be accessed within JavaScript code.

Name	Description
`escape(char)`	Returns a string with the ASCII encoding of **char** of the form %XX where XX us the numeric encoding of **char**
`eval(expression)`	Returns the result of evaluating the numeric expression **expression**
`IsNAN(value)`	Returns a Boolean value of True if **value** is Not A Number
`parsefloat(string)`	Converts **string** to a floating point number
`ParseInt(string,base)`	Converts **string** to an Integer of base **base**

Reserved Words

The following are reserved words which can't be used for function, method, variable, or object names. Note that while some words in this list are not currently used as JavaScript keywords, they have been reserved for future use.

abstract	else	int	super
boolean	extends	interface	switch
break	false	long	synchronized
byte	final	native	this
case	finally	new	throw
catch	float	null	throws
char	for	package	transient
class	function	private	true
const	goto	protected	try
continue	if	public	typeof
default	implements	reset	var
delete	import	return	void
do	in	short	while
double	instanceof	static	with

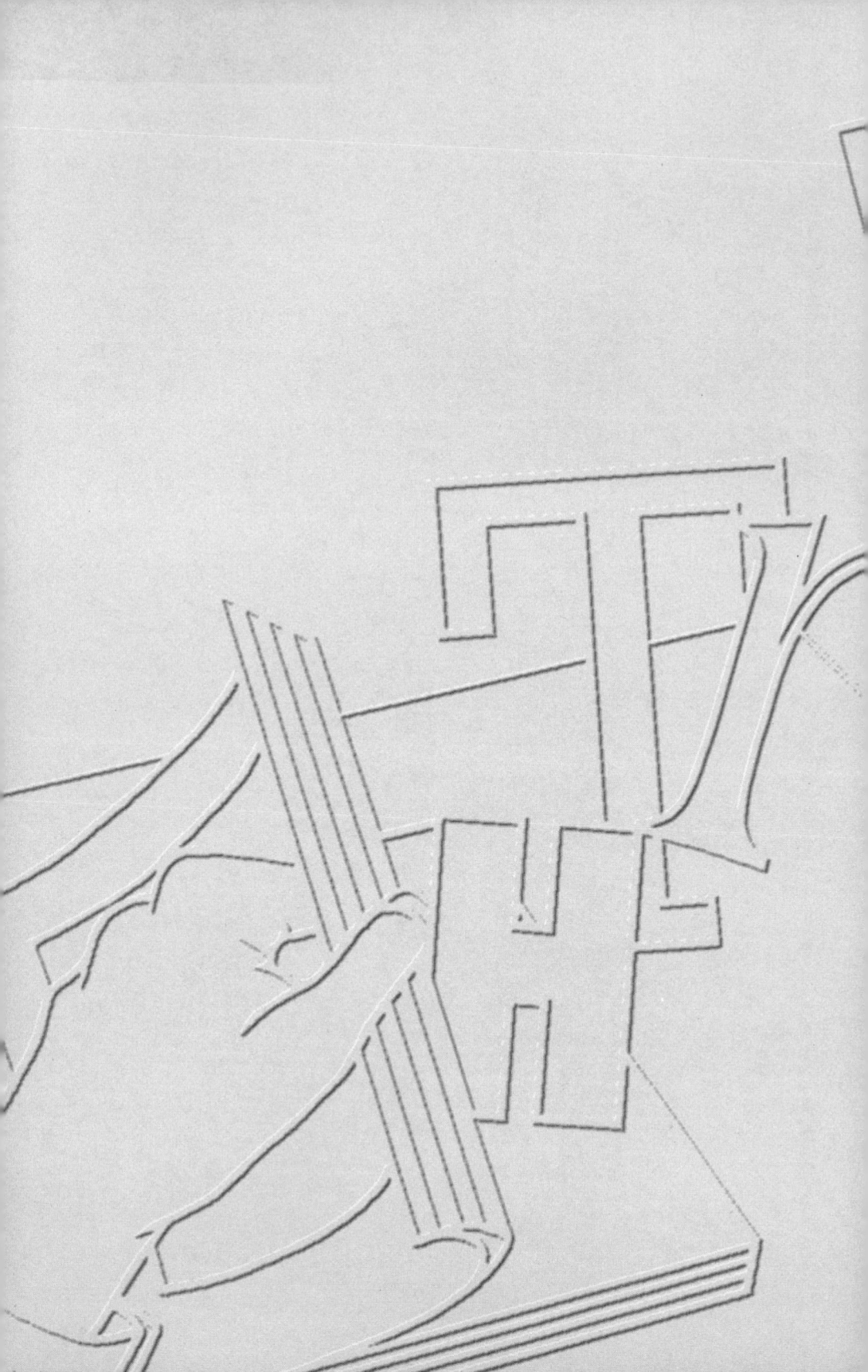

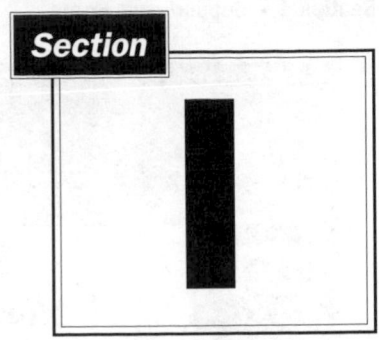

Section

Support and Errata

One of the most irritating things about any programming book can be when you find that a bit of code you've just spent an hour typing simply doesn't work. You check it one hundred times to see if you've set it up correctly and then you notice the spelling mistake in the variable name on the book page. Grrrr! Of course, you can blame the authors for not taking enough care and testing the code, the editors for not doing their job properly, or the proofreaders for not being eagle-eyed enough but this doesn't get around the fact that mistakes do happen.

Greatly as we try to ensure no mistakes sneak out into the real world, we can't promise you that this book is 100% error free. What we can do is offer the next best thing by providing you with immediate support and feedback from experts who have worked on the book and try to ensure that future editions eliminate these gremlins. The following sections will take you step by step through how to post errata to our web site to get that help:

- Finding a list of existing errata on the web site
- Adding your own errata to the existing list
- What happens to your errata once you've posted it (why doesn't it appear immediately?)

and how to mail a question for technical support:

- What your e-mail should include
- What happens to your e-mail once it has been received by us

Finding an Errata on the Web Site

Before you send in a query, you might be able to save time by finding the answer to your problem on our web site, **http:\\www.wrox.com**. Each book we publish has its own page and its own errata sheet. You can get to any book's page by using the drop down list box on our web site's welcome screen.

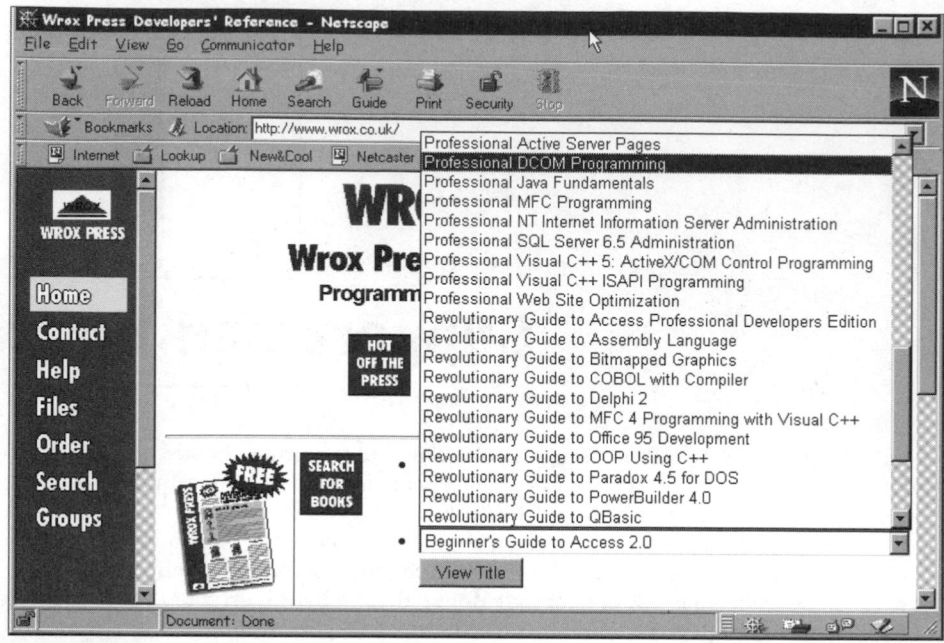

From this you can locate any book's home page on our site. Select your book and click View Title to get the individual title page:

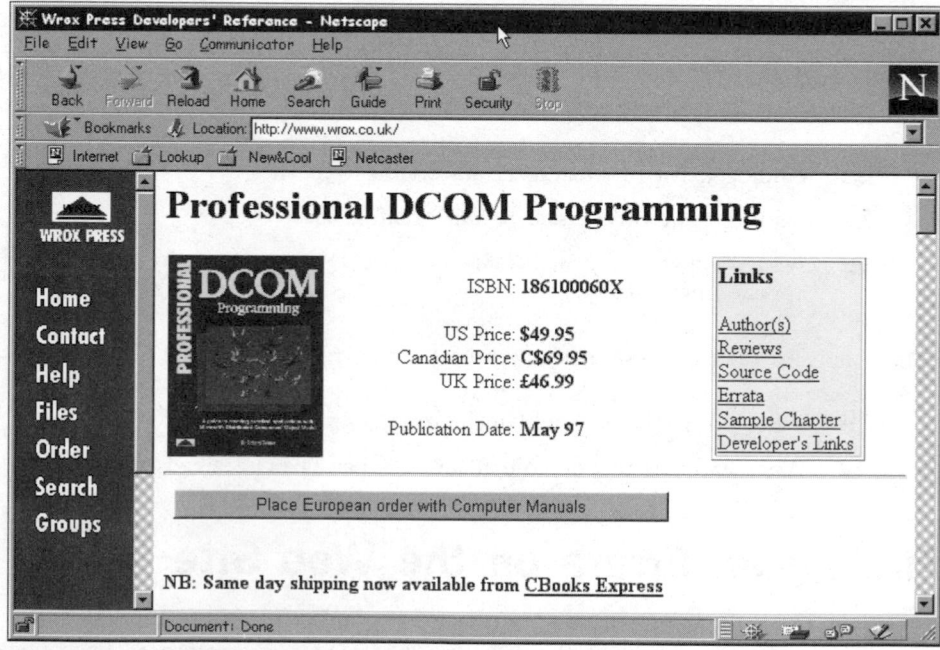

Each book has a set of links. If you click on the Errata link, you'll immediately be transported to the errata sheet for that book:

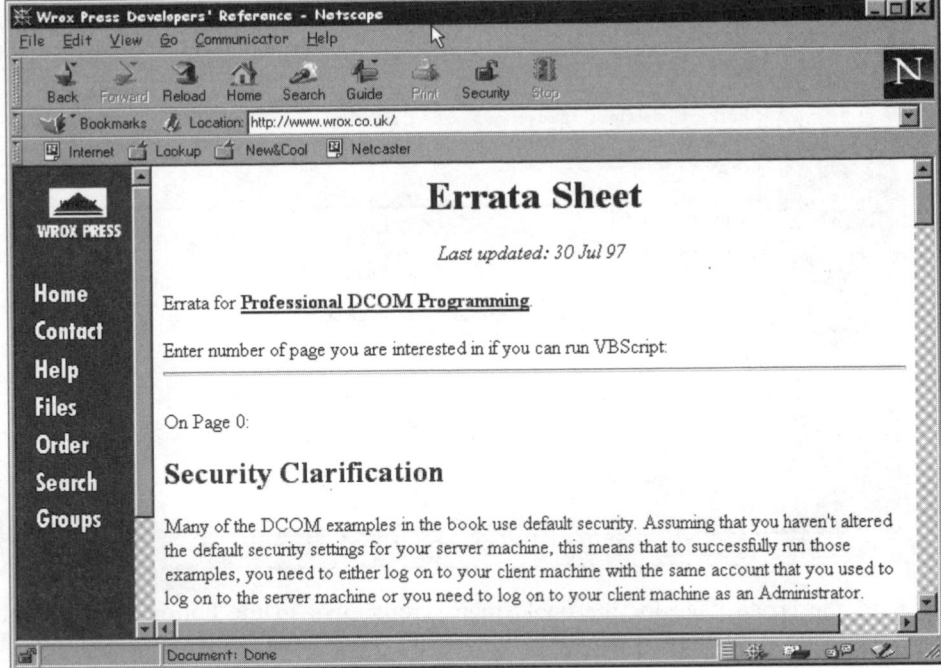

If you're using Internet Explorer 3.0 or later, you can jump to errors using the text box provided to browse the errata more quickly. The errata lists are updated on daily basis, ensuring that you always have the most up-to-date information on bugs and errors.

Adding an Errata to the Sheet Yourself

It's always possible that you may not find your error listed, in which case you can enter details of the fault yourself. It might be anything from a spelling mistake to a faulty piece of code in a book. Sometimes you'll find useful hints that aren't really errors as such on the listing. By entering errata you may save another reader some hours of frustration and, of course, you will be helping us to produce even higher quality information. We're very grateful for this sort of guidance and feedback. Here's how to do it:

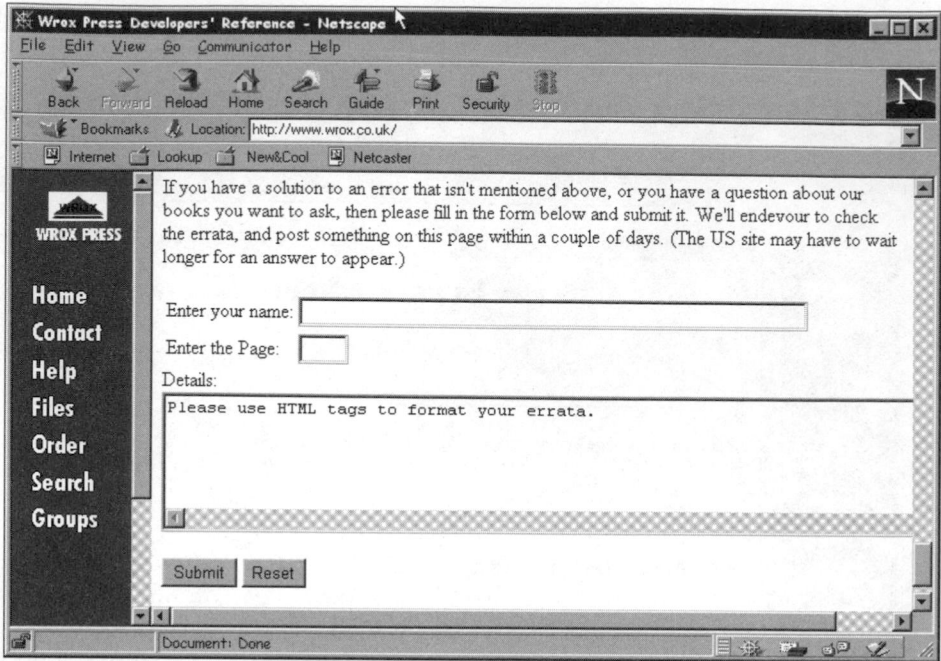

Find the errata page for the book, then scroll down to the bottom of the page, where you will see a space for you to enter your name (and e-mail address for preference), the page the errata occurs on and details of the errata itself. The errata should be formatted using HTML tags - the reminder for this can be deleted as you type in your error.

Once you've typed in your message, click on the Submit button and the message is forwarded to our editors. They'll then test your submission and check that the error exists, and that any suggestions that you make are valid. Then your submission, together with a solution, is posted on the site for public consumption. Obviously this stage of the process can take up to a day or two, but we will endeavor to get you a fix up sooner than that.

E-mail Support

If you wish to directly query a problem in the book with an expert who knows the book in detail then e-mail **support@wrox.com**, with the title of the book in the Subject and the last four numbers of the ISBN. A typical e-mail should include the following things:

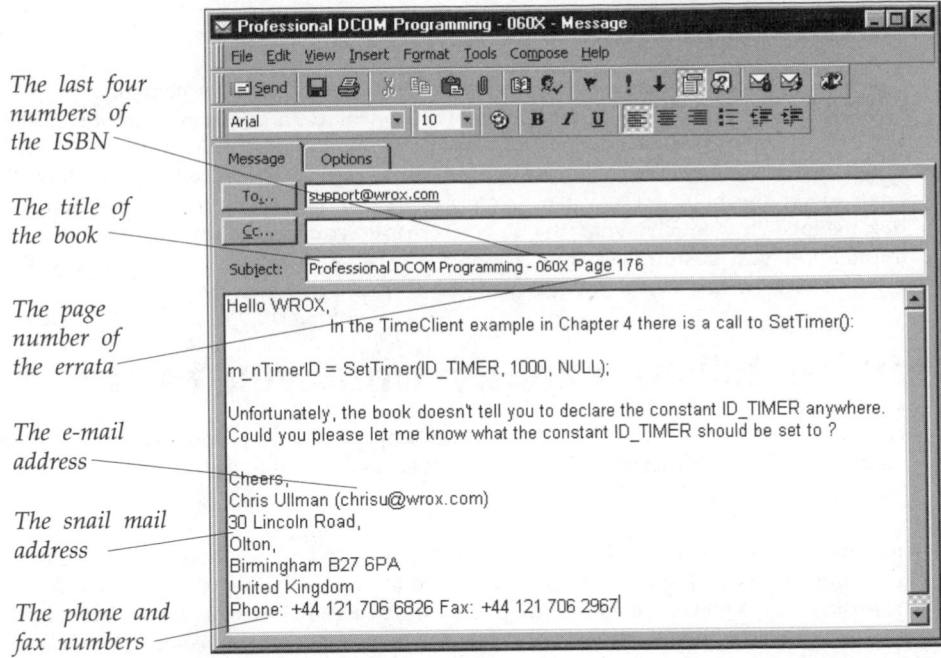

The last four numbers of the ISBN

The title of the book

The page number of the errata

The e-mail address

The snail mail address

The phone and fax numbers

We won't send you junk mail. We need details to help save your time and ours. If we need to replace a disk or CD we'll be able to get it to you straight away. When you send an e-mail it will go through the following chain of support:

Customer Support

Your message is delivered to one of our customer support staff who are the first people to read it. They have files on the most frequently asked questions and will reply immediately. They answer general questions about the books and web site.

Editorial

Deeper queries are forwarded on the same day to the technical editor responsible for that book. They have experience with the programming language or particular product and are able to answer detailed technical questions on the subject. Once an issue has been resolved, the editor can post the errata to the web site.

The Author(s)

Finally, in the unlikely event that the editor can't answer your problem, he/she will forward the request to the author. We try to protect to the author from more distractions from writing. However, we are quite happy to forward specific requests to them. All Wrox authors help with the support on their books. They'll mail the customer and editor with their response, and again, all readers should benefit.

What we can't answer

Obviously with an ever growing range of books and an ever changing technology base, there is an increasing volume of data requiring support. While we endeavor to answer all questions about a book, we can't answer bugs in your own programs that you've adapted from our code. So, while you might have loved the help desk system examples in our Active Server Pages book, don't expect too much sympathy if you cripple your company with a live application you customized from chapter 12. But do tell us if you're especially pleased with a successful routine you developed with our help.

How to tell us exactly what you think!

We understand that errors can destroy the enjoyment of a book and can cause many wasted and frustrated hours, so we seek to minimize the distress that they can cause.

You might just wish to tell us how much you liked or loathed the book in question. Or you might have ideas about how this whole process could be improved. In which case you should e-mail **feedback@wrox.com**. You'll always find a sympathetic ear, no matter what the problem is. Above all you should remember that we do care about what you have to say and we will do our utmost to act upon it.

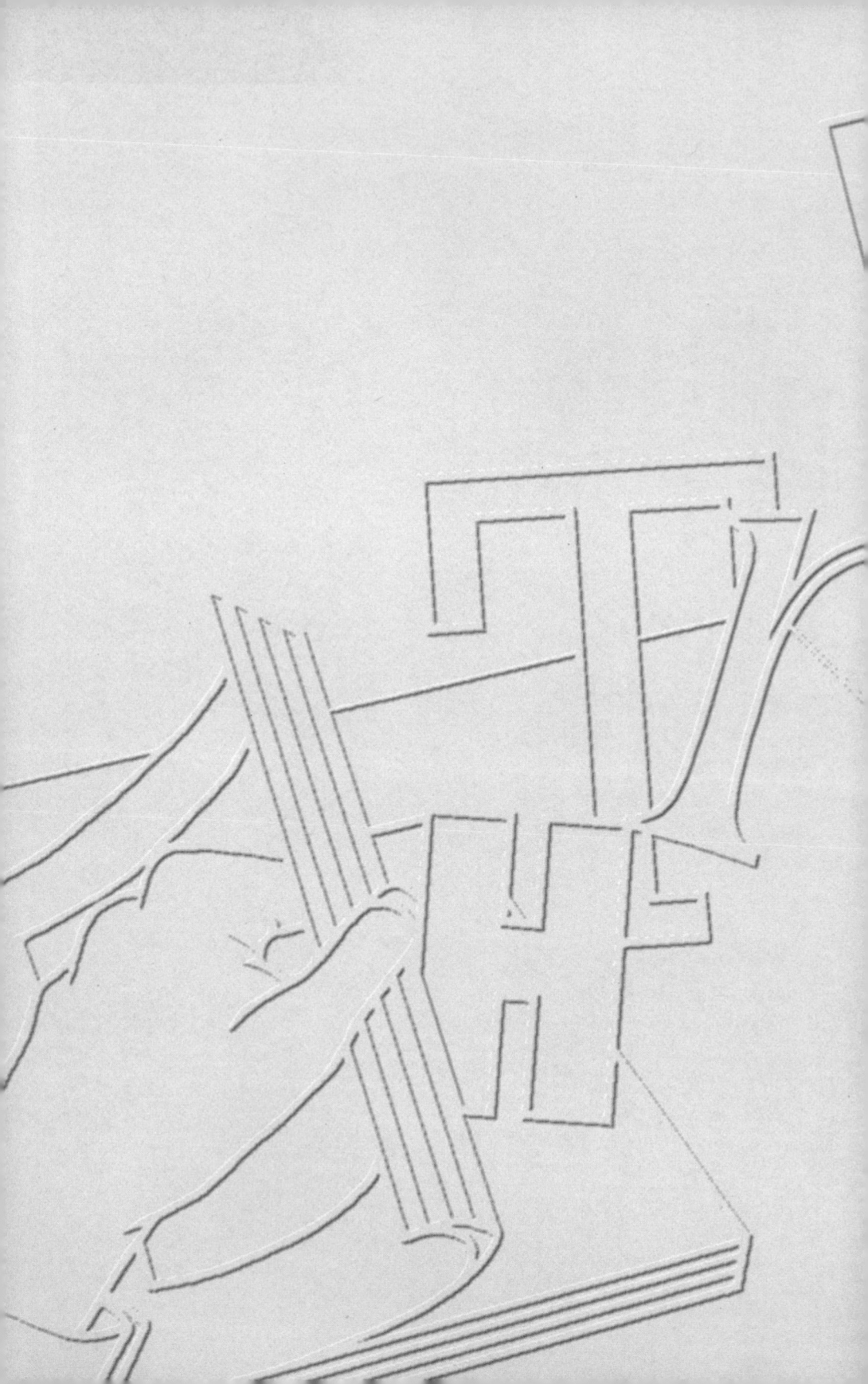

Dynamic HTML

Index